An Italian Journey

A Sort of Latter-Day Mini Grand Tour

David M. Addison

authorHOUSE™

1663 LIBERTY DRIVE, SUITE 200
BLOOMINGTON, INDIANA 47403
(800) 839-8640
WWW.AUTHORHOUSE.COM

First published by AuthorHouse 07/15/05

ISBN: 1-4208-6930-2 (sc)

Printed in the United States of America
Bloomington, Indiana

This book is printed on acid-free paper.

Pour CLAIRE

à ma française préférée sans qui ce livre n'aurait jamais été écrit.

…it is a tale
 Told by an idiot…

Shakespeare.

Macbeth Act 5 Scene 5

Table of Contents

Overture

The first *Italian Journey* was written by Goethe. But even before his time, it was fashionable to conduct what was known as The Grand Tour. From the 18th Century, right through the Victorian period, a tour of the famous cities of Europe, focusing particularly in a study of the Classical and Renaissance sights of Italy was considered an essential component of a young aristocrat's education. Since Goethe, countless writers have recorded their experiences. And now there is me. I am neither young nor an aristocrat - just a wrinkly on a package tour, like hundreds of others - because they make it so easy for us nowadays.

Back then, the trip might last one or two years and was not without its dangers. My illustrious ancestor, (well namesake anyway) Joseph Addison, the founder of *The Spectator* is said to have made a spectacle of himself by falling into the harbour at Calais. History does not record if he was drunk or not. Well, that is not going to happen to me. For a start I am not going to Calais and secondly, if I do fall, it will be onto the tarmac like a pontiff but unlike him, I may possibly be just a *teeny-weeny* bit tipsy, for I have my hip flask with me. Have hip flask, will travel, that's my motto. No point in paying the exorbitant prices the airline charges. As we are a charter, all I need is the price of a mixer for the gin (bad enough, but I also need the ice and the plastic cup) and a window seat to lessen the chances of detection by the stewardess.

We are going directly to Naples, my wife and I, which surprisingly, was the culmination of the trip for the Grand Tourist rather than Rome, which for us will be the last port of call. So, perversely, on this latter-day, mini grand tour of Italy, I am beginning at the end.

Another difference is my trip is going to last two weeks rather than two years. How blessed is the modern Grand Tourist who can be whisked off to Naples from Heathrow in three hours or less! In just one week, we can visit Naples, Pompeii, Assisi, Florence, Pisa, Siena, and Rome and spend a second week in Sorrento from where it is easy to visit such attractions as Vesuvius, Herculaneum and the Amalfi coast. Thanks to the marvels of modern transport, we can cram in so much more in a fraction of the time it took to rattle over those rough roads in carriages all those centuries ago.

But first we have to get from Falkirk to Edinburgh and from Edinburgh to Heathrow. And that was where our troubles started. Troubles that the original Grand Tourist never dreamed of – not even in his worst nightmares…

Yes, they make it so easy for us nowadays.

Chapter 1
Con Molto Panico

Like Jane Eyre for whom there was no possibility of taking a walk that day to get some air, there is a distinct possibility that we will not be taking to the air today. The panic began about 9 o'clock the night before departure when the telephone shrilled. I seldom answer first as I don't need to ask for whom the bell rings: it's hardly ever for me. If anyone does want to speak to me on the phone, it is usually only to sell me something.

"Get that will you!" It's not a question; it's a suggestion, a suggestion which I can't refuse. It's my wife, Iona, otherwise known as La-Belle-Dame-Sans-Merci. She's got one of the cats on her lap and can't disturb it to answer the phone, naturally. Better to disturb me.

"Hullo?"

"Is Iona there?" I knew it wouldn't be for me. It's my mother-in-law and there is something about her tone of voice which spells trouble.

I could tell her the truth but Iona would just say I was making a catty remark, so instead I say: "I'm afraid not. She has come to her senses and run off with the window cleaner. Will I do or can I take a message?"

"Have you seen the news?" Mother-in-law treats my attempt at levity with the contempt it deserves and her queen-like Essex accents vibrate unfalteringly down the line. She is a TV addict and her TV is never off, unlike ours, which is rarely on. She even tapes programmes whilst she's watching them, just in case the phone rings. Since she lives alone, she knows that it will be for her.

"No. Why?" I don't like the sound of this. Something dreadful must have happened for her to phone us about it.

"BA is on strike and there is chaos at Heathrow."

"Bloody hell! I don't believe it!" That's what I think but in fact, I do believe it all too well and what I actually say is: "Oh no! Thanks very much for letting us know."

We are supposed to be flying to Heathrow with BA to catch a connecting flight to Naples with British Midland. I remembered that at Easter, on our trip to Tuscany, we had just missed a strike by Italian baggage handlers by 24 hours and I had counted my blessings then. Counting blessings doesn't challenge my lack of arithmetical skills as they don't happen that often. It looks like we are not going to be so lucky this time.

I switched on the TV and looked up Ceefax. Right enough – flights cancelled left right and centre due to a wildcat walkout by check-in staff. I rang the help line but it was engaged. It took an hour to get through. The girl at the other end sounded harassed and wasn't much help.

"It's a very fluid situation," she said. "The situation could change at any time. Best thing to do is phone back in the morning."

So that night we went to bed, not knowing whether or not we would be travelling in the morning, or at all. It's enough to drive you to drink. Just as well that I was quaffing the Chilean Cabernet Sauvignon when the phone rang and it was to hand.

*

Although our flight is not until 11:15, I am awake by 5:45. By 6:05 I have just about enough energy to drag myself out of bed and call the help line. As I expected, the line is engaged. This could take a long time but I have a cunning plan. I grab the cordless phone, key in the number and climb back into bed. All I need to do now is keep my finger poised on the redial button. I have not many skills, but laziness is one of them. I could write a book on how to be lazy, but I am too lazy to start.

I know I won't sleep but at least I can stretch out and rest my eyes. God knows when I might be able to do that again. I have visions of being stranded in the airport for hours, fighting for a bit of floor space to lie down on. Sometimes the number starts ringing out and my hopes are raised, only to be dashed again when no one answers and the line goes dead, but mostly I just get the engaged signal. I am getting repetitive strain injury on the redial finger.

It's 8:10 when I finally get through and it takes me utterly by surprise. The female voice at the other end sounds as if it's suffering from repetitive larynx injury and wants to know my flight number. I give it to her, having committed it to memory.

"There is no such flight number," she says with absolute certainty.

"What?"

"There is no such flight number," she repeats. Her tone is on the cusp of intolerance. She's probably been up all night talking to enraged customers and now she's got some moron who doesn't even know his flight number and the elastic of her patience is stretched to snapping point.

"No, I'm sure that's right," I tell her. By this time I am out of bed and trying to find the computer print out which is our evidence of purchase. We had got a good deal over the net.

"Where are you flying from?"

"Edinburgh to London."

"Just a moment."

Now I am downstairs and scrabbling amongst the travel documents. At last I locate them, and discover that I have

3

given her the flight number for the Naples flight but it doesn't matter - she has already found my flight number.

"Your flight is on time and leaving as normal."

"What!" I can scarcely believe it. "Are you sure? 11:15 from Edinburgh?"

"The flight is at 11:05 and is leaving on time. You should get there an hour beforehand." I can tell she is itching to get rid of me. She doesn't want an argument about it; she's probably had hundreds of others already.

"Yes! Yes, of course!" I cannot believe my luck. I can feel the relief coursing through my veins. All that panic for nothing! Thank you, mother-in-law, thank you very much indeed! But for you I would have gone to bed blissfully unaware that anything was amiss and got up this morning hopefully refreshed and looking forward to the start of our mini Grand Tour.

They make it so easy for us to panic these days.

I check my print out and it does say 11:15. Hmm. They must have changed it I suppose. I don't mind when it leaves, just as long as it does leave and gets me to Heathrow in time for my connection. The chaos there should not affect us as we are not travelling out with BA. All's well that ends well. But what about our luggage? Will the BA baggage handlers unload it? It's a niggling worry but I dismiss it - it's the check in people who are on strike, after all, not the baggage handlers and she said it was all right, didn't she? So why worry?

I have a shower, after which I deem it not too early to phone Ben and Eileen who are taking us to the airport and who, like me, don't believe in getting up a moment too soon. They are at breakfast and I tell them the panic is off and that the flight is actually 10 minutes earlier.

To our disappointment, Ben is at the wheel. He is 78 and his eyes have the dimness of cataract. He limps with a stick. He is waiting for a knee operation and that is on his good leg. The other one has never been the same since he got *Necrotising Fasciitis,* that flesh-eating bug in it and had a chunk cut out of it. Numerous skin grafts later, it is not a pretty sight, puffy and a blotchy deep brown and purple colour which looks only a couple of shades lighter than gangrene. I get the feeling he would not be too good at an emergency stop, if he saw the emergency in the first place, that is. We are grateful for the lift but had hoped Eileen would be driving. She is only 74 and doesn't even wear specs. I think that's because she doesn't need them, and not because she is too vain, though she is always immaculately turned out and takes great care with her appearance, looking more like 54 than 74.

As he swings out of the drive, the wheel slips momentarily out of Ben's hands and he nearly collides with a parked car outside my gates. It's not a good start and it's the only time he comes close to the left hand side of the road. I knew he had right wing tendencies but hadn't realised that he carried them over to his driving. He drives well over on the right so oncoming cars have to pull hard left. That's all right as long as they see him coming; just as long as they are paying attention and not texting or looking at girls with tight T-shirts. Sometimes we can hear the road markings rumble under the wheels and he pulls marginally over to his side of the road again. Iona and I, in the back, look at each other askance.

Ben asks for suggestions as to the best way to the motorway. When I tell him, he disagrees. I suppose that was why he asked. No, no, such and such is a much better way, he insists. Eileen is on our side. She tells him where to go but not in the pejorative sense of the expression. We wish more than ever that she had been driving. Ben has control, well sort of, and there's no way of telling which mad way he'll go and delay us for God knows how long. The argument rumbles on, like the tyres on the white lines.

Iona is beginning to panic. She has a phobia about getting to the airport in time after the taxi we had hired two years ago arrived late and then compounded the felony by taking a convoluted route to the motorway. When challenged, the driver had said this was the best way to avoid traffic. I was not convinced; after all we live here, but it soon became clear why we were going that way. Before we could stop him, we were off the roundabout and heading up the motorway in the opposite direction to Edinburgh and the way we wanted to go. Even at our united cries of protest, he argued that *he* was right and we *did* want to go to Glasgow and it was only after juggling with his schedule as he was speeding us in the wrong direction, that he finally did believe us. It was a crucial error. Even at that late stage, we may still have made it, but it was several miles before we could turn round and as a result, we missed our flight to London and consequently our connection to New Zealand.

"You're not going to catch that flight to London," was one of the most chilling sentences I have ever heard. Even after the assurances I had been given on the phone this morning, I half expect to hear it again, especially as Ben has had another idea. He thinks if he takes a left down this road it is a short cut and it will take us out through some industrial estate. Iona and I know for a fact that it is a cul-de-sac.

"No! No!" we cry in unison. There is a rising tone of panic in Iona's voice. "It's a dead end. It doesn't go anywhere!"

Ben argues that they have opened it up.

"Look, Ben!" shouts Eileen, slapping both hands down hard on her thighs. "Will you just do what we tell you to do! And go where we tell you to go!"

Ben is silent and does what she says. I like obedience in a man, especially that man and at this time. Iona sighs with relief and I breathe a little easier but I am still willing Ben to keep into the side more. We are on our way to the motorway

6

and in good time which is just as well as we may need the time. I still can hardly believe that the BA strike is not going to affect us. I'm not so much a pessimist as a realist.

And how right I am! But the gods tease us for their sport and to begin with, it looks all right. There is the BA check-in desk and there are people actually being checked in! There is a girl at the tail of the queue with a clipboard looking at people's tickets.

"Where are you bound for?"

"Heathrow, then Naples."

"I'm afraid that flight is cancelled - don't worry, we'll get you to Naples tonight." She must have seen my stricken face. "We're using other carriers. Just join that queue over there. I will warn you, however, that it is rather a long queue."

"But I phoned this morning and was told my flight was on time. And where are these people going?" I indicate the passengers being processed at the desks in front of me.

"That's the 11:05 to Gatwick."

The horrible truth dawns on me with a sickening clarity. On the phone this morning, I had foolishly said I was going to London, rather than Heathrow and the girl hadn't noticed the discrepancy in time, or had she? This explains why she said my flight was departing and 10 minutes earlier than I had expected. I should have known not to believe it. I curse myself for my foolish optimism. In the light of previous experiences, I should have known better.

The sooner we get into the queue the better and I'm glad that we arrived so early; it might make a crucial difference. We walk on and on, pulling our cases behind us. This is the mother of all queues all right. We take our places at the end. BA staff are handing out free drinks and muffins. That's a bad sign, a very bad sign indeed. It looks like we could be here for some time and so it proves, for an hour later and we have moved about 10 feet and the queue has, like Topsy, grown behind us. It is worrying and boring and tedious. The only bit of excitement is when our relatively straight formation is transformed into a series of S bends to let incoming passengers through.

I stroll to the head of the queue trying to work out how many people are ahead of us. Not counting the people who have made it to the desk where presumably passengers are being re-routed, I reckon there are at least 42 ahead of us. It's a bit hard to tell couples from groups but I estimate it's going to take 14 hours to get to the head of the queue and my arithmetical skills are so unreliable, it could be a good deal longer than that. Certainly not less. There's no way I can see us getting to Naples tonight.

Then news filters down the queue that there are no more flights going out that day and passengers are being put up in hotels. Then someone says that he's heard that British Midland is running flights to Heathrow. I decide I'll go and investigate. Apart from missing a day of my holiday (at the most optimistic), a flight to Naples might be too late for us as we are on a tour and our group may have moved on to Florence by then and how would we be expected to get there? Besides, the first day is a visit to Pompeii and for me, one of the highlights of the visit, and I don't want to miss it.

The girl at the British Midland desk tells me she has two seats left.

"And will that get me to Heathrow in time for my flight to Naples?"

She says it will be a bit close but she'll mark our bags priority and we should make it.

"Right. How much are the tickets?"

"£155."

I gasp and even if I suspect I already know the awful truth, I have to ask: "That's return, right?" We had only paid £179 return for both of us.

"No," she says. "One way -" then so that there should be no misunderstanding, she adds with emphasis, "- each."

Bloody hell! That's going to add another £310 onto our holiday! You can practically *get* a holiday for that. Maybe it's not such a good idea. Maybe I should take my chances in the queue even if the thought appals. I voice this to the British Midland girl.

"No," she informs me. "You're on a split ticket. All BA is contracted to do is get you to Heathrow. You haven't got a ticket with them to Naples."

Worse than ever! If I'd stood in that queue for 14 hours to be told that, I swear murder would have been done. "Can you hold those seats for me?" I ask. I must consult Iona about this. She nods.

Iona and I have a brief consultation. If we take the British Midland flight but fail to catch the connection to Naples, we'd be stuck in London. Yet if we don't go for that flight, we are definitely not going to be in Naples tonight. But if we come out of this queue and have to rejoin it, it could set us back another 10 hours at least. I'm not good at making decisions at the best of times, like what to choose from a menu and when it comes, I usually wish I'd picked what someone else has. This is a decision with far more serious consequences and I am in a lather of indecision. But better some action than standing in this queue in the terminal, interminably. If we're going to go for it, the sooner we go, the better. Now, having made up my mind and having left the queue, I worry that maybe the British Midland girl hasn't held the seats for us and has sold them to someone else.

"You're holding two seats for me on the next flight to Heathrow," I tell the girl, just to remind her. I hold my breath as she looks at her computer screen. Please God, let them be there!

"That's fine. And how would you like to pay?"

The relief makes me jocular. "Through the nose."

She looks at me sharply. I give a wan smile. "Just a weak joke," I explain feebly. "Visa of course." I add, humbly.

She is coolly, if not coldly professional. I gather up the tickets and visa receipt in some confusion. I want to get away from here after my *faux pas* and I'm smarting from the pain of signing the visa. I fully intend to claim compensation from BA. Whether I have a chance or not, I don't know, but it would improve my mood considerably if I thought I'd get the money back. I am already composing the letter in my head.

It is also mollifying to discover that we are travelling business class and that partly explains the high cost of the ticket. At the check-in desk across the hall, our bags are marked priority and we are advised to split up at Heathrow – one to go to the check-in and one to go to baggage reclaim. This sounds a bit scary. I didn't think we'd be that tight for time, but the British Midland girl hasn't finished with dispensing the bad news.

"Because you are on a stand-by ticket," the check-in girl explains, "there may not be a meal for you on the plane."

What! I'm paying all this money for a seat and I don't even get a meal! And, what's more, this flight may not even get us to Heathrow in time to catch the flight to Naples. It seems that since this morning, it's been non-stop stress and I am reeling.

"In that case, is there any chance I can get a reduction on the price?" There is some serious intent behind my question, but I put it a jocular fashion, so that when she says no, I can always pretend that I was joking all along.

She stops what she is doing and gives me a withering look. "I'm afraid not." Like her colleague, whom I presume is called Victoria, she is not amused. "At least we are getting you there," she says between clipped lips, with a glance to the BA desk on her left at a young man who has just had a horrendous fright or, who, more probably, is a slave to fashion and, regardless of how much an idiot it makes him look, has gelled his hair so it is standing up on its roots.

Maybe it's not so much me she's peeved at, but BA – she and a few thousand others. Or maybe she's having a private vendetta with him. Maybe she's going out with him and they've been having an argument about his hairstyle.

"You may make use of the business class lounge upstairs." She dismisses us like naughty children after a reprimand.

I phone Eileen to tell her what's happened and then we proceed to the lounge. I have only travelled business class once before, when I went to the States with my daughter's ex-boyfriend, which some people thought rather an odd thing to do, but it was just that he'd won a couple of free flights to anywhere in the USA and needed someone to accompany him. As it happened, Iona and I had completely different Easter holidays that year and as I said I'd pay the accommodation, Graham found my offer irresistible, especially since I'd been there before and knew my way around.

Well, I thought I did, but we got horribly lost in San Francisco. The motorway, or highway as they call it, just stops before the city and you have to go through it before you pick up the highway again. I thought the point of motorways was to go *round* cities.

The first night we stayed with an old friend of mine. Old merely in terms of the length of time I had known him. It happened to be his fortieth birthday and he was having a party. There turned out to be quite a number of gay people at it. (Well, it was San Francisco after all.) If some people thought we were an odd couple, I was gaily unaware of it at the time and it was only later it dawned on me that a number of people probably assumed that Graham and I were an item as well.

Anyway, on that trip, we did not have occasion to visit the executive lounge and so I am unfamiliar with the proceedings. A lady checks our tickets to ensure we are bona-fide business class passengers.

"What are the facilities here?" I ask. I could always look around but I am paying for it, so I may as well ask in case there are things like free phone calls or something I wouldn't know about and might miss.

"Newspapers behind you. Tea and coffee ahead of you and there's a bar if you would prefer anything stronger." The tone is polite but I suspect behind her cool professional exterior she's thinking: *Who are you? Some sort of moron? Can you not see for yourself?*

A bar, eh? I'm ready for a drink after all this hassle, even although it is a bit early, even for me. Still, somewhere in the world, the sun must have gone down over the yardarm and I could be there in spirit. There's a problem though. I know Iona is not going to be amused if I choose the whisky rather than the coffee. But I have already failed to amuse two ladies already and may as well go for broke and make it three.

It's no surprise then to find it's my Chinese wife, Scow Ling, who greets me with a look, when after we get settled in a corner, I return from the bar, bearing a glass containing the golden-coloured restorative. She doesn't say anything. She doesn't need to.

It's very ambient surroundings, this lounge. Quiet, muted colours, comfortable chairs, lots of personal space. There is the quiet drone of a TV somewhere, golf by the sound of it, and some people on the Internet. This is more like it. But how am I going to get another drink? I have already finished that one. It was hardly enough to wet the bottom of the glass, coming from a microscopic optic measure. I should have had a double but couldn't find a glass big enough to take it with the American Ginger. I know, I'll go to the toilet and pick one up on the way back. But where is it?

With a feeling of déjà vu I have to ask at the desk, "Where are the facilities?" I'm sure, in a posh place like this, that's what they are called. Unbelievably, they have all the drinks here: whisky, rum, gin, beer as well as soft drinks, and coffee and tea, but nowhere to get rid of them. We have to use the toilets outside, those used by the common herd. £155 and you don't even get en-suite facilities. That's a bit rich!

When I come back, I successfully root around for a bigger glass and make it a double. There is a notice which reminds us that it is an offence to be drunk on board an aeroplane. I know this only too well because I have a cousin who has been refused permission to travel for this reason – on two occasions that I know of at least. The things people do to prolong their stay.

I also bring back packets of nuts and pretzels. If we are not going to get any lunch, I may as well dose up on the nuts. Now for the tricky bit – facing the wrath of the boss. Hopefully she'll not realise that I've got a double.

"Well, I may as well get value for money," I say in answer to the frosty stare which meets me on my return and before she protests that it's far too early to start drinking. She just can't seem to realise that I am only doing it to reduce the cost of the ticket.

"In case you hadn't noticed, we are paying through the nose for these flights. Here, would you like a nut?" I offer a packet as a peace offering and diversionary tactic.

"Nuts to you!" she responds without humour. "How many have you got in there?"

"About twenty, I should think." I examine the packet carefully. "Warning. This packet may contain nuts." I read. "But it doesn't say how many nuts are in the packet."

She snorts. "I was referring to the glass, not the nuts as you know perfectly well," but maybe the logic of my argument has prevailed because she goes to get herself some more coffee and shortbread.

Now that the drinks issue has simmered down, we are in an oasis of peace and tranquillity. I am gorged on nuts (although they have not made me gorgeous as a German friend of mine once said as he helped himself to another slice of cake) and I am also mellowed with whisky. This travelling business class is not too shabby. In fact, I think it really suits me. My glass is empty but I dare not get any more whisky. Apart from fear of La-Belle-Dame-Sans-Merci, I know that this is just a pleasant little interlude, the eye of the storm, that beyond these doors lies the real world and that at Heathrow we are in a race against time and I need to have a clear head.

At last our flight is called. Just time to stowaway some more nuts, just in case we get hungry.

But there is a meal on the plane after all – chicken chasseur and I choose a bottle of French Chardonnay to go with it, although my German wife, Frau Ning, hurls a look at me across the passage. To my surprise, in these security conscious times, the cutlery is real metal, the sort that you could attack pilots with, but of course, we business class people wouldn't dream of using such things in such a way and we have real linen napery instead of paper napkins and because there are not many of us in business class, service is a lot more speedy. I don't know what the plebs in cattle class are having, maybe just a sandwich, because a curtain is pulled across to preserve our superior status and privacy.

I get talking to the woman beside me, as you do. She's from Pennsylvania and has paid extra for this flight, like me, in order to catch her flight back home. She says she always travels BA. She's been staying in Edinburgh with relatives and I wonder if she would not have been better staying there. It wouldn't surprise me if her transatlantic flight were grounded too, but I suppose she has checked that out. Still, that doesn't mean to say you can believe what they say, as I have just found out. I tell her I travel with whoever is the cheapest and, as she seems to be such a big fan of BA, I don't tell her of my misgivings either. It won't be long before she finds out.

When we come to a standstill, Iona and I get off to a flying start. That's another good thing about travelling business class; because we were at the front of the plane, we get off first.

It seems miles to the terminal building. Maybe that's why they call it the terminal building – because some people practically are by the time they get there, especially if they are in a hurry like us. I make for the baggage reclaim whilst Iona goes off to check in and hold our place in the queue. At the carousel, I stand at the point where the bags, like projectile vomit, come spewing up from the tarmac. It could save vital minutes. I stand and wait. And I wait. Although I have been first at the carousel, I realise that there was no need for haste – it looks like the whole plane has got here by now. That's the thing about carousels. On the great roundabout of life, they are a great leveller.

At last the carousel churns into life. The gods conspire to ensure that my bags are amongst the last to emerge from the nether regions. I am relieved to see them all the same and hurtle off with them on a trolley. The passage to the central concourse is wide. Like a crazed geriatric with a Zimmer, I pass slower passengers. No rules of the road here – I overtake and undertake and avoid oncoming traffic, all without mishap. Breathless, I arrive at the hall where all the shops are and the check-in desks and God knows what else.

The hall is heaving with humanity. Perhaps it is worse than usual due to the strike, but to me it is always like a scene from *The Inferno.* Hell could be no worse than this. It's certainly as hot as hell is reputed to be, no doubt due to a combination of the body heat inside, augmented by the sunny London weather outside. All shapes, sizes, colours and ages are here. It is the world in microcosm and it looks as if the gods have contrived to send the whole world to Heathrow, all at the same time: *Heh! Heh! Heh! Look at this, lads! Pure pandemonium, eh Pan!*

My objective, through this human maelstrom, is to find, and reach, Point Q. Way down there I can see M and N and O. There's plenty of queues all right, but no sign of any Q. Where the hell can P and Q be? If I can find the ladies' toilets that's where they'll be - in the queue to pee.

I head off down the hall towards O. There is a choice. I can either go down the left side or the right. I know whichever one I choose, it will turn out to be the wrong one like in restaurants. I hope that the decision to come here was also not the wrong decision, that the plane to Naples has not already left.

I pick the right because it looks less crowded and sure enough, it's the wrong choice. I soon get behind someone ambling along, the least stressed person in Heathrow, the person in the least hurry in the entire complex. Overtaking is impossible and speed is not really possible either, even for him, due to the pressure of people, but he could go faster than a snail recovering from a hip replacement for God's sake. I grit my teeth and mutter death messages at his back, driving my trolley to within a hair of his ankles, urging him, willing him to walk faster. Wherever he is going it doesn't look like he's going to get there today or even this century, the way he is ambling along, like a stroller sauntering along a summer lane. At last I am able to cut down a side aisle and sure enough, the left hand side is less crowded now and I make much swifter progress without any dawdling geriatrics getting in my way.

Iona is at the check-in desk and agitated because in her panic to get there as quickly as possible, she had somehow taken a wrong turning and has just arrived. There is no queue at the desk. That's a bad sign. Please, God, don't tell me that it's closed, that the plane is already on the tarmac. Bloody hell, all that money for nothing and what do we do now? Try to get a flight back to Edinburgh, at more expense, or find a hotel here, but for how long? Or do we just find a bit of floor to camp on like the pictures you see of travellers at Bank Holidays? With a sinking feeling in my heart, we approach the man at the desk.

But it's all right. Presumably everyone else on the flight has already checked in. There are no seats together so we are allocated aisle seats opposite each other but not to worry – the main thing is that we have made it. As our bags disappear from view, the relief is as tangible as if we had been physically relieved of their weight. I wipe the sweat off my brow. We have finally made it! We will be in Naples tonight after all.

They make it so easy for us nowadays.

It must be comedy night in heaven, for after all that, ironically, the flight is delayed by an hour. The monitor screen in the departure lounge shows flight after flight cancelled so one would have thought there would have been no delays with all those empty skies. It doesn't look good for my travelling companion from Pennsylvania. She could have had more time with her relatives in Scotland but now, at best, she's going to be put up, fed up in a Heathrow hotel.

We had thought the departure lounge would be less crowded than the central concourse but it turns out to be just as crowded, if less frenetic. Probably it's full of people waiting for a BA flight to be transferred to another carrier. God knows how long they have been waiting. But in the best piece of news I have read for some time, there is our flight up there on the monitor. For once I am not moaning at the delay. An hour seems nothing after what it might have been, had we not caught that flight.

With time to kill, I go for a walkabout and come across a BA customer enquiries desk. To my surprise, it is not ten deep in irate customers, so I go back for my printout. It would really make me feel a whole lot better if I were told that I could claim the British Midland flight back. A search through my pockets and camcorder bag fails to unearth the visa slip. Bloody hell! I've lost it already. Maybe in my haste, I never got it in the first place. I'll worry about that later, but I would like to know if in principle, I am entitled to any compensation or not. My fear is that I will only be refunded half of the ticket I did not use – about £88.

The woman at the desk is helpful when I show her the flight I have missed and tell her what I have been obliged to do but she doesn't know the answer.

"It's unknown territory," she says. "Nobody knows what's going to happen." She gives me a leaflet and says I should write to the address on it.

"So, has the dispute been settled?" I ask. I am worried that the action could flare up again and we could be in the same situation on the homeward leg.

"It was," she says, "but when we came back we were getting such abuse and some of my colleagues were spat upon so we walked out again."

I express my shock, horror at this.

"Really," she says. "They expect us to work in this heat and take that sort of abuse and send us home for a couple of hours then call us back in again. And you know what the traffic's like here. It was 110° in this place yesterday."

I agree that that certainly is hot. It's hot enough in here now without all those hot tempers flying about. The lady seems prepared to go into more details, but Iona materialises at my side to say that we are to proceed to the departure gate. I wish the lady good luck with her dispute. It has less to do with altruism than a more selfish desire to have it settled before we come back.

"If I were you," she says to my departing back, "when you get to Naples, I'd advise you to confirm that you are using the return part of your ticket."

What! How am I going to do that? What kind of parting shot is that to make, for God's sake! So, as I walk down the passage to the plane, instead of feeling a slight sense of euphoria, there is a black cloud hovering over my head. We could still be caught in a backlog when we come back, even if the dispute is settled. I hope it doesn't mean another £310 to get home.

We are at our gate now. The people here will be our fellow passengers and some of them are bound to be on our tour. It is interesting to look at them and speculate which ones. It's mainly an older looking crowd. The ones with the suntans will be the Italians, going home. I scan the palefaces. I am looking for any carrying portable radios with CD and tape players which I regard as a pestilence. They never seem to play good music, only bad music very loudly to the invasion of my privacy and intense annoyance. I am paranoid about being allocated a room next to one of these. There doesn't seem to be any, and from my vantage point, I can see just about everybody.

It's impossible to say who might be on our tour. There are no tell-tale luggage labels to give me a clue. There's an attractive lady in a pink top, about my own age, with short blonde hair. Hope she's on our tour. If the church architecture gets a bit boring, as it might, I can always pass the time by studying her superstructure. From where I'm standing, it looks pretty good to me.

There's a younger couple on my right. When I sit down beside them, leaving a spare seat between us, he steadfastly refuses to make eye contact and stares, like a Buddha at a spot on the ground. Some people are like that. Maybe he thinks I'll ask him for money or something. I don't mind. I'm like that myself sometimes, especially in the mornings when I just haven't the energy and I can't be bothered with conversation. I'm likely to snarl at anyone who does try to speak to me, especially if they are cheery. If there's one thing I hate, it's people who are cheerful in the morning.

His partner gets up and goes to the toilet, I presume. When she returns, she picks up my passport and boarding pass which I have placed on the seat between us, in readiness.

"Hey!" I shout in panic, but even before the words are out of my mouth, she realises her mistake, apologises and hands them back to me. She probably thought that was her seat and they were hers. I smile in forgiveness. Losing my passport *before* I start out is a new departure for me. I quite often lose my visa card while on holiday which is why I am insured for such an eventuality, but I've never lost my passport before. I've had quite enough stress today already without this, thank you very much.

Now we are boarding. We shuffle forward. Somehow I always end up at a wing and this time is no exception but it doesn't matter a great deal anyway, as I am at an aisle seat. I prefer a window seat as I like to look at the mountains especially and try to identify places below. Iona is across the aisle and my fellow passenger looks like the sort of person who plays rugby or who is a pugilist by profession, or he maybe he just likes fighting for a laugh. He has a barbed wire tattoo motif on the bulging bicep that is next to me. He's probably the only tattooed person on the plane. Mind you, his female travelling companion looks a bit scary. She's probably got tattoos and piercings in places you'd have to take her clothes off to see first. No thanks, and it's not just the fear of being bashed either. She looks the very antidote to desire. I bet they have a ghetto blaster concealed in a bag in their hand-luggage. I can't understand how I failed to pick them out at the boarding gate.

The plane fills up and the curious thing is that the row behind me is completely empty. Strange, because Iona and I were told that we couldn't sit together. Anyway, it suits me because I can put my seat back with impunity, without feeling that I am impinging on the limited space of the person behind me. Actually, the space here seems quite roomy. With my seat reclined, I can stretch out straight. I am built for theatre seats and planes because although I am the same size as normal people sitting down, when I stand up, I am short because my thighs are short, shorter than Iona's, although I am marginally taller when we are standing up. It is one of my defects but I have the last laugh when I am in the theatre or flying. I pity those six-feet-plus people in planes. Shorter is smarter as far as flying is concerned, unless you are business class of course. I come in economy size for economy class. Pint sized so I can drink pints.

My plan is to have a couple of gins, eat my delicious British Midland meal, put my seat back, close my eyes and wake up in Naples. I don't know why I have these fantasies. I can't even sleep in a bed, let alone a plane because I am an insomniac. The gins might have lulled me to sleep but I am not going to have any, sleep or gins. Since I have already had three whiskies, La-Belle-Dame-Sans-Merci doesn't think I need any more.

When the drinks trolley eventually reaches us, predictably amongst the last, for we are at that point where the trolley coming down meets that coming up, contrary to orders, I buy a couple of cans of tonic. Across the aisle it is Frau Ning, my German wife again. She can't say too much however without creating a scene, but she bangs her book on her lap and turns round in her seat as far as space allows, to present her bristling back to me. I hope she'll have got over it by the time we land - in about three hours.

No doubt, gentle reader, you are wondering why the dear trouble and strife should be so aerated about my purchase of two cans of slim line tonic. That's because she knows I am going to mix it with the gin in my hipflask. I prefer to do this when I am sitting at a window seat as an aisle seat leaves me rather exposed to discovery by stewardesses and the prying eyes of other passengers, whom you never can tell, might tell on me: *Please miss, that man with the red face is drinking his own booze.* But I decide to risk it. My tattooed neighbour doesn't look the type to tell and after all the hassle we've had today, I think I deserve it. Besides, it makes the time go faster. By the time the gins are finished, it will be time for the meal and then, perhaps, who can tell, I may fall asleep.

Actually, the meal *is* surprisingly good. It is our national dish as revealed in a recent national newspaper poll – chicken tikka masala and now that everything has been cleared away, it is time to try and get a little nap. I put my seat back and close my eyes, hoping the gin and food will lull me to sleep.

But it's no good. After ten minutes, I give up. Perhaps if I read something. I can't be bothered with my book, so I begin reading the in-flight magazine where I learn that President Kennedy suffered from Addison's disease. Amongst the symptoms are tiredness, vague stomach pain and weight loss. I'm not like what's-his-name in *Three Men and a Boat* who, reading the medical dictionary, discovered that he was suffering from everything except housemaid's knee, but now I come to think about it, I *have* got two out of three. I certainly don't have weight loss but I am always tired and I am aware of some discomfort in the abdominal region. Perhaps it was the curry or too many free peanuts in the business lounge or perhaps when the two met in my stomach they didn't like each other and started a fight. Whatever it is, my stomach is churning like a washing machine.

What's that smell? Where did that come from? It surely wasn't me was it? Perhaps I am just imagining it, but Tattooman's nose is twitching; now he is rubbing it. He slips me a sidelong glance which I pretend not to notice. Do I pretend that I can't smell it, or do I wrinkle my nose and pretend to locate the direction myself to unmask the foul perpetrator? You can never be sure from whence these things come, though I tend to suspect the person in front. Maybe that's what Tattooman will think. Maybe he'll think he's imagining it if I show no signs of discomfort. I grip my magazine tightly as if my life depended on holding on to it and try to focus on the print swimming before my eyes. Above all, I must avoid eye contact in case he flexes his muscles and says: *Look here, mate, would you mind stopping that?* And if I had the courage and the presence of mind, I could reply: *Certainly. Which way did it go?*

I know I am blushing furiously which will be taken as an admission of guilt, compounded by an already florid complexion due to the damage years of quaffing Cabernet Sauvignon and malt whisky has done to my capillaries. In fact, my friends in Montana used to sing *Dave, the Red-nosed Reindeer* to me at Christmas time. But Tattooman doesn't know anything about that and will certainly assume it was me, however innocent I am.

My mind is racing with fear, embarrassment and panic. I feel certain now that Tattooman thinks it's me. What can I do? Perhaps I can shift the suspicion on someone else - Iona for instance: *I'm terribly sorry about my wife. She can't help it. She suffers from Addison's disease, you know.* She is absorbed in her book. Such an innocent pose doesn't look as if she's responsible for gassing flight whatever it is, bound for Naples, to death. A surreal image floats before my mind of the consternation when the plane lands in Naples with all the passengers and flight attendants dead, apart from one American passenger who manages to gasp before he expires:

It was horrible! It was a weapon of ass destruction! And the mystery of what happened to flight 666 from Heathrow to Naples becomes a sort of *Marie Celeste* of the skies.

It is a relief to touchdown at Naples at last without any further air turbulence. We are amongst the last off the plane and squeeze onto the bus for the 200-yard drive to the terminal. Why we just don't walk it, I don't know, but we're amongst the first off the bus, being the last on.

At passport control there are two queues. Iona goes into the right but I shift to the left when I see it is shorter. Wouldn't you know it! The man in front of me has a problem of some sort. Up till now it had been flowing freely, a quick flash of the passport and the traveller passes through. I don't know what's going on but it looks like some form-filling is going on. Meanwhile the other queue is proceeding smoothly. Typical! It happens in supermarket queues too. You join what looks like the shortest queue but there's always some old lady who looks completely dumbfounded that she has to pay, then she has to find her purse and painstakingly count out the exact money with rheumatic fingers, only to find she doesn't have it after all and hands over the note she ought to have handed over in the first place.

Anyway, what does it matter here? We won't be going anywhere until the last person has recovered his luggage. Probably me by the looks of it.

Whilst Iona waits at the carousel with a trolley, I go to the toilet. It's not for what you think; my guts have settled down. But as I leave, there is a man performing peculiar contortions at one of those inefficient warm-air hand-driers. At least they are *meant* for hands and sometimes faces, but this man is trying to dry his leg! In a sort of ungainly reverse arabesque, he is drawing the attention of a small crowd by holding onto the wall and trying to place his leg in the blast except he's not supple enough to get anywhere near it. I've sometimes seen people dancing to go to the toilet, but not *after* they've been and I've often seen people's oxters stained with sweat but this is the first time I've ever seen anyone with such a severe case of it in the groin.

We are amongst the first to reclaim our baggage and the reps direct us to our bus. It is practically empty and I choose the seat just behind the driver just in case there is anything to see on the trip into Naples. But for now there is nothing to do but watch our fellow passengers. I can see them coming and wonder which bus they'll go to. There is no sign of Tattooman so far, which is good. Ah, here comes the blonde lady in the pink top. I'd forgotten all about her. She'll either go right to the other bus, or left to ours. She goes right, of course.

"Hard luck, David, she's going on the other bus."

Bloody hell! How does she do it? Has she got some kind of radar or something? I am sitting at the window seat, so she cannot see my face. How did she know what I was looking at, let alone know what I was thinking? I could have been looking at any number of people and thinking all sorts of elevated thoughts.

"What? Eh?" I inject a puzzled tone into my voice.

"She's getting on the other bus."

I look at Iona and raise one quizzical eyebrow, like I haven't got a clue what she's talking about but she merely gives a snort of derision at my naïvety and doesn't say anything. I deem it wiser to say nothing either, but for the moment, I keep the look of perplexity on my face just in case that does make her think she has been barking up a wrong tree and may have been mistaken after all.

It is getting increasingly hot in the bus and I am beginning to sweat. Eventually the driver switches on the engine to operate the air-conditioning and illogically leaves the door open. It soon becomes apparent why he does so – to allow the diesel fumes to come in.

After a while, when she judges we've had a sufficient, but not quite lethal amount of lead poisoning, the rep comes aboard herself and takes our names. It looks as if we are complete. We will be underway soon, the door will be closed - no more diesel fumes, only nice cool air. But no, there is a problem.

"Mr and Mrs Guttings?"

No answer.

"Are Mr and Mrs Guttings present?"

It sounds like school. You ask a question and answer came there none. Looks like they are not here but maybe I wouldn't admit in public to that name either but until they are found, we are not going anywhere unless to an early grave with an ingestion of diesel fumes. The bus driver is no fool either: he's outside in the slanting evening sunshine talking to his mates while the rep goes back to the terminal building. If I'd any sense, I'd be out there too. Even the smell of aviation fuel from departing aircraft would be better than being kippered in here.

At last I can see our rep coming back with two people. They don't appear to have any luggage. So that's why they weren't on board the bus: they have been forlornly watching the carousel go round and round, willing each revolution to miraculously produce their luggage, but deep down inside they know it is hopeless. Everyone else from the flight has long since departed. There will be one bag which is going round and round which the baggage handlers have thoughtfully put on the conveyer belt and which no one claims, so you can count how many times it goes round and round without producing your own luggage. I know that feeling. It has happened to me, but fortunately not on the outward-bound trip. That's bad enough, but to start *off* without your luggage is the stuff of nightmares and the problem with this trip is, since we are on the move, the errant luggage might possibly *never* catch up.

As they draw nearer, I recognise them as the pair I was sitting beside at the boarding gate lounge, the one who was staring into space whose partner lifted my passport. I feel very sorry for them. We've had our problems today and I'm substantially out of pocket, but at least we are here now, we can put that behind us and hopefully enjoy our holiday. But how could you even *begin* to enjoy your holiday with just the clothes you stand up in and wondering when and if you would ever be reunited with your cases? In the brief second when they pass our seats, they don't look as sorry for themselves as I feel for *them*.

The joys of modern travel, eh? You go on holiday to forget the stresses of your job and then this happens. I bet losing your luggage didn't happen as often in the days of the Grand Tour when you and your luggage had a practically symbiotic relationship, strapped to the back or roof of your coach. The gods have a cruel sense of humour all right: *Thinks he's going for a nice holiday, eh? By Jupiter, we'll soon fix that. Watch this!*

The trip into Naples is not that interesting, like most motorway journeys and in any case, it is beginning to get dark. Even the driving, by Italian standards, is not that exciting, although our driver makes it potentially more interesting by hanging his hairy left arm out of the window to dry. One small hand on a very small man seems rather inadequate to be in control of such a large bus.

Angela, our rep, who by her vowels, hails originally from Scotland, points out the financial quarter which, with its glassy skyscrapers, looks just like any other financial quarter of any major city I have seen. It would have been nice to see Naples for the first time, from the sea, the way Nelson saw it when he came to support the King of Naples and sort out the French and where he met the love of his life. Maybe that could have happened to me - one out of three wouldn't be bad – if I'd approached by sea.

But now that we are in the old part, Naples is taking on its own individual character and, I have to say, first impressions are not too favourable. The buildings may have had a certain glory once, but now they are dingy and dirty and many are crumbling. The whole place has an air of decadence, not helped by the fact that there does not appear to be any street lighting. What lighting there is comes from the shop windows and car headlights. It gives the place a semi-deserted, half-closed sort of look, as if the inhabitants have had enough of this squalor and are in the process of evacuation, turning off the lights as they leave. When I ask Angela why there are no lights, she has a conversation with the driver and reports they are conserving electricity because of the drought. It has not rained since early May. We are more than half way through July.

It was a good choice of seat for, from our position above and behind Enrico, the driver, even if the architecture is not very appealing, we have the compensation of a grandstand view of some fine examples of mad Italian driving.

It is not for the hesitant, driving in Naples. Those who hesitate will never move. There appear to be no rules. Angela says that traffic lights are for decoration and pedestrian crossings are street paintings and nobody pays any attention to either. That also applies to Italy's attitude towards EU legislation.

"The Germans make the laws, the British obey them, the French ignore them and the Italians have never heard of them," Angela informs us. Many a true word spoken in jest. "They've just introduced a seat-belt law," she adds. (God knows how many years we've had that!) "They're also supposed to wear crash helmets on their scooters but no one bothers. You'll often see a man and his wife and his son, sometimes even a dog on a scooter and no one is wearing a crash helmet."

"Except for the dog," I wittily remark to Angela, who is just across the passage.

She does not think this witticism is worthy of passing on through her microphone to the bus at large, though she had passed on the information about the lights. That's three unfunny jokes I've made today. I should start a collection: *Jokes I have told and no one laughed (In three volumes).* Anyway, I think the surreal image *is* rather amusing. In fact, I have seen people with crash helmets that do have long floppy ears like rabbits' and I thought them rather quaint. I had thought about buying a scooter, just so I could wear the helmet.

It's not quite true though, as there are one or two who are wearing crash helmets, and there is a boy with bare feet standing on the platform between the handlebars, holding on to them in a casual sort of way, as if he has been doing it for years which he probably has. Interestingly, the father is wearing a crash helmet. He apparently has less faith in his driving than his son or maybe he thinks what's the point of getting him one when he's still growing and he'll get one when he stops growing – if he ever does grow up.

The object of driving in Naples seems to be to get as close as you can to the car in front without touching it, but by the looks of it, this doesn't always work judging by the number of vehicles with bashes in them. It's dodgems without the protective rubber bumpers. It is the survival of the one who blinks last. Amazingly, after more close shaves than all the Wilkinson Swords in Italy, Enrico does not seem to be losing his temper with all the cars, all the scooters which are cutting him up. It's like David taking on Goliath and we all know who won that one, so maybe Enrico knows when he's beaten. Here size gives way to mobility. Might does not get the right of way automatically. Enrico cannot blast his way through the Neapolitan traffic willy-nilly. It is comforting to reflect that size does not always matter.

The truth of this is being demonstrated now. Smaller *is* better because now Enrico wants to turn right up a small street but he can't because his bus is so long it will not allow him to make the manoeuvre without slicing the side off a parked car on his right like the lid off a sardine can.

It seems we are outside a bar. One of the habitués comes out and directs Enrico, like one of those people you see at airports with table tennis bats and earmuffs who guides planes into parking bays. Enrico has his door open and by the sound of it is saying: *Piss off you bastard, I am driving this bus and I'd thank you not to stick your bloody nose in where it is not wanted* or else he is saying: *If I could find the bloody moron who parked here I'd have his bloody guts for garters.* All is confusion.

Angela, over her microphone says, "Welcome to Neapolitan life! Now the whole street is going to become involved!" She says it as if she relishes it and I have to admit, I find it interesting. We northern Europeans, sun-deprived in our cold climate, mind our own business, but these southern Europeans, hot-blooded with a superfluity of sun, cannot wait to get involved. The street is alive with the sounds of excited Latin voices. Is it cursing or advice? We haven't a clue what's going on and that is the romance of being in a foreign place. This is not the sort of scene which you would see in, say Glasgow, and certainly not in Aberdeen, that most staid of all Scottish cities, the home of my *alma mater*, the granite city, the impenetrable, with the tough exterior where you would rather die than reveal your feelings. Besides, it's too bloody cold to hang about the streets there.

This is the warm south and the gentle Neapolitan air is filled with the sound of shouting and commotion that doesn't sound so gentle. There is a lot of hand waving and gesticulating going on. Meanwhile Enrico carries on manoeuvring, moving forward until there seems to a coat of paint only between the front of the bus and the car in front of him to the left, then the bus rocks on its brakes and Enrico switches his attention to his offside mirror and puts the bus into reverse. Iona is shutting her eyes and cringing.

"I don't like this seat."

At the other side, where I can't see properly, there seems to be a crowd gathered round the car on the right. The roof is rocking wildly. They seem to be bouncing it and lifting it to make a bit of extra room for the bus. It takes me back years ago, when as a schoolboy, my colleagues bounced the French *assistant's* Citroen Deux Chevaux from the back of the school to the front. Any car that looks like an upturned pram is just asking to be rocked.

Here presumably, they can't find the owner, or maybe this is the more fun way of doing it and that's the owner over there who is shouting more vociferously than all the rest: *Hey, get your filthy hands off my car?* It looks as if a street fight could break out at any time but it's maybe just a Neapolitan street party. Who can tell?

At last Enrico manages to swing the bus past the offending car, and somewhat belatedly, the self-appointed director of traffic gestures to Enrico that he can get past. Enrico is saying something but it is impossible to judge by his tone what it might be or to whom it might be addressed but he doesn't give any sign of acknowledgement for the director's "help" so I assume Enrico has thought him a spare part all along.

We give Enrico a round of applause but his part is not over yet. A hundred yards or so up this street with cars to the left of us, and cars to the right of us like the cannons flanking the 600 in the Valley of Death and with us all holding in our breath as we pass up the middle, Enrico stops again. It is too narrow to pass. He gets out and folds back a wing mirror of a car on the left, then he inches forward, then shunts, comes forward, reverses again. By inches we are getting there.

This time there is no audience to applaud the deed, and although Iona and I have ringside seats, she cannot bear to look. I notice that most of the cars, if they have wing mirrors at all, are folded in. The cars they belong to are bashed and like the city, laden with dust. Perhaps although it looks like a street, it is really a Neapolitan scrap yard. I wonder why Enrico doesn't just add another bash to these cars, but I expect he is bashful about bashing his bus.

At last we have arrived, the Hotel Golfo di Napoli, Naples. We sit in the lounge whilst Angela gets our rooms but before she does that, she comes round and asks us our names and ages. Bizarre procedure to need our ages, but none the less it provides a modicum of entertainment as I earwig as nonchalantly as I can, to the responses of those within my (limited) hearing range. The results can be enlightening: *My God, is that all he is? He looks at least ten years older than that. He looks older than me for God's sake!*

Angela moves out of range and then my attention is focused on a man to my left. Once having been made aware of him, I can't take my eyes from his face for I am looking at the living embodiment of Rameses the Second. I have a picture of him at home in a book somewhere. He does not look too well which is not surprising as he has been dead for three thousand years, give or take a few hundred. Now here he is in living flesh and blood, the same in every respect but looking a much better colour. The mummy walks again, or rather slouches in his armchair presenting that aquiline nose on that emaciated face at such an angle that the nostrils are clearly visible as two black tunnels like those *galleria* which perforate the Tuscan hillsides.

I think (I hope, I pray) from the angle of his head that he is only asleep but the pose is uncannily death-like - the skull beneath the face is too horribly obvious, the prominent nose, the sunken eyes, the teeth like tombstones in an ancient graveyard, discoloured and not two leaning the same way, just like that of Rameses in my book. I have never seen a living person look more like a cadaver in my life.

I nudge Iona and with a nod in his direction, I intone sepulchrally, "Rameses."

What on earth is she doing now? She is fishing in her handbag and finally produces a scrap of paper. She scribbles a few words on it and passes it over for my perusal. It says: *How old is Rameses?* Her hearing is a lot more acute than mine. In fact, she has very cute ears indeed – one of her best features, like she tells me my legs are my best feature. How low can you get?

I write: *3,500 approx.* Iona writes: *47!!!* I look: *You are joking!* Iona looks: *Oh no I'm not!*

Here is Angela with the keys at last. A chance to pick up some names of our fellow travellers, but I can't take them in; they don't mean anything to me and I forget then as soon as I hear them.

At last our name comes and we join the mad scramble for the lifts. We are not the first in the queue by any means. There are only three of them and with the luggage, only space enough for two, so this is going to take some time.

We are on the ninth floor. We have asked for a quiet room – Iona is a very light sleeper and I don't sleep much at all, so we like a quiet room. This should be quiet, not even the noisiest Vespa should penetrate at this height.

It's much like any hotel room layout, and the bed looks comfortable enough. It's certainly large enough, the kind Iona likes where we are twenty feet apart. The view from our window is across to a block of flats. Well what do you expect in the middle of a city? Anyway, we are not here for the view from the hotel. Tomorrow we are at Pompeii and the next night we will be off.

We unpack as little as we can get away with but when we have done that, the pristine room is transformed into a bombsite. Tidiness is not one of our virtues but we are both untidy so we don't get on each other's nerves. As a result, however, we tend to get twice the mess.

Angela had said that she'd see all of us at the bar at 8:15. I am not sure if that means we have to go because she wants to impart information or not, but there may be a free drink in it, so we wander down.

Nothing much seems to be happening – Angela doesn't look as if she is holding court and regrettably there doesn't seem to be any free drinks either but there are bowls of nuts on the tables so I buy a beer and Iona has a gin and T. She doesn't feel like going out for a meal. We seem to have been snacking and eating at odd times all day and her appetite is ruined. (Great! Discount a meal from the £310 extra this trip has cost us.)

By chance I find myself standing next to a young couple from Scotland who are in a similar position to us. They too bought seats from British Midland but because they were on an earlier flight, their seats were even dearer than ours. Once again, the old adage that there is always somebody worse than yourself proves to be true and that nonsense about early birds is a load of rubbish. We agree to exchange addresses at the end of the trip so we can keep tabs on how each of us is faring with our claim for compensation from BA.

There doesn't seem to be much happening here. Iona is tired and wants to go to bed but from the window at the end of the corridor on our floor, I have seen a very impressive fort-like building which looks as if it would be scarcely a step from our hotel and I want to go and explore. She goes upstairs to get some more suitable footwear. Meanwhile the girl behind the bar is giving me queer looks which I assume is because I am scoffing all the nuts. Either that, or she has got a squint and she's really looking at Rameses and his wife, who, by definition, must be Nefartari, who are sitting with another couple at an adjacent table. Actually, she is rather a comely wench - the bar maid, not Nefartari. It's difficult to imagine anyone who has *fart* for a middle name being irresistible, but apparently the real one was.

The barmaid's stare unnerves me sufficiently to stop me eating my free meal. She goes through a door behind the bar and I dive into the nuts again. It is a trap. She is back instantaneously and catches me. Her look says, no translation needed: *Hah! Caught you, you greedy bastard!* My look says: *Look I know what it looks like but I have had a pretty hellish day and I'm down £310 and I can't afford a meal and I've got a big fat stomach to support.* But I know it loses something in the translation and she just thinks I am a greedy pig.

When Iona gets back, we head out into the soft Neapolitan night. This is what I adore about the continent, to go out, to stroll on an evening that would be considered a blisteringly hot day in Scotland.

We go through a park which is full of people; even little kids who should be in bed long ago, are up. Now we need to cross the road but that is easier said than done. If Rome is the Eternal City and New York never sleeps, Naples is where the traffic never stops. Getting across the road is something the stupidest chicken would never contemplate here and it's like a game of chicken trying to cross at this point, or more like Russian roulette to be precise.

It's no good. We are just not going to be able to cross here without laying our lives down on that black and white stripy piece of contemporary art which the drivers treat with disdain. We retrace our steps and come at it from a different angle and this time we are successful. We are as close as we can get to this fort. Apart from the towering crenellated walls, what impresses me about it is the way the massive round towers fan out at the bottom, like the pleats on a tennis skirt, which I have always found very sexy.

Somewhere, in the distance, down by the port, there is the sound of music from an open-air concert. Some people would call it music I suppose, but I don't and I'm sure Rogers and Hammerstein wouldn't either, but I have to admit, it does add a certain ambience to the evening. To our left, high up on the façade of a building is a neon sign which indicates the time and the temperature: *22:22 28⁰ C*. Perfect. Just right for a stroll.

But La-Belle-Dame-Sans-Merci puts her foot down with a heavy hand – no way is she going to walk all the way round this massive edifice. Now we are at one of the corners, I have to admit it does look rather a long way and next to a busy street and with the irritating buzz of the Vespas for company, it doesn't look the most appealing or romantic of walks, so we head back in the opposite direction and discover a bridge with an arch at the end of it. I just have to cross it and see what's at the other side. Once through the arch, we come to the front of the building.

There are three massive towers, but incongruously, linking the central two is a two-tiered marble arch with a *tympanum*. I may not know much, but I do remember a bit of my classical culture and this is a bit of Roman copying, if ever I saw it. This structure, with its Corinthian pillars and elaborately carved figures and especially the contrasting marble whiteness against the austere grey of the towers, looks as if it does not belong there at all, but was added as an ill-thought-out afterthought. To my untutored eye, the styles look centuries apart and the marriage is not a happy one. I should have looked in my guidebook before I came out, but if I don't start heading back soon, it's not the only unhappy marriage there is going to be.

As we leave by a path which looks as if it will avoid Brands Hatch, we come across a brown sign which tells us what we have been looking at – Nuovo Castel, XIV e XV c. I should have guessed. This is the new castle. Most of the buildings we saw over Enrico's bald pate looked a lot older than this.

Not far away, there are a couple of small boys with two blue plastic basins which seem to be full of empty beer bottles. I wonder if they are collecting them to sell. But who would want them? Maybe they are full after all, but who would want to buy warm beer either? They are at least ten years too young to be selling alcohol, but I don't suppose that is a prohibitive factor in Naples. Whatever the case, they must be trying to raise a bit of cash. Unemployment here is at a staggering 30% compared to Italy's 11% and crime is rampant. I have noticed some cars with some very sturdy anti-theft devices indeed. Yet I feel completely safe and the warm air with its gentle breeze, and even the distant strains of the music from the concert, create a very ambient atmosphere.

At the top of the square which we had come through earlier, and occupying its whole length, is an impressive yellow building with olive-green windows. It is an elegant symphony of symmetry. There are some flags lazily flapping and a brass plaque which my translation of the Italian takes to be the Town Hall. I can't speak Italian, but I reckon I can read a fair bit of it with what I remember of my Latin and French. Our hotel, on the other hand, has nothing to recommend it architecturally, being a cornflake box with holes in it for windows, but it does have the advantage of height and its flat roof does make an excellent vantage point, so just before we turn in, I suggest to Iona we go up (it's only two flights from our floor up the open staircase) to soak in a little more of the atmosphere.

The floodlit Nuovo Castel dominates. Despite its glaringly white triumphal arch gateway, I think it is one of the most splendid buildings of its type I have ever seen. Away down in the park where the lighting is soft and yellow in contrast to the stark white illumination of the Castel, the sound of the laughter of the ant-like children comes filtering through the trees. Further away, down by the port which is obscured by darkness, the sound of the concert is wafted up on the breeze which even the thrumming of the myriad of invisible cicadas fails to drown. Some twelve hours ago I doubted if I would ever see the sights and sounds of Naples this day but here I am, breathing in the warm wisteria-scented air, looking at them now. Who would have thought it, a mere twelve hours ago?

Yes, I am glad they make it so easy for us nowadays.

Chapter 2
O Sole Mio!

There is every possibility of taking a walk today. The alarm bell, really our telephone, began our day by ringing at 7:30. We are being picked up at 8:30 for our half-day trip to Pompeii and in the afternoon we have a walking tour of Naples, so we shall be doing plenty of walking all right. I groan and turn over, pull the sheet over my head. I must look like a mummy and feel like death warmed up. Although the trip to Pompeii is what I'm looking forward to most in the entire trip, I am not at this precise moment. Not at this time; much, much later. I am not an early morning sort of person.

Iona and I have this agreement – she gets to use the shower first in the morning. It's one of the many little kindnesses and courtesies that I unselfishly shower upon her. But she comes back all too soon. She's probably saving water for Italy on account of the drought.

"Come on, get up!"

"Uh huh!"

There is the sound of the hairdryer blasting away followed a few minutes later by: "I said get up, you lazy pig!"

"Uh huh!"

Suddenly, the hair drier noise stops. It was so soothing. There is a bang as it is slapped down on the dressing table and without warning, too late to grab it, the sheet is suddenly whisked off me and I am lying there, not naked but unashamedly terrified.

"I said get up! Before I lose my temper!" She is standing over me holding Humphrey the Hedgehog hairbrush poised to strike and if she does, it will be the spiky side, not the smooth back which will make contact with my back or side and I know it will be sore, because I've had it before.

There is no possibility of any more sleep today, so I meekly roll my trotters out of bed and hobble to the bathroom, bleary-eyed. My ankles are always very weak in the mornings. Like me, they take a bit of time to get used to the day.

When I am finished my ablutions, the cruel tyrant is already dressed and ready for breakfast.

"See you up there," she says. "And don't forget the key."

The dining room is on the roof where we were last night. But what I can see this morning is the Bay of Naples with that arch troublemaker, Vesuvius, dominating everything: the sea, the shore, the sky. Wow! All this was here last night and I never saw it! Away round to the left, hazy in the distance, like a pincer on a crab, must be the Sorrento peninsula where we shall be next week.

What an inspired choice for a restaurant! It's open to the air, on a dais, with a canvas roof but at this time in the morning, the sun is not high enough and a number of tables at the front are in full sun where the rays, even at this time in the morning, come blistering down over the sparkling, shimmering blue waters of the bay. To add to the general ambience, there is even a man playing a piano in the main dining room inside, but the soothing sound easily filters outside through the wide open doors. It seems quite perfect.

"Your wife is sitting over there, sir."

This from the maître'd. How the hell did he know that I wonder? Has she told him: *By the way, if you see someone who looks like a lazy pig - that will be my husband?* Or maybe she has warned him about my *pantouffles* for he is certainly looking at them in a most peculiar way, as if they were peculiar. In fact, there is nothing peculiar about them whatsoever. They have wine bottles on them with *Burgundy* and *Beaujolais* and *Chardonnay* and *Chablis* written on them. Iona got them as a stocking filler one Christmas and as they are so light they have become an indispensable part of my travelling wardrobe ever since, though Iona prefers me not to wear them outside the privacy of our apartment.

She has chosen a table which is in partial shade. She has chosen it to suit us both. She likes the shade, whereas I'm like it says on the back of some seed packets: *Prefers full sun.* That's probably why I didn't grow very tall: I didn't get enough sun. Or perhaps I overdid the watering.

I thank the maître'd and make my way over to the table. "How did he know I am your husband?" I ask as I sit down at the sunny side of the table.

"Don't know. Just asked for a table for two and said you were coming."

"Sure you didn't mention my *pantouffles?*" I mutter suspiciously.

"No, why?"

"'Cos he looked at them most peculiarly."

"I'm not surprised."

He's giving them another good old stare as I go up for my buffet breakfast, as if I were bringing the tone of the place down and if it were up to him, he'd throw me out.

If there's one thing I like to do on holiday, it's to have a good breakfast and if there's another thing I like better than that, it is to get value for money. Thus I have fruit juice, muesli and fruit, cold ham and cheese, (I would have had

41

bacon and egg but it's not on) a couple of croissants and two cups of coffee.

"I'll see you downstairs. Don't be late." Iona isn't waiting. I am still on the second croissant and the second cup of coffee. I don't feel there's any need to hurry. The sun is warm, the scenery is stupendous and the downbeat music from the piano encourages one to linger. I nearly missed all this and I want to drink it in, luxuriate in it. In any case, there are still some people I recognise from our tour. There's the young Scottish couple and the black man with the blonde who've just arrived. Actually, they may not be with us at all, as some of our number on the bus yesterday are going on a cruise whilst the rest of us go on the bus tour. They're so late in coming for breakfast, they probably are early birds for the cruise.

Back in our room, Iona has already gone. We've been told to put on sun cream and I do it here so I can wash the grease off my hands. I change out of my *pantouffles* into my nice blue canvas shoes which I have specially bought for this trip. They have a nice nautical-looking knot motif on the front and they only cost 50p out of Lidl's and I am very proud of that price. I decide to change out of my green T shirt with *Türkiye* written on it into a short-sleeved green cotton shirt, not only because it looks cooler but more sartorial. With my darker green shorts, (actually Speedo swimming trunks) I am a vision in green.

I gather up my camera and the water bottle and set off. I look at my watch. Still plenty of time. When I get into the lift, I don't know what it is, but some inspiration reminds me that I have forgotten my Panama and we have been warned that a hat is essential, especially true in my case, being somewhat follically challenged as they say, since for a number of years now I have been forced to adopt the tonsure as my form of hairstyle more through necessity than force of habit you might say.

I nip out of the lift before the jaws of the door have time to bite and sprint down the corridor to our room, grab the hat and sprint back. The lift has gone and doesn't want to come back. I wait and wait and still it does not come. It's past 8:30 by now and still the bloody lift will not come. Should I run down? But that's what the gods are waiting for and will send it up as soon as I set off. But we're on the ninth floor and as long as it comes soon, it will still be quicker to wait for the lift. I'll give it another minute…Oh, to hell with it; I am going to run down. I set off towards the stairs and far below, I think I can hear it coming. Fooled it! That's what I should have done long ago – pretended that I was taking the stairs. Ping! Here it is at last.

When I emerge at the ground floor, there is no one from our tour in the foyer. That's not a good sign. Now the stupid electronic doors won't open until they are ready to release me and delay me by what can't be more than a couple of seconds but it seems for ages. There is the bus at the bottom of the steps and nobody is hanging about. This looks bad. It is. La-Belle–Dame-Sans-Merci is beckoning furiously from a window near the front and mouthing: *Hurry up!*

By the time I take my seat, we are five minutes late. Angela doesn't turn a hair, though maybe she's seething inside. But I doubt it - I can't be the first person who's ever been late on these trips.

"Don't dare embarrass me like that again!" Iona hisses. Although I am the one who's late, she's the one who's blushing furiously and I get the idea that her complexion has more to do with being furious with me than embarrassment at me.

"It's not my fault. The bloody lift wouldn't come," I plead in mitigation. When in trouble, blame a machine if you can – it can't defend itself. "Besides, *somebody* has to be the last," I point out logically.

I'd like to look back and see if the black man and the blonde are here. I was relying on them to be last. Surely they couldn't possibly be here, not unless they only had a cup of coffee for breakfast. They must have been on the cruise after all, but I'm too embarrassed to turn round and check in case I meet people's eyes and they are as mad at me as Iona is.

When we get to Pompeii, there they are after all but my holding the bus back doesn't count at all, because there's clearly a problem. Angela is on her mobile because our guide has not turned up. She tells us that he is on his way, that there has been a misunderstanding. That probably means he is still in bed.

Meanwhile we evacuate the bus and loiter at the street corner. Most people are in the shade, but I hang about at the edge of the group, in the sun. There's a few stalls selling books and souvenirs and across the road, a stall selling water. Whilst Iona looks at the books, I go across to get some more water. Judging by the heat already, it looks like we could need it.

"Una grande aqua fredo, per pavore." I have no idea how correct that is but I do know that confusingly, in Italian, *calde,* which you would expect to be cold, is actually hot. Maybe I am mixing up my little Spanish with my little Italian. But maybe it's too good because the vendor ripostes with a torrent of Italian as if he expects me to understand.

I haven't a clue how much, but I deduce that he is telling me how much it costs. I can only look at him like an idiot. "Eh?" I am conscious of sounding and feeling like Manuel in *Fawlty Towers*.

He repeats it. I nod sagely, as if I had understood and rake about in my pouch for some coins. I can't get at them for some notes, so I take the notes out and put them down on a wooden table. I hand over some coins and he gives some of them back to me. This could be the dearest water in Italy - I haven't had time to get used to the euro and haven't a clue what I gave him or what I got back. I slip the change into my pouch, zip it up and turn to go. I've only gone a couple of steps when, with the second flash of inspiration I've had today, and it's not even 9:30 yet, I remember the notes. Phew! That *really* would have been the dearest water in Italy.

Iona has bought a book which shows Pompeii then and now. It's a great idea. Facing a page illustrating a ruin, there is a colour transparency which you slip over the scene as it is now and, hey presto! you have an artist's impression of what it looked like at the time of the eruption – brilliant! She shows it to some of our fellow tourists and they like it too and buy one for themselves. If only she had had commission, we might have had ours free.

At last our guide arrives. He's apologetic in a lilting sort of voice in which he stresses the ends of his sentences. I suppose that's what they do in Italian. It seems some employees at Pompeii are on half-day strikes and he had been told the strike was scheduled for the morning instead of the afternoon. Seems everybody is on strike these days. He is carrying his hat rolled up like an umbrella, so when he unfurls it, and plonks it on his head, it looks like a pleated lampshade.

We set off towards the *Scavi* but before we get there, he stops and gives us a talk about the eruption and how Pompeii differed from Herculaneum. Whilst Pompeii was buried by ash, Herculaneum had been engulfed by mud. I think, had I had the choice in 79 AD, I'd rather have been a resident of Pompeii. On that fateful day, they were still rebuilding from an earthquake in 62 AD and restoration was still not complete when the cinders and ash rained down.

Standing under the shade of the pines, if we look to our right along the grove of oleander, we can see Vesuvius sleeping peacefully now. It has been having a nap since 1944 but one of these days it is going to rouse itself again.

Probably the first sign will be an earthquake, like the stomp of Iona's feet when she marches across the room to get me out of bed, but unlike me, who am mild-mannered and biddable, even when disturbed from my repose, Vesuvius is going to get up in a very bad mood indeed and everyone is going to know about it.

I hope it will not be when we are here. We were in Sicily in October 2002 and to our disappointment, left just a week before it erupted. From our hotel roof in Gardini Naxos, we would have had a grandstand view of the pyrotechnics and would have been perfectly safe at that distance even if the lave flow came in our direction since it flows so slowly and we should have been well out of range of any lava bombs. But Vesuvius is a killer. 2000 people died that day, including some gladiators who were chained up and could not flee. Ironically, that which had killed them, also preserved them and their city.

Before we get to the ticket booths, our guide picks up a book like Iona has just bought from a stall but does not pay for it and tells us this is the last chance to buy water. We have to buy our own tickets, as some people may be old enough, or young enough, to get in free. That might just apply to two of our number – a boy of 13 or so and an attractive Pakistani girl who could be about 16. There are only 18 in our number now, the rest who were on our bus from the airport, having gone off on a cruise that I never noticed in the brochure. It's a good number because we can all gather round the guide and he doesn't have to project as if he were, as Queen Victoria said of Gladstone, addressing a public meeting.

It is a bit disappointing to enter the city along a wooden ramp instead of treading where Roman sandals trod nearly two millennia ago but I needn't have worried. Once through an arch, actually the Porta Marina, we are on the actual cobblestones, though to call them cobblestones calls to mind our puny little ones and doesn't do these monsters justice. I'd like to see rioters digging these up and throwing them at the police! These are enormous and irregular with gaps between them which much have made riding in a wagon or cart such a bone-shaking experience that it's a wonder that anyone chose to ride in them at all.

Marco, our guide, pulls us up a side street, and ushers his flock into the shade, though I am able to find a spot in the sun where I can still hear him, and points out to us ruts where the carts have worn grooves in the stone. At the end of the street are massive blocks of stone which seem to obstruct vehicular passage. According to Marco, these are stepping stones so that people carrying heavy loads, suspended from poles over their shoulders, don't have to step off the high pavements and climb up again and break their necks in the process. And here's the cunning part, the height of the stones is sufficiently low to allow clearance for the axles of the carts to pass through.

It is our first introduction to Roman ingenuity and it is easy to look at this cobbled street with its high pavements, its rutted cart tracks and the stepping-stones and project oneself back 2000 years and imagine ordinary life, the hustle and the bustle there must have once been on this street. Now, two thousand years later, these same streets are still bustling and sandal-trod (unless of course they happened to get a bargain like me.) But what would the Pompeian's make of those, like some in our group, who are wearing sandals *and* socks? Some strange new sect? And what would the punishment be for such sartorial impropriety? Exile or death? Anyway, shockingly socked and sandaled or not, as the case may be, we set off to follow in the footsteps of the last inhabitants of Pompeii and explore their town.

Appropriately enough, it turns out, the first stop is the Basilica. This of course is long before Christianity became a popular cult, so it has nothing do with churches, though Christian churches pinched the architectural idea for their great cathedrals. This is a secular building, a meeting place, but principally, the law courts. An immense structure, intimidating in itself, but with the podium where the magistrates sat, so high from the ground that it must have made any defendant standing beneath it feel like an insignificant little ant upon whom the full force of the law would soon be about to descend: *You are charged with wearing white socks and sandals and making yourself look like a right pleb. Because of the gravity of your offence, you are sentenced to attend a course on wearing appropriate footwear so you do not offend public decency in future and 200 hours community service.*

The place is pretty ruined now, one of the places they didn't quite get round to restoring completely after the earthquake of 62, so Iona's book with the transparency comes in pretty useful as I can see just how awe-inspiring it was in its heyday.

But apart from the huge scale of the building, the thing that captures my interest particularly here is, because of its ruinous state, you can see the construction of a Roman pillar. Made of cheap brick, the whole thing is then covered in plaster and then given a coating of marble dust and - transformation - you have what looks like a column made of marble! Put a lot of these together and you create a place of elegance and apparent affluence, perhaps even opulence. Imagine all those northern industrial streets with the back-to-back houses, faced with powdered marble! Now that would be something, wouldn't it!

We're off to see the forum. Then, as now, it is a large open rectangular area, and was the heart of the city, a market place and where religious and civic functions took place. At the northern end once stood the Temple of Jupiter and behind the ruins, looking surprisingly near, shouldering into the cloudless azure sky, is the hulking presence of Vesuvius.

It is a pedestrian precinct (another idea we have nicked from the Romans) bounded by the remains of colonnades. The great artery which extends from the south eastern end of the forum, The Via Dell Abbondanza, terminates here in three massive blocks of stone. This far can the vehicular traffic come and no further. Turning must have been a nightmare as there is no turning circle. And if another cart was beside you, and another twenty behind, what did you do? Traffic jams: yet another idea we got from the Romans. I can imagine them all, shouting and gesticulating, telling the cart driver how to manoeuvre, like Enrico with his bus. I wonder if they had rules of the road then, or did they do what they pleased, like the Italian drivers of today? Perhaps we should understand that that was how it was then and that is why it is as it is today. *Plus ça change* and all that.

In one of the market places off to the right of the forum are some frescoes and more interestingly but grimly, enclosed in two glass cases, are two victims of the eruption. The first of these, we are told, is a boy of about 15. The expression on his face is one of agony; he is probably trying to breathe but suffocating from the noxious gases. In his contorted posture, it is a reminder of how grim it must have been that day, how great the panic, how desperate the struggle to flee, to take to the ships, to escape what must have seemed to them, the wrath of the gods. From his extended hand, I can see the bones of his fingers emerging from the grey plaster, for this is how he has been resurrected. He would have been covered in ash and there he would have lain for eighteen hundred years until the first archaeologists poured plaster into the cavity created by the decomposed flesh and thus preserved him forever.

It reminds me of a similar idea I saw a number of years ago in the Dordogne region of France. A dead pig had been immersed in running water and slowly the corpse was being calcified due to the heavy concentration of limestone in water. I thought then and still think now, what a wonderful way to dispose of a corpse! I could be put out in the garden as an ornament – think of the variety of artistic poses I could be twisted into once rigor mortis had worn off – or instead of an artistic use, I could be something practical, like a hat stand or an umbrella stand, though they are not as common these days as they once were. Or perhaps what fun the grandchildren could have playing a game of quoits with grandfather! I am sure I could be put to some use dead, perhaps more use in this condition than alive.

But I suppose there will be some stupid EU rule against it though, in Italy, perhaps, I could realise my ambition. After all, since I am a lazy pig, I am practically there already and although I'm not quite dead yet, my feet are dead tired and it could spread up.

Next stop are the baths. We are going to the Stabian baths, the oldest in Pompeii, dating from 2BC. I am already familiar with the principle behind Roman baths, having been to Bath and many other Roman baths beside, though as I would expect, these are in a much better state of preservation – some have been little more than stumps of pillars in the ground.

First there is the *apodyterium* or dressing room, but it should really be the undressing room. Here you can see the holes in the walls where once were the shelves where the patrons placed their clothes and belongings. Next is the *calidarium* or hot room containing the *alveus* or hot tub and the *laconicum* or steam bath. The whole system is operated by a hypocaust or underfloor heating system (another idea we have nicked from the Romans) though I think we tend to have given that one up now. There are men's and women's sections and the women are wimps because they do not have the *frigidarium*. There was none of your mixed bathing here: it is a common misconception that Roman baths were scenes of debauchery and depravity. This only happened in the latter days of the Empire and Pompeii never survived to see that.

The baths are swarming with people and two hot dogs, dead to the world, are oblivious of all the commotion around them, their sides heaving rhythmically in deep slumber and their tongues lolling out loosely with the heat. That shows you how stupid these dogs are - they should have picked the *frigidarium* for their nap – it would have been a lot cooler there. This place is as hot and crowded as Heathrow airport on a strike day. How they can sleep amongst the constant tramp of feet just centimetres past their ears together with the Babel's Tower of guides' voices as they explain to their tourists the key points to observe, shows how dog tired they must be.

In fact, it is quite hard to hear Marco amongst this mêlée, so it's as well that this is the area of Roman architecture I need to learn about least. However, the one thing I do learn, which intrigues me, is that the roof in the *calidarium* is grooved, like a Nissen hut in the Second World War, which allows the condensation to run down the channels instead of dripping onto the patrons below. Clever people these Romans, eh?

The Stabian baths are near the brothels and that's where we are off to next, via the House of the Vettii. We can't get in there today as it is under restoration, but Marco takes us up a side street so we can peer through a grilled iron gate at a famous pornographic fresco. It looks like a grocer weighing a leek and a couple of onions but in fact, it is Priapus casually weighing his phallus, as you do. It is poking out obscenely from beneath his tunic and reaches to his knees. He's not looking too happy so I presume it's lost a bit of weight. I think he should cheer up a bit. I don't know what effect it had on the horses, unless it was to make them jealous, but I bet it certainly frightened the ladies. But perhaps he's discovered that like Enrico's bus, size isn't everything and perhaps he is glum because it *has* put on weight.

Marco wants to know what Iona thinks of it. She gives it a brief glance and him short shrift.

"Disgusting!"

Marco seems disappointed and says that it is only recently that women have been allowed to see this fresco and others of an erotic content, implying Iona is very lucky indeed to get to see this. If he had hoped she would find it arousing, he's sadly mistaken. Iona certainly doesn't think so. Quite the reverse in fact, and looking round the rest of the women in our party, I can't imagine any of them rushing back to the hotel in a fever of sexual arousal either. Unless the blonde one...but not because of the fresco. Perhaps that's why she was late down to breakfast, or maybe she doesn't do breakfast, just bed.

Ironically, next stop is Modestum's bakery. You can see the holes where the wooden shafts were threaded through the grindstones to be turned by the slaves, poor devils. The oven is still here too. In fact, the whole place must have seemed like an oven what with the combined heat from that along with the temperature from outside as well. Talk about slaving over a hot oven. Amazingly, archaeologists found 81 carbonised loaves here. Marco shows us a picture of one in the book which Iona has bought. It is divided into segments like a sponge cake and I must admit that although it looks a trifle well-fired as the supermarkets call it when they sell them off cheap, I like the look of it better than the loaves Iona bakes in her bread machine. We are on our third bread-maker now and I think we are down to £27:10 a loaf, but sums aren't my strong point, so it could be a bit dearer than that. Anyway, man cannot live by bread alone, and we're on our way to the brothel at last.

Was it like this then, I wonder? I hope not, for the poor girls would be worn out as there are massive crowds outside, waiting to go in, funnily enough like the queues outside the bakers in my home town, only worse. It's at a three-way intersection and they are queuing up from each direction. Most of the streets in Pompeii are built in a grid design (another thing we got from the Romans) but this brothel is on one of the few twisty streets in Pompeii. Marco says it's so people can't see where you're heading – as if they wouldn't have guessed!

Actually, because of its location, the building itself, never mind what's inside, is very interesting. Forming two arms of the Y, it's a two-storey building and shaped like the prow of a ship, the upper storey hanging over the ground floor and extending so far as to overshadow the narrow pavement. I bet this building was high on the list for restoration after the earthquake of 62 and by the looks of it, appears to have been given a lot of attention since the disaster of 79. It looks the newest building in Pompeii, as if the restorers knew this is what would draw the crowds. There must be something about brothels which intrigue us; even the baths were not as busy as this, and everyone has been to the baths.

When we eventually get inside, our time is regrettably all too short as we are being processed along a conveyer belt of humanity. There isn't time to stop and look properly unless you want to be trampled underfoot by the perpetual motion of the stream pushing to get in from behind, so to speak. Above each door is an erotic fresco. The idea seems to be that the speciality of the prostitute is advertised, like a sign above a shop door. There is one of a woman with very small breasts sitting astride the man. Unfortunately, or fortunately for Iona, the fresco is badly damaged in the vital area. He has his right hand raised. Perhaps he is telling her to stop: *Stop! Stop! You're giving me a headache!* or else he is waving cheerily at someone who has just come into the room: *Hello, dear, it's not what you think. I'm just doing a bit of research for this novel I'm writing.*

We are not allowed upstairs unfortunately. I get off the conveyer belt by slipping into one of the rooms to my right. It's not roped off or anything. I am alone. So this is where it all happened, happened, happened. I wonder how many *sesterces* it cost to get in here? What sounds of ecstasy had these walls heard? What sights had the walls of this little cubicle witnessed, on this hard little bed? And it *is* little, even for one as short as I am, and it *is* hard because I can't resist lying on it, trying to ignore the stares of the tourists trooping by, trying to get a feeling for the past. How many people had lain here and what speciality did the girls who entertained their clients here, perform? I had not time to look before I came in. I'll look on the way out.

It couldn't have been very erotic in here, I reflect. It is windowless and cramped, and even although that unappealing bed would have had a straw mattress on it, it still looks hard and far from conducive to sex, especially with other patrons passing by within feet of you, although there presumably was at least a curtain, so they didn't get a free show.

"What on earth do you think you are doing?" It is La-Belle-Dame-Sans-Merci.

I leap up in confusion. "Em...er...just trying out the bed." I thought she was ahead of me and had already left the establishment.

"Pervert!"

In my confusion and hasty exit, I haven't time to notice the erotic fresco above the door, and before I know it, I am out into the open air of the brilliant Pompeian sunlight and being given a lecture on being an embarrassment and sexual deviant.

"I just hope none of our group saw you!"

No chance of what happened in the brothel happening to me tonight then, that's for sure. I have really blown it because it's one of Iona's eccentricities, that apart from anniversaries, birthdays and religious festivals, such as

Christmas, she likes to consummate each new place that we go to. As for me, I just like travelling, but even if I like a place a lot, I tend not to go back as there are so many interesting places in the world to go to. And this is my first visit to Naples.

By the time we get to our next location, however, the big theatre, the heat seems to be less on me and concentrated more on the arena. It is more baking hot in here than it would have been in Modestum's bakery. Pompeii had two theatres, side by side, and a porticoed quadrangle behind them (later turned into a gladiators' barracks) where patrons could go during intermissions. The big theatre, seating about 5000, staged dramas, whilst the smaller Odeon, seating about 1200, was used for musical concerts and poetry readings. How cultured were these Romans!

And how modern too! They had fast food shops, so close to the road that you could purchase your food without getting out of your carriage, and I had thought that the Americans had thought of drive-in takeaway joints first! You can see the marble counters in which are set the *amphorae* which once held the hot food but which now contains the killer ash. Marco says they put the ash in there as people were using the *amphorae* as rubbish bins. I take some of the ash and put it in my pocket as a souvenir and to add to my geological collection. I have stones and pottery shards from all over my travels, but in my laziness, I have never labelled them so I'm not sure where they come from any longer, though there are one or two I recognise such as a bit from The Great Wall of China and a white stone from the shore at Abu Simbel. This will go with my bit of lava from Etna. I won't get them confused, even although Etna was smoking vigorously when we left.

And when it comes to houses, the houses of the rich make my house look like a slum. The basic structure consists of an entrance hallway which the Romans called a *vestibulum*, which leads to the *atrium*, a porticoed area open to the elements with its *impluvium* to catch the water. Then there is the *peristilium* which would have been my favourite part of the house. This is an open courtyard area, a sort of inner garden from which the other rooms opened off. What a grand design to have a garden inside your house and how cool to have a water feature too, but of course, totally impractical in Scotland.

As we pass The House of The Tragic Poet, so called because of a mosaic in the *tablinum*, or main room, used for receiving guests, I notice a mosaic behind another of these barred gates like at The House of The Vettii. It is in black and white and shows a chained dog with bared teeth, ready to pounce. At the bottom, it says: *Cave Canem*. It's of interest to me because I know it well – it was an illustration in my Latin book at school, and to this day is about all the Latin I remember, apart from *amo, amas, amat* and *mens sano in corpore sano,* which for some reason has stuck in the brain, along with *festina lente.* That, I regret to say, is the sum total of what I have to show for three years of studying Latin. Well, actually, that's not quite true – I remember *homo sum* but whenever I said it, I used to get queer looks or I kept meeting the wrong sort of people, so I gave up saying it. I regret my hatred of the subject now, which I thought pointless then. How did I know that 40 years later, I would see this mosaic in real life and be addicted to Roman culture but unable to read the inscriptions on all those triumphal arches I've seen all over the Roman world?

We visit The House of The Faun so called because there is a diminutive bronze statue of a bloke with a tail in the middle of the *impluvium*. There is a transparency of this in the book and I can see just how sumptuous it is. What's special about this house, is that it contains not one, but two peristyles and an *exedra,* a recess with seats, where conversation could take place in the peace and tranquillity of

56

pleasant surroundings. It must have seemed a million miles from the Via Della Fortuna which is the main thoroughfare on which it stands. I adore its open spaciousness, how you can look from the atrium to see the peristyles beyond and when you think of all the mosaics and frescoes which would have surrounded you, it must have seemed like paradise. I think of my own poor home and think: *These Romans knew how to live. Wonderful houses, baths and theatres and plumbing better than in French campsites, even today.* But of course you would have to have been rich and I would have been one of those poor slaves pushing the grindstone at the bakery or a porter tripping over the stepping stones with a heavy load and not enough money to go to the bordello at the end of the week, so there's no point in feeling jealous, especially if you were there in 79AD.

On the way to our exit through the badly damaged Temple of Venus, Marco points out a public drinking fountain (another idea we adopted once, but, no doubt due to the advent of the canned drink, we have since abandoned) and on the road, a sign. It is a phallus, with its tip pointing to the left to indicate for newcomers to the town that the brothel is the first on the left. How thoughtful! You don't have the embarrassment of after tramping around aimlessly looking for it and eventually, in frustration, of having to ask directions from someone whom you think is not going to be morally outraged, and have him looking you up and down thinking: *You dirty bastard*! Nor do you have to go looking up at the sky, pretending to be an ornithologist, looking for the brothel sign. Instead, you can keep your head down, just in case there is someone here who might recognise you, and keep an eye out for the signs. Clever people these Romans; they think of everything!

Marco hands his book with the transparencies back to the vendor from whom he borrowed it. Ah, so this is how it works! The vendor tells us that we can buy this book for less than the marked price. Damn! Why didn't we wait? But it's all right. It's the same price as we paid. They mark it up and sell it cheaper and everyone's happy: you think you've got a bargain and they get a sale and all the vendors agree on the same price, so it doesn't matter where you buy it.

It's time to say *ciao* to Marco – our trip to Pompeii is over. But we haven't seen half of it! It should have been a whole day, but having said that, my feet are *loupin'* as we say. We must have walked for miles, on hard surfaces, but more tiring still, was when we were standing listening to Marco, not because what he said was boring, far from it, but because I was more conscious of the weight on my legs. I watch as his slim, lanky frame with the lampshade hat on the top disappears down the street, for all the world like a walking standard lamp. There he goes, as Burns said: *a burnin' and a shinin' licht,* having illuminated for me some of the fascinating story of Pompeii.

There is nowhere to sit down, but the drinks being sold at the stall where I nearly lost hundreds of euros on the water also sells drinks which look most refreshing. There are *bolsas* of oranges and lemons hanging round the stall waiting to be wrung out to the last pip and mixed with crushed ice. Iona is a sucker for lemons. She adores lemon-flavoured things and at the moment she is looking like one of those hot dogs in the caldarium. If she were a dog, her tongue would be lolling about her knees like Priapus, except it wasn't his tongue that was lolling about. I think I see a way I might redeem the day and how Naples may be consummated after all.

"Would you like a cool lemon drink, from freshly squeezed lemons?" I know she won't be able to resist it. I can be a real creep, a Uriah Heep sometimes. At least I didn't call her darling: I have some self-respect.

So, there I am in the queue, with a €10 note at the ready. I am not going through all that *parliamo Italiano* again. I haven't a clue what these things will cost, but it's an investment after all, and €10 should cover it. I would never do this at home, buy something without knowing the price first, especially in a tourist trap, such as this. I choose an orange drink as I like the look of the deep orange colour much better than the pale yellow of the lemon. Perhaps I'm drawn to it because I'm a more colourful character.

I point to the lemon cooler and then the orange, "Una, una," I say, aware, as I say it, of how simian it sounds. However itchy they are with sweat, I must resist the urge to scratch my oxters.

It works! He is giving me one from the orange and one from the lemon. This pointing and grunting is a lot better than attempting to *parlare Italiano*, though it doesn't sound so musical, but you've got to sacrifice something in the interests in communication. I hand him the note when he rattles off what I presume is the price in his native lingo, although, like before, I haven't a clue how much it is. It seems I can't do numbers even when they are words.

He takes my note and moves on to the next customer, behind me, whilst I stand waiting. Did he say: *Hang on a minute whilst I get your change* or was it: *Thank you very much for your most generous payment.* Surely it couldn't have been: *That'll be €10 if you don't mind me robbing you in broad daylight?* Conscious of the fact that the longer I hang around, the more it will look as if I have just dropped out of the trees, or in Woody Allen's memorable putdown - *just started walking erect that morning,* so I move away thinking: *€5 each! What's that in real money? Divide by three, multiply by two, roughly. Oh, God, that's too difficult! Call it €6 each, that's easier. Right, 3 into 6 goes twice, multiply by 2. Oh no! Surely not! That works out at £4, take off a bit, it still means that it must be over £3 doesn't it? Each!! Bloody hell!* For that price, I could practically buy a bottle of gin at Italian prices I imagine, though of course, I've not had time to investigate that yet.

In the meantime, let's hope for some value for money in the form of appeasement with the administration of the lemon juice. She sips, she tastes, she smiles, she says, "Delicious!" I taste it. It's bitter to me, but she thinks it's sweet. With this injection of sourness, she is sweet again. I think I may have pulled it off. Perhaps Naples will be consummated after all. It's tonight or never because we are off to Pisa tomorrow but sleeping in Florence. Will the juice last out till we get to the hotel?

"Excuse me." It is a young American girl talking. "Which is the better, the orange or the lemon?" She must have seen me tasting Iona's. "I can't make up my mind which to get."

I wonder if I should ask her how much money she has in the bank but I tell her the orange is better. "Here, taste it for yourself."

"Oh, no! I couldn't take all your drink!"

"Who said anything about the whole drink? I was just offering you a taste. Go on, try it. It's as good as a kiss." I heard somebody say this once and it seemed to go down quite well, so why is it, when I say it, it falls flat? When will I realise that saying extremely witty things to females is not one of my skills?

She looks a bit alarmed and backs off. "No, no, it's all right."

"It's only a kiss I was offering, not wild, passionate sex!" Well, I didn't actually say that, I just thought it. "Go on, have a taste." I proffer her the plastic cup, but the thought of putting her lips where mine have just been is too horrible a thought. I keep an eye on her as she gets in the queue. Which will she buy? The answer is a lemon. Somehow I thought it might be.

It's time to board the bus and we seem to be all present except for Angela. Someone says she heard her say she was going back to do some laundry. She told me she loves her job but I'm not sure I would, and keeping on top of the dirty washing would be one of the reasons. Imagine touring from March to October, endlessly re-visiting the same places without a day off, your only break away from your clutch of tourists when you hand them over to another guide and there's bound to be some awkward customers amongst the hundreds she must meet. No wonder you would want to get some time to yourself, and then when you do, you have to spend it in such mundane tasks as washing out your smalls and hoping they get dry before you move on to the next place. We wait a while for her, getting hotter and hotter in the bus, then, when she doesn't appear, we set off.

It takes quite a while in the bus, and although the air-conditioning is on, the sun streaming in the window is making me drowsy, especially after my early start and all that walking. In fact, the woman in front of me is doing an impression of Rameses, her mouth gaping open, catching flies and her husband's head is nodding. It's a talent to be able to sleep like that. I wish I could do it. Maybe this time, I will.

As we get into the centre of Naples, we drive over cobbles; it's included in the tour, apparently, this re-creation of experiencing a chariot ride in Pompeii. But the motion, combined with my drowsiness, is having an alarming effect on me which I am powerless to control, like the schoolboy who was told not to look at bare ladies or he would turn to stone and when he did, panicked when he thought it had started when he experienced a natural reaction. Even on the smooth road, there is no improvement. I am starting to panic as we are very near the hotel now. I try to think of off-putting things: dog poo on my shoe, a plate of mushrooms, Tattooman's wife – but it's no good.

The bus stops, the doors open with a hiss and I know what I must do. Fortunately, I am near the front of the bus so I don't have to pass a great deal of people. I have to get off first, while my fellow tourists are occupied in collecting their belongings and their attention diverted elsewhere. And thank God for my hat. I know now how the man at the airport must have felt, pirouetting in front of the hand drier, without a hat to hide behind.

Iona is astonished to see me get up so precipitously. It's not like me to be so quick off the mark. "Here, where are you going? Don't leave me to carry all this!" She hands me the water bottle and a guidebook. I am already holding my camera bag in one hand and my hat in the other. I have no choice but to use my hat hand to take the articles being thrust at me. A look of horror appears on her face.

"Oh never mind," she snaps. "I'll manage! Just go!"

Like The Gorgon in reverse, fear of La-Belle-Dame-Sans-Merci is beginning, belatedly, to break the spell and I can tell that I am being released from my state of Priapic petrification. By the time I get to the foyer, it's as if it had never happened, as suddenly as it came, it has gone. It's just the gods having their little joke again.

*

There are still hours to go before our afternoon walk. Our feet are recovered from the pavements of Pompeii, so we decide to pound those of Napoli instead. The objective is to go to the National Museum to see the artefacts which were removed from Pompeii. I think it is a pity that they haven't built a museum in the vicinity of the *Scavi*; it would have been fitting to have spent the afternoon there, having visited the places where they actually came from. The trouble is, I can't find any information about buses and I'm too poor to afford a taxi, and to tell the truth, I'd rather not have the hassle of negotiating a price with a taxi driver because I think I may as well have *I'm a tourist, rip me off* written across my T shirt. Besides, I'm on an economy drive after the British Midland flight.

So we set off on foot. According to a digital display on the street, it is 34°. It's cooled down by two degrees since we got back. From our hotel, we take the Via Monteoliveto. It's as if we are not together, Iona and I. We are chiaroscuro: I walk on the sunny side of the street, whilst she walks in the shade. Apart from matching our dispositions, I like to feel the warmth of the sun on my back. Of course it makes conversation a bit difficult but there is nothing to say, unless it is to comment on the tattiness of the buildings or, as we pass the side streets, one of the images I had of Naples, the yards of washing hanging like bunting from the tenement flats.

At the junction with the Via Toledo, police are lying in wait for unsuspecting motorists. Here's one poor devil being flagged down by a cop with a table tennis bat. He's taken round the corner where another policeman armed with a clipboard advances upon the hapless driver. I know how bad this feels, but will the motorist take it as calmly as I do though I feel as sick as a parrot inside? This is Italy and Southern Italy at that. This could be interesting, so I lurk about to see what happens. It seems they really are taking this seat belt legislation seriously, with the zeal of the newly converted now they have actually heard of it and it doesn't look like it's just a warning either as there are pages of paperwork being completed, which, to my disappointment, the transgressor takes with Anglo-Saxon sang-froid.

We come to the Piazza Dante, which, being oval, would be a very attractive square, but for two things. Firstly there is an extremely ugly Metro station there, all Perspex and tubular grey steel and secondly, there is some exhibition or other going on, so most of the square and the buildings behind it are obscured. There is a very attractive semi-circular building with a triumphal arch in the middle and flanked by two wings. The roof has a balustrade dotted with statues, but it's impossible to get an uninterrupted view of it now, like the Louvre with its pyramid. Well, the exhibition will go, but the Metro is there to stay. Dante, on his pedestal, has his back to the exhibition and is loftily ignoring the Metro as if he doesn't approve of such modern contraptions. It would be nice to take a leaf out of Dante's book and ignore them, concentrate on the architecture and imagine the square without all the scaffolding, canvas and clutter but it's easier to imagine a scene in Pompeii than this.

The Museo Archeologico Nazionale is a grand, pink building. There is a big banner strung across the front proclaiming a special Pompeii exhibition. Great! We didn't know it was on, but it's just what we want. We stand around inside, dithering. It isn't clear if we can just go to the Pompeii exhibition or whether we have to pay for admission to the main museum also. It's €10 for the museum and €6 for the special exhibition. There's a kiosk selling tickets and another which has tickets for the Secret Cabinet which is where they have put all the erotic art from Pompeii. We've only got an hour, we reckon, if we are to be back in time for the walk. It doesn't seem a long time, especially if we want to go to the Secret Cabinet. Well, I do, but Iona won't, so it's no use bringing that into the argument. We decide that if we can just go to the special exhibition, we'll do it.

I show the cashier a leaflet Iona has picked up. I point to where it says €6.

"*Due, per favore.*"

The LED on his till says €20. That's almost £14.

"No! No!" I say. "This one. €6."

He shakes his head and points to the till. It must mean that the special exhibition is six extra. I am not going to pay that amount of money for an hour, plus another £4 each to get to the special exhibition. We'll have an opportunity to come back for a longer time next week when we stay across the bay at Sorrento but it's no use explaining that to the man. I don't know what he's going to do with the tickets and the sale he's rung up and I don't want him to tell me, so I smile apologetically and shake my head and beat a hasty retreat. I feel, rather than see the daggers he is throwing at my back.

So we have come all this way for nothing. Well, not quite. What else would we have done anyway (though I am sure I could have thought of something) and as we are leaving, someone thrusts a leaflet into Iona's hand. It is an advert for a restaurant. It is offering a pizza with beer for €5 and as an additional enticement, it declares that it is in *pleasant gardens, surrounded by greens.* We had decided that since Naples is the home of the pizza, that was to be our fare that night anyway and who could resist sitting in a garden surrounded by cabbage, broccoli, and Brussels sprouts, especially at that price?

We retrace our steps down the Via Santa Maria de Constantinopoli which has a pavement wide enough and trees enough for Iona to walk in the shade and for me to walk out of it. Down a side street to our right, we can see some greenery, which according to the map on the leaflet which Iona got at the museum, should be the pizza place, so we decide to check it out. It looks as if it would be pleasant enough, sitting outside, even although the promised greens are only leylandi and oleander. Yes, I think this place will do very nicely. But in the meantime, my eye is attracted to a huge arcade at the top of some steps off to the right.

It is an elegant shopping centre, a *galleria*, but empty because it is a Sunday. Iona sits outside on the steps to study her map whilst I go in to explore. Apart from the litter strewn across the floor, I have the place to myself. It is a shopping mall, built in the shape of a cross, each entrance like a triumphal arch decorated with carvings and mouldings that would not have been out of place in a Roman villa. Elaborately carved Corinthian pillars separate the shops and an elaborate frieze distinguishes the ground floor from the one above. The roof is an arched, elaborate affair of iron and glass, the sort you see at railway stations. It belongs to an age of elegance and refinement. It is certainly a lot grander than any of the shopping malls I am reluctantly dragged to from time to time.

Iona is till sitting where I left her, on the steps, which is peculiar really, as there is a big comfy armchair on the pavement. There is, there really is! My 50p shoes from Lidl's don't have much in the way of cushioning and I'd dearly love to sit in it and have Iona push me back to the hotel but it doesn't have a seat belt and we'd probably get pulled up by the cops when we hit the Via Monteoliveto. Probably you need a crash helmet as well to ride in an armchair and they'd really throw the book at me, so I don't bother to suggest it.

Yes, the cops are still pulling people over for not wearing seat belts. For a change, we carry on down the Via Toledo and when we come to the painted cannon balls and the rusty windmill, we know that that is the top of our street. We only have a few minutes to take the weight off our legs when our guide comes to take us away on the walking tour of Naples. Oh my poor feet, or as the Neapolitan song has it: *O sole mio.*

In the foyer, Angela introduces us to our guide, an attractive young lady named Sophia and leaves us. It's her afternoon off. As I suspected, the first stop is the Castel Nuovo. It's a bit difficult to concentrate on the guide because she is not long launched into her exposition when an urchin interrupts her. He could be one of the boys with the bottles we saw last night. She tries to ignore him, but he is persistent. I expect he is asking her to ask us for a handout. Whatever he said, she is giving him short shrift. I can imagine she said: *Look piss off you little plook and leave us alone.* But perhaps she said something a bit more subtle because he falls quiet and listens to her more keenly than I do, as I'm more interested in what he's going to do next. I don't suppose he understands a word of it, but if he did, he would have learnt that the castle is trapezoidal in shape, with five great towers, built by Alphonso V in 1443 who also was responsible for the Arco de Trionfo, that triumphal arch which sits between the massive cylindrical towers like a sore thumb wrapped in a bandage.

Our little urchin, who has been listening patiently all this time, harangues our guide as soon as she is finished and moves us on. The urchin follows her, haranguing her, until finally, she fishes in her purse and gives him what looks like a euro, whereupon he leaves quite happily. I suppose it's a kind of mini protection racket really: *I'll go away and leave you in peace to get on with your job if you give me a euro.*

Now we are in the Galleria Umberto 1. From the roof of our hotel, I had thought it was the botanical gardens or something. It's like the Galleria I was in near the Museo Archaeologico although it differs in some important respects. Built in the same cross shape, the arms of the cross here are of equal lengths and it is altogether much bigger. The floor is much more ornate with marble geometric patterns and pictures, though the facades of the shops which here have three tiers instead of two, are much less decorated.

It is certainly a magnificent structure and because of the glass roof, tremendously light and airy. It is also not empty. There are blacks selling handbags, leather goods, jewellery and trinkets which they have spread out on the floor. According to Sophia, if a policeman came, they'd be off like a shot. I can believe it, yet it would be hard to see how they could pack up all that stuff and avoid arrest at the same time. I suspect it's just another law that the Italians ignore. Probably they'll get fed up of catching people not wearing seatbelts soon and life can go back to normal.

We have come in the entrance which faces the Real Teatro San Carlo which in fact, is an integral part of the Palazzo Reale and one of the oldest opera houses in the world. The Charles in question is the Bourbon Charles I and the theatre was completed in 1737 which makes it some 40 years older than La Scala in Milan, so put that in your pipe and smoke it Milano!

We go out the entrance which faces on to the Via Toledo and outside the Gay-Odin chocolate shop, which I presume caters for those of a certain sexual persuasion, Sophia tells us that Rossini lived in this street and had to be locked in his room by the theatre manager because the maestro was more interested in sampling the delights of Naples than getting on with his composing. Never mind Rossini - I am just glad that the chocolate shop is well and truly locked and that Iona can not get in to sample those delights, as that is her form of temptation.

We skirt the Piazza Trieste E Trento which faces the Teatro San Carlo. It's just as well that the Teatro is not on our agenda as the piazza is pretty wide and there is a car parked on the pedestrian crossing across to it anyway, but of course nobody bothers, least of all a patrolling police car. Instead we pass the Caffè Gambrinus where waiters with long aprons are flitting about the patrons sitting at the pavement tables. It is of interest to me because, as well as being the present day haunt of artists, musicians and writers, it was frequented by two of my literary heroes, Guy de Maupassant and Oscar Wilde. I'd like to drop in there for a drink later, just so I can say I have drunk from the same watering hole.

Now we have reached the Piazza Plebiscito. Now this is what I call a piazza! It is vast! On our left is the Palazzo Reale, an austere edifice taking up one side of the square, and on the right, the church of San Francesco di Paola. Now, that's what I call a church! The problem is that there has been a concert here the night before. (What! Here and the one down by the port as well?) It's hard to hear Sophia over the intrusive sound of cascading scaffolding. Why is it that can you only see the best buildings Naples has to offer, except through a screen of 21st century clutter?

This is without doubt, the best building I have seen in Naples so far. Perhaps it has something to do with scale; in fact, I am sure it does. The church is so huge it takes the breath away but it has also something to do with contrast. The Palazzo Reale is so austere, so forbidding, so plain, that it hopelessly upstaged by the classical lines of the San Francesco di Paola. It is styled after the Pantheon in Rome and there is something very pleasing about the combination of the magnificent portico with the graceful curves of the cupola rising behind it like a moon and seeming to dwarf it - but for me it is the great sweep of the colonnades on either side, embracing the other side of the piazza that gives the building its awesome elegance. We are told that it was conceived by Murat, Napoleon's brother-in-law, but unfortunately he never saw it, the French being booted out of Naples in 1815. It just goes to show that the French weren't all wrong.

A long time admirer of classical architecture, I think I have rarely seen anything so fine as this, in spite of the ugly scaffolding which masks the façade and which last night supported the bums of the music lovers of what? Verdi? Puccini? Mozart? Probably not. More likely some modern cacophony or other, making the very foundations of this magnificent building quiver and recoil in horror.

The much younger Palazzo Reale was begun in 1600 and not completed until 1843, not so surprising when you look at its vast scale. It's difficult to hear what Sophia is saying about it thanks to the scaffolding being dismembered and to tell the truth, I am not that interested. Perhaps it's better inside. It almost certainly is, because apart from its size, it holds little fascination for me. The most interesting thing is there are statues of the kings of Naples in niches at the base and apart from the fact that none of them appears to be Italian, judging by their names, it's a lesson in stone of fashion through the ages.

Sophia tells us that if we want a pleasant walk in the evening, we should walk this way, past the Palazzo and follow the bay round to the Castel dell'Ovo or egg castle so called apparently because of a magic egg supposedly hidden somewhere inside it. According to legend, this egg had originally a spell cast on it by Virgil, and it was believed that as long as the egg remained intact, the castle and Naples would be protected from disaster. Must have been working in 79 AD anyway, but in 1503 the castle was practically destroyed by Ferdinand II of Spain so by that time, it looks as if someone had had an omelette for breakfast.

"I have often walked down this street before," I croon to Iona, except croak is a more appropriate term for the vocal activity I engage in and which in others, is called singing. I have a song for every occasion and the reason for this unmelodic utterance is that we are trailing up the Via Toledo again. We are heading for the Spaccanopili, a long straight street which runs like a gash through old Naples. It is famous for its churches, but we are only going to visit two, thank God. To be honest, as far as I am concerned, it is two too many. I'm footsore, weary and hungry and what I really want to do, is get the weight off my feet. The good thing though is that we are heading towards the cheap pizza place, so when we get done with the churches, we can just nip up there, even although it is a bit early to eat.

Our first church is the 15th Century Gesù Nuovo. I wouldn't call the façade beautiful to look at, but with its top to toe diamond point rustication it certainly makes a point – about 2000 of them, I should think. There is a service going on and the congregation, for some reason, appears to consist entirely of Filipinos.

We follow Sophia as she skirts round the side and we come to a room which is covered from floor to ceiling with silver ornaments, except they aren't exactly ornaments, they are body parts – legs, arms, breasts like poached eggs, even guts and brains - they are all here. There are so many of them that the walls look as if made of silver and indeed they have run out of space, because there are bundles of them hanging on hooks. I have a closer look at one of these. It's paper-thin. I am not a metallurgist but it doesn't look like silver to me. Anyway, there must be a nice little business somewhere in Naples churning these things out. There are also some words expressing thanks for a cure and in the chapel beyond there is a man on his knees praying. Perhaps his wife has cancer or one of his children is ill. I hope he's going to have to buy one of those silver things later anyway.

He is praying to Naples' very own saint, and a very new one, Guiseppe Moscati who only died in 1977 and was canonized ten years later. You can see his study and his bedroom preserved behind glass. What? He didn't really work and sleep here did he? On the way out, I see a statue of him and a woman is lighting a candle to place beside scores of others at his feet.

"Pray for my soles, father," I say under my breath as I pass by.

If there is anything else of interest in the church, we are not going to look at it, maybe because of the service going on or maybe because Sophia's time is almost up. I suspect this may be the case, as when we cross the street to the Santa Chiara, which she tells us is 14th century, she doesn't take us in and show us anything there either. I am not complaining because of my aching feet and this means I'm going to be able to rest them all the sooner. She leaves us outside to our own devices.

Having come so far, we may as well go in. It's pleasing in its Franciscan simplicity, to my taste much more preferable than all those fussy, over the top baroque churches I have visited. In the middle of the back wall is the tomb of Robert of Anjou. I suppose he's one of the kings of Naples and a famous dead person, but I've never heard of him before so I don't suppose he can really go in my collection. It's one of my hobbies, visiting the graves of famous people, especially literary figures, but since I don't keep a record of them, I've no idea of how many dead people's last resting places I have been to. I know the last one was Jane Austen though. Poor maiden aunt Jane! I imagine I gave her a bit of a fright when I stood over her grave in the nave of Winchester cathedral in my kilt.

Leaving the church and the rest of the group behind, we walk down the Spaccanapoli a little way, past the church of San Domenico Maggiore and emerge, by chance, at the Piazza Bellini. There are some ancient-looking walls here and a statue to Bellini as you might expect, but what I like about it is all the cafés here are surrounded by "greens". Pity our cheap pizza place is not here; it would be lovely to stop here in this green oasis, but €5 is €5 and I didn't get where I am today by passing up the chance of a cheap meal, so we pass by these cafés and plod wearily on.

Only the gods are playing one of their little jokes again. It is too early and our cheap restaurant isn't open yet but the café further up is and we are too weary to go back to the Piazza Bellini, so we settle for that. With relief, I take the weight off my feet and order a *birra grande* for me and a glass of wine for Iona whilst we study the menu. We should have a Margherita I suppose. Our guide had told us that it was for the queen of Umberto I that this pizza was invented. Up until this time, the pizza was the food of the poor with a topping of tomatoes only, but for the Queen, mozzarella and basil were added to recreate the national colours of Italy and the pizza never looked back. Food fit for a queen, but it sounds a bit boring, so in the end, I opt for a *calzone*, a folded over pizza.

It takes forever to come, so I order another beer, this time a *media* because by this time, I have seen the price and a *grande* costs as much as our whole meal would have cost at the other place. The *calzone* costs €7.50 and when it comes, I see why it has been so long – they have been burning it. One corner is quite blackened. Not to worry. I cut off the burnt bits and open it up to remove all the nasty mushrooms, so it may just as well have not been folded over in the first place. I give them to Iona, so nothing is wasted, not even the burnt crust which I fling away to keep the low-flying pigeons out of our hair, especially Iona's as she hates them.

*

Now we are rested, night has fallen and I want to go out again, to walk down to the Castel dell'Ovo and drop in to the Gambrinus on the way back. Iona is not for it to begin with, but reluctantly comes along to keep an eye on me.

The Piazza Plebiscito is mobbed. It looks as if all Naples and his wife and children are here, most heading in our direction, towards the bay and the castle.

"Italian television *must* be rubbish," I remark. "I doubt if there is anybody left at home." I've heard that it's the worst in Europe, if not the world and it looks like the strategy of game shows with housewives taking their clothes off is not working any more. Or perhaps they have come where the real action is. Everywhere you look there are lovers eating each other's faces off. There's a pair next to us right now. They look as if they've not been fed for a month. That's bad enough, but they accompany it with a sound like water being sucked down a sink.

"Why don't you just rip her clothes off and do it, right here in the street?" I ask. Of course I don't really. Even if I did, I doubt if they would hear me. They seem totally oblivious, not only to our proximity but to everyone else around them. Maybe if we stuck around it might happen. After all, this is Naples and it's a warm sultry evening, but Iona is fed up and wants to move on.

We run the gauntlet of Latin lovers and presently turn onto the Via Partenope. There are some very swanky hotels down here, and there floodlit, is the bulk of the Castel dell'Ovo sitting on its own little promontory like a ship heading out to sea. It has massive towering walls but none of the charm of the Castel Nuovo. It's impressive, like the Palazzo Royale, for its sheer size but it is too square to be really interesting and the buildings on the top look decidedly modern.

To get to the Castel you have to cross a bridge guarded by two impressive square towers but La-Belle-Dame-Sans-Merci is palely loitering. This is a bridge too far for her, but to me it looks so inviting down there. There are some classy-looking restaurants and on their reflected light, a flotilla of boats and yachts are bobbing gently while Vesuvius looms darkly in the distance. The bridge is thick with lovers and the sound of the kissing drowns the cicadas. Maybe it's not such a good idea after all, having to pass all these smoochers, but Iona decides she'll come after all, (as if she's not walked far enough today already, she complains) so it's not going to be a romantic little stroll. To show we are an old married couple, we do not even hold hands. None of this romantic rubbish is going to rub off on us. We are Scottish, not lascivious Latins and it takes more than a soft evening and a splendid setting to make us go gooey at the knees.

The view was better from the bridge after all and even the Castel looks ordinary. From here, all we can see is a soaring wall, so disappointed, we head for our hotel via the Caffè Gambrinus. I've still got that to look forward to.

There is a door at the side off the Piazza Plebiscito. Inside, it just looks like a posh hotel, except there is no one about. I have a feeling that I am not meant to be here, so I beat a hasty retreat before someone comes along and throws me out on a torrent of irate Italian and rejoin Iona who was too cowardly to go in and who is waiting outside on the pavement where all the clientele appears to be. It's a bit of a disappointment. I can't imagine Oscar and Guy sitting outside on the pavement here drinking their lattes. There's no sense of their presence here; their ghosts have gone. Oscar's may have gone to the Gay Odin shop but as for Guy, I don't know if he was that sort of a guy, so where his ghost may be, I couldn't even hazard a guess.

I pick up one of the menus from a table and put it down again hastily. I don't see any point in sitting at the pavement paying these sorts of prices. It's not really the Gambrinus, just a piece of pavement. I may not be able to say that I've drunk at the same place as my heroes after all, but after this long walk and although it may be a cool evening for the Neapolitans, it's still warmer than a hot summer's day at noon for us, and I could murder a pint. There are several *trattoria* along the way with tables on the pavements and not so posh as the Gambrinus. We stop at the Rosati. It's nice just to watch the people pass by and sit out in my shirtsleeves at this advanced time of night and above all, take the weight off my legs.

There is a young couple behind me. I can't see them, but Iona can and she is giving me a running commentary of what's happening. Thank God the date is not going well. I'd have had to get up and move if they were going to do drain imitations in my ears.

Then an alarm goes off in a shop on the Via Toledo and a police car comes down with its lights flashing and ignores it. The city is just coming to life: the *passeggiata* is still parading, the lovers' lips are still smacking and if I don't finish my beer soon, that's what I'll be getting. Iona has finished her lemon drink and wants to go and I should make a move before its sweetening sourness wears off. Naples has yet to be consummated.

I need to go anyway. We have to get up at 6:30 tomorrow morning and I need a lever to prise me out of bed at the best of times, let alone in the middle of the night.

But first, I go up on the roof for a final look at Naples by night. There are a myriad of lights all round the bay as far as Sorrento and I can just make out the dark hump of Vesuvius, now I know where to look, and the Castel Nuovo with high up on one wall, and something which I hadn't noticed before until this afternoon, signs of damage as if in some battle, long ago, a cannonball had smashed into it and splattered the stonework with the impact.

I breathe in the warm scented air. Goethe, in his *Italian Journey* memorably remarked: *See Naples and die.* I hope not, not for the time being at least, but I know what he meant.

Chapter 3
Con Molto Fresco

"Pronto." If my Italian is improving, my common sense is not. I am talking to a machine, but according to the digital display on the TV, it is 6:27 in the morning and it is pitch dark, so how can you expect the brain to work at that time in the morning? It is our early wake up call, but already the bed beside me is empty. Iona is already in the shower. Damn! That means I'm going to have practically no time to think about getting up.

"Get up!"

There is a certain resonance in the timbre of her voice which even my befuddled brain knows means serious injury to my person if I procrastinate. I don't want my skin perforated like a tea bag by Humphrey the Hedgehog hairbrush. I daren't, I just daren't be last on the bus for the second day running. My trotters are trotting to the bathroom just as fast as I can make them trot.

The *pantouffles* receive the same hostile stare as before, but what do I care? I shuffle past the maître d', consuming both breakfast and lunch at one sitting, fuelling up for the long journey ahead and (incidentally) getting my money's worth. I'm not going to be intimidated by some maitre d' I'm never going to meet again. What's he got against my *pantouffles* anyway? It doesn't make me a bad person.

To my relief, I am not the last person on the bus. Angela's things are on the front seat and the Guttings are sitting behind the driver, so we sit in the seat behind where

Angela will sit. It should give us quite a good view. Besides, Iona doesn't like sitting at the back as she is prone to travel sickness, in a bus especially.

"*Buon giorno*!" says Angela in far too frisky a voice for this time in the morning. "Our driver today and for the rest of the trip is Giancarlo. *Buon giorno*, Giancarlo!"

"*Buon giorno*, Giancarlo!" we all chant in that lugubrious way that children greet their teachers. It sounds a lot more musical in Italian than the "Good morning, Miss Prune!" that I used to say. Her name was Brown, but Broon in the Doric which my young ears misheard as the wrinkled plum, unconsciously associating it perhaps with her appearance, which to me appeared ancient though, in actual fact she had probably yet to celebrate her fortieth birthday.

Somewhere on the way out of Naples, I see a petrol station, right by the side of the road, the sort of thing that was outlawed years ago, when I was still in short trousers, long before the days of the Common Market even. Things move exceedingly slowly in Naples it seems, except for the traffic of course, which is why it is not a good idea to have a car parked on the street being refuelled whilst the traffic manoeuvres around it.

Later on I discover a lever by my seat which allows me to recline the seat. Whenever I think of that word, it brings a smile to my lips. It's about my friend who had much more success at pulling women at dances than me. Whenever I asked them to dance they declined - well what they didn't actually speak but gave me a look which said: *Piss off short legs*! But my friend reported that first one reclined, then the next and the next. What a talent! Such power over women to bowl them over like that! Wish I had it, especially now I really am in my declining years.

Vesuvius is plumb ahead of us as we thread our way through the traffic in search of the motorway which will take us north to Assisi. Angela tells us that what we call

Vesuvius is the larger of the two peaks we see. The lower one is actually Monte Somma and was the original volcano, so strictly speaking, it was Monte Somma which actually did the damage to Pompeii and Herculaneum. It is a bit disappointing to look at it now and know that that was not what the Ancients saw. It has changed with successive eruptions, the last being in 1944. The gods were angry with Mussolini I imagine.

"The ground is very fertile," continues Angela, "and they grow a famous wine on the slopes called *Lachrima Christi*." She doesn't say it is a good wine though. It *is* a very good name though and I should try it though I am not a big fan of Italian wines as a rule. Some of them are thin and watery; others are so rough, they bring a tear to my eye, let alone Christ's.

As we hit the motorway, Angela says she's going to let us sleep. Because we are 18 in a 42 seater bus, we have room to spread out. Iona slips across to the seat opposite. She's sitting behind the Guttings which means she can't see them as well as I can. They are sitting motionless like automatons, not talking, just staring expressionless, straight ahead.

I'd like to sleep, but I can't sleep in a bed, let alone a bus. I try closing my eyes, but it seems only a few minutes later there is the sound of furious clicking. It is Giancarlo flashing his lights at a slower moving vehicle on which we are bearing down like a juggernaut. That word also takes me back to the past – to one of my jokes, to an occasion when we were first married and Iona put a jug containing custard into the oven to keep warm. It was a plastic jug and when she took it out the oven, it was so melted I told her I wasn't sure if it were a jug or not. It was one of my first jokes in our life together and for some reason it fell flat. The subsequent ones never seemed to be appreciated very much either, but I don't let that get me down. I keep on trying.

We are in the middle lane and there is space in the overtaking lane to his left, but it seems Giancarlo and buses aren't allowed to use it, (and he probably daren't in case Angela tells) so the only solution is to bully the car in front out of the way. It doesn't seem to be working, so Giancarlo gives him a blast of the horn and slowly, as if it's just a co-incidence, as if he had been thinking of changing lanes for quite a while really and had only decided to pull over at that precise moment, just for a wee change, the driver switches lanes and as we sail past, the driver gives Giancarlo a retaliatory blast of his horn: *Stick that up your tailpipe and smoke it!* He can fume as much as he likes but we are already leaving him to follow in a wake of exhaust fumes.

The Guttings watch this quite unmoved. If the car in front had performed a wheelie and stood up and saluted, I doubt if it would have registered with them. Maybe they are thinking about their luggage. I don't blame them for being miserable. Naples was so hot and humid, their clothes must be sweat-impregnated, even if they didn't go out as much as we did, which I don't think they did. Guttings has a beard growing because of course, he doesn't even have a razor and I realise that they won't even have a toothbrush. All they have is what they stand up in and this is their third day of wearing the same clothes. They probably chose, altruistically, to sit at the front of the bus hoping no-one would sit too close downwind of them.

Angela has been busy on her mobile and I can understand enough of what she's saying to realise that she's making enquiries about their luggage. I look out the window, pretending that I'm not ear wigging and you would think it were my clothes which were on holiday by themselves in some unknown location, because Guttings is not showing the slightest interest in the proceedings – he's still staring straight ahead as if the road unravelling ahead has hypnotised him. I can tell from Angela's tone, that it's bad news. She leans over and says that there's no news of the luggage, but she'll take them shopping in Florence. Instead of provoking looks of delight, or relief or even dismay, Guttings receives this with only the merest inclination of the head to indicate that he has received and heard the message. He barely looks at Angela. It's like he daren't take his eyes off the road because Giancarlo is using *his* eyes to drive.

And so the countryside of Campania slips by. The bus settles down. Out of curiosity at the silence, I turn round to steal a glance at my fellow travellers and most of them have either copied me or discovered for themselves, the reclining seats, because they have them in that position and seem to be dozing, most of them. Nobody seems to be talking. It's just after eight in the morning after all.

From time to time, Giancarlo flashes his lights and blasts slower vehicles out of the way. When his mobile phone goes off, he has an ear-piece which allows him to talk without taking his hands off the wheel, but it is impossible for him to talk without using his hands. He is waving his right hand about like a conductor. (Doesn't he know he's the bus driver, not the conductor?). Perhaps it is his wife giving him a hard time because it sounds animated: *Look, I told you, she means nothing to me. I am an author manqué. I was just doing a bit of research...Because sex sells, that's why. I'm doing it for you too, dearest...think I want to spend my life driving some crappy bus, even although it is new and my seat has hydraulic suspension when I could be with you more often?* It's true – it is riding up and down to each minute bump and ripple in the road. *Look, I've got to go now, there's a guy behind me at the moment – I can see him in the mirror- and he's giving me the creeps. His eyes are just boring into the back of my neck the whole time...No, I am not going to do any more research in Firenze! Ti amo! Ciao!* It's amazing how I am picking up Italian.

It's going to be a long time yet until we stop for a coffee and toilet break, so I amuse myself by studying the driving habits of the lorry drivers we are passing as the scenery unrolls. I soon discover that there are a variety of driving styles. There is the talking on the mobile style: *Hi, babe! Just left the bitch...Yeh, I'm just out of Napoli. Should be with you by 3. Get the bed warmed up... Heh! Heh! Heh!* It sounds as if he's talking to a younger woman, but these days you can't take anything for granted.

There is the talking on the CB style: *Hey, Limp Leaning Tower, some ugly bastard with a red face just passed me in a flashy bus... About two seats back from the front. He just kept staring at me. Think he must fancy me. He's gonna pass you soon. Give him the fingers for me will you pal?* My Italian and my lip speaking are really coming on.

As we pass the next bus and I look to see what driving style this driver has adopted, he turns out to be a gorilla. Although they may not have heard of many EU laws, in some ways the Italians are away ahead of us. As far as I know, we have not yet started to train primates to drive. He grimaces and raises his hirsute left hand in a salutation which some may think a bit insulting. Either he is waving at me in a friendly way and saying: *Handsome tourist, welcome to Italy – I hope you enjoy our country,* in such a lazy fashion, that he can't be bothered to use all of his fingers - or he is acting on instructions from the previous driver. Anyway, he has one finger waving at me and the other holding his radio, so both hands are off the wheel. It seems the further we leave him behind, the better, even although he may be friendly. We could never have had a meaningful relationship anyway. My gorilla is even less fluent than my Italian.

But what about this hairy one reading a map? To be fair, he does have both hands on the wheel, because he has it spread over the wheel, grasping both ends to stretch it out. His lips are moving in frustration: *Where did that Simianne say she lived? I can't find it on this damn map.   Funny address anyway. Said it was her he male address -whatever that is. Damn!*

Then there is the steering with the elbows style, which requires you to hunch forward so that your arms are sticking out at right angles from your side, the hands overlapping in the centre of the wheel. He's got his window wide open and the hairs from his oxters are whipping round his bosoms like a Lombardy poplar in a hurricane. He's obviously using the steering wheel as a prop to dry them out. I say he, but by the size of the bosoms, (38 C by my estimation, not that I'm an authority in these matters) it could be a female, albeit a very hairy one. The balance of probability is it's a bloke, however. Surely, on the grounds of safety, they wouldn't allow women to drive topless would they? But when did the Italians ever hear of driving safely?

Or there is the foot up on the dashboard style. This is particularly relaxing as all you need are a couple of fingers hooked over the wheel to steer. He's not thinking of his wife or his mistress or planning a trip to the zoo– he's so relaxed his mind has gone to sleep. He's brain dead now. His body will catch up later.

Then there is the Buddha style but for this you need to have a 44- inch waist, a shaven head and a bare chest. What you do is, you slot the wheel in the space between your overhang and where your belt starts, then all you need to do is swivel your body from side to side to turn the wheel. Now, the beauty of this method is that it leaves your hands free to feed your face and ultimately, oil your steering mechanism. Mainly those who adopt this style, are eating pizza but there was one eating a Chinese take-away with chopsticks. Actually, that is a porky pie, but the only reason it doesn't happen is because the Italians resist foreign cuisine since they think they have no need to since theirs is the best in the world (and maybe they're right).

The favoured form of attire seems to be the singlet, but topless is *de rigueur* also. But they all must have to pass a hairiness test before they are allowed to take to the road: *Turn round, Antonio...anyone can grow hairs on the chest, but it takes a real trucker to grow hairs on his back side.* There is a regulation half inch of hair which must escape the confines of the back of the vest and stick up like a crest on a cockatoo. If you don't have a doormat on your shoulders, you are wasting you time taking the trucker test.

This anthropological study (not forgetting the Guttings who still have not moved or spoken) keeps me happily entertained until we reach our toilet stop. I am built like a camel in reverse – they don't take water in frequently and I don't expel it frequently. I also get the hump when I am travelling with people who are not built like Bactrians who want to stop every half hour and let all the slow moving lorries I have passed get ahead of me again.

It's deceptive, being in the coach. (Musn't call it bus – it's far too posh). It looks a nice sunny day from our air-conditioned cocoon but as soon as we step outside, the heat hits like a hammer. The good thing about sitting at the front is we can get off first and get to the front of the queue without having to wait in a tiresome queue. This gives me more time to get outside and grab some rays. I buy a couple of cans of Coke and move a seat into the full sun while Iona can stay in the shade. But even that is too hot for her and she moves away into deeper shade, where all the wimps are. All, that is, except for the Scottish couple who are enjoying the rare chance like me, to feel the sun on their faces.

We have stopped at a family-run motorway café at a place called Cassino. Up there, high on the hill is Montecassino, famous as the site of a famous siege in World War II. The monastery which was founded in 529, suffered destruction three times in its life – first by the Lombards in 590, then by the Saracens in 884 and then by an earthquake in 1349. They might have thought their luck was in after three attempts, but nearly 600 years later it suffered extensive damage from the Allies. I remember seeing a television programme about it and how impregnable it was, which is why it suffered such extensive damage. And impregnable it looks, perched like an eyrie at the top of the spur but, from here, even through my binoculars, there is no sign of damage at all, although there is a crane standing like a stork, one legged, at one of the corners. If you hadn't known, it might have looked as peaceful as this for the last six and a half centuries since it was rebuilt after the earthquake.

There is a road sign which captures my attention. It is the SS 7 to Formia and Gaeta and underneath it says Via Appia. What a shame we are on the A1 to Firenze. It would have been cool to have travelled down the famous Roman thoroughfare - just as long as they had smoothed it out of course. I don't want another ride over cobbles, thank you very much.

Meanwhile, Iona has been networking. She is able to tell me that the boy with the lap top is called Dick and he's been saving his photos onto a CD. He has kindly offered to do the same for Iona as she went camera-crazy in Pompeii and thinks that the 166 capacity she has on her digital camera may not be enough. (She had just got it, before we left, especially for this trip. Her biggest fear is she does something by mistake and wipes out the entire lot). Dick's parents are called Tom and Mary, so collectively are called Tom, Dick and Mary. And Mary is hairy, so she is almost Harry, so that's what I shall call them, Tom, Dick and Harriet, in deference to her sex. I mean, I have no idea how hairy Mary's legs are like, let alone her oxters, but Mary *is* hairy in the sense that for a woman of her age, she wears her hair long, like I imagine, in the style favoured by Lucretia Borgia, down to her waist. It would probably suit her shorter. As a matter of fact, I can remember seeing her from the opposite side of the carousel at Naples and thinking that she bore a resemblance to Ben and Eileen's daughter.

To tell you the truth, I think God has only got a certain amount of templates – a good number of templates I admit – but I think He runs a bit short of ideas sometimes and repeats them. In our travels, we constantly see people who remind us of people we know. Take my own case for example: I have often been accused of being the same idea as George W. Bush. Even Iona would be hard pushed to be as insulting as that, but it is true, because many of my pupils have called me George and first name intimacy is not something I would encourage nor something to which they would aspire, so I know it is the deepest insult their puerile minds can devise. We have got the same broad nose, caused my mother said, by picking it too much, but most scary of all, the same close-set eyes. You really cannot trust a person with close-set eyes. You really can't. I've got them and I should know and if you don't believe me, ask Iona. My mouth is different from his though: I don't go opening it, putting my foot in it all the time. Actually, now I stop to think about it, I think perhaps I do. My jokes don't seem to be going down too well recently, I recall.

From her accent, I deduce that Harriet comes from Kent or somewhere down that way and by profession she must be an infant teacher because after years of speaking to little ones, the habit becomes ingrained and they find it impossible to talk to adults in any other way than slowly and precisely and in words no longer than two syllables which always makes me feel as if I'm wearing short trousers, which of course I am, or would be, if it were not for St Francis and the rule that says we have to wear long trousers in the basilica, so I'm sporting the longs at the moment.

Iona has also talked to another couple who also come from the south of England somewhere: in fact, the ones who were sitting in front of us when we came back from Pompeii and one of the ones who, as a result from Iona's introduction, had bought a book with the transparencies; the ones who could sleep for England, who slept from Pompeii to Naples whilst I was having my rude awakening. Their names are Pat and Bill.

First off and last on, I leave it to the last minute to get back on the coach, smiling to my fellow travellers as they pass my sunny spot. I can tell they think I am a mad dog. If they have heard me speak, then they'd know I'm not an Englishman, so that just leaves a mad dog who would sit in the sun like that, even although it's not mid day yet. The annoying thing is that, because of St Francis I cannot get my best feature, my shapely legs, tanned.

Back on the coach, I pursue my anthropological studies but do not spot any more driving styles unless you count dangling the left arm out of the window, and the smoking and the drinking water, but that's so commonplace as not to be worth mentioning. The Guttings are still staring straight ahead, still expressionless. Somehow, I can't imagine them having sex. It would have to be Tantric if they do. Actually, I have a feeling that they might just be newly married because when she comes down the bus steps, he is there, helping her down or up. And yet, they just sit there, like bookends on a shelf, never looking at each other, or exchanging a word.

"Where were we two years ago tomorrow?" says Iona from across the passage. She does this to me. Just because she has a memory like an elephant, and I don't, she plays this humiliating trick on me. Two years ago! I can scarcely remember where I was two days ago, never mind two years. She plays this game with me on holiday every year, but of course, I can never remember the answers and each year there in another one to remember so it gets progressively harder. I suspect it is some sort of senility test and if I fail to come up with the answer, she'll be applying for power of attorney. I have one clue though: tomorrow is our wedding anniversary. I may not remember much, but I never forget that. I'm too scared to.

"Come on, it's easy!" She is exasperated by my amnesia and can't believe I haven't got it already.

I close my eyes and try to think. What did I do on my anniversary two years ago apart from the presumed usual consummation, it being one of the permitted days on the calendar? Was that the year we went to New Zealand or not? It seems a bit further back than that. Let me try and work it back. Where the hell were we this time last year? It's incredible! My mind is a complete blank.

"Just leave it with me," I tell her. "Don't tell me!"

It gives me something to think about as the surprisingly English-looking countryside of Lazio unravels outside the bus window, for we have left Campania behind now. Lunchtime comes and I still have not got it. I am not hungry, having had my lunch at breakfast as usual. Angela has taken us here because she says it's a family restaurant with home cooking. As usual, we are at the head of the queue and it's just as well that I'm not hungry, because there is not a great deal of choice. I sit down at a table with a big bottle of beer and some sort of tomato salad; then I notice that people are carrying laden plates of pasta like lasagne and spaghetti and grilled aubergines which I like the look of but had never noticed. It dawns on me that this is a case of the early bird not catching the spaghetti worms. It seems we had come a bit earlier than expected and they didn't have it all out before I was served.

I decide to have some of the grilled aubergines, but no matter how often I sidle up and down the counter, I can't see them. Perhaps they are under one of the chrome lids. Pity they don't arrange these dishes alphabetically. O for aubergine as they were spelt in my local supermarket once should mean that they are near the lasagne, except I don't know what they are called in Italian.

"Aubergines?" I try hopefully.

The server looks at me in alarm. Maybe aubergines in Italian means: *Has anyone told you what a fine moustache you have for a woman?* I repeat it, pointing to the lid. She looks even more puzzled: *What, here, now on top of that, in front of all these people?* Impasse. What do I do now? Just then Angela materialises by my side.

"What's the matter? What do you want?" Her tone sounds as if I *have* been suggesting something improper. She rattles off the Italian for are there any aubergines left or maybe she's saying: *What did he say to you? Is he harassing you?* and then tells me what I have already suspected – aubergines are off. Not to worry. I feel I've been let off another embarrassing encounter relatively lightly.

The toilets are a sight to behold. They must have been tiled in the seventies - that worst decade for fashion and design since the twenties. Great swirling blobs of luminous orange and yolk yellow and mucus green, but it is the orange which dazzles. Surrounded by it on all walls, is like being inside some psychedelic nightmare. They could drive people mad by shutting them up in here for an hour. It wouldn't take any longer.

"Have you been to the toilets yet?"

As I come back up the stairs, the young Scottish couple are standing in the foyer and I can't help but want them to enjoy this unique spectacle of bad taste also. Without waiting for an answer, I plough on. "You really must go! They are fantastic!" Pause. A sudden silence. Uh! Uh! It's as if I have committed some grave solecism, like being sick on the carpet at some booze-fuelled party or putting the living flame gas fire out with one's portable fire extinguisher. Or maybe they think I am some sort of perv. The silence could not be more absolute. From the shocked look on their faces, they clearly *have* been and thought them a disaster.

"I mean fantastically bad, of course!" But it doesn't matter how much I try to reclaim the situation; my havering has put me down for a poor mad boor whose taste is all in his mouth. My only hope is they think I must be colour blind or just blind drunk.

Outside, it is sweltering. Most of my companions are sitting inside in the air-conditioned cool and I want to be outside, building up my tan. But there is nowhere to sit down outside: the few chairs which are available have been taken. I linger, palely loitering and eventually a couple, not of our party, get up and leave. I grab the plastic chairs and move them down to a sunny spot at the end of a path which also affords Iona full shade.

I open up my shirt and roll my trousers up as far as I can. I don't need a knotted handkerchief because I have my Panama. In spite of what the young Scots think, I am not a complete boor. The punishing sun beats down relentlessly: there is not a smidgeon of a cloud to offer the slightest respite. Before very long, rivulets of sweat are beginning to course their way down my chest and form a pool in my belly button. I know my fellow passengers are behind me, watching. I know they think I am mad but here's the thing – I can't stand up in front of them all and say: *Phew! It's a bit hot* because they will look at me condescendingly as if to say: *We could have told you that, you bloody moron!* There's only one thing for it – I have to stay until the bus goes and pretend I am enjoying every second of it.

The sweat is just drippin' off me tits as Susan, an Aussie we met on the Nile Cruise memorably remarked to the ship's company at large in a voice like silver paper on your fillings. The oxters of my short-sleeved shirt are several shades of blue darker than the rest. My hair, underneath my Panama is plastered to my head, and beneath my trousers it's a tropical rainforest. The back of my shirt is probably the same colour as my armpits, the way it is sticking to my back. Iona passes me a tissue and, just in time, I absorb the dam of sweat which was just about to overflow down the front of my trousers. Major catastrophe narrowly averted. I might have had to try out some ballet steps in front of the electric drier.

I have wiped myself down but I'm springing sweat from every pore even as I look, like water out of a colander. The tissue is soggy; it cannot possibly absorb any more. Fortunately people are beginning to drift back to the bus. I dash down to the toilets and struggle out of my shirt and wash out my pits. I can't do anything about washing out my bottom, or should I say, lower pits. I'm just going to have to sit in the damp. Revolting thought - I bet if you wrung out my clothes and the Guttings', I'd have more perspiration in my underpants than all their clothes put together. I'm just glad that the stain has not shown through.

I look as if I have just stepped out of the shower and put my clothes on without drying myself. If I don't stop sweating soon, I'm going to have to find a plumber. It will be good to get back to the bus and let the air-conditioning dry me off though I'll probably get pneumonia. Iona gives me a look which is enough to turn the sweat to icicles. I'm last onto the bus again but at least she has stopped the sweating. Everyone is waiting and will have seen me coming on the bus looking like a lump of leaking lard. I should think I've made good progress today in making my fellow travellers think they've got a lunatic on board and Iona is not amused at being taken for the lunatic's wife.

As the bus settles down for its siesta and I idly pursue my anthropological studies, the answer comes to me out of nowhere. I wasn't even thinking about it - it just drifted into my mind.

"Estonia! Tallinn!" I say triumphantly across the passage. Anyone close enough to hear me, like the Guttings for instance, would have had any lingering doubts as to my sanity instantly dispelled.

Iona nods in assent, but what does her expression mean? It could mean: *Amazing! That only took you about three hours!* Or it could mean: *Damn and blast! He's not quite brain dead yet. Can't get control of his money yet.*

It's amazing that I could have forgotten, because apart from the time we missed our flight to New Zealand, this has to qualify for the second most stressful travelling experience we have experienced. I had met my friend from Narva in Tallinn when our ship docked there and she had arranged for a taxi to show us about. We just caught the ship by the skin of our teeth. Our fellow diners had told us that there had been three announcements over the Tannoy, the last being from the captain: *If Mr and Mrs Addison are on board will they report to the purser's desk **immediately.*** When our taxi drove up to the quayside, there was only a plank for a gangway and a coterie of white-shirted officers waiting for us. Their body language said: *Where the hell have you been? Get your arses on board right now!* What they actually said was: *Mr and Mrs Addison? We're leaving **now**!* No time to negotiate with the driver - $100 – it was all my dollars. And we had spent so long visiting other places, like the boring TV tower, we had no time to visit the charming old town and because I had no dollars left, it meant we had no money to buy souvenirs the next day in St. Petersburg. And it didn't stop there, because, when I contacted my friend when I got back, I discovered the taxi driver had charged her as well. It was incredible to me that I could ever have forgotten it, but of course, I hadn't really: only the date of this nightmare.

At last, we leave the A1 at Orto and join the *superstrade*, the E 45. There is nothing super about it except the bumps and potholes. Giancarlo's seat is bobbing rhythmically like a cork on water. Assisi is getting nearer, but here is a sign to Bastardo. I catch Iona's eye. I know what she's thinking, so I get in before she has time to say it: "I know. I should live there."

Assisi is visible for miles, tumbling down from its elevated position on a ridge high to our left. If Pompeii was my anticipated highlight of the trip, Assisi was my expected least favourite part. Churches are not my favourite places in any case and religious art either unless it's Hieronymous Bosch. Further evidence of my weirdness according to Iona because I am also a Salavador Dali fan. But, I must admit, I am looking forward to seeing Giotto's famous frescoes, though they would have to be quite outstanding to rival Pinturicchio's which we had seen in the Piccolomini Library in the Duomo of Siena at Easter. Painted in the early 16th century, the colours look as fresh as if he had just laid down his brush yesterday. But who has heard of Pinturicchio? And who hasn't, of Giotto?

We pass the Basilica of Santa Maria degli Angeli, according to Angela, the seventh largest church in the world. From the distance, we had seen the gold statue of Mary over the portico, flashing in the strong sunlight, like the beam from a lighthouse. But it's not its size that interests me so much (I've seen bigger in Malta and who says size matters anyway?) - it's the place where St. Francis died. Of course he did not actually die in that building, but they built a chapel in the place where it supposedly happened 330 years earlier which they call the Capella del Transito. We are not going to be visiting that, but that doesn't bother me as long as we visit his tomb. That would be a good one for my collection, for as I already said, I am a grave man. No, seriously, I really want to go there and I'm not even religious.

Our guide, Paulo, is waiting for us. The good thing about this visit is that we are going to start at the top and work our way down. Just as well: the temperature today is 36 according to Paulo. The bus has taken us quite high, but in response to American visitors, no –I just made that up-but it could be true for all that, there is an escalator to take us further up. It's the first time I can remember being on an escalator in the open air, though this is more like riding through thick jungle as we are levitating through a tunnel of leafy vegetation. It's a good idea anyway, as it's a pretty steep climb.

We enter Assisi through the Porta Nuova and make our way down the Via Borgo Aretino. It's an attractive street with geranium window boxes a splash of red against the warm brown stonework. At the end of the street I can see two spindly cranes. Apparently reconstruction after the earthquake of 1997 is still progressing.

In the shade of the enormous flying buttresses of Santa Chiara, Paulo points out where the damage had been repaired and explains that they gave the church a facelift at the same time. It's a bit difficult to hear him as there is some sort of commotion, chanting and cheering coming from the piazza round the corner. As we move round to the piazza, I can see what it is. Some American students are trying to build a human pyramid on the central fountain and making more noise than a combined choir from Bedlam lunatic asylum as somebody tries to take their photograph if only they would stand still and be quiet enough. I can imagine it in the album later: *This is us really getting up the noses of all the tourists in Assisi by creating a disturbance by acting like assholes.* Thankfully they finally get their photograph and boisterously go off to annoy some other people somewhere else and the piazza returns to relative peace.

Giving my attention to the church, I see a beautiful rose window, like a lace doily on the plain façade. Beneath it is a simple arched door. The flying buttresses on the left are balanced by the convent on the right, fortunately, or it would have looked distinctly unbalanced. As it is, it still does not look quite right – the buttresses are so thick and solid making the façade look thin and delicate in comparison and the curves of the buttresses are not echoed in the squat, square shape of the convent. But, in its fresh pristine condition, it looks attractive in its plain simplicity. I get the feeling that I am seeing it as the builders saw it in 1265 but I have to imagine it without the buttresses as they were only added in 1351 when the structure began to crumble. I like the buttresses. I am sorry they had all the effort of it, but I think they are very impressive: I'm not sure if I don't almost prefer them to the church itself! I am sorry about the earthquake too, but I am glad that I can see the church in its newly restored freshness. Just like Pompeii, their disaster is others' good fortune.

It's dedicated to St Clare, the founder of the Poor Clares, the female branch of the Franciscan order. We are going in to see a cross which supposedly spoke to St Francis before he became a saint. In fact, he had been a bit of a lad at one time until a year in the clink made him alter his ways and after the cross spoke to him, well that changed him even further. What the voice said, three times, so there could be no mistake, was to repair the Church which had fallen into disrepair.

I am struck with a resemblance between me and St Francis. Iona has often to tell me three times to do things as well and she's quite cross with me too at the moment as a matter of fact. She has been bleating on about the conservatory roof which is leaking even more than my sweat glands at lunchtime. I'm going to have repair it when we go back. And it could be a life-changing experience for me too, if it stops her nagging and I can get some of St Francis' peace and quiet.

There are frescoes of Biblical scenes and scenes from the life of St Clare on each side of the nave, but we scarcely spare them a glance. Imagine that! Some poor bugger has spent years probably painting these things and we don't even look at them! But time is limited and Paulo probably doesn't want us to give us fresco fatigue before we get to Giotto's.

We make straight for the cross which is in a side chapel. It's in the style of a Cross of Lorraine, except the top bar is at the very top and the bottom bar broadens out to form a squat T behind the Christ figure before it tapers again below the knees. There is no mistaking the awe of reverence which permeates this place. Well, well, whether it talked to St Francis or not, he certainly *thought* it did and he saw it and I am looking at it now. It's about the one thing left in Assisi that he would recognise. It's very dubious if he would approve of the enormous basilica built in his name and much else beside if he could see it now, which perhaps he can. I bet St Clare can. She's the patron saint of television. She has this dubious honour - especially dubious in the case of Italian TV- because it is said that she foretold the time and circumstances of her death, describing it in glorious Technicolored detail as if watching a screen. Not a skill I aspire to.

We make our way, through the throng, up the gentle slope of the Corso Mazzini until we emerge in the Piazza del Comune. Who need the basilica of St Francis, this place makes an immediate impact. I love the rustic warm brown stone of the buildings and their style and character. It's a charming place, worth coming to for its own sake, if only it weren't for all the people. Even the hordes of people wouldn't be so bad if only they made less noise. In fact, I'm starting to feel a grudge against St Francis. As well as giving me nappy rash, he's responsible for bringing all these people here, including me of course, but I don't count: it's the other tourists that are the problem.

The Torre Comunale is visible before you enter the square and with its crenellations, and two tiers of arched windows is very pleasing, and so is the town hall to which it belongs. If only ours had been built in the 13th century instead of the

20th it might have had a chance of looking as attractive as this instead of looking like a packet of abandoned condoms laid on its side.

But as you enter the square, the attention is drawn from the Torre down to the building next door which is at least a thousand years older. It looks like a Roman temple with six massive Corinthian pillars and pediment. In fact, it *was* a Roman temple, the Temple of Minerva and predates the birth of Christ by a century. It's a church now of course. Never mind St Francis' reactions to how Assisi has changed, what would the Romans make of their temple now? Maybe not that much actually, since the Christian religion was grafted on, in many cases, to the pagan beliefs. Minerva was the goddess of industry, commerce and schools. Now it's Mary who's in charge but I don't know if they changed her job description when they rededicated the church to her: *OK now Mary, you gotta make these little brats pay attention in school and not cheek the teacher, right? And bring us lots of tourist euros as well? That OK with you, Mary doll?*

Embedded in the base of the Torre are weights and measures which they used in the medieval period. Paulo says one of them is a cubit, but there is so much noise from passing vehicles and chattering tourists I can't make out what he's saying properly. It's annoying because it would have given me an idea of how big the ark was, if I could remember how many cubits Noah used in the first place. It would be nice to know my height in cubits too, but I don't suppose I qualify even for one.

We take the Via Portica out of the square, past the Museo Civico with its arched windows and attractive porch reached up a short flight of steps. It's not a building of note apparently, but I like it very much. The whole Piazza, in fact is very pleasing. It's easy to like Assisi. Wonder if the tourist wallahs would be interested in buying my slogan? What's the point? With St Francis, they don't need to advertise. How many people would be here if he had not been?

This too, is a very attractive street with little inviting alleyways. The houses, of weathered brown stone look warm and inviting in the sunshine, the side where I am walking. Everyone else is walking on the shady side of the street. There are boxes of geraniums everywhere and terracotta pots over-spilling with them to add to the general ambience.

The Via Portica has turned into the Via San Francesco and there is an ancient fountain, like a trough with weathered and worn coats of arms from the centre of which the pipes emerge. We arrive, coming down, as a party of backpackers arrives coming up. They've probably just come from the Basilica of St Francis and after being made to be quiet for so long, they are letting off steam. They don't speak, but *shout* at each other and adolescent girls scream in that ear-splitting way that only they and stuck pigs can. I'd cheerfully like to hold the heads of each and every noisy brat under the water. One thing about Assisi, it's certainly not quiet and I think even the Saint himself might approve of my giving this lot a ducking, if it restored the peace and tranquillity he was reputedly to have held so dear.

Adjacent is the Oratorio dei Pellegrini, or pilgrims' hostel. I like this for its delicate arches supported by slender Arabian style pillars. There are frescoes in here too, but we're not going to bother with them either. Just then, a backpacking Franciscan friar strides past unconscious of any incongruity between his ancient habit and the 21st century rucksack on his back. So that's what the well-dressed pilgrim is wearing nowadays. I notice he is wearing sandals *without* socks.

There is an interesting house further down. It may be medieval, I mean, it is certainly medieval, but I wouldn't mind living in it. I can imagine it from an estate agent's point of view: *Bijou toilet, all ceramic, portable, with handy carrying handle and in case of noisy pilgrims, just empty over the bastards' heads.* That would sort them out. Much better than a ducking. It's the Casa dei Maestri Comacini. Their coat of arms is visible beneath the projecting upper story floor which is supported by wooden beams. It has diamond shaped leaded paned windows with the inevitable geraniums in terracotta pots suspended between them. I like it a lot – despite the sanitary arrangements.

From here, the campanile of the basilica is peeping over the rooftops of the houses and a few paces on, Paulo gathers his brood about him and issues us with gadgets like hearing aids. It's called talking in whispers and the idea is that when we enter the basilica, he is able to talk to us in a low voice, so we can all hear him. It's to create an atmosphere of awe and reverence, an attempt to preserve a sense of the numinous in this hallowed place.

From the vast Piazza in front of the church, looking over the colonnades of the even more vast Piazza Inferiore of the lower church, for the basilica is built on two levels, three if you count the crypt - you can see the vast Umbrian plain stretching out towards hazy blue hills in the far distance with the great dome of Santa Maria degli Angeli with the gold statue on the top, looking like a pimple ready to burst. It's here in the Piazza Superiore, if there are any, I should see the beggars. I am half expecting them because of Norman McCaig's poem *Assisi* which, as practically every pupil in Scotland knows, satirises the attitude of the Catholic church to the poor, and thus paradoxically misses the whole point of Giotto's frescoes depicting the saint's life.

The façade of the basilica resembles that of the Santa Chiara pretty much, the main difference being that here the door is a double door, split by an arch. We pass through this and we are inside.

As soon as we enter, there is a sibilant SSSH! which would have stunned us into silence, had we been saying anything. I can't see who said it, but clearly, it can't have been directed at us in particular, but at the multitude inside in general. It's so loud it must have been through a microphone, though I think it sounds unaided somehow and so fierce that everyone instantly falls silent – even the guides who are talking in whispers. There's probably some fierce nun who has been getting lessons in crowd control from the Captain Bligh school of discipline or is it like the Wizard of Oz and is there amplification and in reality it's just a tiny wee wifie who looks as if a gust of wind would blow her over?

But here's Paulo looking at me. Someone has just come up to him and whispered something in his ear and into my shell-like comes: *Take your hat off!* I hadn't realised that I was still wearing it or I would have doffed it but the whole group of course get the broadcast and Iona gives me another withering look. After my performance at lunchtime and now this, the consummation of Florence is receding by the minute. But what's really bugging me is that there are lots of men going around wearing shorts and I've been encasing my unhappy genials (because they occasionally make Iona happy) in the hothouse of my trousers all day till, as Susan from the land of Oz would have said, if she had had the right bits: *The sweat's just drippin' off me* – never mind, it's just too horrible to imagine.

There are 28 frescoes by Giotto down each side of the nave, but the whole church is frescoed like Ray Bradbury's *Illustrated Man* was tattooed, leaving no part of white space uncovered. It's not so much a church as an art gallery and the comparison is appropriate, because what we get from Paulo is an art lesson. We are invited to sit down in the pews whilst he tells us about them with the use of a laser pen to point out details.

Man who have sweaty botty should sit in own pew as Confucius would say, but we are a group and Paulo must talk in whispers, and we must crowd together, so phew, it's a relief that I should find myself next to the Guttings and we therefore cancel each other out.

(SSSSSSSHHHHHH!)

Giotto's frescoes have been restored and the colours are quite vivid, more vivid than I had been expecting. What Paulo is telling us is that Giotto was the first to use life-like human figures, with a real sense of movement and space, so that they seem to stand out from the flat surface and that is why, I suppose, he is more famous than Pinturicchio. Everyone has heard of Neil Armstrong and even Buzz Aldrin, but who knows the names of the others who have set foot on the moon unless it is their special interest?

From this distance, it's hard to see if Paulo is right, but I'll take his word for it. Perversely, I still like Pinturicchio better, maybe because I saw his first and they still look fresher than the restored Giottos but I suspect, he was nevertheless the more accomplished painter and it's not his fault he was born too late to invent the technique. Plus of course, St Francis' life is of a great deal more interest than that Pius the Second's who was Pinturicchio's subject, or at least, a lot better known.

(SSSSSSSSSHHHHHHHH!)

Presumably it is a command for the company to be quiet, but I have an uneasy feeling that someone has been reading my mind and I am in grave danger of receiving a lightning bolt through my unprotected un-Panamanian cranium for my heretical views on the respective merits of Giotto and Pinturicchio.

Paulo picks out some of the frescoes for our attention. If we discussed them all, we'd be here all night, but there's the one with the talking cross. It looks just like the one we saw in real life. So we go round and that's the story of Francis'

101

life, told in pictures so the illiterate can understand it. Like they watch TV now instead of reading books.

The Giotto frescoes were unaffected by the earthquake. Paulo shows us how the frescoes above the door through which we entered have been damaged. They are in the process of being restored, but truth to tell, I think, they are so high up, if they had to be damaged so that Giotto's frescoes could be refurbished and Santa Chiara cleaned up, well, maybe it was the shock they needed to restore their unique heritage. I am probably seeing them as the Grand Tourists saw them 200 years ago, maybe even better than that. It's a thought to think how many famous eyes have seen what I am looking at now, apart from Goethe who, apparently, perversely avoided the place.

We're going to the lower church now and like the upper, it is full of frescoes but a lot more gloomy a building than the one above. Paulo shows us some Byzantine frescoes, pointing out how stiff and unnatural they are, compared to the Giottos. The significance of these two churches is it has such an array of different frescoes by different artists, it's possible to study the development of Italian art.

He stops now before one fresco by Cimabue and tells us that this is a true likeness of the Saint himself, not an idealised portrait. I can believe that all right. If you were doing an idealised portrait, you'd paint somebody a lot more handsome than this. Of course, the hairstyle doesn't help – that big baldy bit in the middle must have been adopted by him after he'd reformed, to keep the birds away, unless of course they were sparrows and other birds of that ilk as he chatted *them* up all right. I know it works because I am tending to that sort of hairstyle myself these days and I've not had an offer in years. To be frank, even when fully thatched, I wasn't exactly snowed under with offers. Actually, hair apart, he's not that bad looking, but he has a pair of ears, especially the left, which would not be out of place on a milk jug.

There are one of two frescoes of St Clare too. She's got a long face but probably that is exaggerated and she might have been quite comely. One thing though, both of them look pretty miserable. It looks as if being a saint is a serious business. I've never sat for a portrait, funnily enough, but equally strangely, I think I may possibly be designed for sainthood my self because in every photograph taken of me, I look as miserable as an alligator with the toothache. And recently, I have been suffering from a very itchy back in the region of my shoulder blades which might signal the sprouting of incipient wings but when I showed the doctor, she said she couldn't see anything, not even a pimple. And there was a feather in the bed one day, but Iona, who's more of the opinion that she's more likely to be a saint than me, having to put up with me, said I was an idiot and it must have come out of the pillow. There's just one thing- we have synthetic pillows. So make of that what you will.

We are visiting the Vatican later in the trip and if I could wangle a meeting with Pope John Paul II who has created more saints in his reign than all the others put together, it could be my best chance of getting a definitive opinion. Maybe if I could perform the miracle of leaping out of bed first thing in the morning, Iona might testify on my behalf but she'd probably prefer the Miracle of the Giving up of the Chilean Cabernet Sauvignon or the Miracle of the Abstaining from Malt Whisky. And if I ever did give them up – that truly would be a miracle.

I have to confess, I'm frescoed out and I'm not really listening to Paulo, though I can hear him clearly with my earpiece, though I recognise with interest, the famous one of Francis preaching to the birds. It's not by Giotto, but by an unknown artist, so they call him Maestro di San Francisco. The fact is, I have seen a sign which points to the crypt and the tomb of the Saint. It's drawing me like a magnet. I've had enough of frescoes. Surely we are going to go there? We're not going to miss this out are we? After all of this, the very reason why we are here, why practically everyone in Assisi is here – St Francis – surely we're not going to miss out paying homage at the Saint's tomb are we?

But, incredibly, it looks as if we are. We are already heading for the exit. I arrest Paulo in his tracks.

"Are we not going to the tomb?"

Paulo looks at me sadly. Sad because we are not going, or sad because of the request?

"Is it OK if I go?" I hope I am keeping the sense of urgency out of my voice, as if it's a casual request and it doesn't matter to me one whit that I am on the point of missing one of the most famous dead persons who ever lived from my collection.

Paulo looks at his watch. "Yes but you don't have long." He clearly does not want me to go, but I'm off already, obeying the laws of Italian logic by going down the exit stairs to save time. Just before I make my descent I can hear him say: *Give me back your earpieces* then I lose radio contact with him. Either he's switched off or I am already out of range. I don't really know what I'm looking for, but I expect I will recognise it when I get there. But the truth is, I don't. I wander round the chapel, but I can't see anything that looks like a tomb. Perhaps if I came in the proper way I would have seen it. It's too late now to go hunting – I've already been some time and I daren't be last for the bus two times in a row. Deeply disappointed, feeling frustrated and internalising involuntary curses, a terrible thing to do in this art gallery of a church, I make my way with the traffic this time out of the church.

But when I plunge outside from the cool dimness of the church into the blinding heat of the sunlight, there is not a sign of my fellow travellers, neither to left nor right nor straight ahead. Bloody hell! I'm in real trouble now. What am I going to do?

Surely they would have made their way down the gently sloping Piazza Inferiore towards the town? Surely they couldn't have gone that far in the short time I have been gone? But there is not a sign of them. I know I can't miss them because the whole, immense Piazza is empty. It's incredible! Before, you couldn't move or see the buildings for people as thick on the ground as in a Lowry landscape and suddenly, I have an eerie feeling that I'm in some Sci-Fi movie and I'm the last person left alive. Where have all the people gone?

I'm in too much of a panic to admire the emptiness of the scene, the magnificent colonnades framing the piazza and looking back, the bulk of the basilica with its campanile blocking off one end and at the other, an arched gate which must lead down to the town. I set off towards it. If I were in a cartoon, it would show my little trotters revolving in a blur.

I've probably gone half way down the Piazza when I hear a familiar voice calling me. I hear, but I can not see her. Perhaps I have actually died, been struck down for cursing in the church or suggesting that the obscure Pinturicchio is a greater painter than Giotto? The truth is, I have so many sins, it's hard to say which one may have struck me down. And would La-Belle-Dame-Sans-Merci really call me from the other side? Well, she might if, in order to access our bank accounts, she needs to know my mother's maiden name or our pet's first name or our first pet's name or the first school I attended. She'd never remember Brakoden. I bet there's not fifty people on the planet still surviving for whom that is the correct answer. Which just goes to show you what a rare individual I am and how lucky she is to be married to me. Or should that be was? Maybe that's why it's so empty and so hot. I'm in the first circle of hell. Well, I knew it would catch up with me sooner or later. I'd intended to be better, but nearer the time.

Then I see Iona emerging from the colonnades to the left, waving at me furiously which I imagine has as much to do with state of mind as manner. It seems they have all stopped for the toilets and those not engaged in that pursuit are sheltering from the sun under the umbrella afforded by the roof of the colonnade which is why they were not visible from where I exited the church. I am so relieved to see them, rejoicing that's it's not too late yet to try to be better, that I have lost my fear of Iona and being last to the bus, for the second time that day. Being a pest is not nearly as bad as being *non est*.

"You're a slug, give me a slug of water," says Iona in greeting and surprisingly, without malice. It's true I am the water bearer, Aquarius, though my astrological sign is Cancer, the crab and why Iona, in another of her witticisms, says I'm so *crabbit*.

But what if the Hindus were right all along and I have been transmogrified, from for example, a frog? Our house is full of froggy things, most in the worst possible taste and because people think I like them, they keep adding to my collection. For those who are not frog admirers (and there are not many who are) I would point out that being a frog was promotion from the toad I used to be. If I am now a slug, perhaps I *have* died and am sliding down the evolutionary scale again. It's so difficult to be good. But thank God I'm not a snail. Not much chance of improvement there with everyone trying to squish the life out of you to bring the drought to an end: *I'd rather be a slug than a snail. Yes, I would! Yes, I really would!* I really do have a song for every occasion.

Carrying the water is one of my few uses on holiday. My other two uses are I do the driving when on the continent and I bargain for things, which just about makes me redundant on this trip I should imagine. You don't bargain in Italy. Well, I hadn't bargained on doing so anyway.

"You didn't hand your earpiece in," Iona accuses, refreshed after her slug of water. It's better than a frog in your throat anyway.

"I know."

"Paulo has been looking for you." It sounds sinister, like something out of a Mafia film. I have a feeling that Paulo isn't best pleased with me.

But Paulo isn't here. He's gone ahead to hand in the other earpieces which means I'm going to be in even greater trouble when he comes back. Angela is not in a good mood either. We have only 50 minutes' parking time and the toilet stop is taking an age. At least it means that she wasn't waiting for me, I think selfishly.

When Paulo comes back, he does a good job of not wanting to strangle me, though when he says it doesn't matter, it sounds a trifle strangulated. I offer abject apologies, like a penitential pilgrim but he just takes the earpiece and strides back down the town again. I call after him I hope he doesn't have to go too far, but I can tell he's already going to great lengths to restrain himself from expressing his opinion of some stupid buffoon who wanted to go and see where some dead person is buried. With each step, he's probably thinking of all the ways he'd like to kill me before he buries *me* somewhere.

On his return, the toilet stop is *still* in progress. It's taking an inordinate amount of time. We have been encouraged to drink a lot of water and perhaps there's only one toilet for all the ladies. Angela looks as if she is wetting her knickers. Maybe that's the protocol, under P in the guide's handbook, having to wait till last, or maybe she's getting really agitated about the time. If I had known about this, I could have spent more time in the crypt looking for St Francis. It was a bit of a dead loss really. I suppose you could say where his remains are will just have to remain cryptic.

At last we set off at a cracking pace, but it doesn't matter how fast Angela marches, the group begins to stretch out and stragglers are soon far behind. For one thing, they don't want to hurry in the heat and for another, there are just too many photo opportunities. There is one splendid view in particular, looking back up at the churches from below with oleander bushes in the foreground. It's just too good to rush. I remember telling the lady from Pennsylvania on the plane that Assisi was the part of the trip I was least looking forward to and she said that Assisi was wonderful. I doubted her judgement at the time, but I certainly don't now.

We are one of the first back at the bus. Angela is looking at her watch and walking up the aisle counting heads. Suddenly, there is a commotion.

"You can't eat that in here!"

I look back the bus and see that other chiaroscuro pair, the black man and the blonde woman, walking sheepishly down the aisle holding ice-creams. They've been put off the bus for eating an ice-cream! Clearly the strain has been getting to Angela. Who would be a travel rep with hooligans like that to deal with and people who are late and deadlines to meet, and nutters who want to meet dead people? It's still not as bad as being in charge of a school trip though.

At last, we are all together. We say goodbye to Paulo and in a scatter of dust and with a residue of diesel fumes, we leave him and Assisi behind.

Whilst I was in search of St Francis, Iona was taking the opportunity to do some unrestricted shopping and has bought a book on Assisi, one Paulo has recommended and as I flick through it, I realise that I have visited the grave of the Saint after all. I recognise the picture which has the caption: *The tomb of St Francis.* His bones lie in a stone sarcophagus at the top of a pillar in the chapel. I hadn't thought, in my haste to look up! According to the book, his body was hidden there in 1230 to prevent violation and in 1818, Pius VII permitted the area to be opened up. The crypt was hewn out of the solid rock and opened to the public in 1820.

If that is good news, the book contains some bad news for me. I may have bagged the bones of St Francis, but I have missed the body of St Clare. You can actually see her blackened corpse it says. Imagine not taking us to see that! Just one more reason I'm going to have to come back to Assisi.

As we skirt Perugia and head north, towards Florence, the names on the signs begin to become familiar from our visit to Tuscany at Easter. Lake Trasimeno where Hannibal took on the Romans, Cortona and Arezzo.

There is a moment of excitement when a car overtaking us has to slam on its brakes to avoid crashing into the rear of a braking car in front. There is a cloud of smoke as the rubber burns but, as usual a catastrophe is averted by the narrowest of margins. The Guttings observe this unmoved, as if it were such a regular occurrence that it had become tedious, like watching an advert, no matter how well constructed. Why there are not more accidents, in Italy I don't know, as they drive so fast right behind the car in front. They don't seem to have heard of braking distances. Perhaps they haven't got to Italy yet. Maybe they don't apply to Italy at all: that must be why there are so few accidents. Like the rules of the European Union, the rules of physics in Italy must be different.

*

So now, finally, we are in Florence, or maybe it's a field in Flanders. We've stopped outside our hotel but there are earthworks and ditches with purple and yellow plastic entrails disgorging from them. We are in a three star hotel here, a star less than the firmament in whose circles we normally revolve. Angela warns us that it is not up to the standard of the Golfo di Napoli, but it is clean. This sounds like more of an apology than a recommendation to me. In other words, it's not sounding too promising.

We crowd into the small foyer whilst Angela gets our keys. It's another chance to try and learn the names of our travelling companions.

"Bennet and Simpson!"

The black man comes to get the keys. I'm going to call him Gordon until I find out his real name.

We're amongst the first to have our names called out, so my education is curtailed. Just as well, as the lift is extremely small, with barely enough room for our cases and us. We're on the third floor. The room looks out over the street and the earthworks and although the finishing is not of a high quality, the room is spacious enough and the bed feels suitably comfortable if not quite as wide as Iona would have liked. We might accidentally touch in the night.

Whilst I am studying the room and the view, Iona is in the toilet. When I go in, it is flushing like Niagara. The flush is operated by a handle the like of which I've never seen before. To operate it, you turn it upwards and it doesn't stop automatically, you have to turn it upwards again to shut it off. Looks like another instance of Italian logic to me. No wonder there is a water shortage in Italy, if all the tourist technophobes are wasting water like this.

We are going to meet Angela in the lounge and then go somewhere to get something to eat, so we get changed and lock our valuables in the safe. All other hotel safes I have used have a digital system which takes you half an hour to understand, but once you have, you can't lose the key. All you have to do is remember your number. But this is the old fashioned type, with a key for me to lose. Actually, it's going to be hard for me to lose this key, not with half a

Con Molto Fresco

hundredweight of metal attached to it. The bloody barrel
has come out with the key when I locked it.

"You are a little barrel of laughs, aren't you?"

The key to a successful relationship with broken
mechanical things is not to lose your temper. Don't let
them see that you're annoyed with them. Pretend that you're
enjoying the joke, cajole them, try to get them on your side.
Don't let them see that they have got you over a barrel, so
to speak.

"Look, you little bastard, if you don't stay in this time,
I'll bash your bloody brains out!"

I've spent five minutes trying to get the barrel back
minus the key and my good humour and patience has run
out. Which just goes to show you that violence, or the threat
of violence, has its place if the pacifist approach doesn't
work, for would you believe it, this time I manage to get
the barrel back, the key out and the safe locked. I suppose
it's safe to say it's still a victory for the barrel because I've
spent longer with this than working out how to operate the
electronic system. Anyway, at last we can go.

I am surprised how compact Florence is. Angela says
it's only 10 or 15 minutes' walk to the city centre where there
are a variety of eating places. Somehow, I had imagined
Florence to be vast and sprawling, a place for the motorist
to avoid which is what we did at Easter, especially since we
knew we were coming in the summer, but actually it doesn't
seem so daunting after all.

We decide we'll keep the delights of Florence till the
next day. Besides, the restaurants in the town centre sound
flashy and expensive whereas if we stay in this locality, we
should get just as good a meal for a fraction of the price in
the sort of place that is patronised by locals, not by tourists.
Angela says if we turn right out of the hotel and then turn
right again we should come to a *trattoria.*

At the top of the street, there is an enormous structure which looks as if it had been one of the gates of the city at one time, but the walls have disappeared and it has a distinctly forlorn appearance in its new role as a roundabout. Our *trattoria* is just down the street facing it. I am not too impressed with the menu. For one thing it is all in Italian and secondly, it is handwritten, so between them, this makes it a dangerous place to eat. What if I got tripe or liver or kidneys or something else awful?

We decide to walk on and try somewhere else, but it soon becomes apparent that there is nowhere else. The street is long and straight and there are no neon signs proclaiming another eating place. When we come to the first intersection and see nothing up that street either, we decide to head back. It's not all bad because the tables seem to be arranged on pallets outside even although there are no greens.

There is a native sitting having a solitary meal. That's a good sign. Not good that he's solitary; I actually feel very sorry for people who eat alone in restaurants. I'd rather eat alone in my lonely garret than put myself under public scrutiny like this. This one for instance, has he not got any friends or has she walked out on him: *Huh! You expect me to believe you love me and you take me to a crummy place like this, you cheapskate! And expect me to give you a good time afterwards? Well, you've got another think coming!* No, I mean it's good that natives eat here – that's always meant to be a good sign. Of course they do not suffer from the handicap of not being able to read the menu. It's not busy but that doesn't mean a thing for 8:30 is early by Italian standards to begin eating.

The menu arrives. It might just as well have been like the one we had in Chinatown in Vancouver once, where we were the only Caucasians among the clientele. It was written completely in squiggles and to my horror, the first course I ordered at random turned out to be dead hen's feet, turned to a warm golden brown with claws intact. Did they expect us to order these or had I inadvertently ordered toothpicks for a starter? The rest of the meal went down from there. We sent something unrecognisable back, untouched, and the waiter called the manager who accused us of sampling the delights of whatever it was. I think it was duck of some sort. Anyway, I ended up getting a big bill for some not very appetising food. I suspect this is going to be somewhat similar.

Iona, whose language skills are more honed than mine, can work out some things but we have left the book behind and most of it is incomprehensible. Even the bits that I can read, like *Salad Toscana*, I don't know what it actually *is*.

The native next door is crouching over his half bottle of wine and his meal, looking as if it would choke him. I recall an Italian proverb which I had picked up in Sicily last October: *He who eats alone strangles himself.* How true! Well, maybe he's learned his lesson now: he should have taken her to one of the flashy tourist places. Poor bugger! I feel a bit smug. I don't need to go through all that wining and dining rubbish. It's Florence and neither of us has been here before and tomorrow is our wedding anniversary – I even know the number –31- so I can't fail. It's one of these rare conjunctions of the planets. If it's not tonight, then it certainly has to be tomorrow. I feel invincible, even immortal. It's written in the stars. It could even be a double eclipse if such a thing exists, because my misdemeanours of the day seem to have been forgotten, if not forgiven.

I order the *Salad Toscana* (when in Tuscany…) and since I am not a pasta fan, the *gnocchi* in a tomato sauce which I've had at home and which Iona says is made from potatoes. But maybe she is just telling me that to get it down my neck, a sort of inverse of my mother telling me that marzipan was made out of chicken fat, when she caught me pinching it before it could be put on the Christmas cake.

The main meal, as far as I am concerned, is the wine. I order *Vernaccia di San Gimignano*, not so much because of its price (€12), but because from my previous trip to Tuscany, I know that it is not only one of the best wine producing areas of Italy, but one of the most enchanting places I have ever been in my life, with more towers left standing from medieval times than phallic factory chimneys in a Lowry painting.

When the *Salad Toscana* comes, I look at in dismay. It is a cold meat platter consisting of something that looks suspiciously like liver sausage and a meat with great big chunks of white fat in it. In fact, there is so much fat if it's not already called fat sausage, it bloody well should be.

Whilst I am surgically removing the fat from the meat, Tom, Dick and Harriet come past, and seeing us there, before I can say fat sausage, they take this as a recommendation and ensconce themselves forthwith.

Presently along come Gordon and Blondie, and seeing us and Tom, Dick and Harriet, decide to walk on. I don't blame them. A bit like Groucho Marx who wouldn't want to be a member of a club that would accept someone like him as a member, I wouldn't want to be seen in a restaurant where the only clientele are people like me either but in a few minutes they come back. They have found that there is nowhere else.

Now we are seven as A.A. Milne nearly wrote. If we keep this quiet from the rest of the group, we could be the Secret Seven and perhaps we could have a jolly exciting adventure together but there is no chance of that, for along with the *gnocchi* comes the Yorkshire couple. His face has a lived-in look, like W.H.Auden's only his looks as if it's been inexpertly ironed, so that while some of the creases have been erased, some seem to be as deeply etched as striations on a block of sandstone. He has a bit of a cast in one eye too which looks as if it might have been the result of some previous pugilistic encounter. His face doesn't make him a bad person, but he looks the sort you wouldn't want to tangle with in a dark street on a dark night.

He is speaking to me. I nod and say it's all right and there's nowhere else anyway. I hope he has been asking me what this place is like, not challenging me to a fight because he doesn't like the look of *my* face. He could be because not only does he sound and look a bit aggressive, but his thick accent appears to be delivered through a mouthful of cotton wool, so deciphering what he's actually saying is just an educated guess on my part. I have a suspicion he is drunk. Amazing! Those hundreds of people I saw on the *passeggiata* in Naples and not a single one drunk or even slightly the worse for wear! Yes, it takes an Englishman in Florence to show these wimpy Italians how to drink.

They sit down at an empty table at the other side of the lonely Italian.

"Whadyizbindoinzisevn?" He is determined to be friendly. I think he's asking me if I've consummated Florence yet. Not waiting for a reply, he volunteers the information that they've been in their room *Havnfewwhishkies*. I thought as much. My national drink has made him loquacious and friendly as it can do sometimes. Sometimes it makes people want to fight the whole world. Tonight he is in mellow mood. Fortunately, the waiter interrupts us before this distant and difficult conversation can really get into its stride.

The *gnocchi* in tomato sauce is all right but there is rather a lot of it and I'm struggling a bit. Meanwhile, the waiter is bringing something that looks very tasty and interesting to Tom, Dick and Harriet. I wish I'd ordered that, but then I always like the look of what other people choose better.

Now there is a couple choosing a table to our right. The woman is one of God's repeats. I catch Iona's eye and look towards the newcomer.

"The same idea as Claire," I whisper. I think she may even be French which would make the resemblance even more of a carbon copy. Their speech doesn't sound like Italian anyway but they are talking in such a low tones it's almost as difficult to decipher as the form of English promulgated by my Yorkshire friend. For all I know she may be saying: *Comme il ressemble Georges Buisson!*

When her food comes, she gets the sort of thing I would have dreaded – a mound of steaming dark green vegetation, the sort of thing that looks as if it had been freshly deposited by a not very well cow. I don't know what it is called in Italian, but on the menu it would have translated as cooked spinach. Imagine eating a whole plate of that by itself! Look-a-like-Claire probably is French after all. Next to the Chinese, the French are the nation most likely to win the if-it-moves-eat-every-bit-of-it contest. I bet they think something that looks as if it's just come from a cow's bowels must be good for the bowels of those who eat it.

My food may not be good, but the wine is. I give up on the *gnocchi* although it is against my principles of waste and value for money and fill up my glass and savour what Keats called *a beaker full of the warm South, /Full of the true, the blushful Hippocrene* and devote myself to a study of my fellow diners.

Ironic really. Now that the lone Italian has gone, all the customers apart from Claire and her companion are Brits and I had thought I was going to avoid the tourists! The Yorkies are attacking their *coperto*; Tom, Dick and Harriet are sitting next to Gordon and Blondie and they seem to be getting on well together. It's a little corner of England in this corner of Florence.

When the wine is finished, the bill and the tip paid, the latter out of habit rather than for services rendered, we have to make our way past Tom, Dick and Harriet. I can see that Harriet is eating some sort of meat dish smothered in gravy.

"That looks good," I remark. "How did you know what to ask for?"

She flashes me a surprised look, as if I were some sort of idiot who was too stupid even to work it out for himself. "I just asked the waiter what the menu said - in English!" she says.

You can carry this when in Florence, Tuscany, Italian thing a bit too far sometimes, I reflect as we make our way back to the hotel for our first night in Florence. I may not have had a good meal by my determination to enter completely into the spirit of Italy but there are other compensations. The *Vernaccia di San Gimignano* was very good and for once I don't seem to have annoyed Iona for quite a while. There is too much light pollution to see the stars but they look propitious. I can see the moon however and by some optical illusion, it looks as if there are two of them – the old and the new. Could this be the double eclipse, the double whammy of my dreams? And then, unbidden, the lines from that great ballad, Sir Patrick Spens comes floating into my mind:

> *I saw the new moon late yestreen*
> *Wi' the auld moon in her airm*
> *And if we gang to sea, maister,*
> *I fear we'll come to hairm.*

What does it mean? I have a horrible feeling that disaster may be lurking around the corner – not that I am superstitious of course, but it is our 31st anniversary and 31 is only 13 turned.

Instead of stepping towards the hotel with a heightened sense of anticipation, I have a sudden feeling of foreboding...

Chapter 4
Con Anniversario

Groan! The telephone is clamouring persistently demanding attention, like a spoiled brat. With my eyes still closed, I grope for it, pick it up and promptly drop it back on the cradle without speaking. A moment later, I reflect that in this downmarket hotel, it may have been a real person. If it was the friendly, pretty receptionist who gave me my keys last night, that's too bad. She'd only be telling me to get out of bed anyway, not issue an invitation.

Best begin this anniversary day without Iona having to bash me with Humphrey, make it a special day for her without her even having to tell me to get up. At the last possible moment, I swing my trotters out of bed and am waiting to slip into the shower, trying to look as if I'd been bright-eyed and bushy tailed for hours, but I know my eyes are small and piggy and tired. If she was surprised to see me already up, she doesn't say so.

"Bathroom's free," she says, plugging in the hair dryer. Maybe she thinks I'm so bleary eyed I can't see that for myself.

By the time I am finished, she has already departed. I slip into my *pantouffles* and catch the lift to the ground floor then descend further stairs to the dining room. For some reason of Italian efficiency, the lift does not go down all the way to the dining room. Here, my *pantouffles* excite no comment. This place is apparently not posh enough for them to cause offence.

Having said that, the food is just the same as at the Golfo di Napoli. I'll have my usual breakfast and lunch combined, fruit juice to begin with - but I can't find any bowls for the muesli, or any plates for the cold meat and cheese either. I circle around thinking it's probably me, still too tired to see what's right in front of me. No one else seems to be having a problem. I catch sight of Angela talking to someone who may be the maître d' only he's not dressed for the part and by the looks of it, they are having a serious conversation. I hover, not liking to interrupt, but after a while it starts to get a bit embarrassing, standing about in my *pantouffles* and swimming trunks like this whilst they are too engrossed to notice me. God knows how they can't see me as I feel everyone else is looking at me, wondering what I'm doing hanging about like a lemon.

An apposite comparison, for today I am a vision in yellow. I have been wearing my green swimming trunks for two days now and I deem it time for a change; no need to show sympathy for the Guttings by imitation. Besides, they probably went shopping last night whilst we were all at the *trattoria* and they will be kitted out in different outfits.

Before we left, Iona and I had a discussion about my yellow shorts. I thought I had been very fortunate to find them in one of my chain stores as you can never be sure what stock they will carry and it had taken weeks of dedicated hunting to track these down. They are the very same as my green pair, only in yellow, and I like them because, although they were intended for water, in my opinion, they work very well on dry land being nice and light and letting the air circulate. They are a very violent yellow, I have to concede, brighter than I would have chosen if I had had a choice and perhaps a little young for someone sporting my kind of tonsured hairstyle, and, it has to be admitted, girth, but once I got my tan going, I thought, they would show my bronzed beer belly off to advantage. In my chain store, a choice of colour is a luxury dispensed with in the interests of economy. My chain store trades under various names: Oxfam. Help the Aged. PDSA. The British Heart Foundation. Imperial Cancer Research etc etc. .

However, when I proudly displayed my purchase, Iona's reaction was as violent as the colour.

"You are *not* wearing those! No! Definitely *not*! People will laugh at you! And I'm certainly not having them laughing at *me* being seen with you. No! Certainly not!"

£2:50 wasted. She just would not listen to reason, refusing to see what a bargain they were, what a rarity they were (she agreed with that) and how they would keep my genials (sic) airy and sweat free. But she doesn't share my genial disposition and I know it is hopeless trying to get her to understand. Maybe she hopes all my little tadpoles will be shrivelled to death in the heat.

A few days later, she gets her revenge. She has bought me a pair of shorts for four times the price and which she *will* allow herself to be seen with me. Dreary black shiny nylon things, obscene things, that come down to my knees, though I concede, she has met me half way, in the sense that their intended use is as swimming trunks.

I riposte with: *I'm not wearing those things unless you are burying me in them*! She refuses to take them back and will not give me the receipt. She thinks she has me there, because she knows I will not like the idea of all that money going to waste, but I say: *Give them to George, (our son) because I am definitely not wearing them unless at my funeral and even then, I'd prefer not to be seen dead in them.* There is a pretty good chance of this as La-Belle-Dame-Sans-Merci is looking very murderous indeed.

On the matters of sartorial taste, we do not see eye to eye. I don't see anything wrong with sixties fashions. My philosophy is that fashion is for mugs and it annoys me to see her throw out perfectly good clothes that are not worn out at the cuffs or anywhere else, just because the colour or the hemline or some other arcane matter is out of date.   I still have a T shirt from Montana which is 24 years old. It's got a few holes in it now I admit, and I no longer appear in public in it but it is still serviceable in bed. In fact, I have to guard it carefully as Iona has her eyes set on it as a floor cloth or some such other ignominious purpose.

And so, when it came to packing, surprise, surprise, I could not find the dastardly yellows. But in the end, she had to reluctantly dig them out of their hiding place because the thought of me wearing the same pair of shorts for two weeks on end was something even more horrible to contemplate.

I catch her eye now and there is clearly a glint of disapproval in it. It may be because I've got the yellows on, though I think them very tasteful and co-ordinated with a lemon shirt. I had hoped once she had seen my ensemble she might see the error of her ways and mellow towards the yellow, but it doesn't look like it. But perhaps she's wondering why I am standing about making an exhibition of myself instead of eating my breakfast and making myself last for the bus again. Ha! Ha! Got *her* there! No bus to catch today. Giancarlo's R&R - rest and research day. We are being met by our guide at 9:15 for a walking tour of Florence. But the way things are going, I'm going to have to go on it hungry.

At least Angela and the bloke are talking in Italian, so I can't be accused of eavesdropping. Maybe he's the boss and she's telling him that they are not going to use this hotel next year, in which case my intervention is not going to help him plead his case. It's definitely not up to the standard of the Golfo di Napoli nor, according to the brochure, the others on our trip, but I don't mind really, just as long as I get fed and even more pressing, stop feeling like a retarded lemon. I can't understand why, if the whole of the rest of the restaurant is looking at me, why Angela and her companion can't see me.

Finally, I can bear it no longer and give a little cough. That does it! They give a bit of a jump and look up at me.

"Er…em… there don't appear to be any plates."

Angela says something in Italian. Perhaps she's saying: *Oh God, it's him again. You'd better see what he wants.* The maître d', or whoever he is, doesn't look too pleased as he follows me over to the table and to my horror, long before we get there, I can see the plates white though they are, prominently stacked on the white tablecloth. Surely I couldn't have missed them? I stammer an explanation to the maître d' that there hadn't been any a few minutes ago: someone must have placed them there when my back was turned. He may or may not believe me, merely giving me a flicker of a smile before turning on his heel. I can just imagine Angela saying: *Bird brain. Now it seems as if he thinks he's got to dress up as a bloody canary as well!*

The plates are still hot, so they must just have been washed. This is what happens when you get up too early. The early bird is made to feel like a worm and if I'd stayed in bed until I had been threatened me with Humphrey the Hairbrush, I probably would have arrived just as the plates were being put out. It just goes to show you, it doesn't pay to alter the habits of a lifetime.

Iona has practically finished her breakfast. She's unimpressed by my latest embarrassment and is in a hurry to be gone.

"*You're* the embarrassment," she says with finality, getting up. "And as soon as you've finished your breakfast, you're going to go upstairs and take those things off! Hopefully not many people may have seen you." Then, over her arched shoulder, "And don't be late!" Clearly, it's not an invitation to an early celebration of our anniversary – it's a command, which if I don't obey, means there will be none of that nonsense, as the saying goes, anniversary or no anniversary.

So I'm back in my Robin Hood outfit of Lincoln green when we foregather in the foyer. It's so small, that we can't all get in together and Angela has to move up and down and round pillars to count us. Our guide is Giulia, by far the best looking guide we've had so far, with her short dark hair and brown eyes, which perfectly complement the straps of her cappuccino-coloured bra. I'm not really a coffee fan - I don't see the point in taking antidotes, alcohol being more my drink, but I wouldn't say no to a couple of cupfuls of those.

Our first stop is going to be the Santa Croce church, but first we have to negotiate the Florentine traffic which means that we have to walk a hundred yards in the opposite direction from our intended destination so we can cross the broad boulevard Viale Giovine Italia in relative safety. Giulia says we have exactly 30 seconds to cross before the torrent of traffic pours down again upon the hapless pedestrians. Frustrated by having been held up by this valuable half a minute, I can see the motorists' fingers drumming impatiently on their steering wheels and hear feet revving on accelerator pedals, like the start of a Grand Prix. As far as pedestrians are concerned, it's *De'il tak' the hindmost* for I can see that no quarter is going to be given here. I wonder what the elderly and infirm do here. They must be quarantined within their block or call a taxi to cross the street. We are only 18, so Giulia has hopes of getting all across in one sprinting. She trusts that we are all reasonably spritely, and doesn't ask if any of us are suffering from a heart condition. When the red light comes, we are off and all safely gathered to the other side - just in time. Had we been 20, we could have been down to 18. The racing track is off again, roaring in our ears.

We make our way down the leafy shade of the boulevard and presently we come to the Piazza Piave. Giulia tells us that the structure ahead of us is where, in medieval times, people were publicly executed. It's a bit like the gate we had seen on the way to our *trattoria* last night, a city gate in need of a wall, and indeed that's what it is. The road which we now take is called the Via dei Malcontenti because this is the way that those poor unfortunates, about to go to heaven, made their last walk and, unsurprisingly enough, weren't that happy about it.

Suddenly we emerge at the Piazza di Santa Croce. The church is on our left and we have not seen it coming, so we are denied a view of its façade from the distance. There is a statue of Dante to the left of the entrance, a statue which once occupied a position of prominence in the centre of the square, but which was later moved to the top of the church steps after the flood of 1966. This is another Franciscan church but much more ornate than a Franciscan church ought to be. It is far too fussy and the combination of pink and green marble does not appeal to me but the inside is much better and plainer. Both sides of the nave have massive pillars with pediments which house the memorials to famous Florentines and on these pillars, you can see the marks of where the flood reached. It looks at least twelve feet to me. Incredible to think of that whole piazza and much else besides, under water. Because of the drought, it's not likely to happen this year.

Giulia explains that the idea, in the days of the rival city-states, is that you show your wealth on the outside and most people, who would just be passing through, would marvel at the exterior and be impressed by the wealth of the Florentines, making the church a weapon of mass deception, I suppose you could say. It is said that even today, that some Edinburgh ladies have adopted the same principle, as the saying goes, of *fur coats and nae knickers*, though it has to be said, I have no personal experience of this phenomenon, as ladies in Edinburgh are a pretty rare phenomenon.

The great thing about Santa Croce is that it has lots of dead people in it, so this is a very good place indeed to augment my collection of graves. I hadn't done this part of the homework before we left, so it was a very pleasant surprise that the first thing that I see when I enter the church, to my left, is a monument to that arch heretic, Galileo who, a century after his death, was given a Christian burial in 1737. The memorial is intricately carved with a bust of Galileo with jutting, bearded jaw above a brown marble sarcophagus. Giulia explains that he is not really there at all, but down below in the crypt. That doesn't matter to me – this counts as a grave visit. There is an inscription below, written in Latin: *Galilaevs Galileivs Patric. Flor.* I like the sound of the first two names - they have a ring to them, but I never knew he had Irish blood in him and a girl's name as well, only the sculptor, for reasons best known to himself, cut off the *k* and the *a* of his last names. Perhaps the budget only extended to a certain number of letters and he reckoned those were the ones he could most dispense with. Not for the first time, I wish I had paid more attention to my Latin in school.

Galileo's bust has him looking heavenward appropriately enough, but his memorial has him facing bang opposite that of Michelangelo. His memorial is much more elaborate and according to the Latin inscription, his name is: *Michalli Angelo Buonarroti*. That's some name too. It sounds good to me – the sort of name that would get you into heaven. But I don't think it would work for me; I'd still sound like a sinner. The tomb was designed by Vasari, the same who wrote *Lives of the Great Artists*. At the bottom of the faux sarcophagus are the figures of Painting, Architecture and Sculpture, just three of the things in which he dabbled.

Unbelievable! Next but one down, we have the tomb of Dante. I'm excited because that's a really good one for my collection. Like some philatelists specialise in birds or bees,

I specialise in literary graves and have collected amongst others, Shakespeare, Wordsworth, and, as I already said, poor spinster Jane Austen who, being interred in the floor of Winchester Cathedral was treated to a view up my kilt when I was there for a wedding though I'm not so sure it was a happy occasion for her. I have also been as close as I can get to the even poorer Charlotte and Emily's graves in Haworth but Anne inconsiderately died and lies in Scarborough, so I have not yet done the full Bronte.

Uh! Uh! But wait a moment, Giulia is explaining that Dante was exiled and died in Ravenna in 1321, where he is buried. They erected a monument to him all the same, five hundred years later - even Galileo didn't have to wait that long - and letters from the mayor of Florence to the mayor of Ravenna asking for their boy back fell, as you might expect, on deaf ears: *Get stuffed! You didn't want him when he was alive, and you bloody well can't have him now he's dead. Have you never heard of habeus corpus? Well we have and we're keeping it.* City wars are alive and well in Italy.

The thing about Dante is, apart from being arguably, Italy's greatest poet, he was the one who unified the language, so that the Italian of today and perhaps indirectly, the unification of the country, is thanks to him. But now, there are some in Italy, who would like to see the rich north secede from the poor south and who's to say that in the length of time it takes the Florentines to erect a memorial to one of their most prestigious geniuses, that it couldn't happen, European Union or no European Union? If it could happen anywhere, it could happen in Italy.

Four memorials further down, we have that of Machiavelli. I had thought they may not have displayed him so prominently, maybe put him on the floor under some pews somewhere, so the descendants of those of the downtrodden, could stand on *him*, every Sunday, if not every day, if they so choose. In fact, under my feet there are other graves who must have been somebody important once, but I give up trying to read them, there are so many and anyway, if they counted for my collection, they'd be bound to be up there on the wall. To be honest, I don't like my graves all gathered in one place like this, like Poet's corner in Westminster Abbey- it makes it too easy. I prefer the joy of the hunt and occasionally, the serendipitous discovery.

From where I am standing, I can see the memorial to Rossini, the very same who had to be locked in his room in Naples before he would do any composing. Now he lies decomposing in the crypt of Santa Croce in Florence. I wonder if he's happy about his proximity to Machiavelli? Maybe he's not next to him down there though. Rossini might have made it to heaven, his peccadilloes notwithstanding, but it's hard to imagine old Niccolò up there looking up the angels' skirts. He's more likely to be warming his bum at Auld Nick's fire. It seems curious to me to make such a fuss of him compared to these other great men, but it's certainly true he was a writer and philosopher and has certainly achieved immortality through most would agree, immorality, his name being synonymous for duplicity and cunning. It makes me wonder what happened to that other man whose name has passed into the language and sums up excessive pride in one's country. Not surprising, that he was French. I am referring to none other of course, than Monsieur Chauvin. Does he have some elaborate cenotaph somewhere, to mark his contribution to the world's lexicon?

But Giulia doesn't seem to be interested in Rossini– she's not taking us to his memorial. Maybe even Italian TV screened *The Lone Ranger* and she's still traumatised by hearing the *William Tell Overture* at five o'clock every Saturday tea-time though that was hardly poor old Rossini's fault. Instead she is taking us to see a pulpit. It's a very fine pulpit indeed, very intricately carved by Benedetto da Maiano with scenes of the life of St Francis - of course.

Another treasure, possibly the most famous in Santa Croce is Cimabue's *Crucifixion* which was the most famous victim of the 1996 floods. But it doesn't look damaged and it is so high up, well above the watermark. What we're looking at is a copy - the original we are going to see later. Unfortunately, just two months before the flood they had decided to restore it and laid it flat in the refectory. Now two thirds of it is damaged. I'm sorry about that. Giulia says it's a masterpiece but I much prefer Salvador Dali's *Crucifixion*.

Behind the cross, at the back of the church, there are two chapels which contain frescoes by Giotto. I don't know if she knows we've been to Assisi or not, but she invites us to look at the realism of the faces, at the lines and wrinkles and points out that without Giotto the rest of Italian art would not have been possible. I may not know much about art right enough, but I do know that about Giotto. These frescoes do not have the colours of the frescoes in Assisi, looking more like a sepia photograph than a fresco, and I disagree with Giulia – I think most of them look decidedly un-wrinkly for their ages, though apart from that, they look realistic enough. I think I'd probably choose Giotto to paint me anyway as he doesn't seem to do wrinkles. He also seems to do blokes with baldy bits so all I need is a brown suit and I could qualify as a suitable model, especially as I might be getting holy with those itchy shoulder blades I've got.

We're on our way out now, and it is a pleasing view down the whole length of the nave. Wide and spacious, with a relatively plain wooden ceiling echoing the serried ranks of pews on the floor, this is more my idea of a church and less of an art gallery. It's a pity about the façade, which, it seems, was re-clad by some vandal in the nineteenth century, probably under the impression he was improving the place, whereas in fact, he was tarting it up. I wonder what it would have looked like before he "improved" it. I bet St. Francis had a fit in heaven.

We are stopping in front of the memorial to Gioacchino Rossini after all. It turns out that he was the last to be buried in the church and that wasn't yesterday – 1868 in fact and only at the insistence of Mrs Rossini. So, it's thanks to her that he's got this grand memorial in Santa Croce. I wonder what memorial, on what windy hillside, Mrs Addison will provide for me. Small of course, but it would have to be big enough to have my name on it and my dates, (though I never had many of them) and a suitable epitaph. I have composed a verse already like the ones I saw in Boot Hill Cemetery in Tombstone, Arizona for the likes of Lester Moore *et al*:

> *My name was Dave*
> *I was a sexual slave*
> *I am lying below*
> *And I am lying above.*

But that would probably cost too much and anyway, it would not be real life, only a fantasy. I would have to chose something more pithy, something which sums up my life and sayings which I made famous during my lifetime such as: *I never knowingly bugged anyone* or *I am not a sweet person* (I am constantly made to eat puddings because Iona likes them and kids herself she is making them for me). But the inconsolable widow would probably choose something like: *He bugged me all right – he was a right little bugger–* except there's probably some EU law against writing *bugger* on a gravestone. I'll just have to croak in Italy if she wants to write that, preferably here in Florence where they have never heard of rules like that and be buried in the Protestant Cemetery along with Elizabeth Barrett Browning whom I happen to know lies there.

We've come out of the church now and descend some steps to the cloisters. I am a cloistered cloisters lover. I'd rather be out here than in any church, even Santa Croce, but I daren't admit it to anyone. The architecture, I think, is distinctly ancient Roman, but not ruined Roman. I half expect to see someone in a toga emerge from behind a pillar and perhaps that's why I like it so much. In the one part which does not have the two tiers of colonnades, in a section set back from the rectangle of the cloisters so as not to upset the symmetry, shade is provided (for those who want it) by cypresses and their greenness is picked up by two inviting carpets of grass running down each side of the rectangle. This cool green oasis in the heart of the city is given further emphasis by the twittering of invisible birds. Not a single sound from a Vespa is allowed to permeate in here to ruin the peace.

But we're not allowed to loiter here in this tranquil place which is as about as far removed in atmosphere and ambience as it is possible to imagine from the place where Keats's knight-at-arms waited forlornly for his Belle Dame Sans Merci. We are now entering the Cappella de' Pazzi, designed by Brunelleschi, who even I know, designed the famous dome of the Duomo. According to Giulia, this is a perfect example of early Renaissance art. It's based on geometrical multiples of seven, very plain and elegant, though I think it's a bit on the forbidding, unwelcoming side, with its grey stone and even regularity. But for all that, I like the domed ceiling, the arches and Corinthian pillars and the roundels of the saints below the metopes which run in a frieze round the walls.

The Pazzi family were rivals of the famous and powerful Medici family. In the Pazzi conspiracy of 1478, the family were foolish enough to think they could murder Lorenzo, so-called The Magnificent. They wounded Lorenzo but succeeded in killing his brother Giulliano. Naturally the Medicis did not take this lying down and wreaked their revenge, culminating in Pope Sixtus IV declaring war on

Florence with the help of Naples. So it was a pretty stupid thing to do with deep repercussions and the word *pazzo* in Italian means mad or crazy.

Iona gives me a knowing look. I know what's coming.

"You're mad," says she. "I'm going to call you Patsy. Give me some water, Patsy!"

I suppose it's progress from a slug.

Looking back at the Cappella from the cypress trees, I can see the complete exterior façade of the building which we had not seen before, having approached it from the side and I must say, I find it stunning and much preferable to the interior. The dome rises above a loggia with a balcony suspended upon slender pillars. It must be great to look down from there, or even better to look back at the Capella from the length of the cloisters. This place, not the Santa Croce, gets my vote for architectural ambience and harmony.

Whilst I have been admiring this, the group has moved on to see the damaged Cimabue crucifixion. It looks as if this place may have been a refectory once – at least there is a fresco of *The Last Supper* at the far end. Perhaps Giulia has told my fellow travellers about it, but I don't think so. Just another case of some poor bugger painting away for all he's worth before the plaster dries and when he's finished, no one gives a hoot. A bit like knocking out your immortal memoirs to have your wife tell you it's a load of rubbish. Well, I *think* that was the word she used. Maybe she said she was enraptured and I just imagined the silent c.

The Cimabue is indeed in a pretty bad state. Giulia says it is an important painting in the development of art because it shows the real suffering of Christ which was an advancement on the Byzantine idea. I don't know about that. I have to take her word for it because the painting has certainly suffered and Christ looks as if he's suffering all right but from some disease which has left huge brown patches over his body.

As we make our way out of the cloisters, there are two classical statues on either side of a door. The larger one is of Florence Nightingale whose father was an ambassador here and was apparently stuck for a name, so he called his daughter Florence because she was born here. That might be news for the Beckhams who probably thought they had conceived of this idea first. Maybe Posh consummates each new place, like Iona in which case, when she reads this, she will be disappointed to learn she did not think of that first either.

The smaller figure and plaque is to Elizabeth Barrett Browning whom I'd just been thinking about and who died here. Maybe it's smaller because the Florentines deem it a greater honour to be born in Florence than to die here but the interesting thing is, that they appear to have used the same statue, only shrunk Elizabeth's down a bit.

Just time for one last, lingering look back up the cloisters, with its elegantly thin pillars, with the grass, the occasional statue and cluster of cypresses with the Cappella de' Pazzi at its head. Perfect!

The noise hits me like a pneumatic drill. A Vespa roars past in the Piazza Santa Croce. Welcome to the real Florence. Before we set off to wherever we are going next, I wander down the Piazza a bit to have a proper look at the façade of the Santa Croce. No, I don't really like it that much, but at least it doesn't look, with its variegated marble, quite as much as a Licquorice Allsort as the Duomo in Siena does.

As we are walking down the Borgo Santa Croce, I catch sight of Sandra Duncan. I excitedly nudge Iona on the upper arm. I want her to confirm my sighting. It can't really be Sandra as she lives in South Africa, but someone the same idea as her.

"Look, look! It's Sandra," I say – it's a habit I brought back from Egypt where the "guards" at the sites, who apart from sitting napping in the shade, would come up to tourists

and say: *Look! Look!* before taking them to see something
they could see perfectly well for themselves, then they would
hold out a hand and say: *Baksheesh*! Well, I only fell for it
once, but I heard plenty of *Look looks* and as I find it difficult
to think of original ideas for myself, I grafted this onto my
repertoire of memorable phrases and it's what I say when I
want Iona to look at something. Strangely enough, however,
Iona seems to find this another of my irritating habits, traits
I did not possess before she married me.

"Yes, Patsy," she agrees, seizing the chance to make use
of her new soubriquet. "That's Sandra all right."

As we wander along the Via Della Nina towards the
Uffizi and the Palazzo Vecchio, I wonder how long it will be
before she tires of calling me this. The Uffizi is not on our
tour, or at least the interior. If we want to go to that, we have
to go on our own. The Uffizi is another of Vasari's efforts.
In 1560, Duke Cosimo I commissioned him to design a block
of government offices and, now I come to think of it, of
course, Uffizi means offices. After Vasari died, succeeding
Medici generations turned it into an art gallery, not that
they were scared to ask Vasari's permission I wouldn't have
thought.

Giulia points out an arch, startlingly white and new-
looking high above our head with windows so huge, it's
more windows than arch. She says this is the Corridoio
Vasariano (there's that man again) which is more than a mile
long and runs from the Palazzo Vecchio behind us, right
through the Ufizzi, across the Ponte Vecchio, ending up in
the Palazzo Pitti across the river Arno. All this so that the
Medicis did not have to mix with the riff-raff in the streets.
Probably a good idea if there were *pazzo* Pazzis round every
corner, trying to do you in. I would do it myself too if it got
me out of range of what were the equivalent of those bloody
Vespas in those days. Horse poo too I should imagine.

We walk down the Piazzale degli Ufizzi towards the river. On each side of us, in niches, are statues to the famous: Giotto, hooded and looking like something out of *The Canterbury Tales*; Donattello, with a hat like a pudding basin, as if he's about to have the escaping curls chopped off; Leonardo da Vinci, with the best hat so far, like something Jean Shrimpton wore in the sixties, and looking very hairy; Michelano Buonaritti (that's how it's spelt) short-haired and hatless and looking pensive, with his back slightly towards his rival, Leonardo: *Why did they have to put me next to that bushy bastard?* Dante Alighieri looking furious at having the worst headgear of all – a cloth cap like the leather helmets the WWII pilots used to wear with padded ears and then the crowning glory - a wreath of laurel leaves, Roman style, balanced on top. No wonder he's mad. Giovanni Boccaccio in drag, holding up his skirts and also sporting laurel leaves, but this time on top of a hooded cape and strangely enough, not looking as if he minds too much being caught cross-dressing and good old Niccolò Machiavelli is there too, hair cut down to the wood, looking like he's devising another scheme, or wondering where he's put his hat. There are so many more it's like being in a stone open-air Madame Tussaud's.

Turning to look back at the way I have just come, it's a surprise, though it shouldn't be, to see, at the top of the street behind a building completely shrouded in a white sheet and scaffolding, two segments of the famous Brunelleschli dome – my first ever sighting of it in real life. It's not seen to its best advantage from this vantage point, and I can scarcely contain my impatience to get there. Patience is not really one of my skills and I would certainly need more of it than I possess if I were one of those in the queue for the Ufizzi. Giulia says that between the columns of the building represents a 20 minute wait and the queue extends in an untidy snake from the entrance, along the side of the building, turns the corner and across the comparatively short arched span of the Corridoio Vasariano which links the two arms of the Ufizzi, and then runs parallel with the street bordering the Arno for a good 10 yards or more. Not only that, but this multi-lingual human snake, like its animal counterpart, bulges hugely in places, like it's just swallowed a meal.

Because of these bulges and because it extends beyond the columns which provide a rough estimate of time, it's impossible to estimate just how long it would take to get in, but it must be at least two and a half hours, probably three and if I were in it, it would be – at least. Much as I would like to visit the Ufizzi, this is my first visit to Florence and I can think of better things to do than stand for three hours in a queue in the shade, then spend another two or three hours inside looking at paintings which you probably can't see properly anyway, like being on the human conveyor belt in the brothel in Pompeii. It makes me exhausted just to think of all that standing and walking. I hope Iona doesn't want to go, because I certainly don't. But wherever she goeth I go also as she is the boss, especially this day.

So there is the Arno and up to the right, the famous Ponte Vecchio, fortunately about the only bridge that was not bombed in the war, through good fortune or by design, I do not know, but which means that the medieval shops which overhang the bridge's edge can also reflect on their lucky escape and on the still waters of the Arno below, as they have done for centuries. It makes a perfect a photograph – the three low elegantly sweeping arches, the raggle-taggle of shops providing a splash of green, yellow ochre and terracotta except for a space in the middle of the bridge where there are three arches where you can stand and look down at, and along the river. Above, is the Corridoio Vasarino, while below is a mirror image in the placid waters of the Arno which looks as if can not be bothered to flow today. I'd rather make for this bridge than stand in the queue for the Ufizzi, that's for sure, as we are not going there on the tour either.

Now we are on our way to the Piazza Della Signoria.

Thank God for those hundreds queuing to get into the Ufizzi and thank God for the Ufizzi which occupies all those hundreds inside as well. Perhaps it's all to do with crowd control you have to queue for so long because this place is heaving and so noisy, it's practically impossible to hear Giulia speak over the babble of other guides or tourists shouting to each other. It must be hell to be a Florentine – imagine your city invaded daily by thousands of tourists so you can't get across the piazza for people, nor your ears being assaulted by this multilingual blasting. I remember feeling the same about the poor residents of Corfu. Imagine living in paradise only to find that it is overrun for half the year by bloody tourists, some of whom are just there for the beer – and the three S's of course. Still, it provides jobs I suppose and maybe keeps the taxes down, so maybe the natives don't mind the invasion too much.

I don't need Giulia to tell me – I can recognise instantly, me, totally naked and unashamed over there, in front of the Palazzo Vecchio which has a skeleton of scaffolding covering the façade. It's not the real me of course, that is in the Galleria dell' Academia, this is just a copy of Michelangelo's *David*, which just goes to show you, that you don't have to be big to be beautiful, though the statue itself is pretty big, though not as big if Michelangelo had decided to sculpt Goliath instead. *David's* in a wooden frame and not looking too happy about it. Perhaps he's going off for a clean up. It looks as if he could do with it. His marble skin is streaked and grimy and it doesn't look as if you could blame it entirely on the pigeons.

Pity too about the scaffolding obscuring the Pallazo; it looks like a fine building, with its crenellated battlements, which, pierced by arched windows, overhangs the top storey and is supported by tapering struts and in between which are coats of arms. From these battlements rises the campanile tower, which I also find very appealing - plain at the bottom then halfway up, thickening out in a similar style to the battlements, inside which are the four columns of the crenellated campanile itself. Here is the great bell which told the people to foregather for public announcements: *Here come the Neapolitans again with their bloody ice creams!*

David is looking across at another fine building – the Loggia dei Lanzi which contains a number of other interesting statues. In fact, this whole square is like an open-air sculpture gallery. Nearest *David*, is Cellini's bronze statue of *Perseus* standing on the body of Medusa and holding her severed head triumphantly aloft. The message, meant to shock the Neapolitans or any other enemy is: *See what'll happen to you if you meddle with us*! *We're the head bummers about here, OK?* Nowadays, the enemy of the statues and indeed outdoor statues the world over, are the pigeons but *Perseus* has a shock for them. Apparently he has a copper wire somewhere and when the pigeons land, they get a shock. I don't know how it works, but it seems to, as *Perseus* is pigeon-dropping free.

We are not going up to have a proper look at the statues, but the one which captures my attention is fortunately one of the nearest – *The Rape of the Sabine Women.* This was Giambologna, the sculptor's last work, carved out of a single piece of marble. Maybe he thought after creating a masterpiece like this, he may as well retire. The figures are a writhing entwined knot, spiralling upwards to the fingertips on the outstretched protesting arm of the violated woman being lifted aloft by her attacker. Giulia tells us that this is typical of the Mannerist school who like spiralling forms.

On our way out of the piazza we pass another Mannerist sculpture, only I would never have recognised it as one.

It is Ammannati's statue of *Neptune* surrounded by water nymphs. I quite like it. *Neptune* is a big chunky guy, just the sort you might imagine a god to be, but Michelangelo said it was a load of crap, and poor old Ammannati never carved again, which just shows you how the critics can destroy an artist's confidence. I should know.

Further away is another piece of work by Giambologna – an equestrian statue of Cosimo I but we are too far away to see it in detail. Cosimo was the first to unite Tuscany and thus brought a period of peace and prosperity to the region.

We exit the piazza by the Via Calimaruzza and presently come to the Mercato Nuovo. This place is worse than the Piazza Signoria and the Ufizzi queues put together. When I think of all the people who must also be at the Duomo, I begin to wonder if the gods are playing another of their little tricks and have removed everyone in the world from Heathrow and transported them to Florence. It's just as well Florence has all these attractions to thin them out a bit. But this place is a hot spot. As well as being a busy market, the attraction here is a big bronze boar around which scores of people are milling, but it's just possible to see that its nose is a bright, shiny gold colour unlike the rest of it which is a dark brown. Giulia explains that if you rub its nose, your wish will be granted. I have a wish. I wish all these bloody tourists would disappear so I could get close enough to give that nose a stroke as I have a wish, another wish, which I am not going to tell you, to protect the potentially guilty. But it's no good – we're off again this time down the Via Calimala. I'll try and get back to the boar this afternoon – not that I'm superstitious of course, but if there's a chance of me getting my wish, I may as well try it as nothing else seems to have worked so far.

"Here, Patsy, you're a boar," says Iona wittily, "let me rub your nose. I want a wish."

I wonder how she is spelling that? "No chance," I retort. "I am too young to die." I bet she wants me to drop dead right here in Florence so she can put me in the Protestant cemetery and write *bugger* on my tombstone.

We are walking down the Via Calimala and about 12 feet beneath our feet, lies the old Roman road which presently brings us into the Piazza della Republica which used to be the site of the old Roman forum. Now it is a pleasant enough square, bounded on three sides by rather ordinary buildings, but dominated by the massive three-tiered golden-stone structure which rises, sheer, like a cliff, at the far end of the piazza. It is pierced by a monumental triumphal arch in the centre, above which there rises a further tier which, as well as emphasising the central arch, contains a slab of white stone on which is written the legend:

L'ANTICO CENTRO DELLA CITTA
DA SECOLARE SQUALLORE
A VITA NUOVA RESTITUITO

I don't need Giulia's help with this one. It seems that they built this square upon the squalid remains of the old town. I presume they don't mean the Roman era but there's nothing like boasting about your cultural heritage. According to Giulia, through that arch is where all the expensive shops are – Gucchi, Armani and that sort of rubbish. We won't be going there, even if we could make it across the square which looks as if it is a pedestrian precinct except there is a white car crossing it now, cutting a swathe through the pedestrians and scattering them in various directions, like chickens mad for corn.

As we turn into the Piazza di San Giovanni, I gasp at the sight before me. I had expected to see the Duomo but here obscuring it, instead, is something which in its hideousness takes my breath away, an utter monstrosity composed of green and white marble. I suppose you could say I don't care for it very much. Octagonal and ornate - it is none other than the Baptistry, famous for its golden doors. It's not the fault of the Baptistry that it obscures the Duomo as it was here first, as early as the 5th century, though what we see now dates from the 11th century.

We are not going into this either – it looks closed anyway, but the inside can scarcely be worse than the outside, so perhaps it is a pity we are not seeing the interior as it might serve as a bit of an antidote to the exterior, like that of the Santa Croce. Like me, the beauty might lie within, if it lies anywhere. The reason for the Baptistry, Giulia says, is that the church which stood on the site of where the cathedral now stands, was considered too holy for the unbaptised to enter.

As everywhere else in Florence, crowds are milling around, especially in front of the golden doors. These were executed by Lorenzo Ghiberti who defeated Brunelleschi in a competition to design the doors. What we see, not surprisingly, are copies, the originals being in the Museo dell'Opera. Over the heads and the voices of the three deep crowd in front of us, Giulia tries to tell us about the scenes from the Old Testament which are depicted on the panels, but it's a bit of an exercise in futility as we are too far away to see the detail and it's difficult to filter out what she is saying from the competing cacophony. What we are meant to be looking at is the naturalism of the figures and the use of perspective which makes these panels prime examples of early Renaissance art.

And so to the Duomo. I have to admit, I am bitterly disappointed, no – horrified would be a better word for it. If the façade of Santa Croce was bad, this is a thousand times worse. It is made of white, green and pink Tuscan marble but it is the pink which captures the attention the most, even although it may not be the predominant material. It looks like some kid's fantasy birthday cake, something out of *Hansel and Gretel*, smothered in pink icing, topped with white which has run like candle grease down a bottle. The whole effect is so sweet and sickly-looking that if it were a cake it would be stomach-churningly inedible. As a piece of architecture, I merely think it is appallingly over-the-top, with its adjacent matching campanile (designed by Giotto, no less) like the proverbial cherry on the top.

I keep my sacriligeous thoughts to myself. I can't decide which is the most tasteless- the Baptistry (golden doors excepted), the façade of the Duomo, or the campanile, but taken collectively, I don't think there can be a greater collection of great buildings so close together and so incredibly fussy anywhere else in the world. From that perspective, it was worth coming to see, like some people watch a horror film, if only to be repulsed by something obscene.

Poor Brunelleschi. I wonder what he would think of what they had done to his cathedral, for like the Santa Croce, this sugar icing is a nineteenth century 'improvement'. I am sorry for them, Brunelleschi and Giotto birling in their graves at 1000 revs a minute. In all the photographs, in all the postcards, in all the years that I have looked at Florence Cathedral, nothing had prepared me for this architectural abuse, because they all seem to have been of the dome, usually from a distance. Perhaps part of the reason for this is that Piazza del Duomo is so crowded that even photographers' special lenses cannot get it all in, but surely, a more likely explanation is that they recognise that it is truly ghastly. Once again it vindicates my philosophy of life: *Never look forward to anything too much for you will be disappointed. Always look on the worst side of life for it will never be as bad as you fear.* That's what I'd like for my epitaph. Mrs Addison please note.

There is a queue to get inside, a queue which extends almost as far as the Loggia del Bigallo on the other side of the piazza. Now, that's a better building from what I can see of it from here. I like the over-hanging roof supported by timbers, the arches, the plain white façade with a dark brown strip two-thirds of the way up and above which are three sets of shuttered windows. It was here than in the 15th century that abandoned babies were displayed for three days. At the end of that time, if they were still unclaimed, they were fostered out. If they weren't dead first, I imagine. It's good to know they had a thriving child-care policy all those years ago though.

Although the queue is long, it is moving relatively quickly for the Duomo is apparently the fourth largest in the world, so there is plenty of room for all the people. If St Peter's is the largest, (which we are going to visit) and this the fourth, Westminster Abbey must be up there somewhere and when I was in Malta they claimed to have world ranking cathedrals in terms of size, though I can't remember which numbers exactly now, so had I been collecting churches instead of graves, I think I would have been doing pretty well and cursing that I could not get into number seven, the Santa Maria degli Angeli in Assisi. I might have needed just that one to complete a top 10. Sometimes it's just as well not to have a hobby: it can just frustrate you. It frustrates Iona that I don't have one. I have a few hobbyhorses though, but they're not quite the same thing.

Talk about the beautiful inner self! If the outside of the Duomo was meant to impress, then I must agree with Iona and admit I am perverse, for it is a relief to step inside and see how plain it is. If plain can be beautiful, this is it. The side chapels are plain and unadorned, illuminated by pointed windows imitating the shape of the arches beneath them.

Talking of perverseness, how about this? The first thing Giulia points out to us is a clock, decorated by Paolo Uccello in the 15th century, situated in the wall of the façade. It is perverse on two accounts – firstly it has only one hand, though I have seen that sort of thing before, but what makes this really perverse, is that it works in an *anti-clockwise* direction! I mean, how perverse is that! Also, how perverse of Giulia to tell us who decorated the clock, not who made it, which, to my un-mathematical mind, is a far greater achievement - and to make it run backwards as well, which not only confirms my assessment of Italian logic, but which appeals to my sense of the ridiculous and love of the eccentric. Perhaps that's typical Florentine – and it wouldn't surprise me if it were: outward show in preference to the inner beauty. Just imagine all the wheels and cogs that make this thing tick backwards! I wonder if they make wristwatches like that. Maybe Iona could get me one for Christmas. It would be the ideal present for me and it wouldn't matter if, like this one, I couldn't tell the time by it, as I am usually late anyway.

If there are points of artistic interest here, then we are not going to see them – we are making straight for the cupola. When we get there, after several minutes' march, what can I say? Nothing! I am struck totally dumb with the wonder of it, as I was, just half an hour ago by the horror of the Baptistry. It is octagonal, light beaming from a window at the zenith around which swirls, in a myriad of colours, a multitude of figures, executed by that man again, Vasari. It seems a pity to me that he is not better known as the geezer who painted the frescoes on the cupola of Firenze Cathedral, like that bloke who painted the roof of the Sistine Chapel is world renowned. I suppose the difference is that the exterior roof of the Sistine Chapel *per se* is not anything to write home about, whereas the roof of the Duomo most certainly is. Maybe it's that Florentine thing again, the outer triumphing over the exterior.

I am afraid I am not listening to Giulia – I have the binoculars out and am focussing on Vasari's frescoes, particularly on the bottom level to my right, where horned devils are pitch-forking poor souls into the eternal flames.

Perhaps it appeals to my innate Calvinism: *Serves the bastards right for sinning* – they definitely should not have enjoyed themselves with all that sexy stuff and all that drinking. But I think as a Bosch fan, that it is the subject matter that appeals to me. Maybe I'm fascinated by what's going to happen to me one of these days, and statistically speaking, not in the too distant future. But maybe, like the façade of the Duomo, I have room for improvement. It may not be too late to change – but not yet. I'll try and time my reformation to nearer the time.

Here's a curious thing. There's a trio of angels sitting on a cloud, the middle one garbed in golden raiment and beneath him, at the bottom of the cloud there are a couple of cherubs on either side of – an automatic washing machine! (Is it a Bosch?). No wonder those angels have such sparklingly white clothes! I wonder if it's a special one, being celestial, that does feathers. Maybe that's what it is, a tumble drier for their wings - if they are detachable. It reminds me of the painting I saw in a temple in Egypt of an aeroplane. Certainly it looked like a plane, but of course had to be something else, like this is actually an open book with a big round hole through which Vasari's scaffolding was supported.

But fascinated as I am by that, my attention is attracted to the very top tier of paintings, beneath the octagonal window. I don't know whom the figures represent but they are sitting in alcoves, looking down on the scene below, like an audience in private boxes at the theatre. Only these are the most relaxed spectators ever, who have dressed down, rather than up, for the occasion, some wearing nothing but a strategically placed piece of chiffon and sitting astride the balcony as if they are intending to hurl themselves into the abyss. Through the binoculars, it's a 3D effect and it's all I can do to stop my self from crying out: *Don't do it!* Incredible to think that it's all painted on a flat, curved surface.

Beneath Vasari's colourful frescoes, the area is illuminated by eight portholes beneath which are the enormous pillars and arches which support the enormous weight of the dome- except not exactly, for the dome – and this is Brunelleschi's achievement - is built with an inner and outer layer so that the thicker, inner layer, supports the thinner, outer layer, the bricks of which are laid in a herring bone pattern so they are self supporting. No doubt about it, the man was a genius and, what's more, he got the ambitious Florentines out of a hole too, for in what seems to be a bit of reckless one-upmanship over the revolting Pisans and Sienese, they started building a Duomo bigger and therefore better than theirs and left the problem of how they would crown the 40 metre hole in the roof till later. Fortunately Brunelleschi happened to be born at the right time and solved the problem.

Giulia says if we want to climb to the top of the dome, it will require an hour - twenty minutes up to the top and twenty back down (surely it should take less?) and twenty for admiring the view. There are 463 steps and she says that they are not very high but the passage is narrow and warns us that once embarked on the mission, there is no return as it is a one-way system. I am pleased to hear it as when we climbed to the top of the Town House tower in Siena, it *did* take as long to come back down as to go up as we had to stop at corners to allow those going up to pass. I don't know about Iona, but that's for me. Apart from the view, I want a closer look at Vasari's frescoes.

That's our guided tour of Florence finished. Giulia ushers us outside, says goodbye and is soon lost in the throng. Iona and I sit down on the steps in front of the Duomo in the brilliant sunshine and as we do so, the bells begin pealing with an intensity that seems to shake the ground and last for a long time. It's a wonderfully atmospheric sound that must have echoed down the centuries and it's great to be here, right beneath them as they clamour into the air.

We find ourselves next to Bill and Pat, whom, as it happened, were standing in front of us in the queue to get into the Duomo and with whom we had got chatting. Bill is for the climb too and so it is agreed we will all make the ascent. That means another queue. The entrance is round the north side of the Cathedral and the queue is long and moving very slowly. They probably only allow a certain number of people up at one time, and in fact, in Siena they only allow a certain number of people up per day. Imagine queuing for hours to be told: *Sorry, mate, the two in front of you are the last today.*

But before I do the climb, I must go down, down to the crypt because I saw a sign that said TOMBA di PHILLIPO BRUNELLESCHI. I have to get this for my collection, naturally. As far as I know, he's the only one of note down there as the Florentines are pretty picky about whom they bury down there. I am glad to see they recognise their debt to the maestro. I wonder what happened to Vasari as I would love to add him to my collection. It's difficult being a grave man because although it is reasonably easy to find out where someone died, sources don't often mention where they are buried. So while the others wander about, that's where I go.

The grave is barred off but through the bars I can see a slab on the floor with a frame, like a blank painting and behind it is a rectangular slab with a marble plaque, written in Latin which says something about his bones. There are a couple of wreaths, a big bronze cross and a couple of candles. Yes, I like it. Not for him the pretentious monuments in the Santa Croce. This is nice and modest, like the simple white cross which marks the grave of Robert Kennedy in

Arlington Cemetery in Washington DC. and which is also in my collection.

I don't mind the long wait in the queue so much as the fact that for most of it we are in the shade. It seems a bit of a waste of sunshine, but the others are perversely pleased. The long wait gives me time to study this side of the Cathedral. It's not to be recommended. They haven't got round to restoring this side of it yet. The green marble is black with dirt and encrusted with inches of pigeon guano. It looks very seedy indeed. There is some scaffolding erected though, so in due course, they will get round to restoring it to its former ugliness.

As we inch painfully nearer to the entrance, there is a beggar woman in a red dress, shoeless, with a most terrible looking squint, sitting to the side of the door. In fact her eye is so bad, I bet she is blind in that eye and maybe she can't see too well out of the other one either. She has a baby swaddled in the crook of her arm, one hand cupped for donations, the other holding a colour photo of her family and herself, presumably, though it is impossible to recognise her in that photo as it looks like a snapshot of a smartly dressed, well to do, middle-class family.

She keeps up a mantra in a monotonous tone, looking straight ahead of her into the middle distance, punctuated only by the occasional *grazie* as someone drops a coin into her upturned palm. When she comes to the end of her speech, there is a few moments' silence before she starts the whole thing again, slipping the coins, unseen, away into some invisible receptacle in her dress. Her voice is cracked and hoarse. The baby never flinches. I don't count the number of times she goes through her monologue, the only word of which I recognise being *bambino* but we hear it a good number of times before we reach the door.

I drop some euros into her palm and she slips out the *grazie*, born of patient perseverance, with only the minutest interruption to her flow. I wonder if I should give her a 10 note and she could go home, wherever that is, whatever it is like and she could give her throat a rest for an hour or two. God knows how long she has been here, or for how much longer she'll stay or how much she'll make today. So this is McCaig's beggar, only in Florence, not Pisa, and it makes me think of another Scotttish poet, Edwin Morgan who, in his poem *In the Snack Bar*, wrote of another handicapped destitute, this time in Glasgow: *Dear Christ, to be born for this*.

It's a bit depressing, but all thoughts of the beggar woman are banished as the constriction in my chest occupies my mind as I puff up the steps eyelevel with Iona's posterior. You can only move as fast as the bum in front of you but whoever's bum is at the head of the column, it is moving fast enough for me. I am not a bum man, but even if I were, no libidinous thoughts would enter my mind. I just hope that with this proximity to each others' bums no one has had beans for breakfast.

We have barely begun to climb when we come to a place which widens out and there are some statues of what looks like bishops and things, but are probably popes, and some other bits of masonry behind grilles. It's good to pretend to be interested in them, to study the carving minutely until the heaving in the chest dies down and the pain leaves the thighs and it's possible to speak again. Here also is an ominous sign in four languages. There is an arrow and beneath in English, it says: TO THE SUMMIT. It makes it sound like a mountain expedition.

I don't know how many more steps we climb before we emerge onto the gallery. From here there is a bird's eye view of the floor. Beneath the cupola it is possible to see how the octagonal shape has been echoed in the floor, with dark and light strips of marble radiating towards the chapels. It makes me giddy to lookdown at the nave and see the people moving about below. From here they don't really look like people – they are just black specks. Maybe if I had specs on of course, I could make out some distinguishing details.

It gives me a chance to get closer to Vasari's frescoes too. I can see Jesus radiating a golden light with a prayerful Mary at his knee and a heavenly choir of angels gathered about. Every square inch of plaster has been covered and there is so much going on, it's impossible to take it all in or to know where to start looking. We are also very close to a beautiful stained glass window of red, green, purple and blue but what still intrigues me is the topmost gallery with one figure who had better be very careful indeed or else, like the careless fella in Harry Graham's witty ditty, he might overbalance and *land upon my nut*.

We spend a few minutes gazing at the frescoes and the floor before it's time to move on again. High though we are, we are probably only half way up. The gallery is very narrow and to get to the steps I have to pass a stoutish Irish woman, no doubt because she drinks too much of it, and who is having a bout of vertigo. Her husband is trying to reassure her but we could be here all day and already Iona and Bill and Pat who were on the other side of her, have disappeared. She is standing as far back from the gallery rail as she can, with her back to the wall.

"Excuse me," I say as I push past her. Well, I had *intended* to push past her, but she is stouter than I had thought, or my own girth is more than I had thought, for we fatties are stuck fast. I had gone through the gap with my back to the gallery rail, on the assumption that I am thinner from front to back than from side to side. So here we are now face to face, body to body touching all the way up and down like conjoined twins. Thank God I managed to get the barrel off the key to the safe which is presently residing in my pocket or she might have thought I was getting a real thrill out of this.

She's not screaming at least and seems to have forgotten her vertigo, maybe because with me as close to her as this, I would make a pretty good cushion if we went over into the abyss. I've never been this close to a woman before with all my clothes on since I was sixteen doing a smoochy dance at Portsoy town hall. I smile apologetically and wriggle a bit and she wriggles back. Far from being erotic, this is getting embarrassing. We are still locked together and the husband is starting to look belligerent.

"It's all right, I don't fancy her," I want to tell him but realise that he could be insulted more by this than the fact that I am locked in this intimate embrace and knowing the wrath of the Irish, I might find myself suddenly hurtling towards the floor of the cupola. Instead I smile and say to her: "We must stop meeting like this." I hope my breath is all right.

She doesn't find it amusing. My feeble joke at our mutual predicament falls upon stony ground just as my other attempts to create humour in the face of adversity have failed. I should have known. In fact, she's looking distinctly panic-stricken. I can read her eyes which are saying: *What sort of perv are you?* and *Just how dangerous are you?*

I look back: *Look, no offence, lady, but I really am not getting a thrill out of this. In fact, if I were a perv, yours is about the last body I would have picked.*

By some mutual but unspoken understanding, I move to the right as she moves to the left and after a moment's heightened friction, we are free. I expect we had been only been locked together in this intimate way for a matter of seconds, but it had seemed like a living entombment. I mutter apologies over my shoulder as I scarper for the stairs but not before *ya bleedy eejit* reaches my ears. No doubt the language was toned down in deference to being in the House of God.

"Where have you been?" demands Iona when I catch up with her in a graffiti-covered passage. There seems to be a hold-up ahead. Maybe somebody has farted far up ahead and they are waiting for the air to clear, but no one gave us canaries. If I had been wearing my outfit of this morning, they probably would have sent me ahead.

"Oh, just having a close encounter of the Irish kind," I reply enigmatically. I hope we can get going again before they arrive.

It's disgraceful how much graffiti there is on the walls and the stairs. Maybe they think this is their Andy Warhol's 15 minutes of fame. Hundreds, if not thousands of people, must read their names every day. So what? What have they achieved, apart from advertising to the world: *I am a desecrating moron.* Sad to say, the names are depressingly British, I mean English – Chris and Duane (as you might expect) and even, would you believe - a David! Having said that, two in pieces in particular, arouse my interest. One says: *Brunelleschi is magic*, the other: *Fucking steps.* With the pain shooting up my thighs and my chest heaving, it's hard to say at this time with whose sentiments I agree most.

We are achieving our goal now. We have reached the part where we are between the two domes: I can see the curve of the inner dome sweeping up and away in a graceful arc. Brunelleschi's invention. Apparently before he died, he burnt all his papers so no one would copy his ideas. In fact, he was so terrified that he would die before the dome was finished that the workers were paid extra to stay up in the dome and their wine watered down in case they fell over and plunged to a premature death. He need not have worried. The dome was completed in 1436 but he did not hand in his dinner pail until 1455.

To step out into the bright Florentine sunlight with the orange roofs of the city laid out below is an awesome sight.

This is still the highest point in the city. The functional, yet attractive, ribs of the dome, steeply curving to the ground seem inviting. I have an insane desire to sit on one, like a boy sliding down a banister. But I resist the urge. My wings are just beginning to sprout.

From here, the campanile, puncturing the sky actually looks quite elegant and even the Santa Croce looks good from here, now that distance means that the fussy details are indistinguishable. I can recognise the Piazza del Republica and in the distance, the pencil-like tower of the Palazzo Vecchio. Across the river, squat and brown, like a toad, sits the Pitti Palace and the Boboli gardens. Bill has a map and points out what must be the Ponte Vecchio, which from here, just looks like an insect-infested gap between buildings. Curiously, the river doesn't seem to be visible at all. Bill also points out from where he reckons the photographs of the Duomo are taken.

"Just like me, best seen from a distance, in profile."

He laughs politely but I can tell he doesn't understand that what I mean is that you can't see the façade or the conglomeration of buildings that crowd the piazza.

It's been well worth the climb to have this bird's eye view of the city but it's time to go down and I am eager to go before the Irish couple appear, though I would have thought they should have appeared by now. Having got that far, she would have had no choice but to continue. Inside the roofs, on the stairs, there is no sense of height anyway, except there are views from portholes which make a nice frame to an overview of the city.

We come to another gallery, higher than the one we were on on our way up which brings us in close proximity to the frescoes of the devils shovelling the souls into the everlasting bonfire though we are so close it's difficult to see the big picture and from this close, they appear more as swirling patches of colour. There is one fellow though,

I had noticed from below, and now I am within feet of him. He has a double-yolked head with Mr Spock ears and a fine pair of antelope horns and an incongruously bushy ginger moustache. Apart from those ears and the growths on his head, he could be somebody's uncle. He doesn't look anything like me, though I have often been told that I am destined for hell. I can't even feel any lumps on my head, only that itchy feeling in my shoulder blades. Could it be I am destined for higher things or if I had taken that ride down the rib of Brunelleschi's dome, would I have been a fallen angel?

We continue our descent. The whole of Florence awaits. So much to see and so little time. The afternoon lies ahead of us. Where shall we head for next?

Chapter 5
Con Cons

Bill and Pat have gone to spend the rest of the day in the queue at the Uffizi. We have decided that we won't bother on this occasion. I would like to go and stroke that boar's nose for a start but can't admit to something so stupid, so I say instead that I want to find Dante's house. If I can't go to his grave, at least I can see where he lived. The Casa di Dante is located, strangely enough on the Via Dante Alighieri. What a co-incidence and what an achievement for Italian logic!

It's another disappointment. There is a coat of arms on the wall executed in stone with his name on it and that's about all to show he lived there. It's more like a tower than a house, with a huge overhanging roof and great barred windows and doors so it looks more like a prison than a house. It's well and truly shut up and like a lot of buildings in Florence, most of the surface is obscured by scaffolding.

It's incredibly hot and we get a couple of *gelati* to cool us down and sustain us. This will be our lunch. I have cherry and Iona has lemon of course. We eat them as we make our way towards the Piazza della Signora to have a closer look at *David* and the other statues. For my money (and that is the good thing about this place, you don't need much of it as you can look at the art work for free), *The Rape of the Sabine Women* is preferable to *David*. It has so much going on, so much interest and so much movement and drama. *David* just looks forlorn, as if he is waiting to do battle with Goliath and doesn't reckon on his chances too much.

When I have finished admiring Giambologna's masterpiece again, I turn round to look for Iona and find she has disappeared. Like hiding a leaf in the forest, this is a good place to hide, as the piazza, as ever, is swarming with people. I scan the crowds with a mounting sense of panic as I fail to spot her. How will I ever find her again in all this mob? How will she find me? I knew I should not have changed out of the yellow outfit.

It's like something out of a thriller. It would make a good story – about how I am going to have to track her down in a strange city with no money. I would go back to the hotel room and find all our stuff gone and everyone else on the tour gone too. And the friendly, pretty receptionist says she's never seen me before in her life. And what's more, I gave her my passport and like the Guttings, all I have are the clothes I stand up in, my short suit of Lincoln green. It would make a good story, but I can't think how it would go on from there.

Talking of the Guttings, they have been shopping as they are wearing different clothes, but he must have forgotten to buy razors as he still retains the beard. Or maybe he thinks it suits him. It doesn't. If you could disarticulate his jaw, it would make a good lavatory brush though and he doesn't use it much for articulation anyway.

I have enough sense to know that it's no good wandering about trying to look for Iona. If she wants to find me, then she will, if I stand still. Surely she will on our anniversary, won't she? But where the hell can she be?

It seems like ages before she comes back. I am relieved to see her, but of course I don't say so. Instead I say: "Where the hell have you been?"

"I've been over looking at *David.*"

"What do you want to do that for? You can see me naked anytime."

"Don't be revolting. *David's* an Adonis. You're just an Addison."

"That's true. Close though."

"In name only."

Well I can't argue with that.

We stroll down the Piazzalle degli Uffizi. I want to see what progress Bill and Pat are making in the queue. We find them in the U that joins the two arms of the Uffizi. They haven't even made it as far as the columns where they can start to estimate how many hours it will take them to get to the entrance. They don't seem despondent about it though.

We turn right and walk along by the side of the river towards the Ponte Vecchio. This is not very easy, as apart from the pedestrians, most of the pavement has been commandeered by black people who are selling handbags and other leather items, like we saw in Naples, which means that we have to walk on the road most of the time. It would be handy to walk along the Corridoio Vasariano like a Medici. There is also a man who is sticking wire into a crack in the parapet and bending it into the shape of a motorbike. Quite clever really. He has a few parked along the top of the wall, but no one is buying. I think that's because no-one thinks they work.

Across the road we see Tom, Dick and Harriet who are lapping up *gelati*. They too are on their way to the Pitti Palace and are complaining of the heat. Iona agrees. She is looking a bit flushed. She doesn't cope too well in hot climates.

We spend some time in the middle of the Ponte Vecchio, which is heaving with people. There are so many people that they spill on to the road when there is no traffic. The shops which, in medieval times, were butchers and tanners, are now almost exclusively goldsmiths. The jewellery is not to my taste, being big and heavy and chunky with rings which look more like knuckle dusters than pieces of adornment. It looks like the sort of stuff which my ex-companion on the plane, Tattooman, would wear for his pugilistic encounters.

The handbag sellers are out in strength here too, which makes it difficult to get a view from the bridge as they have their wares spread out all over the pavement. I wonder if it were like this in medieval times too. I can imagine it hustling and bustling like this, though thank God, it doesn't smell like it did in the days of the butchers' and tanners' shops - there's just the smell of the leather.

It's not far from the bridge to The Palazzo Pitti. Iona hugs the shade as much as she can but in the vast piazza before the Palazzo, there in no hiding place – the sun bakes the piazza with a greater intensity than any we have experienced so far on this trip and we've had some pretty hot days. A pharmacy signals it is 39^0. I am loving it.

The Palazzo itself is a massive brown structure and looks more like a barracks than a palace. Windows and doors stand in regular, serried rows like soldiers on parade. It reminds me of the Palazzo Reale in Naples in its severe stolidity which is exacerbated by its muddy brown colour. At first sight it does impress, but only by its size and dominating position in the piazza, a giant dwarfing the pigmy buildings facing it. According to our guide – a book which Iona carries in a pack on her back along with sundry other items now that we don't have Giulia (no wonder she is sweltering in the heat) – the façade of the Palazzo was designed by Brunelleschi no less.

How could someone who built the dome, design something like this, though to be fair to him, it was later extended by three times its original length and wings added later still in the 19th century. I think it's improved by the wings but perhaps when all there was was Brunelleschi's original building, it may have looked less formidable than it does now, but somehow I don't think so.

It was the former home of the Pitti family, rivals of the Medici who tried to compete with them by building this pile and who became bankrupt as a result. To add insult to injury, the Medici bought it from them, no doubt at a knockdown price, and in due course it became their main residence. The Pitti must have been *pazzo* to think that they could hold a candle to the Medicis. Pity those who tried to take on the Medicis. They didn't stand a chance.

The entrance is in the middle of the building but in another instance of Italian logic, we have to leave that queue, cross the piazza and join another queue to purchase our tickets.

There's a menu of attractions on offer. We can have an all-inclusive ticket which admits you to everything: The Galleria d'Arte Moderna, the Galleria del Costume, the Museo degli Argenti, the Museo delle Porcelane, the Galleria Palantina and the Boboli Gardens, a name which conjures up images of trees and hedges being trimmed by topiarists into fluffy balls like the heads of dandelions. I have to confess that before we came, I had never heard of them. Iona is not really a garden lover it has to be said, but maybe because it's our anniversary, she is relinquishing power for a day by agreeing to come here or maybe she is not desperate to go and look at paintings and more statues.

But although we have come only for the Gardens, we have to buy a ticket for the Porcelain Museum as well, but it is closed, so we are just going to the Gardens anyway. This may be the place, but it's not the time to protest about the illogic of having to buy a ticket for something which isn't open as Iona is not for hanging about in this heat whilst I hold up the queue, making a fool of myself for the sake of a few euros and for something that would have bored the pants off me in the first place. I'm surprised that no one else has protested in principle though.

As we leave to cross the Piazza again, we come across Tom, Dick and Harriet who have arrived and joined the queue, so at least I can complain to them about Italian logic. They listen politely but don't show any signs of even mild outrage and we pass on to the entrance, flash our tickets and pass through to a colonnaded courtyard. So where are the gardens? There are no signs of them and no signs to them. But in the top right hand corner, there is a café with some tables and chairs roped off from the courtyard. Our water, supposedly kept cool in its insulated carrier is warm enough to poach an egg and we'll need to replace it for our trek round the gardens - if ever we find them.

We prefer fizzy water to still, considering it more refreshing but where is it? I have the door of the fridge open, raking through the bottles looking for *frizzante*, but all I can find is *naturale*. They don't feel that cool either. The man at the till is looking at me strangely, as if he thinks I'm suffering from Asperger's syndrome or something and am arranging the bottles with the labels all facing the same way. He's probably also annoyed that the cold is getting out of the cabinet - besides there is a woman behind me who is shuffling her feet and breathing heavily with impatience.

"They're all the same," she sighs pointedly.

I seize a bottle and straighten up. "They are now."

I give the chiller cabinet a fond gaze as I turn to pay. I'd love to see the look on her face, but I can't because I'm acting so cool and nonchalant. I wish I could say the same for the water, for although it looks deliciously cool in an ice-blue bottle, in fact it's quite tepid. However, it is a lot better than we had before, which I dump in a bin.

We have climbed a curving ramp at the end of the courtyard, bounded by a high wall and find ourselves in the garden at last. Facing us is a huge amphitheatre, tiers of seats, Roman style, arranged in a U with hedges and trees behind them. It was from here that the stone was quarried to build the Palazzo, so presumably the seats and steps are built from the same material, but the curious thing is, that here, in this open setting, the stone has a honeyed appearance and a warmness and attractiveness which is entirely lacking in the house.

The Gardens are shaped like an isosceles triangle. If we turn to our right and follow the yellow sign which says *To the gardens*, we should come to what's called L' Isolotto or small island at the point and from thence we can make our way back up the other arm. We begin walking across a gravelled rectangle towards a huge stage which has battens of lights and speakers five feet tall. Obviously there is a concert of some description held here in the evenings, though I have not seen any advertisements to indicate what it might be. Something incredibly noisy by the looks of the speakers. Glad I'm not going to be there to hear whatever it is.

Over to the right, in front of the Palazzo, there is a woman waving furiously at us and gesturing that we should go back the way we have come. Iona looks at her in disbelief and dismay: *Why should we go back?* I know the thought of retracing her steps over that baking rectangle is filling her with despair.

"Dunno. Stupid old bat."

Is it possible we could have taken a wrong turn? Certainly there is nobody else following us and no one else in sight, but we must be going in the right direction.

"Sod it. What can she do?" She's a good distance away and we have a good start on her. "Come on!"

I continue to cross the area in the front of the stage and the woman becomes more animated: *Get back! Get back!* She is signalling frantically as though we were unwary travellers heading towards quick-sands. I can see no earthly reason why we *should* go back. I give her a wave, as if in friendly greeting and she stops waving and stares with her fists belligerently resting on her ample hips. It's too far away to see the look in her eyes, which is probably just as well. She turns on her heel and stomps back into the building. Perhaps she has gone to call security or something.

In a couple of moments, as we leave the gravel and enter a wooded area, we come to a path but there is a mighty big gate across it and the way is plainly barred. Was that what it was all about? It's not a problem, as we can make our way up a shady incline to our left. It's taking us in the wrong direction, but Iona is glad to be out of the blistering sun. It's very pleasant, surrounded by all this greenery, the sound of birdsong, the hum of insects and no danger of being assaulted by a Vespa. These gardens are the lungs of the city, a far cry from the crowded piazzas. We could be the only two people in Florence for we have not seen anyone else. It seems incredible. Maybe we are not meant to be here after all.

At last the trees thin out and we join a path which brings us in due course to an avenue of cypresses. We know where we are now. This is the Viottolone, planted in 1637 and which forms the spine of the triangle, pointing like a dagger at the heart of L'Isolotto. At regular intervals, there are classical statues set into alcoves in the hedge which borders the avenue. Formal and only partially shady, since the sun is still high in the sky and apart from the statues, lacking interest since it is so long and straight, so at one of the intersections, we bail out and here in the shade, lurking in shady alcoves, we find the lovers. Maybe that's what the woman was on about: *Hey, Robin Hood, that place is for lovers only. I can see from here you're too old and ugly, so get outta here!*

We hurry past them, with our eyes down because our approach doesn't seem to alter their behaviour in any way. Maybe it's true that love is blind. It may be our anniversary, but we are not going to indulge in any of that Italian nonsense, though they do not all look Italian – some look Dutch or Scandinavian with their blonde hair and tanned legs and shoulders. I'm only talking about the women. I didn't have time to notice the men.

When we get to L'Isolotto it is to emerge from the relatively cool of our shady walk to the full glare of the sun. The lake is oval and we can walk round it, but, unfortunately, not across the path which bisects it to the island that sits in the middle, because the way is blocked by ornate gates at each end. This is annoying as according to my book, on that island is a fountain by my new found hero, Giambologna, he of *The Sabine Women* fame. It's a copy but that doesn't bother me, but what does is that I can't get close enough to see it properly. Still, it is only a minor disappointment as this place is lovely. It provides the only colour we've seen so far, as if the designer had said, like Henry Ford after him: *You can have any colour as long as it's green*, except, of course in Henry's case the preferred colour was black.

On the central island there is a splash of pink but the main colour is provided by terracotta pots arranged like sentries along the paths leading to the central island with geraniums, like strumpets amidst all this greenery, spilling their scarlet petals over the rims and reflected in the still, emerald-green waters of the moat. The effect is further enhanced by the arches of the path, which, in their reflected image, form a perfect oval. This is curious because the path cannot be any more than three feet above the water and the arches only rising a few inches above the surface. What's curious about it is that there is a statue in the water of a horse and rider. The horse is rearing and the barebacked rider is foolishly holding on with only one hand, whilst the other arm is held aloft in a victory salute.

There is a photo of this same statue in our book, but there, the water is just clearing the horse's front hooves and lapping at the feet of the rider. Now, the whole belly of the horse is exposed and even lower as I can tell it is a stallion. This must be due to the drought, but that surely means that when the moat is full, it must cover the graceful arches of the path and be perilously close to the edges of the path itself.

It's a perfectly idyllic scene. We have only walked halfway round and sit on a bench in the shade to drink it in. A young couple stroll past. When they are out of earshot, I say, "Did you see? That was the same idea as Claire!"

Iona agrees. "A very common type."

It's a fact: we have seen her twice now.

A couple of blonde Scandinavian women are approaching from the other direction. Iona is slugging some water and fanning herself with the very efficient fan she bought in China. She is pink and perspiring, not looking her best.

We watch the Scandinavians stroll past, golden limbed, lithe and laughing, not a bead of sweat on their brows. The baking heat doesn't seem to be troubling them at all, as if they were used to it every day of their lives.

"It's just not fair!" Iona erupts looking after their retreating figures. "They've just not got the right to look so cool when they are so fair-skinned. I can understand how the Latin types like Claire stay cool, but the Scandinavians have no right to be. Just look at me- I'm a pink blob."

I chuckle until I turn to look at her and see that she is weeping behind her sunglasses.

"It's just not funny, either!"

I've faced this situation before. On the Acropolis in Athens when we were still students and before we were married, she was weeping copiously and silently behind her sunglasses with the heat. It was the first time we had been on holiday together and the first time I realised that she's not good in the heat. Unfortunately for her and fortunately for me, the great Civilizations such as the Greeks, Romans and Egyptians lived in warm countries so she has to suffer for her culture.

She suffered most in Tiananmen Square. It was 42° that day, so hot that she burnt her bum when she sat down on the kerb, much to the amusement of a Chinese family who insisted on taking her photograph and being photographed with her. Even now she is probably a legend in some obscure part of China: *You want to see something velly funny ha ha? This pink blob picture of English lady who sit on pavement and burn bum. She leap up pletty damn quick, I can tell you! Ha ha velly funny.*

"No! No!" I hastily respond. "I wasn't laughing at *you*!" I gaze around for inspiration. "I was laughing at that water gargoyle over there – the one that looks as if he's suffering from projectile vomiting." For indeed, that's what this curly-headed monster with open mouth and arched back looks like he's doing.

"Huh!" says La-Belle-Dame-Sans-Merci. "You were so laughing at me!"

Before I say I'd be too terrified to laugh at her, she gets up abruptly and stomps off, not noticing that she has left her fan behind. No, no, she meant to leave *me* behind, but she has forgotten about her cooling device. I pick it up and the water bottle and hurry after her. I'm going to keep it hidden from her and hopefully I'll get Brownie points for producing it when she discovers its loss.

As we leave the lake behind, we take a path to the right, a beautifully green, shady path that looks as if it should be full of Sylvan coolness: only shady it may be, but cool it certainly is not. It is uphill and more interesting as it is meandering, but we soon sacrifice the meander, Iona because she wants to get to the top of the hill with as little walking as possible and me, because I want to get out into the sun again. So a few minutes later, I am plodding up the steep and sunny incline of the Viottolone whilst Iona is struggling up the path to my side.

"David!"

"What?"

"I've got to stop. I don't feel right. I think I'm going to faint."

But it's like being on the other side of a dual carriageway and I can't get across to help her.

"Can you make it up to the next intersection?" I ask through the trees. I can't see her.

There is no answer, but I can hear her footsteps resuming so I presume she is saving her energy. A few minutes later we come to the intersection and fortunately there is a bench unoccupied by any lovers, upon which she collapses and hangs her head down. She's pinker than ever, not drained of colour as if she were going to pass out. I give her some water.

"It's so hot and I feel dizzy. I've had nothing to eat."

It's true we've had nothing since breakfast, apart from the *gelati* and probably she didn't have the two-in-one breakfast like me either. It probably wouldn't have mattered had it not been for the heat, and God knows how far we've walked, not counting the steps up the Duomo.

After a time she recovers. I give her the fan which she takes without even noticing that she had lost it and eventually we reach the top of the Viottolone, though I eschew the sunny path for the shady lest Iona should need me to pick her up and sling her over my shoulders. God help her if that's what she's relying on. I've enough to do with hauling myself to the top of this hill.

At the top, there is a path to the right which leads to the Porcelain Museum and the Forte di Belvedere. It's either that or take the one to the left and go back down towards the stage and the scary woman. The question is: which one am I scared of most? However, Iona feels fit enough to continue now that we're more on the flat, so we head off towards the Porcelain Museum. No point in going there, so we sweep round to the right and come in a short time, to a splendid vista, arranged in tiers like a wedding cake. At the top of the steps here, we can look straight down the whole length of the gardens to the Palazzo. In the foreground there is a pond as bright green as the water in L'Isolotto, set between trees arranged in a horseshoe shape and in the pond, my book says is *The Neptune Fountain*, by Lorenzi. It just looks like a rock to me. Neptune has gone fishin' evidently.

"You're a frog," says Iona. "That rock would suit you. You could sit on it and admire your reflection in the water." She must be feeling better.

"I don't think so," I reply after a moment's reflection. "I'm not as green as I look. They would have to call it *The Frog Fountain* and what would happen when I croak?"

Beneath the pond, though we can't see them unless we go down the steps to the far side of the pond, there are some formal gardens and then the amphitheatre with the Palazzo in the background. However, instead of making our way in that direction, we turn to the left and head in the direction of the fort. The walls rise sheer above us but we can't see any way in, which is a pity as there might have been a good view of Florence from there. The very place, I suspect, where all the postcards of the Duomo are taken.

As we make our way downhill through trees, we come across what's known as the Kaffeehaus which our guide says was built in 1776. It also says it is open during the summer which is not true as it looks as if it has been closed up for two centuries. Another pity as we might have got a cup of coffee and something to keep Iona fading away from hunger. I wonder what else the book has said which I have taken as gospel.

From here though there is a good view across the city to Brunelleschi's dome which rises so hugely out of the tangle of roofs that it looks as if you could reach out and touch it. Out to the left, there is a mini Brunelleschi dome except that the functional but also decorative ribs are not picked out in white so it loses some of its appeal. This is the church of San Lorenzo where the Medicis worshipped and are buried. Their tombs were designed by Michelangelo and the dome by Buontalenti which sounds more like advertising propaganda than a real name. I express this opinion to Iona.

"You're right," she says. "If it were you, your name would be Buonoperniente."

Yes, I like the sound of that. I told you she had a good, intuitive grasp of the language. David Buonoperniente. David Goodfornothing. It sounds quite musical, in Italian anyway. Which is ironic really as music is another of life's skills in which I am lacking a few crotchets out of a quaver if that makes any sense. I wouldn't know, though I have often been accused of being crotchety by Iona so perhaps I am more musical than I give myself credit for.

We make our way down a steep embankment to save a long trail round by the path. I go first so if Iona slips, I'll cushion her fall. I'd be good for that at least. She's coming down sideways like a crab as her soles are slippy she says. As for me, I'd better look slippy if she starts. I don't really want her landing on top of me - I'd probably break more than just her fall. So as a cushion, I'd not be much good either. David Buonoperniente after all.

We stop and get our breath and drink some water on some steps at the back of the Pitti Palace and decide what we're going to do next. We must have walked for miles round the Gardens alone and now we have the long trek back to the hotel. We could get a taxi but I'm disinclined to do that. Apart from the haggling and the fear of being ripped off – what would we do at the hotel apart from lie on the bed and let our throbbing feet subside? I can't think of anything. It's not the most comfortable of establishments and it seems a pity to waste the sunshine, besides, by a direct route, without stopping to look at the sights, it doesn't look so terribly far, so we decide we'll walk. We hobble out of the Boboli Gardens.

We have not gone far past the non-diminishing queues at the Uffizi before Iona says she can't take this heat. I want to walk along the banks of the Arno, where the sun can beat down on my back and the back of my bare legs, but she wants to walk through the town so she can get some shade from the buildings. We agree that we'll meet at the end of the street we came down this morning. She shows me it is the third street on the left, takes the map and a slug of water because the bottle is too heavy for her to carry and disappears into the maze of streets to our left while I set off along the riverbank.

It's a bit annoying that the wall is just a little bit too high or I'm too short to see the river easily but the sun is very warm and it's quite pleasant and un-crowded down here, which is just as well, as the pavement is very narrow.

There is a group of people coming towards me and I can see that the pavement is not going to take us all, so being less numerous than they, I step off into the road, but just as we are passing, one of them, who is carrying a map, speaks to me.

"You speak Italian?"

He must be in his thirties, with straw-coloured hair, stout and perspiring with the labour of carrying his extra avoirdupois in the heat. He looks as if he has caught a bit of sunburn. He's obviously a tourist. No one else would wear a bashed hat like his in a place where people would know him.

I say no and am about to pass on when he says, "Do you speak English?" We've been talking English all this time and it's a pretty safe bet that someone wearing a Panama hat and dressed like Robin Hood probably does speak English like a native.

"Can you tell me the way to the railway station?"

"I'm afraid not. I'm a stranger here myself." How thick is he that he's asking someone dressed like me the way to the railway station?

"Well, in that case, can you tell me where we are now?"

That's something I can do. "Oh, that's easy! That's the Ponte Vecchio over there." I turn to point it out to him.

He seems to be straining to see it. "Can you show me on the map?" he asks.

"Certainly." I know I'll be able to do that easily.

"Let's cross over the street," he says.

I suppose it is a bit narrow here and the other side may be fractionally wider, but I presume he doesn't know that I'll be able to tell him where we are very quickly and it's not worth crossing the street, but he's already moving off so I follow him over. I look at the map while he stretches it out.

"Right, let me see...There's the river so the Ponte Vecchio must be there... there it is, so we must be here." Simple really. If we hadn't crossed the street, he would have been able to see it for himself.

"Show me your papers. Police."

What? The speaker is a young swarthy man in a baseball cap with two days' growth of stubble on his face. He's dressed in black trousers and a navy polo shirt. He's got a companion who looks older and stouter, wearing lighter clothes and a straw hat, like a tourist, but I don't get much of a look at him before he disappears behind my back.

Oh, no! I am cursing I've not got my passport with me. It reminds me of the time in Nice when I was looking forward to a nice cold beer and a shower after a day of sight-seeing in the hot sun and instead was thrown off the bus by three over zealous and sinister bus inspectors because although I *had* bought my tickets, I did not realise I had to validate them. I stubbornly refused to pay the fine. They wanted to see my papers but I had left my passport in my friend's flat. They wanted to know the address. I couldn't tell them. It was true. I could get there, but had no idea of the name of the street even. I showed them I had no money with me – apart from the secret pocket which did have the cash. They wanted me to go to the bank and get money out with my card. I told them I didn't know my pin number which was also true. If you're idiot enough to get yourself into a mess, there are advantages in being a consistent idiot. That is when they threatened me with the police. *Go ahead,* I said with what I hoped was more insouciance than I actually felt. The leader apparently called them on his mobile. We waited and waited, me under guard in the bus shelter and still the police did not come. I hoped the inspectors were bluffing and they would leap on the next bus, give me up as waste of time and leave me alone, but when the next bus came, it remained stationary whilst they threw more ticket evaders off the bus. To my astonishment, one young lady did the kissy-kissy thing the French do before she paid her fine and again when she left. Well, that's fine for them I thought but there's a principle at stake here. It was my very first day in Nice and I had bought my tickets in good faith and I was damned if I was going to pay a fine into the bargain. I would take it to the British Embassy if I had to. I decided when the next bus came, I was getting on it. Better to provoke some sort of action than hang about here all day. And that's what I did and to my enormous relief, the inspectors made no move to stop me.

Now I have visions of being hauled down to the police station and it taking hours to get it sorted out whilst La-Belle-Dame-Sans-Merci loiters increasingly pinkly at the rendezvous wondering where I have gone to this time. She should never have let me out of her sight. I always seem to get into trouble when she is not with me. I remember the double moon of last night. It was an omen after all. Nothing seems to be going right this afternoon.

To my astonishment, my new companion with the map has produced his passport like a conjuror. I don't have any time to look at it, but it seems to be the same plum colour as a British passport but I think the writing on it was in the Cyrillic script. The young cop takes it wordlessly and flicks through it.

"Your papers," he says to me again.

I shrug my shoulders and shake my head. "I don't have them with me. At the hotel."

He looks me up and down. "I have the right. I'm an undercover cop. Your papers!" he says again, this time with a hardened edge to his voice.

By this time, I have a tight grip on my camcorder. I have no money as Iona has that and I don't even appear to have a watch as I have taken it off as it was a bit tight and sweaty and I had put it in the pocket of my swimming trunks. I consider myself very lucky indeed that the cops should have swooped at that moment, because I realise now that all this rigmarole about the station has just been to get me occupied so I could be pick-pocketed. Only it seems I am wearing swimming trunks and they don't have any pockets, or so it seems. But before he had a chance to find out, Mapman, who must have been under surveillance, had been interrupted by these cops.

But are they? A sudden thought comes to mind. What if they are crooks too and they are all in it together? Oh, God, what am I going to do now?

"I've told you, I don't have them." Then, with the boldness of age – I would never have said had I been his age - I add, "Show me *your* papers." If he was an undercover cop, he could well be dressed and look like this and maybe this is how they operate, on the lookout for pick-pockets – but why here, in just about the quietest part of town? He looks tough enough to be a cop, yet there was something about his telling me he was working undercover that jarred.

He is still looking at Mapman's passport. "Show me *your* papers," I say again, more boldly. I have a feeling something is not right.

He ignores me. Instead he hands Mapman back his passport. "Come on," he says to him and they turn to the right and head towards the Ponte Vecchio, in single file, Black Cop first, followed by Mapman, followed by the mate whom I'd actually forgotten about in all the excitement. I cross the road, unscrew my bottle of water and watch them until they reach a corner. Black Cop turns and looks at me, then they disappear round the corner.

I stand and stare at the spot, scarcely believing it had really happened. Is Mapman under arrest? How many crooks were there? Just one, or three? Whilst I was engaged with Mapman and Black Cop, had the third one, the one I couldn't see, been trying to pick-pocket me? Or had they been after my passport? If I'd produced it, like Mapman, would they have scarpered with it? So many questions and I don't know any of the answers but one thing's for sure, I've just had a close escape and only my timely challenge to the cop had prevented me from being taken for a mug or mugged. They didn't seem interested in my camcorder anyway. Pretty nice people really – they might not have believed me when I said I didn't have my passport and duffed me up for it or maybe the one behind me had been stroking my bum all this time, feeling for my passport and I never felt it.

I continue my journey along the river. By this time, I should think Iona will be at the rendezvous point, but when I get there, there is no sign of her. I loiter for a bit. Pity there's nowhere to sit. After a while, I decide to go and stand at the end of the Via dei Malcontenti which is the street I expect her to come down. There is a posse of tourists coming down it. It doesn't look as if she is amongst them, but she could be. The last stragglers of the tourists arrive and board a bus. Americans. But there is no sign of Iona and I can see right down the Via dei Malcontenti and there is no one in sight who looks remotely pink and perspiring. Maybe she's coming another way, down the Via Tripoli or the Viale Giovine Italia. But there's no sign of her there either. Surely she should be here by now? Maybe she's fainted somewhere or been knocked down by a Vespa? Where the hell could she be? I am beginning to feel like one of the Malcontenti myself. That's twice she's got lost today.

I decide to give her five minutes more, but after three, I decide to go back to the hotel as there is no sign of her coming from any of the possible directions. Hopefully, she has got fed up waiting for me in the heat, with nowhere to sit in the shade, and is waiting for me there with a rolling pin, asking *me* where the hell *I* have been.

I set off up the Viale Giovine Italia, hoping I may meet her on the way but there's still no sign of her by the time I get to the hotel. My next hope is when I ask for the key at reception they'll say that it's not there, which means either we've been burgled, or she is already there. But the receptionist hands me the key without demur.

"Have you seen my wife?"

As soon as I utter the words, I realise how stupid that is. How would he know Iona from Eve? I should have said: *Has a pink blob been in here and left a pool of sweat in the foyer?*

Instead I say, "I mean has anyone else asked for the key?" Maybe she has been here and gone back to look for me, but the receptionist just shakes his head sadly: *Why would anyone ask for your key, stupid? They're not going to want to pinch your clothes are they?*

I decide to go up anyway and see if there have been any signs of recent occupancy but there are none. I'd love to have a shower and a beer and lie on the bed and let my feet reduce to normal size but I daren't. I can just imagine La-Belle-Dame-Sans-Merci storming in, no longer pink and sweaty but furiously red: *Do you realise I have been standing there for hours in the heat waiting for you and all the time you are living the life of Riley here?*

Our anniversary is not turning out to be a very happy one. It's my own fault. I should not have got up early this morning, should not have changed my routine, should not have changed my outfit – I would have been visible for miles. This is what happens when you try to be good, to change the habits of a lifetime. The gods decide to teach you a lesson: *Who does he think he is? We make the rules about here. You're a lazy pig, got it? And don't try anything like this again, got it?*

There's nothing else for it. I am going to have to trail all the way back but I hope I'll meet her before I get there. If only we had taken our mobile phones – except mine might have been pinched anyway after my recent encounter.

But back at the Piazza Piave there is still no sign of her. I wait for ten minutes but when she doesn't show up, I decide there's nothing else for it but to go back to the hotel. I curse myself for wanting to walk in the sun. If I hadn't done that, I wouldn't have had my close encounter with the crooks and I would probably be having a nice cold beer in the hotel bar by now with the pain beginning to leave my soles, instead of pounding even more pavements.

As I enter the foyer, I pray that key will not be there and that I will go up to the room and she will say: *Where the bloody hell do you think you have been?* and other choice words of endearment because that will mean that my ordeal is at an end, once the pain has left where she has hit me –

probably stomping on my feet, one of her favourite methods. But what will I do if she is *not* there?

The receptionist hands me the key and my heart sinks. She *must* be here by now! I take the lift to the room and throw myself on the bed and slip off my Lidl's 50p shoes. Ah, the relief! I may as well have a shower and if she still hasn't come back by then, at least I'll be a bit more refreshed to mount the search again. Just hope she doesn't try to get in the room whilst I'm in the shower and I don't hear her. That could really make sparks fly in what is already a very volatile situation. She won't know that I've been waiting and been back to look for her. She'll just think that I've been enjoying myself without ever a single thought for her and it's going to make Vesuvius in 79 AD look tame.

I am swathed in a towel like a Roman senator, taking the weight off my feet when the telephone rings.

"Pronto."

"Oh, you're there!" It's a familiar voice which replies. She sounds more relieved than furious. "I just wanted to make sure. I'm coming right up. Don't go away!"

It's a bit of an odd conversation. Who did she think would have the key if not me and why would I go out before she got to the room? Maybe she's got sunstroke or gone soft in the head. It's all very strange, especially as she does not seem to be furious with me.

I explain that I waited for ages and had already been back to look for her and she says she had been waiting for me and had even pursued some poor innocent man whom she thought looked like me. Incredible! Incredible that there's someone else dressed like me in the whole of Florence, let alone the whole of Italy. And incredible that we could have missed each other.

"Where were you waiting?" she wants to know.

"Where we agreed – at the gate where the Malcontenti were executed."

"I might have known it! I told you the third road on the left."

"That's where I was. I counted them."

"Well you can't count!"

In spite of her crippled feet, she gets up off the bed and produces a map from her rucksack.

"Look: one, two, three. I always knew you were arithmetically challenged, but I didn't realise you were this bad!"

"Just a minute," I point out, "what about this?" I indicate the Piazza dei Cavalleggeri.

"Well, what about it? It's a piazza not a street."

"Well, I counted it as one," I say humbly in defence.

So it's all my fault. I always knew it would be.

She gets up again, rakes in her bag and pops a pill out of a silver foil bubble and gulps it down with some water.

"What are you doing?"

"Taking a Migraleve tablet."

"Have you got a headache then?"

"No. My feet are killing me."

"I see. So you are taking a headache pill for the opposite extremity?"

She *has* finally flipped. She's probably got sunstroke right enough.

"Well. It's a pain killer isn't it?"

"I'm a pain but if you took one of those pills, I bet it wouldn't make me disappear."

She can't argue with that. I go on to regale her with my adventure and she is impressed with my asking to see Black Cop's papers as she thinks that is what scared them off right enough and she agrees that probably it was my passport that they were after.

There's still time to kill before we have to go out again. No point in suggesting we consummate Florence. She would just say she has a headache. Haven't I just seen her take a pill? No point in another defeat. Besides, my feet are killing me.

*

Most of the meals on the trip we have to get for ourselves, but this evening we are going out for a meal together to the Palazzo Borghese. As we walk along, I tell Angela about my adventure and ask her opinion.

"I know a crime was nearly committed," I ask her," but how many robbers were there? One or three?"

"Well," she replies, "it's true that the police do work undercover like that and it's also true that and they have the right to stop people and ask to see their papers, so they might have been cops but they probably were after your passport. There's a big demand for passports from the likes of Bosnia and Croatia. That's why we say to people to leave their passports in the hotel. If there's a problem, we can always sort it out afterwards."

Did she really say that? I don't remember her telling us that. Perhaps I never heard her. I am often accused of not hearing things Iona has said, especially orders. I wonder what a Bosnian or Croatian passport looks like. Was that what Mapman had flashed?

I change the subject. "By the way, Angela, it so happens that today is our wedding anniversary."

"Oh, is it really? That's nice."

"Yes. And I just wondered if you mentioned it to the waiters, if perhaps they could arrange something..." My voice trails off. I have a bit of a cheek really. I must have been mad to suggest this. I feel Angela is waiting for me to dig a bigger pit for myself. She must get at least one troublesome tourist every trip and it looks like I have elected myself on this one. "It's not for me, you understand – just something to make the night more special and memorable for Iona. She likes that sort of thing." Actually, she does

177

nothing of the kind, as she hates fuss, but I hoped there may be a free bottle of wine in it for me.

"Just leave it with me, I'll see what I can do."

The first time I tried this was on our mini-cruise to Denmark, many anniversaries ago. There was a DJ giving out boxes of chocolates to those with birthdays and anniversaries, so I bribed our daughter to go and say to the DJ: *It's my mummy and daddy's anniversary today.* It wasn't a good deal. The chocolates were not that good and we had to lead off the dancing in front of the ship's company, which was acutely embarrassing. Dancing, along with music, is another of life's skills which has passed me by. I think I must have been in the queue for drinking skills when they were being passed out.

The other cruises, to the Caribbean and the Baltic were better, but on our anniversary we got a cake and the waiters came and sang to us. How embarrassing is that? To tell you the truth, I could have done without both of them as I am not a sweet person as I have already said and I could do without other people making an exhibition of me. I am perfectly capable of doing that for myself. But here I am probably making a fool of myself again, just on the off chance that they might throw in a bottle of wine for us.

I have been so busy chatting to Angela that I haven't noticed where we have been walking and now we find ourselves at the Palazzo Borghese restaurant. Right from the start, I can see that this is going to be a special occasion.

There is a red carpet leading through imposing doors and a guard holding a double-headed axe. He is wearing purple and white striped pantaloons and a tunic with puffy sleeves with body armour over the top. On his head is a red and white plumed helmet.

We pass through a long corridor with statues in alcoves, lit by real flames burning in bowls set in tripods and arrive in a tastefully decorated vestibule with arches and ferns and classical statues, one of a modest maiden covering up her rude bits. I've a feeling it's a famous statue, but I don't know of whom. I might have guessed it was Venus if she hadn't been so modest – I would have thought the goddess of love would have had her wares more on show.

We pass through a heavy gold curtain, mount some stairs and the strains of medieval music are wafted down to us. At the top of the stairs is a bloke dressed as I imagine one of the Medicis might have dressed. He has black boots, white tights and a gold coloured tunic with a ruff at the neck and flared out at the bottom like a skirt. Over that, he has a white jacket sort of thing with puffy sleeves edged in black to match his boots. On his head, like a pea on an elephant, he has a cap with a fold of material hanging over his right shoulder. The things some people do for a living!

We progress further into an elegant room where there is a quartet of ladies dressed in medieval costume. This is some welcoming party! One is playing the harp, one the flute and the other two, who presumably are singers, are standing demurely in line. No doubt their time will come. The music makes me think of Henry VIII and *Greensleeves*, although this is meant to suggest medieval Italy. Maybe our meal will consist of fourteen courses with swan and wild boar.

We leave the ladies to their music and move on through the room to another, then an ante-chamber lit by a massive chandelier (electric) and candles on the walls and tables. They look Louis XIV sort of style, disgustingly fussy gilded bow-legged monstrosities. There is a sofa in the same style with three gilded panels on the back, the larger flanked by two smaller ones. As a sofa, I bet it's not the last word in comfort but there is no mistaking the opulence of this room and the place in general.

We pass through yet another room with expensive-looking red wallpaper, heavy gold brocade curtains, more

179

bow-legged chairs upholstered in gold and some hideous gilt mirrors above equally hideous gilt tables.

At the far end of the room, to the left, one half of a pair of double doors is open. Their basic colour is white, divided into three panels, the bottom and top crescents of gold leaf, the middle a green oval with a white frame but what amazes me is, in the centre, there is a golden face in high relief with golden rays radiating from it like that of some Aztec god. This is the portal to our dining room.

This is elegance. None of that heavy gilded furniture here, but four round tables, set for our feast; an enormous chandelier (probably made of *papier mâché* as I learned this is what the chandeliers in The Hermitage in St Petersburg are made of, otherwise they would be so heavy they would drag the ceiling down); electric candelabra on the walls; a pale blue wallpaper with gold stripes and motifs; a big gilt mirror without the attendant fussiness, and four of those amazing doors.

Iona and I pick the first table in the room. This could be an important moment. Who will be our dining companions? If we get the Guttings for example, the conversation is hardly going to crackle with lively repartee. As things turn out, whether by accident or design, Iona finds herself next to Bill and Pat, then there is a space reserved for Banquo perhaps, then there is Tom and Dick with Harriet on my right. This should be a good enough combination.

But before we get settled however, Angela asks us if we'd like to see Pauline Borghese's bedroom. Getting to see ladies' bedrooms is an experience in which I am sadly deficient, so I don't need any encouragement but I suspect it was a rhetorical question anyway, so off we troop in Angela's wake.

Unbelievable! What a room! It sparkles like a jewel. Gold wherever you look —gold on the walls, gold on the ceiling, gold on the candelabra, gold on the chandeliers, gold on the mirrors, gold on the doors - and light – light glistening and winking like diamonds from a myriad of electric candles, reflected as the points of stars in the mirrors. It's breathtaking.

"So like our own little love-nest at home, dear," I say *sotto voce* to Iona in a parody of Queen Victoria's famous phrase.

"This was the bedroom of Pauline Bonaparte, Napoleon's sister," Angela is saying. "She married into the Borghese family. Up there is the minstrels' gallery." She indicates an inset balcony with an intricate balustrade high on the gilded wall at the far end of the room. "That's where the musicians used to come every morning to waken her up in the morning, but the curtains on the bed were always drawn, so they couldn't see who she was waking up with. (Laughter.) Her marriage did not last long. She was very good at public relations however, especially with men, and a bit of a diplomat. All her receiving rooms and her bedroom had at least four doors, so that none of her visitors could tell who was coming or going!" (More laughter.)

It's true. There are five doors here, as ornate as the one leading into our dining room, but maybe I am deceived and one is really a reflection. I look in one of the mirrors myself and reflect: So, if only these mirrors could, by some feat of technology, play back all the images that have been cast on them, what a tale they could tell! Maybe Napoleon himself was here: *You're a slut Pauline. You're bringing the Empire into disrepute. I was just saying to Josephine the other day...* Perhaps this very mirror which reflects me, has also reflected Pauline doing triple X stuff with one of her lovers. Now that's a thought. If these mirrors were movies, I could be in a porno with Napoleon's sister. Of course, I would have only a small part, naturally.

"Would you like to see Pauline's party room now?" Angela asks unnecessarily.

Would I heck! If this is what her bedroom was like, what on earth would her party room be like? I wonder if they made the chandeliers burn red or pink flames. Will we see any of her outfits – see through bloomers and garters – what did they wear in those days? Maybe there are theme rooms, little alcoves, like in the bordello in Pompeii, where the artistes advertise their wares, carrying on the ancient traditions. Never mind the food. Why not take over Pauline's party room and have a party *à la Pauline*?

Wait a minute! This might not be a very good deal for me, to say nothing of the female participants' opinion of me which might well elicit the response that they'd rather die first. No, whatever Pauline's party room is like, I'll stick with Iona, for Florence has still to be consummated and it *is* our anniversary after all.

As is so typical of life, as I have found it, Pauline's party room does not live up to my expectations. Her party room is nowhere nearly so exciting as her bedroom. After all, this was not where the real action took place; this is where all the flirting and all the sexual innuendoes would have been flying like powder off a wig. I have to imagine bosoms heaving out of tight *corsages*, fans and beauty spots and wigs piled high like Mr Whippy ice creams.

Like the bedroom, this also has a minstrels' gallery, a bit more ornate than the one in the bedroom – I suppose a lot more people would see it – and it has also a painted ceiling and mirrors, two chandeliers and innumerable candelabra on the walls. It doesn't seem to sparkle like Aladdin's cave quite the same as the bedroom; the gilt is more muted which makes the room more tasteful and elegant, an impression which is further enhanced by the classical statues in alcoves dotted around the room.

In size, it looks, if anything, smaller than the bedroom, which is to say, you could still have a greyhound track in it. I wonder why Pauline needed such a big bedroom. Maybe her lovers chased her round and round the room first. Like the bedroom, it is set out with tables draped in white crisp linen. Angela tells us that it is let out for special occasions like weddings and anniversaries (note!), and us. If we had been a bigger tour, this is where we would have been, but instead we have to slum it in the blue room, to which we now retrace our steps.

There are bottles of wine set out and water, as is the Italian custom. We should score here, as Dick is too young to partake of the wine, so that should make a bit more for the rest of us, hopefully me. Banquo's place is taken by Angela.

It's a set menu. The antipasto consists of *crostini* – pieces of toast with puréed tomato and liver pâté and two others in two shades of green, one a pale colour, like sludge, the other so dark that it is almost black. Angela says that they're anchovy and olive. Iona and I do a trade – my pâté for her anchovy. I am hesitant about pouring myself another glass of wine. No one else seems to have had much of theirs at all. God knows how long it will be before they finish and I can fill up again.

The next course, which is the second, is called the *primo* of course, by the rules of Italian logic. It's a ravioli dish. Finished or not, it's time for my companions to have more wine. I attentively offer Harriet some more wine and am pleased to see Bill pouring Pat some more. Maybe he feels like me and was waiting for someone to make the first move.

Now we have *il secondo*, the main event, which is pork. By this time, we are getting into our stride and tongues are a little loosened. It turns out that Harriet and I had the same taste in literature in the days of our youth – Rafael Sabatini, Leslie Charteris and Dennis Wheatley, to name but a few. It's incredible how well we are getting on so well together.

"We have so much in common, we should have married each other!" I say to her in jest.

How to go from getting on like a house on fire to the Snow Queen's Castle in one easy step. How to open your mouth and jump in with both feet and land up to your waist in something rather unpleasant.

"Oh, I don't know about that," says Harriet shortly, the smile disappearing from her face like a cloud over the sun.

How do I do it? I don't even fancy her. I was merely making conversation. But it's too late now. Our conversation continues in a more stilted way. She's obviously wary that I might make a further proposition.

Meanwhile, Iona is getting on very well with Bill and Pat and it turns out that we are all going to be staying in Sorrento next week, and we think it would be a great idea if we could hire a people carrier or minibus and go together to Herculaneum, Vesuvius, the Amalfi Coast and such like. Angela says she can fix it for us with a reliable company with English speaking guides and we all feel very happy.

There's just one thing wrong. We are out of wine, but Bill and I agree to get another bottle between us. Surely he meant each? But anyway, it's a start. The waiter brings it and goes away again. I notice that the other tables are also being supplied with more.

"Is the wine free?" I ask Angela.

She nods. Why on earth did she not tell us this at the start? We needn't have been so parsimonious. Now we can have a really good night. This puts the seal on our new friendships. We have a toast to the holiday and next week.

The *dolci* or sweet is a long time in coming, which is fine – more time for wine. The waiter brings two more bottles, red and white. It's not great wine, but it's good enough and getting better and at this price, I'm not complaining. The waiter is especially proud of this sweet. It's a pastry shell, filled with strawberries and confectioner's custard. Nothing too special about this, but the sauce is. It's a pale blue and perfectly matches the blue in Iona's dress.

The maître d comes round to tell us about it.

"This was created by our chef," he says, "especially for tonight. He was inspired by -."

My thoughts are racing ahead – was this the anniversary surprise for Iona – a sauce made to compliment her dress? It would be known as La-Belle-Dame-Sans-Merci sauce and would be devoured the world over like Peach Melba and we were here at its creation! She will adore me for ever for this inspirational idea.

But the maître d continues, "- by the Italian sky and the wallpaper in this room."

How prosaic and how disappointing! The wallpaper and the sauce *are* the same shade of light blue but as a foodstuff, I find the colour somewhat nauseous. I am not in a hurry to taste it. I have a glass of wine to finish first anyway because I know it will taste terrible after the wallpaper sauce. Just as well it was not named in Iona's honour - I don't think it would have caught on. I offer mine to Iona, who *is* a sweet person, but she refuses it. I don't think I can offer it to any of the others either in case they think I'm a fussy, ungrateful swine. They don't know me well enough to know I am not a sweet person. In fact, perversely, that is the very image I am trying to keep up in front of my new friends, so when the glass of wine is finished, I have to eat the sweet which is a shame, as I regret the misspent calories.

But now there comes a diversion. The minstrels, who had welcomed us, and whom I'd completely forgotten about, now make an appearance again. Angela looks at me: *This is it!*

They must have been pointed out to us: *The woman with the blue bits in her dress like the sauce, sitting next to George Bush* for they look over at us and smile before they go into their routine. This is much better than a free bottle of wine, since that was free anyway. They play some sort of melody with flute, harp and although I can't see it, from where I am sitting, what sounds like two bits of wood being hit together, then they segue into Mendelssohn's *Here Comes the Bride* to much laughter and applause. I think Angela must have gone round the tables and told them what to expect, as Iona seems to be the only person in the room who is puzzled by this musical frog-leap through the centuries.

When it is over, I thank Angela profusely for what she has arranged. It has worked out very well indeed for everyone enjoyed the bonus of the music on top of what has been a pretty good meal in the most sumptuous surroundings any of us are likely ever to dine in again and I could even be in for some Brownie points when we get back to the hotel, but in the meantime, there is still some wine left in the bottles and I hate waste, even although the others don't seem to mind, which is all the better for me.

The conversation and laughter continue, louder and more freely than before. The wine is tasting pretty good by now too. I entertain the table (well that's my definition but Iona, who has seen and heard it all before, thinks I am a bore) with my George W Bush impression, taking my hand down my head, to reveal my face gradually. They agree that it's only when the mouth is revealed, that we begin to differ. Well, as far as looks are concerned. Actually, maybe not just looks when I think of my *faux pas* with Harriet.

As we get up to leave, after the coffees, I look longingly at the half full bottle of white lingering forlornly amongst all its dead companions. Surely it would be a kindness to put it out of its misery? Iona gives me one of her Viagra looks - as hard as stone: *No. Don't even think about it! Just leave it!*

I know when I'm ahead. I won't point out that it probably cost the Palazzo 80p or something, that they'll probably just pour it down the sink, that it's actually ours, that part of the deception is that although we have not actually *paid* for this meal tonight, we have really as it would be included in the price of the tour, so the wine *really* is ours, that it would be nice to have a glass or two before we...er...fell asleep. It's frustrating not to be able to air these cogent arguments but the sight of me walking out with a bottle of wine in front of our new friends is not an image which Iona wishes to impinge on the collective consciousness. It would embarrass her too much and she's already suffered quite enough of that already, thank you very much.

But as we file out the door, I notice that Gordon has a bottle with him. Great minds think alike. I don't know what plans he has for it, but maybe I could help him. I'll keep close to him and maybe he'll invite me to partake.

As we leave the Palazzo, I stop and look at it from the outside. I still don't know what street it's on, but the number on the wall outside is 110 and there is nothing outside to show that it is a restaurant at all. The guard and the red carpet, are of course, long gone, but there is a brown sign which reads: *Palazzo e Casino Borghese.*

Just a minute. I don't have much Italian, but I know that while *Casa* is house, *Casino* is altogether more interesting and it doesn't mean what we mean by it in English – it means brothel. Pauline's party room then really *was* a party room and maybe that explains why she had such a big bedroom, maybe multiple party games were played there too. Well, well, so I've celebrated my anniversary in a brothel! What an understanding wife! I just turned up 200 years too late that's all. I've been late before, but this is my latest ever.

All the rest have gone. I hurry after them and catch up with Gordon.

"Your wife is way ahead somewhere," he says.

"Oh, is she? Damn! I've lost her twice today already. I thought maybe third time lucky."

He's probably had a few wines himself as his teeth gleam whitely in the velvety darkness as he chuckles.

I tell him I admire him for sneaking out the bottle of wine and he says we can share it when we get back to the hotel. That's what I like to hear. I've heard the chimes at midnight – many, many times. I am hopeless in the mornings but I've never missed a chance to stay up all night and party.

Back at the hotel, Gordon and Blondie and the couple from Yorkshire, who it turns out, have also procured a bottle, are just arranging furniture and getting glasses when La-Belle-Dame-Sans-Merci waylays me.

"I've been invited to join them for a drink," I say, knowing as I say it, it's hopeless.

"Oh no you're not! You've had quite enough already. And you've to get up at half past six tomorrow. And I know what you're like in the morning."

Groan! It's true. I can stay up half the night, but just can't get up till half way through the morning. As we pass the party group on the way to the lift, Gordon indicates with his head, a seat he has prepared for me. It will have to be for Banquo. I will be with them in spirit only.

I shake my head sadly, and behind Iona's back make the face: *I've got to go to bed. Anniversary, you know. Wink! Wink!*

Gordon looks back in knowing understanding. I hope he believes me. It would be too humiliating to be unmasked as the underling I really am after only three days' acquaintanceship.

We step into the lift and it takes us heavenward. Well, as far as the third floor anyway. Whether or not I take Iona on to heaven on this anniversary night is another matter.

Chapter 6
Con Molto Citta

Through slits of eyes I see the empty bottles of wine and glasses from the party I was not a party to as I shuffle one *pantouffle* in front of the other out of the lift and head down to breakfast. It is 6:47 and I have been awake since 3 and I am feeling like I would have been had I stayed on for the party. I have the pain without having had any of the pleasure. I don't know why I go on holiday to put myself through these early starts. Strangely enough, because I haven't slept well, it has been easier to get up this morning and my fellow guests are greeting me with cheery surprise at seeing me up so early. I smile at them but it probably comes out more as a snarl.

I make my jaws eat breakfast and lunch as usual, though I can hardly summon up the energy. For some reason Iona doesn't feel like eating much at all, and has departed so I am spared the effort of having to conduct a conversation in Cro-Magnon which is the most I can manage on mornings such as these. Maybe that's the real reason why she has gone - she can't tell my talk from mutter as the margarine advert almost said.

Once we get out of the environs of Florence and on to the motorway, I hope I'll be able to rest my eyes, though I know from experience that sleep will be impossible, as I'm always frightened I'll miss something – like this for example.

We are passing tree nurseries on both sides of the road, extending for miles. Ranks of trees in pots: cypresses and trees with pompoms, destined for the Boboli gardens, or if they're not, they should be; trees twisted into all kinds of ornamental shapes; and orchards of fruit trees and flowering trees loaded with blossom, pink and white, set out as neatly and tidily as a geometric counterpane on a newly made bed.

"Isn't that a tree-mendous sight?" I say to Iona across the passage.

"Oh, shut up!"

I close my eyes from time to time, seeing how long I can keep them shut before curiosity gets the better of me and I have to look. When we draw into Pisa however, the sun is streaming in the window, my eyes are very heavy and I believe I could for once, get to sleep. I feel my head nodding and it's an effort to keep awake, just when it's time to leave the bus. Typical of the gods' sense of humour. Typical of Italian logic too. As Giancarlo pulls into the car park and I gather my stuff together, it seems this is only the car park for the car park, where it takes a quarter of an hour whilst Giancarlo gets the necessary documentation to park somewhere else.

We finally arrive in a vast, practically empty, bus-park - that's a good sign, maybe it will be relatively quiet - and make our way across a field of asphalt to a bus stop where a shuttle bus will take us to the Campo dei Miracoli - the Field of Miracles.

No guide here. We are on our own. Angela tells us that we have to be back at the shuttle stop at 9:45. She repeats the time, like a primary teacher instructing a particularly obtuse class on an obscure point. Is it my imagination, or is she looking at me in particular? We haven't time, she says, to climb the Tower. You have to queue for tickets and then are given a time for the ascent.

Just like that awful time at the Alhambra in Granada when, after queuing for an hour, at 8:30 am we were given tickets for 4:30 in the afternoon. Bad enough, but what got my goat was when we ran into the people who had been in the queue in front of us, (we were life-long friends by the time we got to the head of the queue) they disclosed their time was 11:30. I was furious at the extreme incompetence of it all, especially so as it was bitingly cold, with a bone-piercing wind blowing straight from the snow-capped Sierra Nevada and we had a long way to travel back to the Costa del Sol that evening, so I wanted to get away in good time. I dodged into the head of a queue and to my dismay, had to make my complaint in my limited French as I have no Spanish and the ticket distributor had no English. Eventually a security person took me away to another booth and I was given an earlier time as long as I went away and promised not to speak any more French. Even then, our admission time was not until 2pm. The Italians don't have a monopoly in illogicality evidently when it comes to queuing.

On the way to the Campo dei Miracoli, we run a gauntlet of souvenir stalls. Pisa appears to be entered into a Who-Can-Sell-the-Tackiest-Souvenirs–of-the-Year-Contest. They have every chance of winning, though Lourdes might offer them some stout competition. If this had been Egypt we would have been pestered to death, but here we can safely pass by without molestation from the vendors unless you count the assault on your eyes by the miraculous tattiness of the merchandise.

Unscathed, we arrive at an ancient crenellated wall. We proceed through an arch in this and suddenly, we are in the Campo dei Miracoli. The Leaning Tower is arguably the most famous icon of a city, or indeed a country, in the world, but one rarely sees it with the other buildings on the site. Here it is now, at the far end of a vast grassy area, leaning precariously, or so it seems, but after all the stabilisation work, it is now quite safe from toppling over. Angela had told us on the bus that they could have made it perfectly straight, but the tourist board, quite correctly, insisted that it still retained a lean, so it is now restored to the angle it had in Galileo's day, from where, as every schoolboy knows, he conducted his experiments on gravity and which tourists have been gravitating to ever since.

The lean is best seen in conjunction with the Duomo. The Tower looks as if it is trying to peer over its shoulder at the Baptistry, like a child playing hide-and-seek and peeping out impatiently to see if the seeker is coming yet. It's rather comical really.

The Baptistry is the first structure in the Campo and from what I can see of the three other buildings, I have to agree with Angela who had told us that she prefers it to the Tower and the Duomo. It's a pleasing shape: circular, with a dome which is capped by something that looks like a thing you use to get the juice out of a lemon. It seems perfectly proportioned and although it is rather fussy in the middle with columns and Gothic arches, it is not displeasing, especially as that is counterbalanced by a very plain bottom tier with slim columns in relief, supporting arches in a plain marble wall with windows set between the arches. The thing I like best about it is that it is plain white marble, so it doesn't look like something that has fallen out of a Liquorice Allsorts box. I don't think my eyes deceive me, but like the Tower, it also seems to be leaning - to the left.

The trouble with the buildings on the Campo is that they are built on sandy soil and when we go round the back of the Duomo and look at it from the other side, we can see that it too is sinking, and that the top two tiers are not running parallel. Nevertheless, this Duomo is the best we have seen by a long chalk. There are only bands of grey marble on the two upper tiers, so the effect is not overpowering and the grey tones in harmoniously with the white. The curve of the apse with its columns, echoes the Tower and if you stand in a certain position, you can get the two to touch, as if the apse is supporting the Tower, although they are yards apart from each other.

The façade has a triangular forest of slim columns arranged in four tiers, the top two of which look as if a Roman temple had been plonked on the pediment. The larger, more solid base has some gilt paintings and some squares of inlaid coloured marble, but looking at the façade as a whole, they do not detract too much from the overall impression of whiteness, so that the whole effect is one of restraint and rather pleasing.

The Duomo is closed and anyway, you have to pay for admittance, but the massive brass carved doors are open and when tourists move out of the way, I can see as much as I want to see, I think. Stupidly, I have not brought the guidebook, so I don't know what treasures lie within. In the centre of the apse there is a stained glass window with two tiers of paintings in gilt frames on each side and a huge one, which looks at this considerable distance like St Francis, extending into the cupola, so he appears as in heaven looking down at the mortals below. The nave looks impressive with its sturdy Corinthian columns but it's a bit of a disappointment to see that the upper tiers have the liquorice allsorts stripes, the grey being more prominent here, in the interior. But that is the only fault, for there are slender columns between the stripy ones, creating graceful double arches and the wall they support is pleasingly plain with unornamented arched windows set into it. No doubt about it, Pisa wins the Duomo contest hands down. We've still to see St Peter's in Rome, but somehow I suspect that I won't like it as much as this.

We wander back and look at the Tower. No need to describe such a well-known structure. Even if it were not leaning, which gives it an additional interest, it would still be the best campanile tower we have seen, for its cotton-reel drums are constructed of plain white marble, as are the elegant columns, and devoid of pink or green or grey marble bands, as if they were dressed in stripy pyjamas - in fact pyjamas so horrendous you would only put them on in the dark and pray each night that there's not a fire.

We are lucky to see it as it is. If we had been here a few years before, we wouldn't have seen the Tower for unsightly cables and lead weights which they used to correct the lean, which by the 1990s, was precarious. Now there is restoration work on only part of the campanile as part of it is has screens stretched over some scaffolding, giving it from below, the appearance of some sort of communication satellite, about to be launched from the rocket of the Tower. Wait a minute! It *is* restoration work, isn't it? The Tower is probably the highest point in Pisa, surely they wouldn't use it as a communication tower would they? Surely that screen doesn't hide half a dinner set of satellite dishes, does it?

Whilst I am contemplating the enormity of this, a man asks me to take his photograph and, horror upon fresh horror, leaps over the chain railing onto the green sward and positions himself in front of the Tower.

"Hey, you can't do that! You're not meant to walk on the grass!" No one, but absolutely no one is walking on the grass. It's the grass which adds to the appeal of this place, to see these magnificent buildings rising from its fresh greenness instead of grey paving stones. And unlike the cramped and squashed cluster of buildings in Florence, it gives space to the buildings, so you can admire them without tourists as black as flies wandering about in front of them. To step on its pristine green surface seems almost like a desecration. Besides, there's probably some security people watching all the time and they'll probably think I'm with this person and begin yelling at us any moment.

It's all right though, for he who would be photographed, hops over the chain again and I kneel so I can get the whole of the Tower with him standing beside it, not growing out of the top of his head like a chimney. I hope he will be pleased with the result in spite of me not grassing him up.

It's a splendid view, standing here with the Tower to our left and the apse of the Duomo ahead of us. Running parallel with the side of the Duomo is a sparkling white wall with an intriguing little tower jutting out from the roof half way along. This is the Camposanto or cemetery. Apparently on the fourth crusade of 1203 a cargo of soil from the hill of Golgotha was brought back so the great and the good of Pisa could be buried in holy ground. I stand under the mid-way mini Gothic tower and marvel at the delicate tracery of the stonework which forms the overhanging base of the tower. There are four gargoyles leaning over looking down at me looking up: *You may be ugly, but you're not as ugly as us, heh! heh! heh!* There is a door in the wall here, but if we want to go in, we have to retrace our steps to an adjacent building where they sell tickets, just as we had to do at the Pitti Palace. I wonder why it is beyond the wit of the Italians to think of selling tickets at the point of access.

But even where they do, they manage to create chaos. The confusion at the queue for the Tower of the Town Hall in Siena is all too fresh in my memory. We stood in a ragged queue in front of two booths and watched while one of the sales girls ate a banana and the other polished her nails. Five minutes after they were due to open, Nail-polish girl ceased her blandishments and stuck up two signs over the ticket windows. One said Tower, the other said Crypt. Pandemonium erupted as those in our queue, the Crypt queue, naturally, as I was in it, tried to infiltrate the other queue without having to go to the tail of the other queue, which apart from standing for an hour or so, might well mean we would not get in at all, as they limit the number of visitors each day. And what made matters worse, was that while Nail-polish girl was kept extremely busy, Banana-eating girl just sat on her posterior and unashamedly did nothing but look at us. I would like to have strangled her, but I don't suppose she was responsible for devising this queue-rage system. When, at the Creation, logic was being given out, the Italians were evidently not in the queue. They'd never heard of it I suppose. Nor a queue either.

Butting on to the pristine-looking cemetery wall, is the much older-looking city walls, randomly sprouting vegetation, crowned with crenellations. There is nothing I like better than medieval ramparts. I'd love to have a walk around them, but I don't see anybody else doing it, so they are probably not open and anyway, we probably don't have time.

Instead, we walk over to have another, closer look at the Baptistry. The carving on it really is fantastic. This doorway, for instance – just look at the detail! There is so much going on! Christ and the apostles over the door, each with distinctly individual faces and flowing garments and on the arches, smaller figures, like frames on a roll of film, running between two intricately decorated, swirling patterned columns. You cannot help but admire the sculptor's art. Here, the fussiness does not intrude, as it does in the façade of the Santa Croce for example, but adds interest. I walk round it in increasing admiration and come to an open door. There is a security girl with a radio clipped to her waist standing just inside the doorway. I take the chance to squeeze past her plump posterior and slip inside. I know it's the exit: it's probably why she is manning it, to stop people like me getting in, but it's the time to play the tourist idiot, just so I can have just a glimpse of the interior of this magnificent building. By the time we have found where to queue, then queued, there probably wouldn't be any time left to explore it. God knows what this place is like when the bus park is full – it's busy enough now.

My eyes have not even had time to adjust from the fierce sunlight to the gloom of the interior before the guard speaks.

"Ticket?" She must have sensors in her posteriors.

"Ticket?" I am still trying to look around but all I can see is a vast plain space.

"Yes. You have to buy a ticket."

I let a look of comprehension dawn on my stupid, red, tourist face. I hope she thinks the redness is due to embarrassment. I ask her where I can buy a ticket to add substance to the deception and thank her as I back out. Not really a successful mission, but I think I've seen enough to decide that this is the converse of the Santa Croce, much more interesting on the outside than the inside.

Across the field there is a phalanx of tourist stalls. There is only one gap in their ranks, a banner which proclaims this is the entrance to the Museo delle Sinopie. It has one of those enigmatic one-handed clocks high on the wall, topped with a monumental arch. If I read it correctly, it says we don't have time to go in, so we turn our attention to the souvenir stalls.

They are all a variation on a theme. Here you can buy enough Leaning Towers to fill the Baptistry. You can have them in any shade or colour, in any size. You can have them as lamps, as ashtrays, as toilet brush holders –actually they don't have them for the last two purposes, only they should, as that would be appropriate for their dreadful tackiness. We are incredulous at the extent of the variety and the awfulness of them all.

"Look, look! Here is a really nice one!" I indicate a Tower two feet tall, a lurid purple, dusted with glitter. "And it says that it changes colour and glows in the dark! What else could you ask for? My happiness is complete!"

Iona is entranced by its absolute awfulness. She points to a tray where there are scores of mini such towers piled on top of each other. "Let's get one for Hélène! We've *got* to get one for Hélène!" She's practically dancing in excitement.

I look at her in horror. "You're joking! You've *got* to be kidding! What! Waste €2 on rubbish like that!"

But once La-Belle-Dame-Sans-Merci has made her mind up, that's it. We are now the proud owners of a purple-glow-in-the-dark two inches high Leaning Tower of Pisa, covered in glitter. Thankfully it is wrapped in a brown paper bag, like a mailing in a plain envelope that you don't want your wife to see.

There are further delights in store. You can have a miniature of the whole of the Field of Miracles, the Baptistry, Duomo and Tower all crowded together in your choice of lurid colours. Or what about a mug with a picture of the Tower and wittily sloping at an angle away from the handle so you can miss your mouth and slop your boiling coffee into your lap? Or perhaps the discerning tourist would prefer a tasteful plate of the Tower which you can hang on the wall: *Instructions. To get maximum enjoyment from your plate, you should hang it on the wall at an angle*. Naturally.

We come across Bill and Pat buying a Tower.

"Hah! Hah! Caught you! We won't tell on you, if you don't tell on us!" I waggle our discreetly wrapped package at them.

"I know, they're so awful, they're irresistible aren't they? It's a pity we don't smoke – we could use the tall one as an ashtray," says Pat. Great minds!

"Worth taking it up just to have one, I would have thought."

We move on to another stall. The Yorkies are buying a two inch brass Tower.

"Hah! Hah! Caught you! I won't tell on you, if you don't tell on me!" Once I've got a good line, I don't let go of it readily, even when I shoot myself in the foot, toe by toe, like my flippant remarks earlier to the airport staff and Angela and Harriet. I never seem to learn the lesson to give up when I'm ahead, let alone when I'm not.

Mr Yorkie looks at me with one eye; the other is looking over my left shoulder. "What d'ya mean?" he asks ingenuously, without hostility.

Oh God! What *do* I mean? He obviously *likes* his purchase. There is something about his appearance, his casual but non-conformist attire, the battered hat on his head, the length of his unkempt hair spilling beneath it, that makes Sherlock Addison deduce that he is an art teacher. Not only that, but they did not come with us on the tour of Florence. I think they have probably, in that city of art, been exploring galleries they didn't have time for before, on a previous visit. The fact that he likes this little memento of his trip to Pisa adds further evidence to this deduction. Only art teachers could possibly see any merit in the treasures on display here, seeing merit in what we less artistically educated fail to recognise. The brass model though, if I were on the rack, I would have to admit, has the edge over the purple model we bought for Hélène. I mean, I might allow it room space in a dark corner. Quick thinking is required.

"Oh…er…shopping, instead of using the time to go into the Baptistry or the Duomo or the Museo."

He nods. "Yeah, right!" Does he believe me? I can't tell. As long as he thinks I'm just some sort of harmless nutter, I reckon I've got off lightly.

It's time to start heading back for the bus stop, through the souvenir stalls without the city walls. Iona's attention is attracted by pairs of boxer shorts, hanging like bunting from the canvas roof of a stall. The design is a photograph of the lower part of David's stomach and his dangly bits, so the wearer looks as if he's nude, though of course it wouldn't deceive anyone for a moment. The interesting bits are a dusky white as nature intended for a marble statue, but you can have the shorts in a variety of background colours. The ones that Iona prefers are finished in attractive shades of brown, dark brown at the seat and lightening down to the legs and up to the waist as if the wearer had been afflicted with a severe case of diarrhoea. Of all the tack in all the tacky stalls of Pisa, this is the tackiest and brown the tackiest colour. Iona *has* to have them for George – a snip at €5. After all, you couldn't buy these in Falkirk market, but then again, I wouldn't be so sure. It's one-size fits all the lady says and that clinches it - they are ours.

As we head to our rendezvous point, Iona chortling with glee at her purchases and the anticipatory thought of how appalled her children will be with their gifts, there is an old woman coming towards us, except coming is a totally inadequate word to describe the difficulty she has with her locomotion. She is leaning on a stick and is bent up double, shuffling forward on legs arched like the wishbone of a chicken. Probably she is suffering from rickets. She's dressed in black from her headscarf to her shoes. Her right hand is held pathetically open in supplication. I am already feeling for a €2 coin which I press into her palm as we come abreast. Then suddenly, a man at her right makes a grab for it. There is a moment of sheer panic on her face and quicker than I thought possible for her to move, she clutches the coin to her chest and cowers like an animal about to be struck. The man disappears into the crowd. It's all over so quickly, I can scarcely believe it's happened. Who would steal from a woman like that? The crone continues her journey. Where is she going to? Where does she live? Does anyone look after her? Doesn't the State?

At the bus stop, we are not the last. The Yorkies are missing and so are Gordon and Blondie. Angela is looking distinctly nervous. She keeps looking in the direction of the stalls, hoping she'll see them emerge. In spite of the vast car park, we have only a limited parking time and we must catch this shuttle bus which itself, appears to be late, for there is an enormous queue gathering. Angela says that when the bus comes, we *have* to get aboard, no matter how crowded it is and it will be, she warns. This is going to be fun. We should spend the time sharpening our elbows.

The sun is wonderfully hot already, and there is a wall which provides satisfactory seating. It's a great relief to me not to be in Angela's shoes, to not have the responsibility for getting all these people to meet schedules. I know what it's like, having organised school trips abroad for many years. Next week Angela has a full bus load – 42 tourists to look after. Nightmare! Bad enough getting 18 of us onto this bus – but 42, providing they've all turned up on time in the first place!

Still no sign of Gordon and Blondie, but here come the Yorkies laden with packages. What on earth could they have bought? Maybe they have a lot of relations or enemies they want to annoy but I'm not going to ask.

Along comes a black vendor with a briefcase full of watches. There is time to bargain and besides, I need a replacement for my £4 Rolex from Penang which I lost, or more probably, which someone stole, assuming it to be the genuine article. I last had it at the gym and this loss confirmed my opinion that exercise is not good for you. I look at his wares, but there is nothing to my taste – his watches are all big chunky affairs, with wrist straps like the chains you tie up bicycles with whereas I prefer my watches to be like my women, slim and good-looking. This is the sort of jewellery you could buy on the Ponte Vecchio, except these are copies of course, at a fraction of the price.

His opening price is €45. I puff my cheeks out, roll my eyes, shake my head vigorously.

"Too dear. Cost too much."

"How much you pay?"

"How much is £5 in euros?" I have to ask Iona as I do not have the arithmetical skills to work out such arcane calculations.

"About €7."

"I give you €7." I hold up the same number of digits to drive my offer home.

His turn to snort in derision. "Cost me more than that to buy. €25."

I shake my head. "€7." He'll either let me have it for that or walk away. He shakes his head sadly and walks away. The first bite he'd had all day and he has to meet a Scotsman from Banff. It's a bit like being run over by your own stolen car – nobody deserves to be that unlucky. If I'd really wanted it, I would have bargained further, but truth to tell, it was a poor substitute for my fondly loved false Rolex.

Angela is looking frantic. She asks us if anyone has seen Gordon and Blondie. The Yorkies say they were last seen back at the Campo dei Miracoli, ages ago. Ah, here comes the bus and Angela's nerves go into hyperdrive. As if on cue, Gordon and Blondie emerge from the shade of the stalls over to our right where they have been waiting all the time out of the sun. They have been able to see us, but no one has spotted them. It was thoughtless of them, but presumably they had no idea of the knots they were creating in Angela's underwear. There is no time for Angela to say anything to them – we have to fight our way on to the bus, come hell or high water.

It has to be a joke! As the bus draws up, we look at each other in frank disbelief. Surely Angela cannot be serious about us getting on this thing! It's already full and there's plenty of people ahead of us in the queue if you could call this mass of humanity a queue. Some people are getting off the bus and although the rule is alight at the rear and enter at the front, there is a surge to climb on at the back, so those coming up meet those coming down and they have to struggle to get off. It's mayhem, but at last we are all aboard, or so we think. It's impossible to tell really as there are so many bodies aboard and it's difficult to move without becoming extremely intimate with the person next to you. There's no air-conditioning. It's already hot in the bus and all these bodies crammed together is making the sweat drip off my pectorals as Susan from Oz didn't put it so politely. There's nowhere for me to hold on to, so I plant my feet as firmly as I can on the floor and trust that being wedged in as I am will keep me relatively stable.

We lurch round a corner and I teeter forward into an even closer encounter with a young lady. I offer my profuse apologies. There's still nowhere for me to hang on to unless I cling onto one of my fellow travellers but that would be called an invasion of privacy in this place where no one has any personal space left. The bus careers round another corner and I lurch into her again. If I have to lurch into someone, I must admit, this lady is extremely lurchable.

All the same, it's a relief when we get to the terminus. It's a double relief to Angela to find we are all present and correct. We board our bus and we're on our way to Siena. So that was Pisa. We didn't see a lot really, just the highlights and nothing at all of the town itself, but at least we saw more than we did the last time which was just the airport –which made us probably the only people to come to Pisa and not see the Tower - but we knew we were coming back in the summer. Still, there's a lot more to Pisa than the Campo dei Miracoli and there's a lot more to that than we saw. We'll just have to come back.

We make a stop about an hour afterwards at a motorway stop with red and white oleander growing up the central reservation and palm trees growing in the car park. The air seems to vibrate with the heat. Inside our air-conditioned bus, it's deceiving. It looks sunny but the blast of heat when you stand on the tarmac hits you with the force of a blast furnace. Incredibly, it surprises me every time: it just doesn't look that hot from inside the bus.

It's just a short walk to the air-conditioned shop in the service station. As usual, we are the first to alight from the bus and I am first in the queue at the big cooler cabinet in the corner stocked with soft drinks and water, but when I attempt to open it, it won't give an inch. Gordon and Blondie, who are next in the queue, are looking at me, wondering why I just don't get on with it. I don't like to show I'm such a technophobe that I don't know how to open a chiller-cabinet door, so I pretend I've changed my mind and don't like the look of the cans and bottles in there – that I prefer the identical ones in the cabinet next to it. I move across to let Gordon at the first one (see if he can manage it!) but I've got a problem with this one too because I discover to my consternation, that I when I open the door of this one readily enough, I must have been standing in such a way so that the door is now between me and the interior, so I am looking at Gordon through the glass door of the cabinet. He's standing in front of his cabinet which he has evidently had no difficulty with and is looking quizzically at me across at me through the glass: *You're a bit old to be playing peek-a-boo aren't you?* I grin inanely at him, close the door and come round to the front, standing to the right of the handle so this time I can reach inside when I open it.

Harriet is beside me now at the other cabinet. Hah! Hah! Let's see if she can open this then! She gives it a tug. Nothing happens. She tries again. She's a big strong woman, Harriet, or she looks it. I wouldn't care for a left hook landing on my chin from her anyway. I inwardly confess to some *Schadenfreude* that she can't open it either.

"I can't get it to open," she says in her soft south-eastern burr.

I have got my drinks by now and seizing the handle, I channel every ounce of my strength to it and tug. With the sound like elastoplast being ripped from a hairy leg by a butch nurse, only minus the screams, the door swings open. I can feel the suck of the seal giving way. That is one strong seal all right. Harriet looks at me in gratitude or it could be in admiration of my manly strength. I return her look as if it were nothing, that opening chiller-cabinet doors holds no terrors for me. I can show *them* who's boss. They can't make a fool out of me.

As Siena draws nearer, the landscape and names on the signposts become familiar from our visit at Easter: Empoli, Volterra, San Gimignano and the magnificent medieval Monteriggioni dominating its hilltop. The vines, which were knobbly sticks between thin lines of wire then, are now in full leaf, preparing to bring forth my favourite fruit, though normally I take them in liquid form.

In Siena, we have the same ritual as we had in Pisa, except this time the detour is longer. We go to one park to get a ticket so we can park in another. Oh, well. We are disgorged from the bus at the Porta San Marco and make our way up the slope of the Via di San Marco. We are to meet our guide at the panther, one of the signs which denotes which district of Siena you are in. There are 17 of such *contrade* who compete in the world famous Palio in the Piazza del Campo. As you stroll through the town, if you are observant and look up, you can see carvings of animals on the walls which lets you know you have entered another district.

Here we are at the Contrada della Pantera. We know because there is an iron plaque on the wall which says so and a rampant panther, as they say in heraldry, doing the hokey-cokey. He's had a bit too much to drink apparently as he is putting both his left leg and left arm in at the same time, but he's still standing. He's at a Christmas party evidently, as he's wearing one of those paper crowns on his head.

We are given some free time to get some lunch before meeting our guide and Iona and I finally track down a couple of pastry things so she will not drop down dizzy like she nearly did in the Boboli gardens. Angela has told us that we probably don't have time to sit down in a restaurant, but I see the Yorkies go into one.

We make our way back to the panther and sit on the wall of a fountain which has a bronze crouching panther on the top as if it is bending to drink. May as well rest our legs whilst we can for the walking trail ahead. Our guide has turned up. She's dressed in white with her jet-black hair tied back in a pony tail. If she had her hair loose and wore spectacles, she'd be the same idea as Claire again as she's the same build, has the same shape of face and has the same skin tone. God was obviously running short of ideas by the time he got round to the Southern Mediterranean.

Everyone seems to be here except for the Yorkies. Time passes and there is still no sign of them. The Guttings are sitting side by side on the wall, he staring dejectedly at a point three feet from his feet, she, a little more animated, has her head more raised but neither of them speak. The rest of us are tired of sitting down and are hanging around in small groups, chatting.

Angela is alternately looking at her watch and looking down the street.

"Has anyone seen the Yorkshire couple?" she asks hopefully.

What to do? Do I rat on a fellow tourist or, understanding how Angela feels, do I tell her as it may help her to decide what to do? I know I am a party animal like the panther, sometime frog and, according to La-Belle-Dame-Sans-Merci, often a pig, sometimes the pot-bellied Vietnamese variety in what I take she intends to be an insulting remark on my shape, (actually the normal shape for a man of my age) but which I think is quite flattering really as I think they are rather cute. I don't know what year it is according to the Chinese calendar, but I decide that today is the day of the Rat.

"Well, I saw them go into a restaurant, but that was some time ago," I add in mitigation, the inference being that they might turn up at any moment.

Angela makes a little growling noise in her throat, like Marge Simpson. "I told them there wouldn't be time for that. We've got to meet the bus at the gate on time as there is only limited waiting time there."

Don't shoot me! I'm only the dirty rat who *cliped*. But my sympathies are still with Angela. Who would be a travel rep? And this is an easy week for her as we are such a small group.

At last here are the Yorkies striding up the street. I'm going to have to look out or else I'm going to lose my crown as the group's most unpunctual person. But I wouldn't like to be in their shoes, for by the way they are walking, they know that they have sinned. Before they get to the panther though, Angela marshals her troops and we set off to meet them. The Yorkies will be in no doubt that we have been loitering, waiting for them so long that we couldn't wait another second. I thank God that it wasn't me because La-Belle-Dame-Sans-Merci would have been merciless.

There are colourful flags on the streets now which weren't here on our first visit - left over from the first Palio on July 2nd or in anticipation of the second on August 16th in less than a month's time. Here is the snail flag (surely they never win the Palio?) – red and yellow checks with a blue border and a white shield with a snail on it at the centre and on the corner of the Duomo, there is another, a green plant of some description on a gold background with a white and green chequered edge.

Someone wrote a song *I'm in love with Vienna* and I have sung under my breath and in my own inimitable style: *I'm in love with Siena* but that's in spite of the Duomo and its even more ghastly *campanile*, its only redeeming feature being the arched windows which increase in size and number as it goes higher. If you want to picture it, it's the white one from the Liquorice Allsorts box, but all of them piled up into one black and white striped tower of horror.

Claudia is our guide and she is telling us all about the cathedral, begun in 1136. Does she really like it I wonder? If you are Sienese, out of loyalty, do you think your Duomo is better than Pisa's or Florence's, your traditional rivals? I suppose the façade of this is not too much worse than Florence's, all pink and white Gothic icing on its upper two-thirds and the repulsive zebra stripes on the bottom. To show I'm interested, I ask Claudia who the architect was and she tells me that it was a joint effort. A bit like the camel then, which someone described as an animal designed by a committee. That might help explain it. Camels are not the most handsome of beasts, it has to be admitted and it's another of the animals in Iona's bestiary to which she has compared me, because of my capacity to do without toilet stops. Well, I think that's the reason.

Just inside the cathedral there are some people who are handing out free green ponchos. They are intended for the scandalous women who are showing bare shoulders and calves, but I want one too because it's the sort of material that would be ideal for polishing the car.

God, this place is ghastly! No wonder the row of pope's heads near the ceiling are looking down in such disapprobation. It's dark and gloomy; a good place for zebras to hide somewhere amongst all these stripes.

We pass straight by the Piccolomini Library where Pinturicchio's frescoes of the life of Pius II had captivated me and which had made me doubt if Giotto's could compete with them for colour or sheer artistry. My fellow tourists have passed within yards of these marvels and probably will never be aware of it.

Claudia has taken us to an octagonal stone pulpit, supported on pillars on the backs of lions. She points out to us how realistic they look. They are snarling: *What's that on my back? Oh, the bloody weight!* She puts a coin in a machine and a light illuminates a densely carved scene of figures in high relief. This pulpit was carved, she tells us by Nicola Pisano in 1265. The carvings depict scenes from the life of Christ and they are very skilfully executed, each figure, as Claudia points out, having a unique expression. But it's not so much the quality of the carving which impresses me so much, as the sheer number and complexity of the figures. In this panel for instance, there are horses, full of vigour and movement who nobody seems to notice, are trampling some animal to death, probably a dog, but its head is obscured by a tangle of legs, so it's impossible to tell. And there's what looks like a couple of camels and a host of figures behind these mounted animals, whom, you would have thought, would have been obscured by the mêlée beneath, but I expect their superior position is symbolical.

I don't know what scene from the Bible this is meant to represent, and to be honest, I think it is just too full of figures and I'm not sure about the perspectives either, but it certainly must have kept old Nicola busy and off the streets. Maybe that's why his mother gave him a girl's name - so he would stick in at his sculpture and not go chasing after girls. Imagine the poor bugger trying to pull a girl at his *contrada* dance and the object of his desire says: *What do you do then, handsome?…Oh, really? And what's your name then?…Oh, right!* No self-respecting girl is going to entrust her genes to a bloke called Nicola, so here he is, carving out a name for himself as a sculptor instead. You were right Mrs Pisano.

We follow Claudia over to an area of floor which is roped off. I have already noticed that parts of the floor are covered with plywood and taped down. She feeds another coin into another meter and an area of floor is illuminated. It's meant to be for us, but I can't get *in aboot* as we say in Banffshire for the press of tourists who have already ringside seats: *Hey, move out of the way, fatties! I've got an eighteenth part of a euro invested in this. That's my money you're watching!* But of course, now that the floor is illuminated and they are getting a free talk, if they were thinking of going away, they certainly are not now.

She is describing a marble inlaid picture. She says that Siena is unique as it is the only cathedral that has such decorations: *Hah! That's one in the eye for you, you revolting Pisans*! I can just about hear what she is talking about, but I want to see *what* she is talking about, so I move further away where the crowd is less dense and if I stand on my tippy-toes and manipulate my neck like marionette, I can just about get a glimpse of floor over the heads and shoulders of those in front, but of course I can't hear what she is saying now.

When the light shuts off and everyone moves away, I can at last see what I was meant to be looking at. This is a bloodthirsty scene, executed in white, yellow and that reddish-purple marble known as porphyry, revered for its rarity, but detested by me for its hideous colour which reminds me of raw liver, the sight, taste and smell of which is absolutely abhorrent to me. It's *The Slaughter of the Innocents*. Soldiers with raised swords are raining blows upon their helpless victims. One soldier, with sword ready to strike, has his hand on the leg of a naked baby who is clinging to his mother's breast, while the bodies of other babies lie heaped upon the floor. I haven't heard who the artist is, if we even know, but, no doubt about it, it is certainly a powerful image and sends shivers up my spine, though I am sweating under my car polisher of Lincoln green.

I scamper after Claudia and the rest. I am glad to see that we are going outside by a side door and I can divest myself of the poncho. There are a couple of men receiving them. Do they possibly recycle them? Because I want to retain mine for its new career, I walk out still wearing it as if I'd forgotten to take it off. I emerge from the dim interior of that sepulchral place into the blazing heat of the Sienese afternoon, blinking like a mole coming up for whatever moles come up for. The interior of that place is so indescribably gloomy and depressing.

Claudia is showing us now where the ambitious Sienese had planned to expand the cathedral. It would have made it the largest Christian church in the world. The existing nave - and *that* is big - would become a transept, and a new nave was to be built out to the south. Work was begun on it, and there were some stability problems but above all, there was The Black Death and both money and people ran short. There are markers on the piazza, now a handy car park, to show where the massive pillars would have stood and the other side which did have the pillars and arches completed, has been blocked in with red brick to create the Museo dell'Opera del Duomo. The far end, in white marble, and looking rather ruinous, like a gable-end left standing after the rest of the building has been blitzed, is what would have formed the new façade and entrance. At the bottom is an immense door, at least 30 feet in height and above it, two empty spaces one above the other, which had been destined for windows. One good thing about this plan though, the campanile would have had to go, or rather, would never have been built, at least not there, as it is a century younger than the Duomo. But imagine an interior twice the size as the Duomo is now and in the same style! No! NO! That is a Liquorice Allsorts sort of nightmare.

We walk down the steps adjacent to the Duomo and arrive at the Piazza San Giovanni. There is something about a huge flight of steps that appeals to me and even the Duomo looks good, looking up at it in profile from the bottom of the steps. The Baptistry is here. As expected, it is built in the same style and colours as the façade of the Duomo, if not quite as ornate. Between the stripes there are diamond lozenges, presumably considered to be an attractive embellishment, but actually the points are like arrows pointing up and down, like arrows to the black stripes: *Hey, look at my stripes! Smart, eh?* No, definitely not.

We turn right down the Via dei Pellegrini, an attractive street with huge barred windows and huge iron rings on the walls, which I presume were for tying up horses.

Like Rome (and Sheffield), Siena is built upon seven hills and I know that if we were to walk through this arch to our left and take this little street off to our left, the Via di Beccheria, we could look across to the bulk of San Domenico which reputedly contains the head of that celebrated mystic, Catherine of Siena. It never ceases to amaze me how many bits of body parts of saints there are scattered around the various parts of Europe. Years ago, I went out of my way to a church in Brittany, called St Jean le Doigt on the strength of it proudly boasting to have the index finger of John the Baptist, but when we got there, it was to discover that the finger was immured in a wall and we couldn't see it. The journey, you might say, was pointless. What's the point of a finger if you can't point at it and say: *Wow! Just look at that doigt!*

Although the church looked tantalisingly close, because of the different levels, it's actually much further away than if we were crows and could fly there, and in the end we decided not to bother. The car park was eating up a euro an hour and we might climb up and down dale just to have another separated from the body experience like St Jean le Doigt. We decided not to go ahead with it then and it's not on the agenda this time either as we're not heading in that direction and have walked straight past.

Walking down the Via dei Pellegrini, without deviating, without being lured from the ultimate destination, requires a strong effort of self denial, there are so many entrancing alleyways with houses, their louvred windows open invitingly, with quaint street lamps on brackets high on the brown warm walls, and most appealing of all, arches upon arches, some with slim white pillars and Corinthian pedestals, some enclosed with glass, still more, like flying buttresses, spanning the narrow space between the houses. These are some of the reasons why I'm in love with Siena.

But the main reason I'm in love with Siena is now before us. It's the square known as Il Campo where the Palio takes place, only it is shaped more like a scallop shell, gently sloping down to the Town Hall. I love this gently-curving, scooped shape and how it dictates the shape of the Town Hall, as it follows the curve of the piazza and bends in a shallow arc. I'm also captivated by its windows: pairs of slim Arabian-style pillars form two tiers of arched windows, looking startlingly white against the warm brown stone with, rising above them, its central, square, crenellated tower, flanked by matching bastions on either side. The bottom is constructed of white marble with huge arched windows and, to the left, above an ornate white marble portico rises the stunning bell tower with its white marble tip. It's the Torre del Mangia, Italy's second highest tower and named after the slothful first bell ringer: *Bloody steps, every day, more bloody steps. No wonder I've got bloody varicose veins.*

I notice that across the piazza there is another building which matches the Town Hall's windows, crenellations and gentle concave curve, so that there is a pleasing harmonious balance to the whole piazza. The area in the middle, which at Easter had been black with people, is surprisingly less busy now so that it is easy to pick out the grey lines on the salmon pink, which divide the piazza into nine segments, a reminder of the Council of Nine who got together to design the piazza in 1293: *Nice job boys! You done good!* One example of a committee that did design something better than a camel.

At the top of the central segment there is a rectangular fountain – the Fonte Gaia. I don't know what's gay about it unless it's a rendezvous point for all the people happy to meet each other, in which case, should Iona and I get separated again, we'd better not agree to meet here. And it's not really a fountain either; more a basin bounded by sculptured panels depicting Biblical scenes, the water trickling out of the mouths of crouched and extremely skinny lions or maybe its she-wolves as Siena traditionally was founded by Senius, the son of Remus, who, as every schoolboy knows, was suckled by a she-wolf, before he went on to found Rome. Here, clouds of pigeons come to drink from the water which comes by a 15 mile aqueduct, just as it did in the 14th century.

Claudia lets us drink in the scene and tells us about the Palio. "You stay with your district all your life," she says. "Sometimes a woman will come back to her district, just to give birth, especially if it's to avoid her baby being born in a rival district. Each district has its own special rival and making your rival district lose can be just as important as winning the race."

I wonder what district the maternity hospital is in. I remember at Easter seeing some flowers on a door and a card announcing the birth of a baby. Presumably there are a lot of home births: *You are not going to that hospital. I'm not having my wife give birth to an orang-utan. I want my son to be a slug, just like me.*

"Do you get mixed marriages?" I ask.

Another conversation at the *contrada* dance: *You look like an elephant to me. Wanna pack your trunk an' come outside with me?* or *Hey, you look like a panther to me. How*

214

d'ya like to purr along with me, pussycat? After all, I am a frog and Iona is an elephant. I sometimes call her that. Nothing to do with her size of course – it's her prodigious memory, which, as I have already related, she uses to test me on where we were on a certain day 20 years ago. Just think, if we'd been Sienese, we might not have married at all, or it might have been like Romeo and Juliet: warring families.

"Oh yes," says Claudia, "but it can divide families, especially when it comes time for a baby to be born. You know, we Sienese, we're *pazzo*. You'll sometimes see fighting in the streets between districts and in the race, there are no rules – you can do anything you like to win or make your rival district lose. It's the horse which wins, not the rider, so a riderless horse can win. Cheating is all part of the fun! And the celebrations go on for days."

My God! I thought Glasgow and Celtic and Rangers was bad but it seems they are just beginners, if you please, compared to the Sienese.

"If you want to go to the race," Claudia continues, "You've got to be there early." She unfurls a poster she has taken from her shoulder bag. It shows Il Campo and the whole shell, except for the Fonte Gaia, dense with motley coloured pins which are actually the heads of the spectators. There are massed ranks of people round the perimeter too, so that a wide track, covered in sand, has been created between them. "The race begins at 7:45 but you need to get there at 2pm if you want to get near the front."

Bloody hell! Imagine that! Standing there for nearly six hours and then what do you do if you need to go to the toilet, as you will certainly have brought some beer with you? Well, there's always the Fonte Gaia, if you're close enough or you could ask the big beefy guy behind you: *Em...I'm just off for a wee while. I wondered if you would mind looking after my place and my beer for me?* That **would** be right! Of course it might also depend on your allegiances:

Yeh, sure mate, but tell me first, are you a woodlouse or a stick-insect?

"The race lasts about 90 seconds." What! Did I hear her correctly? "Yes," says Claudia obviously pleased at our astonished reactions. "But you won't be able to leave the Campo till about 8:30." Right enough, with all those people, it's going to take some time to empty, and even then, there could be fights between rival groups of supporters and the crowd could sway with people being trampled underfoot as they try to avoid the fracas. "I told you we were *pazzo! We're more pazzo than the French!* " Claudia says with conviction.

She's *pazzo* and proud of it. But why did she say more *pazzo* than the French? It's true they have some bizarre ideas such as the French way of doing things is the best way of doing everything in the universe - so much so that they had to invent a term for it after the geezer who first dreamed it up: Chauvinism. I thank God that I'm just a mild madman who comes from the boondocks of Banff, thereby having conferred upon me the status of congenital idiot and I don't have to go to the Palio twice a year, or even once a year, or ever, if I don't want to, to prove it.

But these poor blighters of Sienese *have* to go and enjoy themselves or else be considered too sane and therefore a disgrace to the family. Imagine the shame of having an offspring who says: *But daddy, I don't want to go to the Palio and stand for hours in the middle just for something that lasts less than two minutes and have people trample on my toes and pee myself and not see anything anyway because I'm too small and too far back to see over the heads of all the people.*

Of course, in her desire to be considered a complete *pazzo*, Claudia has been rather disingenuous. She hasn't told us that the race is only one small part of the proceedings, for it's really a spectacle of medieval costume and pageantry,

216

with flag twirling and throwing, plus all the atmosphere before and after the race with all the attendant partying. All the same, I am glad that I am not Sienese, even if it is free, to get into the Palio, unless of course you want to pay a pension to get a view from one of the houses or the Town Hall. The Mangia should remember *that* when he climbs his daily stairs – he's got the best seat in the house: *No, I bloody don't. They look like bleeding ants from up there.*

"And what's the prize?" I ask Claudia, knowing as I ask it, that it will be something ridiculous.

"A banner."

Well, why not? We do the same for a silver cup which just goes to show how we attribute some value to the prize when, in actual fact, it's the taking part that's important.

She is just about to roll up her poster when Gordon steps forward and points at one of the pin-heads. "That's you," he says.

Everyone laughs and thinks it very funny and yet if I'd done it, it probably would have been considered the act of an idiot and nobody would have laughed except in an embarrassed sort of way.

That's it then, that's all we're going to see of Siena, at least as far as Claudia is concerned. We've got some free time now and Angela and she stride off in the direction of one of the cafés on the piazza. We've to meet at the panther in 40 minutes. I am really glad that I've been here before as, like Pisa, this has just been the merest of introductions to this fabulous city, its Duomo excepted.

We buy our daily *gelati* and sit down on a projecting wall of the Fonte Gaia to eat them – lemon for Iona, black cherry for me, as usual. We're getting a bit conservative about ice-creams. Must be getting old. Better to stick to what you know and like. Like our marriage, at least one of those is true.

There's not much time to do anything but take in the atmosphere and stroll about, looking at the shops. Iona wants another calendar even although we bought several on our last trip. It's another thing she does - she buys a calendar of every place we've been, for next year, as a souvenir. By the looks of it, she is expecting lots of dates next year. I don't need a calendar.

We make our way up the Via di Citta and as we do so, I am struck by another beautiful building , one which I had not noticed before, but how can that be, since this street is one of the main thoroughfares and we must surely have come this way before? It's built in the same style as the Town Hall, with the same elegant arched windows and crenellated battlements and a tower at the left hand side, though not nearly as tall as the Torre del Mangia. Like the Town Hall, it bends in the middle, following the curve of the street in a graceful arc, but unlike the Town Hall, the bottom two storeys are constructed of white stone, whilst the upper one is of red brick. It's magnificent. Pity the street is so narrow, you can't step back and admire it better. But what is it? A brass plaque provides the answer: Accademia Musicale Chigiana and goes on to say in four languages that the palace cannot be visited. Well, that's logical! Build a beautiful building and ban people. Not to worry, I prefer the outside of such buildings rather than looking at stuffy furniture, but we can at least go into the courtyard.

It's a little gem of a place, one of these occasional serendipitous discoveries that make it all the more worthwhile as no doubt hundreds of people walk past it every day and don't realise what they have missed just yards from the bustling street. There is a stone bench running the full length of the back wall and down the side with two orange trees in massive terracotta pots at each corner providing some greenery and the illusion of being in a garden. There is an ornate well in front of a colonnade facing the back wall.

It's perfect for the restoring of sole-weary shoppers. There's only half a dozen people here and no sound permeates the thick brown walls, even through the wide arch which gives on to the street. On the roof of the colonnade there is a painting like a patchwork quilt executed in vibrant but harmonious colours. Imagine having missed this before! I wonder if any of our fellow tourists will stumble upon it, seeing as we missed it the first time.

It's with a sense of reluctance that we leave and head up the street again. We've not gone far, however, when at the other side of the street I come upon a trio of naked figures rolling about on the floor of an open doorway. No, really they are, except they are twice life size at least and made of some white inflatable material and are moving languidly in response to erratic currents of air and it's not in the least erotic. It's the Palazzo delle Papesse, Museum of Modern Art. Well, what else would you expect?

As we head to our rendezvous with the bus at the Porta San Marco, I in the sun and the rest of the troupe at the other side of the street in the shade, wondering at my madness, when suddenly a louvred window high above my head is flung open, releasing the sound of a female voice screeching in agony as if someone had just plunged a bread-knife into her abdomen. What the hell is going on? Further down the street, from the open window next door there is the sound as of cats having their tails pulled and now the two are combining to form the sort of ear-splitting cacophony that could reduce crystal glasses to splinters at twenty paces and any sane person to a degree of madness beyond the ken of anyone in Siena, or France for that matter. It must be the Academy of Music and these are sopranos limbering up their tonsils, practising their scales. If there's one thing I hate, it's sopranos with their proud voices at full stretch. I hurry on to get out of ear range. And they call that art? I'd rather have the blown-up bare people any day.

*

We're well on the road to Rome now. Since all roads lead to Rome, you would think that Giancarlo could not go wrong, but somewhere along the road he has, because the sun which was on my side of the bus is no longer there and Angela has gone over to stand beside him, scanning the road signs. It looks as if we are heading towards Perugia, in the opposite direction to Rome. My suspicions are confirmed when we come off the road, cross a flyover, and the sun and Angela appear on my side of the bus again. I suppose the corollary is that all roads lead *from* Rome too.

It's incredible how dry the earth is! The ploughed earth looks more like boulders than soil. I suppose this is the colour of burnt sienna that I had in my watercolour paint-box as a boy. I can't imagine how anything can grow here – the parched land is desperately crying out for water. On the other hand, those grapes, ripening on the vines, bursting with sunshine, must make for a vintage crop. I shall say to La-Belle-Dame-Sans-Merci in a year's time: *I'm just taking my vitamins, dear. It's good for me. I just prefer not to take them in pill form.*

The sunflowers – *girasole* in Italian, much more evocative than English, further north, were holding their golden heads up to the sun, but here, as we go south, I notice that their wrinkled heads are hanging heavily, parched, desperate for a drink. Some are burnt black, even.

We pass Orvieto, spectacularly built on a cliff – the sort of place you would love to stop and explore if you were an independent traveller. Angela tells us that it's famous for its sweet white wine. Well, if that's so, I've never heard of it and what's more, they can keep it. I cut my wine teeth on Barsac and Sauternes but would regard them as undrinkable now. I used to be a sweet person in the days when I first met Iona but I've changed - just ask her. A dry, full-bodied red is more to my taste now.

We stop for a break at the ugliest of service stations I have ever seen in my life. I am loitering in the sunshine by the bus, making the most of it, waiting for the stragglers to arrive, when Harriet comes along, eating a *panino*. She knows it's sinful to eat on the bus so she has to finish it before she gets on.

"Isn't it awful?" she says, looking in the direction of the concrete and iron-pillared monstrosity. No doubt, like me, the splendours of Siena are fresh in her mind.

"Well, it was never designed by Michelangelo anyway."

Harriet laughs. "More like a student."

"First year, failed."

Harriet laughs again. My joking skills seem to be improving. But maybe it's just something in the *panino*.

*

Our room in Rome is on the first floor, right above the main entrance. I can see the multi-coloured flags through the brown gauze and brown-tinted windows. It makes the outside look dull and gloomy when in actual fact, it is swelteringly hot and humid. The room looks very comfortable but we're disappointed to be on the first floor – it could be noisy, and I offer to ask for a change, but Iona says just to leave it – she wants food. With regard to that, she's a bit like a grizzly bear and her cub - you don't get between them. And when she says she wants it, she has to have it now and will not be distracted.

Angela says we have a choice, we can either turn left out of the hotel and go straight and we'll come to a posh place, or we can turn left and then left again and we'll come to a good, but cheap *trattoria*. It's not much of a contest.

It would be nice to sit outside but there are not a lot of tables, and they are all occupied, so we are inside, in a sort of corridor which leads to the kitchen, apparently all the room

221

they have left. Not the choicest of tables, but that's probably
a good sign as far as the food is concerned. They certainly
are busy because we have eaten our *coperto* and still we
have not given our order. The wine has arrived though and
I am making steady progress through it or it could just be
evaporating quicker than I can drink it. It's incredibly warm
in here as there's no air-conditioning. Iona is beginning to
look like a prawn.

In due course, Angela arrives and sits alone at a table by
the door. We can't invite her to sit at our table as it's only
for two, but maybe we should invite ourselves over to her
table. Iona vetoes it in spite of the fact that it's nearer the
door and must be cooler.

"No, it's her time off. Leave her alone. She doesn't want
to listen to your jokes or weird sense of humour. Give her
a break."

It's all right for Iona as she can't see her as she has her
back to her, but I keep catching her eye and it seems a bit
rude to let someone you know eat on their own, even if
the price you have to pay is to listen to my patter. But she
lights up a cigarette and I decide she's better off without my
scintillating conversation after all.

The service is so slow that we decide that in order to
save a couple of hours, we will just have *primos* because in
the romantic Eternal City, the city for lovers, Iona wants to
get out of here and get back to the hotel. We've not been here
together before, unless you count the airport 30 years ago,
which I don't, but I know better than to get my hopes up - it's
got nothing to do with adding to her list of consummated
places. She is sweating as much sweat as an elephant would
sweat if an elephant does sweat sweat. The hair at the nape
of her neck is soaking and I don't know about her, but I can
feel a rivulet of sweat trickling between my 38Bs. She just
wants to get out of here. In the first instance, the street has
to be cooler than this and that will sustain her till we reach

the sanctuary of our air-conditioned room. She's lucky that she doesn't have stays and the other restricting clothes ladies wore in the days of the Grand Tour, to say nothing of not having flush toilets and showers.

"I'll just order another bottle of wine shall I?"

The service has been so slow, that I have got through most of the wine before the *primo* arrived and there's barely enough left to have with the meal.

"No you will not! You don't need it!"

"But I do need it! I've got hardly any left to have with my food."

"Well, you shouldn't have drunk it all before the food arrived."

"I needed something to do. The service was so bloody slow. If the service hadn't been so slow, I wouldn't –"

"Oh, all right! Have some of mine!" She splashes a thimbleful into my glass. "But you're not getting any more!" She knits her brows and glowers balefully at me across the table.

"*Ja wohl*, Frau Ning!" I refrain from giving the Nazi salute in this public place as I usually do at home.

She's in a bad mood because she is so hot and doesn't want me to prolong the dining experience by drinking another bottle of wine. It wouldn't do any good to tell her I could drink it pretty fast.

We have a general rule, Iona and I, that if, in a restaurant, there is a seat which faces a wall or very few other diners, that I sit in the less sterile environment so I can observe what's going on. I call myself an observer of human nature. She calls me plain bloody nosy. Anyway, that is why I can see, but she can't, that the very fat man sitting behind her has called the waiter over and he is making some sort of request.

The waiter comes back and gives the fat man a tin of baby powder. I'm not exactly familiar with what baby powder looks like in this country, but that's what it looks like as it's the same shape and size with the sort of top that you twist to open the perforations. The fat man takes it and I can't see what he's doing with it, but it looks as if he is opening up his shirt and dusting himself with it. Right enough, if the sweat is dropping off my bosoms in tiny rivulets, he must be getting a tidal wave with the size of his. But just to open your shirt up and do it in public! Even I, whom Iona occasionally calls a boor, wouldn't do that. And imagine the restaurant just happening to have it handy! Presumably people must ask for it all the time and certainly the waiter just handed it to him as if he'd asked for nothing more extraordinary than the bill. What next? Will he open up his flies and dust in there? Perhaps it's a pesticide and he's trying to kill little creepy-crawlies.

He's finished with it and the waiter picks up the baby powder, casually, in the passing. When in Rome...It's not often you can say that and literally mean it. Maybe I should ask for it too. I could certainly use it and Iona looks as if she'd soak up a whole tin. It's so hot in here, perhaps it's the way this non air-conditioned restaurant deals with the perspiration problems of its clientele, or maybe he's just a sweaty regular and he always asks for it: *The usual, sir! Certainly sir! No sweat!*

Anyway, it gives Frau Ning and me something to speculate about and intrigues me enough so it stops me from sulking about the wine I'm not allowed.

As we leave, we pass Angela's table. She would have been in a perfect position to have seen what was going on, besides it makes a suitable conversation topic as I still feel we should perhaps have asked if she wanted us to join her. But how would we have known if she was merely being polite or not? She probably would have said yes when she really meant: *Look! I'm with you bloody tourists practically the whole bloody day, so why don't you sod off and leave me alone! Especially you, who walks alone on the sunny side of the street.*

After the niceties, and about how hot and humid it is in here, I say, "Did you see that man with the talcum powder? What was he doing with it?"

"It's a stain remover. He spilt his wine. The powder soaks up the wine."

"Ah, yes, I thought so."

As we stroll back to the hotel in the muggy Roman evening, I am so glad I hadn't told Angela what I really thought he had been doing. Of course I should have guessed. I have often done the same trick myself with salt on a table-cloth but always found it more efficacious when I spilt red wine (as I was prone to do) on a lady's white blouse at the parties we used to throw in the days of our relative youth, to pour white wine on top and rub it in. In fact, I used to think it wasn't really a waste of wine to use it in this sort of way, nor to spill it. Of course, being a gentleman, in spite of what Iona thinks, I am not a complete boor - I made sure that when I rubbed the white wine in that I put my hand between the blouse and the lady and you know, it really does work because I never had a complaint about a stained blouse, ever.

So, this will be my first night in Rome. The hub of the Roman Empire. The city for lovers. Or is that Paris? Anyway, tomorrow will be an exciting day, but best of all, I won't have to get up until 8am. What bliss, regardless of what ever happens in what's left of this sweltering, sultry evening.

Chapter 7
Con Romani Antico

"Get up you lazy, pot-bellied Vietnamese pig!"

The not so dulcet tones of La-Belle-Dame-Sans-Merci really mean business this time. She's got nothing against the Vietnamese, nor pot-bellied pigs as a species either. It's just me. It's the third time of asking. She whips the single sheet off the bed, all we need in this air-conditioned cocoon and all I need is a few more precious minutes in bed but that is impossible, with her hovering over me with Humphrey the Hedgehog hairbrush poised like a cloud of mosquitoes with their proboscises or whatever they jab into you ready to strike, so like the dwarfs in the bed who were feeling happy till Happy got out, and then felt Grumpy, I roll out of bed feeling decidedly grumpy myself. Of course I want to explore Rome, but this is meant to be a holiday and I want to do it in my time, in a few hours, not now at the crack of 8am.

The brown gauze and tinted-brown windows makes the weather look decidedly gloomy. Wait a minute though - the weather *really is* gloomy. I don't see any blue clouds and yes, surely those cars have their wipers working and the street looks wet. I wrestle with the gauze curtains to get at the handle of the window and when I open it, I see why we had a quiet night, not a single Vespa or tooting horn disturbing our slumbers: the double-glazing must be three inches thick! The sound of traffic floods into the room. And it *is* raining! For the first time in months, it is raining in Italy!

"Would you just look at this," I call over my shoulder to Iona who is busy at the mirror with Humphrey's primary use. "The weather's just like how I feel this morning."

"What? Bloody miserable?"

"That's what I'm saying! It's raining!" Well I asked for it of course, bringing up Ruskin's pathetic fallacy at this time in the morning, though it is not a fallacy that it was a pathetic attempt at levity at this disappointing turn of events.

The gods, however, are enjoying another of their little jokes: *Watch this! We'll teach him to wander about Italy in swimming trunks! We'll make him roam round Rome in the rain. That'll show him! He's going to need them today, heh! heh! heh! By the way, nice pun and alliteration eh?*

By the time we have finished breakfast, and gathered in the foyer, it has stopped raining. I had gone outside earlier to gauge how hard it was. Not hard Scottish rain, but soft, gentle, warm drizzling Italian rain but which nevertheless would still get us plenty wet if we were out in it all day as we are to be. But can we trust it to stay off? Probably not. Can't afford to risk it which means we're going to be lumbered with humphing our raingear about all day. Then I am struck by an idea which is quite good for me, considering the brain is in first gear still at this ghastly hour. I roll my waterproof jacket up as tightly as I can and stealing up behind Iona who is talking to Pat, I unzip her little rucksack which has the zips conveniently placed for pickpockets. But pick-pocketing or unzipping ladies' bags, or undoing other articles of attire belonging to ladies is, for want of practice, another of the social skills in which I am lacking.

She swings round. "What do you think you're doing?"

"Just putting my jacket in your bag, love of my life. It doesn't weigh very much."

She doesn't want to make a fuss in front of Pat and the others. I'm a burden to her, but today she can be my beast of burden.

Angela is counting us. Gordon, who is near a pillar, slips out of sight behind it, keeping it between him and Angela, then steps out behind her as she passes the pillar. Angela cannot make us add up to 18. You can see her looking perplexed as if she'd counted us before but now one of us is missing, but whom? I feel sorry for her. Gordon is only clowning but I know what it's like to organize a bunch of brats and have one of them go missing, so I shout out in pantomime style: *He's behind you!* and some others take up the refrain. Gordon puts on an act like a scolded schoolboy. After his successful joke yesterday, he's apparently appointed himself group clown.

We had given Angela money last night and now she hands out tickets for the bus and metro. She explains that these are for two days and we must validate them when we board the bus. Yes, nice of you to tell us, but I know that now, after my confrontation with the bus inspectors in Nice.

Like a general, Angela marches us past the *trattoria* where we were last night to the bus stop. We must all get on the bus, no matter how crowded it is. Not for the first time, I wonder how she will possibly manage next week with 42. That's a busload on its own.

"It was so much fun in Pisa that we're going to do it again!" I say darkly to Tom, Dick and Harriet and to anyone within earshot, generally.

"You would have thought they would have hired a mini-bus," says Harriet.

"Not Italian logic," I reply. "Besides, it's more fun this way."

And it is. How else can you get to stand welded to a lovely Latin lady without being arrested? But I am not of course. When I struggle onto the bus at last, I find my closest travelling companion looks as if he's about to give birth to twins and had something horrendously garlicky for his tea last night. The sweat is running down his sideboards and his armpits are a dark pool of colour. Thank God there is no smell – at least not that I notice, but maybe that's thanks to the knock-out garlic and my smelling skills being a bit sub-standard, as an inhaler I mean, not a perpetrator.

It's impossible to move, so we pass our tickets by a Houdini sort of manoeuvre to Donald, the male half of the other Scottish couple who happens to have landed next to the validating machine and like a chain of fire-fighters passing a bucket, we pass our tickets up and down the line.

At long last we arrive at the terminus, I am separated from my garlic-eating Siamese twin and we scuttle through the ranks of buses in Angela's wake before burrowing into the Metro. It's a lot less complicated than London or Paris as it has only two lines – A and B. We're taking the B train. As everywhere, you have to put your ticket in a slot to turn the arms of a stile, but when I push the arm with my stomach, it refuses to budge and my ticket is gone. What's wrong with it? Everyone else before me with far lesser stomachs was passing through effortlessly. Iona, who was in a different line, is already at the other side. I can sense the hostile stares and impatience of commuters behind me. Although at this time in the morning, the rush hour should be over, you wouldn't think it with the press of people trying to get through this bottleneck. I feel tempted to jump over the turnstile but like Macbeth, I prevaricate. It would be easy if o'er leaping this barrier were all; but in all probability, there is the hereafter, which in this case would be the fine. Probably there are cameras trained on this site and I'm going to appear on the Italian equivalent of *You've been Framed* in due course or maybe they've a programme called *Lunatics at Large*. Just then my ticket pops out of the machine again. I take it with relief and abandon the queue with an expression which I hope others will interpret as a *I-don't-like- this-machine* sort of look. I get into the queue for the turnstile on my right and this time there is no problem as my ticket is validated and I pass through.

"What on earth were you playing about at?" snaps La-Belle-Dame-Sans-Merci who has been loitering not so patiently for me. "Come on, hurry up! The others are far ahead."

"Bloody machine wouldn't work."

"Did you put it in the right way?" she asks as we scamper after the others.

"What do you mean - right way?"

"With the magnetic strip down."

What magnetic strip? I'd never bothered to look at it. "Course I did! Bloody machine just didn't like me."

She probably doesn't believe me but she's more concerned with horsing after the others and shortly, in even shorter breath, we catch up with them. If we don't all make it aboard the train, Angela is saying, we are to get off at Colosseo.

"Colosseo," she says again, making it sound like New York, New York and us like mentally retarded Neanderthals. Or maybe it's just for my benefit. Anyone who can't work a turnstile is quite liable to get lost. Unless his wife is looking after him of course.

What we're meant to do when we get there if we do get separated, she doesn't say, but I assume she's got that covered. Whilst we are waiting for the train, I get in conversation with the attractive Asian girl and her family. Because we are talking about the horrendous bus journey, I regale them about my Nice adventure with the unvalidated tickets. I have Usha's undivided attention, like a third year pupil hanging on every irrelevant word. Funny how pupils listen to the peripheral, rather than the substance.

We all squeeze onto the blue train and make our way, on arrival, through labyrinthine passages until we emerge into the open air and beneath the woolly white clouds and blue skies above the ruin that is the Colosseum. Whilst we have been down below, the grey skies have disappeared and it is already very warm. I doubt if we'll need the rainwear today after all. Thank God for Iona's backpack.

Angela is waiting for us with our guide who is carrying a car aerial with a bit of material tied to the end of it, no doubt so we can receive her commentary better. The area round the Colosseum is throbbing with noise and heaving with people. There are touts trying to sell postcards, a good deal - only €1 for 24, even if some are rubbish, I don't know 24 people to whom I would send a postcard, so I am bound to find some in that lot that I could send to those I do. I wish I hadn't bought so many in Florence at 45 cents each. There's a red and a blue pack. I might even blow the bank and buy one of each.

There are some men dressed as Roman soldiers with leather breastplates and helmets with bright red plumes on the top and carrying a sword. I approve of their sandals without socks – who would want to have their photo taken with a Roman soldier wearing socks! They are sweating already with the warmth of their garments and the heat of the sun. What a way to earn a living! But it gives me an idea. Maybe, if the pension does not stretch so far in future years, I could don the swimming trunks and shirt of Lincoln green and hang about Nottingham city centre with a bow and quiver full of arrows whilst Iona, dressed in a bikini made of a spray of oak leaves, leaving little to the imagination, passed a hat around. But I already see a handicap – the English climate would give the scantily clad Iona goose pimples. Mind you, that would be OK at the world famous Goose Fair. Hmm! Maybe.

Yole is our guide for today and tomorrow. She takes us over to stand beneath the broken wall of the Colosseum and a man selling books like the ones we saw in Pompeii with the transparent overlays, hands her one and retreats into the background whilst she explains the Colosseum to us. He will certainly pounce when Yole is finished. They have obviously done this before. I don't mind though. For once, I throw caution to the winds. I decide to buy one and I haven't even seen it yet.

So Yole gives us the razzmatazz about the Colosseum; after the Leaning Tower of Pisa, I imagine Italy's next best known icon and certainly Rome's best known. Although it's big, it's not called the Colosseum because of its size; it's probably more to do with a colossal statue of that fiddle-playing megalomaniac, Nero, which stood near the site. It was originally known as the Flavian ampitheatre. The Colosseum itself stands on the site of a lake which was in the grounds of Nero's palace. It was begun by the Emperor Vespasian in AD 72 to make his mark. Just like a dog I reflect, marking out his territory, extinguishing the traces of the previous incumbent.

It took only 8 years to build and was inaugurated by Vespasian's son, Titus, the next emperor, so the Colosseum became the monument to the Flavian dynasty and a pretty nasty lot they were too. Lots of people and animals had to die nastily in the course of their political shenanigans and to satisfy the Roman bloodlust. Apparently there were 100 days of games when the amphitheatre was first opened and 9000 animals perished.

Yole tells us to look at the architecture. It has three storeys of arches and a top storey of marble with square windows. The arches have Doric columns at the bottom, Ionic in the middle and Corinthian at the top, logically following the architectural development of the classical pillar. My favourite is the feminine Ionic, naturally. It's an impressive building, even today, although it has been knocked about a bit by the ravages of time, but more particularly by subsequent generations of cultural vandals who looted it for building material.

The stadium could seat 55,000 people, Yole says, and they could enter and clear the stadium in minutes through the 80 arched entrances.

"If you look carefully," says Yole, "you can see the number above each arch. The spectators had wooden tags which told them which entrance to use and which seat they were in."

True enough, you can – XL is just behind us.

"Is that for the extra large people?" I remark wittily.

Yole freezes me with a Gorgon stare. I don't believe it! I've done it again. Yole is big: not so fat that if she had a caravan, she'd have to go in sideways, nor is she the stereotype of the Italian Mamma either, but she has enough flesh to make one of Raphael's cherubs look anorexic. She plainly thinks I'm being fattist. Well, maybe I am fattist, but I never meant my remark to be a snide comment on her physique. I hope her husband is not in the Mafia.

"That was *my* joke," she says in a tone which I don't know if she's joking or not.

"Oh, er..oops! Sorry!"

"The spectators were ranked according to class," she continues, unfixing her stare and to my relief, ignoring me. "Naturally the emperor had the best seat in the house and the commoners and women were furthest away from the action. And of course, entrance was free."

If I had attended the games, and I'm not sure that I would - they probably would have said to me: *Come on you miserable little wimp! Christians versus lions today. Should be a good laugh! What's the matter with you? Are you an animal lover or something?* I know I'd want to be as far away from the action as possible. I'd probably be a commoner anyway, if I weren't a slave, but that would suit me as I have read Ovid's erotic verse and he's always banging on about what a good place the games are for picking up women.

That's what I'd be doing: eyeing up the talent in togas and avoiding as much of the bloodbath as possible.

"There was an awning called the *velarium* which they used to keep the sun off the spectators. You can see the holes where the poles used to be up there." I knew about the *velarium* before as I'd seen a TV programme about it, but try as I can, I can't see the holes to which she is referring. I wouldn't have wanted it anyway. I would have wanted a seat in the sun. If ever I go to a bullfight in Spain, like if ever I am given the choice of having my toenails pulled out one by one or being hung from a tree by the gonads, or going to a bullfight, then you'll see me there and I'll be the one in the cheapest seat in the *Sol*, not because I'm one mean hombre but because I'd rather be in the *Sol* than the *Ombre*. I'll probably be wearing swimming trunks of Lincoln green or dazzling yellow and I'll have a Panama hat on, so if you see me, say hello and how much you enjoyed my book and I will allow you to buy me a beer.

We are not going into the Colosseum however. I had not expected it, though some of my fellow travellers are disappointed. We have some free time, but I doubt if we will go there, as there is so much else to see and we are seasoned Roman amphitheatre goers, having been not only to Nîmes and Arles, but also El Djem in Tunisia, and which, like God with people, are all variations on a theme.

Yole is going to take us to the Forum next, along the Via Sacra. "And in order to do so," she says, "we will pass before that arch over there."

It's the Arch of Constantine, the first Christian Roman emperor. Yole tells us that the medallions and statues are pillaged from other monuments and the whole thing is a bit of a hotchpotch. I would never have guessed, I don't think. It looks good enough to me, allowing for the ravages of time. The main central arch is flanked by two smaller ones and there are four statues on top of the four pillars between the arches.

"In the film, *Cleopatra*," says Yole, " Elizabeth Taylor made her entry into Rome through that arch, though it wasn't there then. But of course, the film makers do not bother about that sort of thing!"

Well, that's very true. I wonder how many Scots now believe William Wallace wore woad and accept everything else in *Braveheart* as gospel.

I know Constantine lived in the 4th century AD and Cleopatra at the end of the 1st century BC. It's as if Columbus, arriving in America, found the Civil War over, Lincoln assassinated and Alaska had been bought and paid for from Russia and had joined the Union! But as far as Hollywood is concerned, you don't spoil a good story or a good image by sticking strictly to the facts.

As we pass the Arch, I can see that on the side there is a medallion in perfidious porphyry, enough to condemn it in my eyes forever. Apart from that, however, it looks well enough executed to me. I can see that over the central arch there is a whole lot of writing which doubtlessly says how wonderful Constantine is and between the statues on the pediment there are two panels featuring a whole lot of figures too miniature at this distance to see what they are doing and that the bases of the pillars at either side of the arches rest upon panels of carved figures also. Well, it may be a conglomeration from all over the empire but it looks like a perfectly balanced and symmetrical structure to me. If I knew more about it, probably I'd detect a clash of styles in the carvings which would annoy the purists, but for an architectural ignoramus like me, I am well satisfied with the overall effect.

Now we are on the Via Sacra, on the original Roman road that leads from the Colosseum at the bottom, to the Arch of Titus at the top, which in its turn, stands at one end of the Forum. On our left is the Palatine hill, the snobby part of town in Augustus' day. It's the Palatine, which gives us our word palace. Augustus was born and lived here in a relatively modest house, compared to his successors at least, and so did his wife, Livia, who had a separate wing all to herself. From what I know of Livia, I'd have lived in a separate house from her as well, though that still would have been a bit close. The secret of a successful marriage, Roman style – build your wife a wing of her own, though in my case, it'll be me who moves - to the garden shed. I won't find it too much of a change as I am usually in the doghouse.

Tiberius also lived here but he built a massive palace probably rendering tons of toga-ed toffs homeless and among other famous residents were Cicero and the poet Catullus. It's allegedly on the Palatine that the she wolf looked after Romulus and Remus and it's certainly true that archaeologists have found traces of an Iron Age settlement there, so it's probably historically true that this is where Rome started. I'd like to go there; it looks invitingly green but that also will have to be for another time.

On the way to the Forum, a funny thing happens to me. I'm not just saying this for show - it really does! As we puff our way up the Via Sacra, I find myself in step with Usha.

"Get out of school early? Took a few days off, eh?" I say in what I take to be a playful sort of bantering, teasing tone. I know that when the trip started the English schools, which have their holidays much later than Scotland, would not have yet broken up and her accent makes her undoubtedly from the south of England.

She looks at me suspiciously from under the brim of her floppy lilac hat.

"What do you mean?" she says politely enough, but plainly puzzled.

What does she mean, what do I mean? I feel fear clutch at my heart. I have a horrible feeling that I've done it again.

I don't know how I do it or what I've done this time. Perhaps she's slighted by the inference that she's been dogging school. Maybe her authority finished a few days earlier than the rest. I know that in my experience, by and large, the Asian pupils were the most fastidious, the most polite, the most hard-working. Give me a class of them I used to say.

It's time for another spot of quick thinking, but this time the brain is in shock. I just don't know what to say. I wish I had never started making polite conversation with her. Her parents are on her other side. What if they think I am a paedophile or something?

"Er...em. I just wondered if you'd stopped early. That's all," I add lamely. Oh, God, I feel such a bloody fool.

"No, I've just sat my exams."

That's right, so she would...if she were 5th year or 6th year. But third year?

"Exams?" I hear myself say, gradually groping myopically towards the light, a faint glimmer of which I can see at the end of a very dark tunnel indeed.

"Yes. I'm at vet school. I've just finished my exams," she adds somewhat unnecessarily.

"What year?" It may be ungrammatical, but it's all I can think of to say.

"Just finished second. Hope to go into third," she smiles in a most beguiling manner. It looks as if she has forgiven me for my earlier solecism.

"Aaah!" I say as if that explains all, which it does. But that means that she must be at least 21, assuming she did not have a gap year as they tend to do these days. And I thought she was 14 at the most! She must have the gift of eternal youth or I am a stupid, blind, old git who prides himself as an observer of human nature but who can't even get within ten years of a person's age. But which?

"You know, when I said school just now, I hope you didn't think that I meant you were still at school!" I laugh in suppressed chortling at the very notion of such an outrageous idea.

Her brown almond eyes flash me a look, a look like the one we'd had at the beginning of the conversation. I was in a hole and instead of stopping digging, I had just dug deeper. It wouldn't have said it but for her eyes. They captivate me. I am so keen to make a good impression, I have opened my big mouth and have just ruined all. If she hadn't already guessed, she certainly knows the truth now.

"It's just that when I was in America, I got used to calling university school, as I taught in a school and it certainly wasn't a university!" I laugh hollowly at my own joke. I know if she has the brains to go to vet school, she's not going to be convinced by this pathetic explanation. In fact, I feel limp with the woefulness of it all, and just want to hurry on as I know if I had stayed silent it might have passed for a mild attack of idiocy, but now I had put my lunacy beyond all reasonable doubt.

"I'd better go and see if Iona needs any water. It's very hot today, don't you think?"

It is a rhetorical question. I stride ahead and whether true or not, I feel Usha's and her parents' eyes boring into the back of my neck and, even in this heat, I break out into a cold sweat. It's all Iona's fault. Why does she have to go horsing on, leaving me to make conversation with other people?

We're in the shade of some trees near the Arch of Titus, the son of Vespasian, whilst Yole tells us all this and about the Arch and the Forum which we are about to see. Some lucky people have found some ruins to sit on, others like me, are shifting weight from foot to foot and their eyes are beginning to glaze over.

At the top of Titus' arch I can read the first line of the legend SENATVS and, beneath it, all run into one POPVLVSQVEROMANVS, beneath which there are two more lines of block capitals. It would help to read the writing on the monuments if they didn't run the words together like that and used a U instead of a V like sensible people. This one of course, I do know and it gives me a slight *frisson* down my spine: The Senate and the People of Rome. How many times had I read that in my Latin grammar or history textbook and how many ancient Romans had actually read these very words? Yole tells us that these words, or rather the initials SPQR can be seen all over modern Rome today on all sorts of things, from manhole covers to bus timetables on bus shelters.

The arch was built in AD81 by the Emperor Domitian, the brother of Titus, sons of Vespasian, to commemorate Titus' apotheosis. I suppose being the son of a god, you must have a good chance of being a god yourself. As he lay dying, Vespasian is said to have said: *I think I shall be a god soon.* Ironic having to die before you can be immortal. Being a god now, Titus could look down on it and see that it was good. Well, I think he would think it was good anyway. It's not covered with carvings on the outside as Constantine's, but there are a couple of panels on each side of the interior and the inside of the roof is intricately carved with coffered panels of rosettes in high relief with a big central panel on the top which depicts Titus being carried off to heaven. What I find more intriguing, however, is the marks of cart wheels on the sides of the arch from generations of traffic, which also serve as an indicator of how much the level of the ground has sunk, for now, the striped layers of the foundations are completely exposed, so that when I stand next to them, they come up to my shoulder. Like most of the world's most tiresome people, I am vertically challenged. The foundations might just come to the waist of normal sized people, but at a rough guess, I reckon they must be nearly five feet above ground now.

Looking through the arch in the direction we have just come, the Colosseum rises like a broken giant cotton reel at the bottom of the Via Sacra and when we turn our backs to the Arch, there lies the Forum. I've been all over Europe, visiting Roman temples and monuments, aqueducts and viaducts, and here, at last, from this elevated vantage point, I am gazing at the hub of the empire, which at that time, was the largest empire that the world had ever known - and it's one great big messy disappointment. Here a wall, there another more dilapidated; here a column, there a cluster of them; an arch before us, an arch behind us, a modern looking building without pillars over there, another, nearer, with pillars the way a Roman temple *should* look. Just how do you begin to make sense of all these ruins? There's just too much to take in, too many centuries, too much history in too little space.

The sun is blistering now and the air is thrumming to the beat of the cicadas' wings or back legs, whatever they use to produce that evocative sound which always makes me feel hotter, as if the air is vibrating with heat. You never would have thought that it had been overcast and raining, not even a couple of hours ago, and that Iona needed to pack my raingear.

We had been standing near Titus' arch and now we have to stand again, whilst Yole tries to explain the extensive ruins before us. The truth is, hanging about listening is more tiring than walking and I feel defeated before she even begins. She's giving us a general picture; we are not going to go down there and walk among the ruins as I'd like to do. Although I am not the boss, I'm sure we'll come back here with our guidebook and walk around at our own pace. After all, it is free! So it's really with half an ear only that I listen to Yole's exposition. By the looks on the faces of my companions, they feel the same. Some have even wandered out of earshot, perching on pieces of stone, even if they are in the sun, just to take the weight off their feet. I stay and listen, but hope she is not going to give us a test when she's finished.

On our right is the Basilica of Constantine. It looks as if a complete side has been removed like a doll's house, to reveal three monumental arches, through which I can see right through to the other side where there are windows consisting of three arches which seem to be perfectly framed in the absolutely immense outer arches. The figure three seems to be salient figure, for Yole tells us that in the 4th century it was three times as large as we see it now. Bloody hell, it must have been big then, because it's big enough now. It had to be big though because it housed an enormous thirty-foot high statue of Constantine of which the head, a foot and hand with a pointing finger are still extant. It would have to be a big statue though, if it were to be in proportion to his swollen head.

Next there is the circular 4th Century Tempio di Romolo according to a stone plaque attached for the moment to a very battered wall. It is now part of the church of Santi Cosma e Damiano. It's not on the itinerary; anyway, the big green bronze doors framed by the purple pillars are firmly shut. Like the Church of St Mary in Assisi, formerly the Temple of Minerva, it no doubt owes its existence to being adapted for the new religion, which is certainly the case in the next building we come to, the Church of San Lorenzo in Miranda, formerly the Temple of Antoninus and Faustina, though they did their best to destroy it. You can see grooves cut into the tops of the columns to stop the slipping of the ropes with which they tried to pull the structure down. Great curved steps lead up to a portico of six columns plus a further two to the side. The scale truly is amazing but what's more astonishing is the way that the upper part of the Renaissance church just grows out of and towers over this frame. The façade has two great horns at the top and a central window beneath, so it looks for all the world like the sort of cow

Picasso might have painted looking over the bars of a pen: *Moo! Will somebody get me out of here! I've been here for four centuries, for God's sake! Has nobody in this country heard of European Legislation on Animal Rights? Moo, I forgot. I am in Italy. Moooo!* It's the most bizarre building I've seen since the Pompidou Centre in Paris.

Across the Via Sacra is the Temple of Vesta. I prick up my ears because although it looks as if it would have been one of the more interesting buildings on the Forum, I am more interested in the lives of the virgins. I remember them well from school. The Vestal ones I mean. I know already that their duty was to keep the sacred flame alive and that if it went out, Rome might fall. Looks like someone did let the fire go out. There are only a few columns remaining now, just enough to give the hint of a curve to show it was a circular building, appropriately enough for these nubile nymphs. There were only six of them at any one time and as their name implies, part of the job required them to remain virgins. If they did not, they were buried alive and their partner flogged to death. Yole says there were ten known cases of this happening.

They were of noble birth and the job lasted for 30 years. They were about 10, most of them, when they began their duties, 10 years learning the job (what – keeping a fire going!) 10 years practising and 10 years teaching the new girls. They'd be over 40 when they got out, even I can calculate that. I reckon they probably remained virgins. Why change the habits of a lifetime and anyway, probably at 40 you were considered an old woman in Roman times. Mind you, there were perks for all the fun at the baths and those orgies they were missing. They lived in luxurious accommodation but since their old man was well off anyway, that doesn't sound such a big deal to me and they got the best seat in the house, next to the Emperor at the Games. Even bigger deal. I'd have given my ticket away. Best bit sounds the job – just poking a fire all day. I could do that, sitting around in front of the fire all day. Trouble is, if you let it go out you were whipped and then lost your job. Maybe some did that deliberately so they could meet an old flame, maybe someone they got off with at the Games, one of those gladiators perhaps with the Schwarzenegger torsos. But for me, all things considered, I don't think I would have liked the job. I'd just have put up with the sex. It's not much fun poking your own fire all day.

We're still on the subject of heavenly bodies, though it is only a fantasy of mine that the Vestals were gorgeous young ladies clad in diaphanous togas capering about the sacred flame. Maybe their daddies looked at them and said: *By Jupiter, you look a bit like your mother but are you sure your father wasn't the slave because you aren't half ugly! I'll never get rid of you! Dirty togas on the bathroom floor forever and your bedroom as if a barbarian had burgled it! You're destined to be a Virgin my girl! Besides, if some dirty gold-digger does come along, I won't have the expense of a wedding.*

We're looking at the Temple of Castor and Pollux, of which only three fluted Corinthian columns remain, standing defiantly, but probably reconstructed. There was a temple here in 484 BC, the oldest in the Forum, but what we are looking at dates from the time of Augustus, nearly 500 years later. That's the trouble with the Forum, it kept burning down (probably some Virgin asleep on the job) and kept on being reconstructed, so it's even harder to visualise what it might have looked like at any given period of time. The temple commemorates the intervention of the heavenly twins, who, at the battle of Lake Regillus in 499 BC, led the Romans to victory over the Tarquins. That's what you need in a battle- a vision of a heavenly body, and two, even better. Makes a man fight harder.

At the far end of the Forum is the Arch of Septimus Sevirus. This was built by his sons, Caracalla and Geta to commemorate their father's victory over the Parthians, what we today would call Iraqis. Overcoming their bashfulness, they included their names, along with their emperor father's at the top of the monument, but Caracalla murdered his brother and expunged his name. We are too far away to see it of course, but you can still see where the holes are where Geta's name once was. Another charming, self-effacing, Roman family.

In front and to the left of it, is a very modern looking building with a solitary window ridiculously high on the wall of brown stone facing us. This is none other than the Curia, or Senate House. If it looks modern, that's because it is. It dates from 1937! It's a reconstruction of the original Diocletian Senate House, from the 3rd century AD, which itself is a replacement for the original Senate which was ordered to be rebuilt on this site by the orders of Julius Caesar, no less. It was being built when Caesar was assassinated, so this is not where it happened. Pity. That would have been a good place to go and stand and say: *Et tu, Brute!*

Well that was our overview of the Forum, as now Yole is leading us out of it by a path through the inevitable scaffolding. We emerge onto a broad boulevard, the Via dei Fori Imperiali. At the far end, to our right, is the Colosseum and to our left, we can just see the top of Trajan's column. We turn to the left, and under a statue to Julius Caesar, where there is some shade and some seating for those who had kept up with Yole, but not me, who, like Wordsworth has lingered to look and imagine in solitude, and has had to gallop to keep up.

Yole tries to tell us over the roar of the traffic on the Via dei Fori Imperiali about the extension to the Forum and Trajan's column. They may be extensions of emperors' egos but they were also for the benefit of the Roman citizens

244

whose numbers were expanding in pace with the burgeoning empire. The column is not on our itinerary, but says Yole, we will get a better look at it on our way past, but not close enough to see the detail of the carvings which spiral round the shaft of the column. She says that that was all that previous groups had wanted to see; there was some television programme about it apparently. She looks relieved that she doesn't have to shepherd us across Via dei Fori Imperiali and that the fuss about the column has apparently died down.

The carvings commemorate Trajan's victories over the Dacians, which we call Romania now and are apparently a very rich source of Roman military tactics and warfare. It is 131 feet high, the same height as the spur of the Quirinal hill which was excavated to make room for the Forum. That's an awful lot of earth to move, but they also moved heaven for Trajan.

The story is that Trajan died in AD 117 and his ashes placed in a golden urn at the base of the column which is hollow. You can climb to the top if you want or if your guide will let you. Pope Gregory the Great, seeing a panel on the column where Trajan was helping the mother of a son who had been killed, prayed to God to release Trajan from hell. (He was there undoubtedly as he was not a Christian.) And God said: *OK, just this once, but no more praying for pagans, all right, Greg!* And, even stranger to relate, when they disinterred Trajan's ashes, his tongue was still intact and told of his release from hell and ascent to heaven!

To be honest, there is something about this tale which doesn't quite ring true, which is a bit hard to swallow. In actual fact, Trajan was buried with his wife, Plotina and I bet it was really *her* tongue. Sounds much more plausible to me that a woman would keep rabbiting on than a bloke, even if he were emperor, after all that time of enforced silence. Anyway, it's thanks to this miracle that the pagan column was spared and the surrounding ground actually became holy ground. In fact, Trajan's statue survived on the top until 1587 when it was replaced by one of St Peter.

At the other side of the road is Trajan's Forum and Market and we are not going to waste time waiting for the traffic to stop at the zebra crossing or dice with death either, to go and look at it. We can however, see across the track of death, behind a statue of Augustus, two tiers of arches in a semi-circular red brick building. This Forum, as well as containing as you might expect, temples, also had Greek and Latin libraries. But what probably pleased the ladies most on the site, was not Trajan's column, but a shopping mall consisting of over 150 shops, selling goods such as fruit and flowers, oil and wine, pepper and other spices and a whole range of exotic goods from all over the empire: *I'm just popping down to Trajan's market for some of that firewater from North Britannia dearest...I know it's horrible my love, but it does keep the cold out and it's good for my rheumatism and while I'm at it, will I get you a treat, something special for tea, one of their delicacies, a haggis and maybe some neeps? We could have a North Britannia theme night.*

So that's another thing the Romans gave us. The delights of shopping malls. Thank you very much, Trajan. Thank you very much indeed.

On our side of the racing track is the Forum of Caesar. There's not much to see now apart from some rubble and three columns of the temple to the goddess Venus Genetrix built by Caesar in thanks for his victory over Pompey in 48BC. (He also thought he was a descendant of hers, so she was his granny or great-granny or something. Hmm! Maybe she did look like a goddess in her salad days, but that was before Caesar's time, so how did he know?) To build this and the other structures on the new Forum, part of the Capitoline hill had to be levelled. Talk about moving mountains! No wonder you don't have to be numerically challenged to have difficulty counting the seven hills of Rome if that's what they did to them.

Augustus extended Caesar's Forum to celebrate *his* victory over Caesar's assassins, Brutus and Cassius at Philippi in 42 BC. There's not much to see of this either. The focal point here is the Temple of Mars of which there are just four columns remaining. The statue of Mars in the temple looked very like Augustus and just in case anyone failed to get the point, there was a statue of Augustus nearby. It makes me think of William Wallace and his phallic monument near Stirling and the new statue of him at the bottom which looks uncannily like Mel Gibson. I suppose since we don't know what he looked like, he may as well look like Mel. Better than looking like me and better looking than me if you remember whom I look like, but I wouldn't mind betting there are lots of people think he *did* look like that, because they saw his film and he did look just like that!

Most of the Forum of Augustus is under the Via dei Fori Imperiali. Nothing is sacred, nothing new under the sun, *plus ça change, plus c'est la meme chose*. Mussolini built this road through and over the ruins, trampling centuries of civilisation underfoot, in order to hold his military parades as if to stamp his authority on the past to show he was superior to them all. It was his Via Sacra, built for his own glorification, just like the Via Sacra witnessed all those military parades after the acquisition of a new country to the empire. So does this road, which, significantly, doesn't even have his name, commemorate any victories? It should really be the shortest street in all Italy. And for this, he wiped out two thousand years of history! No wonder the Italians don't give it his name.

It *is* busy though and Yole has to shout to make herself heard over the traffic and the statue of Augustus and Trajan's Market to our right are only intermittently visible, being blocked out by constant streams of tourist buses and heavy lorries. If this road were not here, where would all the traffic go? Maybe *Il Duce's* claim to fame should really be as a forward-planning traffic controller.

The others have moved off, leaving me to ponder these imponderables as I look down at Caesar's Forum and try to imagine the scene as best I can as it was in those days. Gradually, I am aware of a couple behind me, looking at the statue of Caesar.

"Gee, honey, here's a statue of Mr Caesar!"

I don't need the accent to tell me where they come from - the words do it. I wonder what their conception of ancient Roman history is like? Maybe because they have a Senate like the Romans and the office of a President who, being commander-in-chief of the armed forces, approximates to the role of a Roman emperor, they think that the Romans went about putting Mr in front of the word, like they say Mr President when they are speaking to him, especially when they are being deferential, or if they are Marilyn Monroe, singing happy birthday to him. Do they imagine in Caesar's time he went into a diner and the waitress said: *Excuse me, Mr Caesar, did you want your eggs sunnyside, overeasy, difficult, medium difficult, bloody impossible, scrambled, poached, soft-boiled, hard boiled or is there any other way I can do your eggs for you today, sir, these Ides, this beautiful day of 15th of March? ...Or what about a salad, Mr Caesar? I've just invented one and it would be a great honour...Certainly, Mr Caesar. An omelette and I will try to not break any more shells than are necessary. Have a good day, now!*

Unfortunately I can't hear what else they are saying because just then a shiny black 1960's car with fins bigger than a shark sweeps by with horn blaring. I catch a glimpse of a white, veiled figure in the back of the car. The horn is saying: *Get out of my way you bloody morons, I've got to get this bride-to-be to the church in time, or at least, just a little bit behind time!* And she is saying: *Thank you, Il Duce. If it hadn't been for your road over all those piles of boring old stones, I never would have made it to the church before the birth of little Benito here.*

Whilst we have been looking at the Roman ruins it has been impossible not to notice the striking white marble building rising behind them. It's so white, so well proportioned, it looks like a set of new dentures against the brown foreground of the burnt grass and terracotta buildings over which it dominates. Yole hasn't mentioned it, but I ask Iona, who has been before, what it can be. It has to be a building of supreme significance.

"It's the Victor Emmanuel Monument. The Wedding Cake."

I nod in complete ignorance but as if in full cognisance of the significance of her response. She thinks I am an ignorant boor and there is no point in providing her with more proof than necessary. I can pretend that having seen it only in profile I have not been able to recognise it.

Now we have come round to the front of it. Well, it's a monument all right. I can see why they call it The Wedding Cake. I can also see why they call it The Typewriter - a curved arch of columns above a solid base which, if I were looking at a photographic negative, would remind me very much of my father's black 1942 *Royale*, which my mother bought for him in Egypt. It is built of Brescian marble which has the quality of never fading, of never weathering, of never mellowing and blending in with the surrounding buildings so it will, despite the best efforts of the pollution from the Roman traffic, remain pristinely white and dazzling like an advert for denture cleaner.

It's a sort of multi-purpose building. Completed in 1911, it commemorates the unification of Italy in 1861, as well as being a monument to the first king of all Italy, (well nearly all present day Italy) Vittorio Emanuele II. (I believe I saw one of his films once, but didn't tell Iona – she wouldn't have liked it. I think it was the one where he met the wife swappers). And it also houses the tomb of the Unknown Soldier. In the foreground, there is a statue of the King himself, mounted on a mount of white icing, like the diminutive figure of the groom you see on the top tier of a wedding cake.

You get the idea Vittorio would like to get his horse into motion and ride off into the sunset: *You didn't tell me that I'd have to marry the bloody country as well as be king and certainly not that you were going to bake a cake!* Five Italian flags are hanging limply in the still air: *We don't care. Nothing to do with us where you put us. We're not getting in a flap about it.*

The view from the top of the semi-circular colonnade is supposed to be spectacular. I can believe it is probably one of the best views in Rome because when you are standing on it, you wouldn't be able to see the monument. You can't have your cake and heed it. Needless to say, we are not going up there and anyway, there are big iron gates across the bottom of the entire flight of steps.

Across the Via San Marco is a much more pleasing building. It is the Palazzo Venezia. It has a rectangular tower which rises above three storeys. The lower windows are arched, the middle storey larger and rectangular and the top storey, smaller and square and all are picked out in white which is very effective against the burnt ochre. There are overhanging crenellated battlements to complete the overall harmony and rhythm of the building. Maybe it gains something too from the comparison with its flashy neighbour.

It was built in the mid fifteenth century for Cardinal Barbo who subsequently became Pope Paul II and later it became the Venetian embassy but of more recent interest to me is that it was Mussolini's headquarters and there, in the centre of the middle storey is a green door with a balcony so small, it hardly seems to be worth the bother, but it was from this tiny balcony that Il Duce, who must have completely filled it, harangued the masses in the Piazza Venezia below.

It is through this Piazza that we make our way now. At the far end, on the left of the Via del Corso, is the Palazzo Doria Pamphilj and on that building, a green covered balcony on the first floor which extends round the corner. There are louvred shutters, all closed. Apparently this is where Napoleon's mother used to sit and when she heard of her son's death in 1821, the shutters were closed and have never been opened again since. My eagle eyes spot however, that it's a convenient spot to place one of those increasingly ubiquitous Orwellian cameras. Napoleon's mum may be gone, but there's someone else watching now, seeing what she would have seen. She would have seen, could scarcely have avoided seeing, the Victor Emanuel Monument. Had she been alive in 1911, she may well have pulled the shutters down then anyway.

On the Via delle Vergini, Yole stops us in the shade of an arcade and tells us that we are approaching the Trevi Fountain. There's no shade there so she's telling us about it now. The name Trevi comes from *tre via* or three roads which meet here. It was designed by Nicola Salvi and completed in 1762. The water comes from the Aqua Vergine and there's a panel on the fountain of the virgin herself showing some Romans the source of the spring. It is a huge baroque affair, like a theatre set, using the back wall of the Palazzo Poli as a backdrop. I am prepared not to like it, having seen it most recently on a friend's postcard and thought it hideous. It was said that if you drank the water, you would return to Rome, but someone, probably from the Tourist Board, had the bright idea that you should throw in a coin instead. I knew that already, but Yole says that if you throw two coins in, you will get a lover and if you throw in

An Italian Journey

three, you will get a divorce. I am looking for two coins,
but as I rake in my pockets, I find that I've got three single
cents. It is a sign as usually they don't bother with anything
smaller than a 5 and I don't usually have any money at all,
so I fish them out and wordlessly hand them to Iona, who
unsuspecting, takes them.

Gordon is creased up with laughter. "Might as well, get
her to divorce me, then she can pay for the costs," I whisper
to him over Yole's oratory.

La-Belle-Dame-Sans-Merci draws me a look which
says: *Shut up!* I can't be sure if it's my joke she's annoyed
about in principle, or that I'm so mean I won't pay more than
3 cents for a divorce or because she can't hear what Yole
is saying or because I am not paying attention. I shut up
anyway or my life won't be worth tuppence.

At a corner of the Piazza, now we can see the Fountain,
Yole describes the details we should notice. Neptune is in
the middle, riding a seashell being drawn by two sea horses.
They're not like sea horses as we understand them, more
like real horses with horrible bat-like wings growing out of
their shoulders. The one on the left is rearing up and being
difficult, whilst the other is tame and docile. This represents
the two moods of the sea apparently. They are being lead
by a couple of Tritons. They are splashing through puddles
amidst some very rough rocks over which the water tumbles
in cascades into a basin of ultramarine water.

It's the roughness of these rocks I think that shocks me
the most, rather than the carved figures. On each side of the
alcove from which Neptune is apparently emerging, are two
figures which represent Abundance and Health and above
them two panels depicting the discovery of the source. And
all this in a façade of something that could have been a sand-
blasted Buckingham Palace. Towering over the centre is a
fussy armorial shield supported by a couple of angels and
below that a panel with some writing in block capitals of

which I can only read the first line: CLEMENT XII PONT MAX. The rest of the writing is too small to read, but it probably says what a great Pope he was to give us this splendid fountain.

Funnily enough, now I have actually seen it, I find it less offensive than I had thought I would. The colour of the water is very nice and the sound of the rushing water, apart from invoking the need for some to visit the toilet, is rather pleasant. Although every tourist in Rome seems to be here, there is plenty of room for people to sit on steps or benches. Yole says we have half an hour to recover before we move on to the next part of the tour. I've been in a lot worse places than this for a pit stop.

I am despatched for *gelati*, but what I really want to do, is sit down and get the weight off my legs. I also want to throw a couple of coins in the fountain. It could be money well spent. Hopefully I will get some small coins in change from the *gelati*. I don't want one of those expensive lovers – a nice cheap one will do me fine. It's my lucky day. I get some small change and secrete them in the pockets of my swimming trunks.

The trick with eating *gelati* in Italy is to eat them faster than they melt in this incredible heat, especially if you are like me and want to sit in the sun at the same time. So I am perched on the rim of the basin in full sun, whilst Iona is on a stone bench in front of me, in the shade. No matter how fast I lick, the ice cream is running down my elbow and my hands are stickier than an interrogation from La-Belle-Dame-Sans-Merci after she's discovered I've had a whole bottle of wine to myself. No problem with all that water behind me. I rinse my hand and arm in it and scoop out a couple of handfuls to wipe over my face. Lovely! How cool! How refreshing!

It's then I think how lovely it would be to dangle my feet over the edge. I have already slipped them out of my dusty plimsolls to give them an airing and to let the fresh air perhaps dilute the aroma from my shoes which by now is of rather mature proportions. No one else seems to have thought of it and no one else seems to be cooling off in that oh so refreshing water, but I can't see any notices prohibiting it. If Anita Ekberg can go paddling about in it, at least I can give my poor aching feet an immersion. It's the work of a moment to swing round and hang my feet over the edge.

Bloody hell! What was that? It sounded like someone blowing a whistle right in my ear behind me. It's enough to give you such a fright you might fall in if you'd been of a nervous disposition. I swivel round, my feet still in the invigorating water to see a couple of policemen dressed in white gesticulating at me and one blowing a whistle fit enough to crack his cheeks. There is no mistaking what they want me to do. I get my feet out of the water as if it were scalding. Oh, God, I am thinking, what if they come down and give me a fine? I'll not throw money into the fountain as a penance. That will pay a couple of cents of it. How much will it be?

But to my relief, they just move off. I am off the hook except everyone is looking at me, or it feels that way, but Iona certainly is and glaring is more the *mot-juste*. I know she is longing to come and stomp on my offending feet as this crime is of such a public shaming magnitude, that I deserve no less, but the thing in my favour is there is nothing to link me with her unless she blows her cover. She is sitting beside Bill and Pat, so they know but there are so many other people, it's impossible to tell if anyone else who knows us has witnessed this public humiliation. It's impossible to tell what Bill and Pat think but their impassive faces suggest that they don't wish to know me either. I am going to be in trouble when we get out of here. I'll just sit where I am. I feel in my pockets for the coins. I should maybe invest more than a couple of cents. I think I may need to look for a new

Mrs Addison before this holiday is over. There is still more than a week to go.

As we meet at the corner of the Piazza where we are to meet Yole, I keep a respectful distance between me and the, for the moment, present Mrs Addison. Respectful because I respect her wish to not be identified with me. As we troop out of the square, I walk alone along the Via di Muratte. I can't walk with Bill and Pat, I can't walk with Usha or her parents, and I'd rather not walk with the Yorkies after Pisa. It's no good walking with the Guttings – they don't talk. I think Harriet has forgiven me for my solecism at the Villa Borghese, but best not to give her any cause for alarm by appearing to be too friendly again. I'm running out of companions. Maybe Gordon likes me. He acts the goat but I *am* the goat. He liked my divorce joke anyway. Well, I thought it was a joke at the time. What a difference half an hour makes.

Presently we arrive at the Piazza di Pietra. We are dwarfed by eleven massive Corinthian pillars, nearly 50 feet high. It is the Temple of Hadrian, the same who built a wall to keep us out, he was so scared of us, the Caledonians, except we weren't a nation in those days of course. It has certainly seen better days. Pigeon guano lies thick at the base of the columns which are black with age and pockmarked with pollution. This temple is to mark Hadrian's deification. Not another one! It's beginning to look as if being a god is part of the job description of a Roman emperor.

The Temple was dedicated by his son Antoninus Pius in AD 145. Ah, yes, he's the one with the temple/church which looks like a Picasso painting of a cow in a pen. And guess what! The Temple of Hadrian is now La Borsa, the Italian stock exchange. So it hasn't changed its function then. They once worshipped Hadrian, though God knows he was not that great a god if he couldn't hammer us Caledonians. And now they worship Mammon in the very same place and has it never occurred to anyone but me, that this could be the very reason why the Italian economy has gone to the Wall?

Emerging from the Via del Seminario, we arrive at the Pantheon, the imitation of which we saw in the distance, through a web of scaffolding, in Naples. At first glance, I have to say that the imitation is better than the original. This looks very tired and grey, as if it would benefit from a good scrub. I look like that and I'm a lot younger and my feet, despite their immersion in the Trevi, could do with a good scrub also. Now I think about it, where does the water from the Trevi go? Maybe the Romans have to drink that water. (Look for an attack of dysentery in the papers in a few days' time.)

The Pantheon dates from 125 AD, the oldest most complete structure in the Roman world. On the pediment it says: M. AGRIPPA.L.P.COSTERTIVM. FECIT which I take loosely to mean: *Mmm. Get a grip. This is taking too long and costing too bloody much.* Marcus Agrippa actually, was Augustus' son-in-law and general and to whom in fact Augustus owed much of his success and power. Intriguing that he seems to have picked up an Irish accent somehow. Unfortunately, or maybe not, it was burnt down and what we see now is a complete rebuild by Hadrian who obviously fancied himself as a bit of a builder.

To enter the portico is to enter a petrified forest. The 16 massive Corinthinan columns completely dwarf and overwhelm, making me feel like a pigmy (as if I didn't suffer enough from that already) in the land of giants. Incredibly, they are monoliths and came all the way from Egypt. There used to be a bronze roof here, but what was left of it from an earlier pillaging, was stripped off in the early 17th century to make the *baldacchino* which covers the altar in St Peter's which we are going to see tomorrow. That act of vandalism having been said, like many of the other buildings that have survived, it is thanks to the Christian Church that the

Pantheon itself survived. There was a Christian church here from as early as 609 AD – the church of Santa Maria ad Martyres.

However impressive the portico is however, it is the circular interior of the Pantheon which makes it the remarkable building it is. Someone once said it's not the breaths that you take that you should measure your life by, but the sights that take your breath away. This is one of these moments. To enter the Pantheon for the first time is an experience, which by definition, can never be repeated and for which you can never be prepared, like seeing *Hamlet* for the first time. You feel as if you are in a globe and the reason for this is the symmetry of the proportions. The height is precisely the same as the diameter - 43.3 metres. The dome is the largest in stone ever constructed, even bigger than St Peter's and is coffered to reduce the weight, but what immediately draws the eye is the great hole at the top – the *oculus* which is open to the elements. The floor is gently cambered and there are channels which lead any rain water into brass holes in the marble floor. I don't suppose a lot of water comes in anyway. At the moment, there is a broad shaft of sunlight striking the floor like a spotlight on a stage. It's incredibly light in here and it shouldn't be with that the only source of light, but the remarkable thing is – it is! There are pillars and niches around the whole circumference, but the dome is entirely self-supporting. Amazing!

We are free to roam at will and meet in the portico in twenty minutes. Great stuff: there must be some famous graves here, surely! That big semi-circular niche over to my right for example, with the two rose coloured pillars and what looks like the largest candleholders in the universe, more than twice the size of the guards standing like sentries beneath them, *has* to be someone important. I can't wait to be unleashed and find out who it is. It *has* to be one for my collection.

There is a big black sarcophagus on which is written in gold lettering: VITTORIO . EMANVELE. II and below PADRE. DELLA. PATRIA. So this is where he ended up. I hadn't heard of him this morning, but I'm only a pot-bellied Vietnamese pig, sometime frog, sometimes a camel and an animal like me can't be expected to know everything. I just hope if I'm ever on a TV show like *Who Wants to be a Millionaire*, they ask me, for even a quarter of a million: *Who was the first king of Italy?*

Right, bagged him. Now what about the niche over at the other side, if a circular building can be said to have sides? A person of great importance evidently as they have planted the poor bugger in porphyry, which is considered a great honour. It is the tomb of Umberto I: *Ah! Right! I visited your shopping mall.* I hadn't heard of him either before I came to Naples, but he is the son of Vittorio and as far as I'm concerned, never mind less famous than his father, less famous than his wife. For she is Margherita, of pizza fame, and it really is my lucky day, for written on the wall behind the hideous sarcophagus, is: Margherita, Regina d'Italia. That's good enough for me – I have visited the grave of the most famous pizza person in the world!

Now, who else is there? Not far away is a real find. There is a statue of the Madonna and child and set below this in the black and white marble base of the statue, is a pane of glass which is illuminated from within, so it's rather like looking into an aquarium. No fish here of course. It contains a sandstone sarcophagus on which are carved wreaths and scrolls and on a plaque at the bottom, his name in Latin: SEPULCHRVM RAPHAELIS SANCTII. I have stumbled upon the tomb of Raphael.

Not a bad haul, I reflect, as failing to find any other graves, I head out into the shimmering heat of the mid-day sun. I don't see any of my fellow travellers in the portico yet, and after a glimpse at my watch, there's still some time left, so I hurry out into the Piazza della Rotonda. There is a fountain there and what looks like an Egyptian obelisk standing upon an elaborate marble base of dolphins or some large fish spewing water. And I also want to get a view of the Pantheon from a distance because from the angle we approached it, we have seen nothing but the massive portico and I want to see if any of the rotunda is visible, or, if from straight on, the portico conceals it completely.

I have just set out on this quest, have got only as far as the fountain – no, at this distance all I can see is portico, when my eye is attracted by some movement – Uh! Uh! Iona is waving furiously at me and some others are merely waving, indicating: *You're going the wrong way! Not that way! This way, over here! You bloody moron!"*

I don't understand how this could have happened. I trot towards them as far as dignity and fear will allow. I am really for it now, this coming on the heels, so to speak, of my transgression at the Trevi.

"Where the hell do you think you were going?" La-Belle-Dame-Sans-Merci hisses. "You were told to be back for twenty past!"

"I thought twenty five past. She said we'd twenty minutes."

"She said we'd to be back outside at twenty past. You weren't listening as usual. Where the hell did you think you were going to anyway? You walked straight past us."

Could it really be possible I had walked past them? It was dark in the portico and they could have been behind those enormous pillars and I was in too much of a haste to look properly, not expecting them to be there anyway.

"Thought I'd save everyone any more trouble and go and drown myself in that fountain," I mutter, miserably.

"Oh, shut up and give me some water, before I turn into a god."

"You would be a goddess, darling. In fact, I have always worshipped you." I can be obsequiously patronising when the opportunity presents itself to speak with forked tongue.

"Look, just don't try my patience any more, right! Just give me the water, for God's sake!" She's never in the best of moods when she's hot and bothered.

At the corner of the Corsia Agonale, Yole tells us our tour is nearly over. She's going to tell us about the Piazza Navona and then the rest of the day is ours to do with as we please, like go back to the hotel and collapse. We must have walked miles on these unforgiving Roman pavements.

Typically, the square is not square at all, but rectangular with curved ends, just like a race-track which, as it happens, is what it was. In a previous existence, it was the Stadium of Domitian where they used to hold athletic and chariot races. The floor of the piazza was concave in those days and was flooded so they could hold mock naval battles, or *naumachiae*, as they were called. Their descendants also made use of this facility up until the 19th century when it was flooded in the summer, to cool the feet of the horses pulling the carriages of the clergy and the rich, and the feet of the poor, and in the winter, if it were cold enough, to make ice for skating.

But no paddling for this poor person in the sweltering heat of this Roman afternoon, for the focal point, the fountain in the middle, the Fontana dei Quattro Fiumi, by Bernini, is barred with heavy metal fences. It's another bit of propaganda. Commissioned by Pope Innocent X, the four gigantic figures represent the great rivers of the world, the Nile, the Danube, the Ganges and the Plate but above them is the Pope's coat of arms, the dove and the olive branch, so it's saying, just like the Roman emperors before him: *I am the boss of the world. How great I am.* It was paid for by taxing bread which is where he departed from his predecessors and made his big mistake, for whilst the emperors kept the people happy by giving bread away, free, Innocent, eponymously and erroneously supposed he could get away with taxing it and he was unpopular to the end of his days.

Anyway, he's not the boss, because there is a towering Egyptian obelisk on top of that and on top of that a pigeon, craning his neck and eyeing up the pedestrians below: *Now, who shall I bomb today? Ooooh! I like the look of that Panama hat.*

The River Plate has his arm outstretched as if to hold up the façade of the church opposite, the Sant' Agnese in Agone by Borromini, to prevent it from collapse, while The Nile has his hand raised, covering his face, according to legend, in horror at the façade of the church. It seems Bernini and Borromini were rivals, and rivals for the fountain too which it is said, that Bernini only won by bribing the Pope's mistress. I see! This tells me two things: firstly he was lying when he called himself Innocent and secondly, it should be *her* coat of arms on the fountain.

But this is only making a story out of the well-known rivalry between the two B's because the church was not even begun when Bernini's fountain was completed and the symbolic reason for The Nile hiding his face is because at that time, the source was not known. Unfortunately we cannot see the façade of the church as, typically, it is shrouded in scaffolding, but it is built on the site of a former brothel, where in 304 AD the thirteen year old St Agnes was stripped naked in front of the crowds and flung inside because she refused to marry. Her dad sounds a complete nutter. Imagine *wanting* to pay for a wedding! Anyway, her modesty was spared, because she miraculously grew her hair with which she covered herself up. Presumably, she was a very well developed girl for her age.

The *Agone* of the church's name does not refer to Aggie's embarrassment as one would suppose. As anyone knows, who did not like me, read a book below the desk during

Latin lessons, *agone* refers to the athletic contests held in this stadium, and the name of the piazza itself, Navona, is a corruption of *in agone*. Well, if you say so, Yole. Though Agnes' modesty was preserved, her life was not. She was martyred here but not buried there. That does not surprise me. I expect bits of her are all over the place. There is however, a statue of St Agnes on the façade of the church. She is looking pitifully at The Plate: *Yes, my child? Do you want to go to the toilet? It's OK, you can take your hand down now. Just do it in the water - no one will notice. Oh, and by the way, my church won't fall on top of you in the meantime.*

Adjacent to Sant' Agnese in Agone is the Palazzo Pamphilj, designed for Innocent X by Borromini: *Beak to you Bernini, I got to build his palace!* It's too far away to see clearly and we can't go in anyway, as it's the Brazilian embassy now. It's a wonder that this piazza is not called Piazza Innocent X, because as well as the palace and the Fontana dei Quattro Fiumi, he was responsible for restoring the two other fountains in the piazza, the Fontana del Moro and the Fontana del Nettuno. There's nothing more satisfying than spending other people's money for them, especially if you spend it on yourself, building your dream house and your own memorial.

So that is Yole finished. We'll see her tomorrow in another place at another time –another country, in fact, at the Vatican. But for now it is time for a sit down and some refreshment. We head for the nearest café. I don't know about anyone else, but my feet are *in agone* and if I don't rest soon, I think I'll soon become a god myself.

Chapter 8
Con Romani Moderno

Ah, the relief, just to sit down! Bill and Pat are with us, so I am outnumbered and have to make do with a seat in the shade. Out there, in the heat of the piazza there is a young man standing completely motionless on a gold box, dressed head to toe in a close-fitting gold Lycra costume, and wearing a mask of Tutankhamen. I can tell it is a male because the costume is really tight. I hope he doesn't fall in love with any skimpily clad tourist who catches his eye. I suppose he is inspired by the obelisk on the Fontana dei Quattro Fiumi - but hopefully not too much. At the other side of the Fontana is still another still figure, this time, completely in silver, and that includes the face, a hat, and a loose fitting coat. In this heat!

To complete the trio of odd personages, there is a Roman soldier with a helmet crested with a bright pink plume: *Come hither you Caledonian bathdardth. I'm going to give you a jolly good thrathing*! He is waving his *gladius* limply, non-threateningly, at pedestrians as if he is directing them through the piazza. Thank God it's only his *gladius* he's waving about (if he's got the good sense to be ventilated like a Scotsman) and not his weapon of mass reproduction, though in his case, probably it isn't. He must be mad to dress like this in this heat and it must be the sign of an overheated brain that he doesn't seem to have anything to collect any money for his efforts, nor does he seem to be trying to collect any. Perhaps, realising that the brain needs oxygen, perhaps he keeps his under his skirt where La-Belle-Dame-Sans-Merci often accuses me of keeping mine. Certainly no one could accuse my favourite organ of being endowed with too much intelligence.

I order a beer, a *grande*. I don't care how much it costs, probably a fortune in this location. Whilst I pour that down my throat, the others pore over the map. No point in having a dog and barking yourself. Iona does all my navigation as she was a geography teacher and is used to maps. She knows what I want to do which is to go to the Spanish steps and visit Keats's house, and as she doesn't have any better ideas, that's what we're going to do. From the map, it looks as if we can walk there and on the way, we can visit Augustus' mausoleum and I'd like to have a look at the Tiber too. Bill and Pat say they'll come as well.

Iona goes down to the toilet and reports that you can see the original pillars of Domitian's stadium. Unfortunately, she doesn't tell me about it until we have left and are making our way out of the piazza, towards the Fontana del Nettuno. If only I hadn't been so bladder retentive, I could have seen them too. Imagine having pillars from the first century in your basement!

I suppose we should have gone down to the other end of the piazza and looked at the Fontana del Moro and the façade of Innocent's palazzo, but it wasn't on our way, and no one seems to have thought of it, so here we are at the Fontana del Nettuno instead. There is Neptune about to stick his spear into some snaky monster octopus of the deep which is wrapped around his godly thighs. Now, I really like this, almost as much as *The Rape of the Sabine Women*. The movement here though, by contrast, is downward. There is real power in the thrust of Neptune's shoulders as he is about to drive his spear home. Better be careful though as he is nude and we wouldn't want any accidents. Still, he'd be dead unlucky to hit *that*! What's the point of being a god if you can't be better endowed than that? *David,* the giant killer, was meant to be small, but for the god of the sea you would expect a bigger muscle than something that could curl up in a mussel shell.

There are sea horses and all sorts of other figures on the periphery. I like the overall effect and this fountain appeals to me a whole lot better than Bernini's Quattro Fiumi which is meant to be the outstanding work of art in the piazza. But I would of course. It comes from being a crab. Cancerians like to be in the minority apparently. I should probably trek to the other end of the piazza to see the Fontana del Moro, the central figure of the moor which was also designed by Bernini and which gets a bigger write up in the guide book than this one. Our book says that Neptune was made by Antonio della Bitta. I think you deserve more credit, Antonio, if you're listening.

We turn right out of the Piazza Navona and presently come to the Via della Scrofa which in due course changes its name into the Via di Ripetta for no good reason, apart from the rules according to Italian logic. To our right now, is the Palazzo Borghese. It was bought by Camillo Borghese round about 1605, when he was a mere cardinal, but when he became Pope Paul V, he extended it as befitting his new station in life. There's meant to be a beautiful porticoed courtyard which we might be able to get a glimpse of.

The palazzo was called the harpsichord of Rome, apparently, because of its shape, and the concave façade to our right, must be the keyboard or *la tastiera.* It looks a tasty enough building to me. However, when Pauline Borghese came here, she didn't like it and refused to live there, saying it was too cold and damp and complaining about the lack of sanitation. I bet it was really the size of the bedrooms that she was complaining about: *How do you expect me to strike the right chord in this 17th century dump? My bedroom's*

only got two doors and there's no mirrors on the ceilings!
How do you expect me to see what I'm doing?

The bit we're looking at forms the junction of three streets and must be the narrow end of the harpsichord. There's a balcony at the top with climbing geraniums spilling between the balustrades and dangling into space, whilst below that there is another balcony which has been enclosed entirely in glass. I don't suppose that was there in Pauline's day though, just like the Spanish flag fluttering from the uppermost balcony. It's the Spanish embassy now. From there, there should be a good view of the river, over the tops of the trees.

For the river Tiber is behind us. We cross the road to have a look at it. To our right is the Ponte Cavour, named after Vittorio Emanuele II's right hand man and to our left, the Ponte Umberto I. The water looks very green and, I would say, looks about the same in width as the Seine. We're nor far, as the crow flies from the Castel Sant' Angelo, another of Hadrian's building projects, designed by him as his mausoleum, but over the centuries it saw service as a mausoleum for other emperors and their families, a papal refuge, a prison, a garrison during the Napoleon era and finally, what it is today, a museum. And behind that is St Peter's but they are both hidden by a bend in the river.

"You're round the bend," says Iona, "so how come we can see you?"

Very witty. Very amusing.

We retrace our steps and on the ochre wall of the Palazzo is a little plaque of a boat on top of wavy lines presumably a floodwater marker. On the top it says: 2 FEBRV 1805 and below the boat, FLVMEN. If Pauline were there then, no wonder she thought the house was damp, because the wavy lines come up to my shoulder.

As we make our way down the back of the harpsichord, down the Via dell' Arancio, we look in vain for the fabled courtyard, but there is no sign of it. You probably have to be inside it to see it and that's not possible as it's closed to the public. Why do they put it in the guidebook then?

What we do stumble across though is a cylindrical water fountain that looks like the barrel of a cannon on its end, with a red beret on its head. It looks as if it is made of lead, but what's of interest to me is that above the spout it bears the letters SPQR: *Come and get your lead poisoning here folks.*

At last we have arrived at the first of our two goals – the Mausoleum of Augustus. What a disaster! It has been allowed to fall into a terrible state of disrepair. It's little more than a weed-strewn mound, like a bowl sitting in a saucer. You can see the entrance and an arched window above, but the saucer, or outer wall of grey stone has a pair of locked iron gates. Clearly, we are not going in here either.

There is a board which shows you what it would have looked like and tells you some of the history of the place. It was circular with four concentric passageways, linked by corridors and two obelisks at the entrance which have been removed to grace two piazzas somewhere else. Augustus built it for himself in 28 BC but he was not the first inhabitant. That dubious honour went to Marcellus, his nephew and the husband of Julia, his daughter, and who was probably poisoned by Augustus' wife, Livia who, in a moment of mad matriarchal misguidedness, thought her son, that arch lecher, Tiberius would make a better emperor than Marcellus. Augustus did end up here in AD 14 however and was succeeded by Tiberius who rapidly saw that Augustus had some company.

What a pity that, like Hadrian's mausoleum, it was used for different purposes: a medieval fortress, a vineyard even (I hope they didn't use the ashes as fertiliser: *Ashes Augustae* - a very dry white) and a theatre. It would have been good for my collection, all those Roman remains, but a bit too easy, so perhaps it's just as well they are gone nobody knows where.

To our left, between us and the river is the Ara Pacis. It wasn't on our map, so we didn't know about it till now. The whole thing is covered not only in scaffolding but in canvas as well, but there is a representation on the canvas of what lies beneath. It's the Altar of Peace, commissioned by the Senate in 13 BC after the defeat of Gaul (which the French must have found galling) and Spain (which the Spanish must have found as painful) but which brought peace to the Mediterranean. Four walls surround the altar, two of which depict a procession of the Imperial family in Carrara marble, like a family portrait. It's a real pain that the restoration isn't ready yet. Just another reason to come again, I suppose.

It's still a bit early, so instead of walking due east to the Piazza di Spagna, we take the Via del Corso towards the Piazza del Popolo. In the other direction, it would take us back to the Wedding Cake. All the roads in this area seem to funnel towards the Piazza del Popolo. In fact, it is known as the Trident, with the Via del Corso forming the middle prong of this spear pointing into the very heart of Rome. It's meant to be a very smart street, one of the smartest in Rome, so of course that's why I am here, in the lemon outfit.

If this is the heart of Rome, then at the very heart of Rome is yet another Egyptian obelisk. Rome seems littered with obelisks. If it had not been for the fact that no one had tried to sell me anything, I might have begun to think I was in Egypt. Of course this obelisk did come from there originally and is 3000 years old, brought back as spoils of war by that peace-loving first emperor, whose Ara Pacis we have just not seen, after his conquest of Egypt. But apart from that, this obelisk has special significance as this used to be in the Circus Maximus, where the charioteers turned to begin another lap.

There is a monumental arch beyond the obelisk at the far side of the piazza and beyond the arch, if we were to undertake that expedition, only it looks such a far way away, and we have already walked for miles, we'd find the Via Flaminia, one of the ancient Roman roads which connected Rome with the Adriatic.

Flanking either side of the Via del Corso, are twin churches. We sit on the steps of the one to our left, the Santa Maria dei Miracoli, with the Santa Maria di Montesanto on our right. Both appear to be closed, presumably because it is siesta time. I'm beginning to think it will be a bit of a miracle if we find anything open today at all. I bet when we get to the Piazza di Spagna, Keats's house will be closed too.

I sit on the steps to read the guidebooks. One says that the Porta del Popolo was designed by Nanni di Baccio Bigio and the other says it was by Bernini. I'd like to think it was the nanny of big Baccio who did it. I can imagine him sitting on her lap, though he is a bit big for that sort of thing: *Draw me a triumphal arch, nanny.* She's probably been drawing arches all morning to keep the little monster quiet. I did that myself when I was small to an aunt who had spent ages drawing me buses. At last she tired of drawing buses: *No, David, I think I've drawn you enough buses for just now.* The young David was not to be deterred: *Draw me another bus, you bugger!* It was my first recorded swear.

"Tell us all about it, David."

"Er…what?"

Bill indicates the guidebooks. "Tell us what we're meant to be looking at."

I stand up and face my three companions sitting like the three monkeys on the steps of the church and give them the benefit of what I've just read, like a real guide. When I get to the bit about the Porta, Pat interrupts me.

"My book says Michelangelo designed the gate."

There's always some smart Alec in the class who thinks they know better than the guide.

"Well, he didn't! He's designed quite enough things already and it's time he let someone else have a go for a change." And I tell them it was big Baccio's nanny who really did it.

My audience has grown from the original three to more like thirty. The other people on the steps, for want of anything better to do, are listening to my free description of the square.

"You are sitting on the steps of the Santa Maria dei Miracoli. (This I pronounce with an impeccable Italian accent, to my unmusical ears anyway.) If you look at the church to your right, you'll see that it is a mirror image of this one. They were designed by - (a quick glimpse at the guide book) Carlo Rainaldi. Although they appear similar, in fact they are not. The Santa Maria di Montesanto to your right has actually got an oval dome. That was because the space in which he had to build it was smaller than this one and he solved the problem by building an elliptical dome. Smart, eh?

"There's another church over at the other side of the square. Guess what its name is? Yes, another blooming Mary, the Santa Maria del Popolo. What's wrong with these Italians? Three churches in one square and all called Mary! Can't they think of any other names? How many dates ended in failure because they agreed to meet at Santa Maria's, and waited at the wrong one, eh? It's probably closed just now, but you should try to go in there because there are some frescoes by Pinturicchio. Forget your Giotto; if you want to see some real frescoes, Pinturicchio is your man –"

Suddenly I am drowned out by an almighty amplified blast: *Allo! Allo!* followed by some Italian. I had noticed scaffolding over to the right of the piazza, (you could scarcely not) and a stage and this person is obviously testing the sound system. The funny thing is, his voice is just like the Pope's. In the 18th and 19th centuries the popes used to hold executions here. He can hardly be here can he? Was it something I said? La-Belle-Dame-Sans-Merci has got her Viagra eyes on, a stare as hard as the Gorgon's and just as petrifying - a sure sign that I have over-stepped the mark again in some way. I make the interruption the closest thing I'll ever get to divine intervention and sit down on the steps with my back to my audience, who, no doubt are devastated at the abruptly curtailed commentary.

I was going to tell them that one form of execution was to bang people on the temples until their brains ran out. (Ah, but what if, like me, they kept them somewhere else? It would have been terrible if they found out though as that would have been really, really sore.) And I would have told them that the greenery behind the person who had so rudely interrupted me and who has now been replaced by someone on a keyboard is the Pincio gardens designed by Giuseppe Valadier, who, as it happens, also redesigned the piazza, giving it its present oval shape. We could walk through the gardens to the Piazza di Spagna, attacking it from the rear so to speak but the others are not for this because it means a steep climb to reach the gardens from the piazza. I am outvoted by the wimps so we retrace our steps down the Via del Corso.

Just as well though as I would otherwise have missed number 18, the Casa di Goethe. It was at this address that Goethe lived for two years and wrote his *Italian Journey*.

"Why don't *you* write a book about *our* trip?" says Iona. "Give you something to do now you are retired. Keep you off the streets." It annoys her, who has so many hobbies, that I have none, apart drinking and looking at women. Except she doesn't know about the last one and doesn't think the former qualifies as a hobby, so that's why she thinks I don't have any. Although, when I think about her remarks about

Pink Top at Naples airport, maybe she does have an inkling about my covert extra-curricular activity. Maybe that's why she wants me off the streets.

"Yes, I might just do that."

The Piazza di Spagna is an essential destination for the modern Grand Tourist. My goal, probably only second in importance to Pompeii, in the entire trip, is to visit Keats's house, which my guide book says is the pink house on the right hand side at the bottom of the steps. As well as collecting graves, I also collect birthplaces and of course, it goes without saying, death places, though in my experience, I find the latter rather rare, but one of the best, incidentally, is at Haworth where you can actually see the couch on which poor Emily Bronte hacked her lungs to death. Here I have the opportunity to visit the room in which Keats actually died, carried off at the tragically early age of 26 by the same coughing which afflicted poor Emily.

But Keats was only one of the many writers and artists who inhabited this area, such as Hans Christian Anderson, Balzac, Berlioz, Elizabeth Browning, Byron, Henry James, Rubens, Shelley, Tennyson, Wagner, to name a few and, to complete this otherwise alphabetical list, Liszt. They all lived in this area, not forgetting Goethe of course, but unlike Keats, they survived - for the time being at least.

I am mildly surprised to find that the Casa di Keats is not pink, but a much more tasteful two-tone affair in apricot and cream and looking good enough to eat, if I liked cream, which I don't. I am, however, not in the least surprised to find that it is closed. Just my luck, typical, but it should be open, according to the notice, at 4 o'clock which will be in half an hour. Well, we'll see. It'll be Italian time anyway, so if it opens at all, it won't be when it says it will, so there's plenty of time to explore the piazza first.

The obvious thing to do, weaving one's way through the crowds squatting on the steps, is to climb to the church at the top, the twin towered Trinità dei Monti, from which there should be a good view of the steps and the entire piazza, but there's further rebellion in the ranks. Iona and Pat protest they are too tired and too hot to make the ascent, but Bill is made of sterner stuff and says he'll accompany me.

It's not a difficult climb. The stairs, which would not be out of place in some grand baronial mansion, sweep down in an elegant cascade, flanked by villas of pink, ochre and yellow and there is a balustraded balcony half way up from which one can admire the view and get your breath back if you're packing what Iona calls a *puku* like mine. *Puku*, by the way, in case you don't know, is a Maori word for the way in which normal middle-aged men spread out at the middle.

I stop for a moment, looking in particular at Keats's house and wondering if he ever had the puff and energy in his last few consumptive months of life here to climb the steps, even this far. And when I emerge from my reverie and look around, Bill is gone. I thought he had stopped too, but perhaps he hadn't. After all he doesn't spread out in the middle like me and is certainly not as Keats-fixated. Perhaps he had said he was going on and would see me at the top. If he had, I hadn't heard him, but no matter, I'm bound see him up there.

Only when I get to the next balcony, he is nowhere to be seen. Not to worry. There are more steps to be climbed for the asking, the steps up to the door of the Trinità dei Monti itself, which of course is closed, but nevertheless, there should be an even better view from there. These steps are a lot steeper, but there aren't so many as the grand Spanish steps, but quite enough after the 137 of them, to make it bloody annoying when I am almost at the top, to have my Panama rudely wrested from my head and be sent tumbling and spinning down the steps, with me careering after it before it disappears from sight for ever, or is picked up by some passing mendicant with a good taste in millinery. Where did this sudden gust of wind come from anyway? When we are at the Wedding Cake, there wasn't a breath of wind to flutter the flags. Maybe it was windy after all and they were too ashamed to fly after all. Or it could be the gods are at it again.

They are all right, for when I get to the top, this time exposing the thinly thatched cranium to the full force of the Roman sun, and clutching the escapist Panama tightly in hand, what should have been a good view and photographic point down the entire length of the steps, as well as the piazza and the city beyond, is obscured by the pedestal on which yet another Egyptian obelisk is residing: *Heh! Heh! Heh! The steps we take to have a laugh at you poor puku people puffing and panting up the steps for the view and there isn't any! Heh! Heh! Heh! Hey, what did you think of the alliteration this time by Jove?*

There's nothing to do but retreat. For the sake of variety, I take the right side down the stairs, keeping an eye open for Bill, but without success. Even when I get to the bottom, there is no sign of him or the ladies either. I am lost again. Well, not exactly. I know precisely where I am and what I want to do. It's not my fault that they've wandered off and left me alone. All of a sudden, I have a blinding flash of revelation, an epiphany - surely it hasn't been a plot to abandon me here in central Rome whilst they have gone back to the hotel? I know Iona is not so keen about the Keats house as me, nor the others either, but then they didn't teach him for years like I did. If they have run off and left me as a joke or for some other arcane or puerile reason, I am in trouble, for not only do I not have any money, but I haven't the foggiest how to get back to the hotel because, to be honest, I didn't bother to listen when Yole was telling us as I thought Iona could do that for me. I know I have tried her patience particularly severely today, perhaps beyond endurance. Perhaps she'd rather not be in the society of a person whose priority is to be in the death room of a dead poet. Oh, well, she's got the map, but I have the guidebook, so I'll worry about getting back later.

At the bottom of the steps is a fountain, so the guidebook says. Ah, yes, I believe I can just about see it under all the people swarming around it. It is called La Barcaccia, designed by Bernini senior and is a bit of a joke, apparently. It's a half-sunken barge, the water supplied by the Aqua Vergine, the same which feeds the Trevi. If I could get close enough to see, maybe some of the silt from my feet will have arrived here by now. Anyway, there was not enough pressure to have spouting jets of water, so here we have this half-sunken wreck instead. In the middle there is something which looks like a bird-bath from the centre of which there spouts a stream of water, similar in volume to the drinking fountains which used to grace the streets of my youth, but which now seem to have disappeared entirely. The inspiration for the fountain is said to have come from such a barge which was stranded on top of the Pincio hill in 1598. If that is true, then that was some flood and Pauline Borghese should have been around then to see what a really damp house was like, because that means it must have been at the same height as the Trinità dei Monti is now.

I stroll off towards the left, towards the Piazza Mignanelli, keeping my eyes skinned for my companions. I want to have a look at the column in the square. It's a Roman Corinthian column, and on the top is the Virgin with a halo of stars hovering round her neck, like a cartoon character who has just received a severe blow to the head or as if she had been elected patron saint of the European Union. She looks as if she is reeling from the shock.

The statue dates from 1857 and commemorates the Doctrine of Immaculate Conception, an idea thought up by Pope Pius IX, namely that Mary was the only person ever to be born without original sin. Well, I didn't know that before and neither did a lot of people up until a century and a half ago. I wonder how many of my Catholic friends know how recent an idea this is; I wonder how many of them have heard of the idea at all; I wonder how old Pius himself found out. Perhaps it came to him in a dream. I wonder how he can have a dream and it comes true. I have a dream too but it's not very pious. Maybe that's why it hasn't come true and I have to go stroking boars' noses and throwing money away in fountains.

There's not the time to speculate any further about impious matters such as these. If I am to catch the late opening of the Keats house, it's time I was heading back to miss it, as the way my luck is going, it's not going to open anyway. However, I can't help but miss it by some more as my attention is drawn to the department store on the right. If the obelisks made me think of Thebes, this makes me think I am in Amsterdam, for the whole wall, all three storeys, is given up to little illuminated windows just big enough to take one person, in which women are displaying their wares. But I am impervious to these weapons of mass seduction – it's only mannequins modelling clothes.

At the other side of the street at number 66 is another, less interesting store, but with a very tasteful ornamental archway over the door and which once was the residence of Byron. Sitting on the pavement in front of it, licking *gelatis* are my lost companions. I prolong their happiness by pretending not to see them and head down the street to see if the Keats house is open yet. It is not. I look at it sternly.

"Come on, it's time you were open you bugger!" I command, like Aladdin, and would you believe it, there is the sound of a bolt being drawn back and the door swings open to reveal a slim girl in her early twenties who is the same idea as my son's ex-girlfriend's sister. I don't know which surprises me most, that, or that the door opened just then. I am overcome with confusion. Did she hear me or not? I can't tell from her face, as to cover my embarrassment, I turn my face away from her and semaphore across the piazza to the others that the house is now open. But they are more concerned with their *gelatis* and apparently totally unconcerned about my whereabouts, for after flapping and waving my arms around as if I were beating an invisible bluebottle to death, I realise there is nothing else for it, but I must go over and tell them. When I turn round to explain this to the girl, she is already gone.

When the prodigal returns, there is no killing of the fatted calf, nor any great sense of disappointment either, it has to be said. I don't bother to ask Bill what happened to him, my disappearance and reappearance seeming to be an event of supreme apathy.

We are requested to leave our bags under the table in the room where we purchase our tickets. I have no bag, but I stow my Panama in homage. We are given an information sheet and we step into a long room with books and paintings from floor to ceiling. One of the paintings shows Shelley's body being burnt on a windswept beach with a handful of mourners huddled round it for the heat.

In the room to the right, which was the bedroom of Joseph Severn, Keats's friend, the painter, is a display cabinet containing various artefacts, especially hair. There is some of Keats, naturally, and also Shelley, prematurely grey and, intriguingly, in a scallop-shell locket which apparently belonged to Pope Pius V, the same who excommunicated Elizabeth I, strands of hair which once were attached to the heads, presumably, of two unlikely bedfellows - John Milton and Elizabeth Barrett Browning. This lock of Milton's hair, apparently, after Milton was finished with it, became the property of my illustrious namesake, Joseph Addison.

It's amazing whom you, or bits of you, might end up next to when you're dead. Stan Laurel for example is next to the bloke who played Lt. Tragg in the *Perry Mason* series on TV in the late 50's, early 60's. Not a lot of people know that I imagine; it takes a grave or seriously sad man like me. Anyway, Joseph's heirloom makes me think I should think about getting a lock of my hair preserved for posterity. Whilst I may still be here, my hair may be gone tomorrow and you never know with whom I might be locketed with forever. Marilyn maybe. I might get lucky when I'm dead, which is just the sort of luck I *would* get.

There is also an urn which supposedly contains some of Shelley's bones which were not consumed by the bonfire on the beach, but there seems to be some doubt if they are Shelley's at all. They could belong to a body which was burnt the day before.   So it seems to have been a regular occurrence to burn bodies on the beach. Imagine that, going down to the beach with your bucket and spade: *But mummy, I'm cold, why can't I get dried in front of the fire over there?*

Next door is *the* room - the room where Keats drew his last breath. There is a bronze plaque on the wall which tells you he died on February 23rd 1821. It's an austere little room, smaller that Severn's but Keats had a great view of the Steps from here. I am looking at them now, the window open and the shutters flung back as I imagine he would have had them and standing where he would have stood. From here, you can get a better view, looking down over the heads of the throng on the Barcaccia at the bottom of the Steps, which, now I can see it better, looks more like a gravy boat and dish than a sunken barge. But I suppose that's why the dish you pour gravy from is called a boat.

There's no bed, nor any other original furniture left, it all having been taken out on Keats's death and burnt in the street, by papal orders. There is however, a glass case with two plaster casts of Keats's face. The one on the right, we are told, is a life mask, the one on the left, a death mask. I am hard pressed to find any difference between them – he doesn't look very well in either of them. Perhaps they did it just before he died: *Say, John, we're just going to make a plaster cast of your face. Try not to cough will you, till the plaster dries. Then when you hand in your dinner pail, (which doesn't look long) we'll make another one and charge tourists to guess which is which.*

It's only fitting that I should have my photograph taken with the great poet, by one who is named after one of his most famous and enigmatic characters, La Belle Dame Sans Merci. It's a digital camera and so we can see the result instantaneously. Because of the reflection from the glass of the case, it's not very good, or maybe it has more to do with the subject matter. I would never have made it in Hollywood. One of my eyes is shut and I do not look very happy to be there.

"You look the worst," says my Belle-Dame-Sans-Merci without malice, as if judging a sculpture for a competition.

I couldn't argue with that.

At the other side of the house, in another little room, there is, amongst a display of books and other artefacts, another mask worn by Byron at the Carnival of Ravenna in 1820. He looks a bit of a ruffian with short-cropped hair and a week's stubble on his chin and a broad nose which looks as if it had been flattened by countless brawls. It looks infinitely more scary than Keats dead or Keats alive or David Addison or George W. Bush for that matter. A masked ball obviously would be my best chance of pulling a bird, especially if I picked a handsome face, but Byron picks an ugly one, hopefully to scare women off so he could have a night off, but knowing his luck, he probably ended up with pulling a woman who liked a bit of rough.

At the far end of the long room is a bookshop where you can buy some of Keats's poetry of course as well as that of

Shelley and some other Romantics. There is also a visitors' book.

As I stoop to write my name, I read the entry above. It's by an American from Pennsylvania who has written: *I teach Keats and I love him so much that I even called my son Keats!* How sad is that! I know some people call their children after football players, sometimes after whole teams which I think extremely pitiful, but which may give the recipient a certain cachet, though in the transient world of football, rather unlikely. But to be called Keats! If you're saddled with that as a forename, you have every chance of being bullied in the playground once the other boys find out you have been named after a poet. What if the son grows up to hate poetry, and Keats in particular, as there is every danger of him doing, given the revolting nature of teenagers?

I look around to see what this perpetrator might look like, but there is no one here but us and a young couple in the room with Byron's mask. He must have already left. I sign my name and in the space for comments, I'd like to write: *Poor kid!* with an arrow pointing to the offending comment above, but maybe he likes being called Keats. But all things considered, I think I'd rather be called Nicola and I wouldn't mind betting he would too.

We are footsore and weary, so it is time to head back to the hotel. We make our way to the nearby Piazza San Silvestro where we can catch a 53 bus. According to the timetable, there will be one in a few minutes. Just enough time, if we are quick, to get a bottle of water at the little shop on the corner. Bill and I dash across the piazza. We are just in the process of paying when Iona appears at the shop door for an instant, frantically flapping her hands at us before disappearing just as suddenly. Bill and I abandon the bottles on the counter and set off in pursuit, scattering pigeons in a flurry of flustered feathers.

We make it. Oh, we make it all right. The bus driver has abandoned his post, presumably he's one of those in that bunch by the kiosk in the shade, chatting and laughing like schoolgirls. Twenty minutes later we are still there. There would have been time enough to have carted a Trevi Fountainful of bottled water by now, but we dare not leave. The woman on my right, on a seat on her own, is starting to get a bit annoyed. She turns round to give the woman behind her a torrent of irate Italian. I wonder if she knows her or is just getting it off her chest to whoever's nearest, actually me, but she knows she wouldn't get a sensible answer from someone dressed like me.

I'd love to know what she is saying. The cry is taken up by someone at back of the bus and Mrs Barrett's husband, Browning, comes to mind as the whispering grew to a murmuring and the murmuring grew to a rumbling and the rumbling grew to - a sudden eruption. The woman is out of the bus and across the piazza far faster than a flow of lava but with a temper just as hot. What fun!

I watch in appreciation as she tears into the group of bus drivers and a moment later she comes back with two captives. One of them disappears into the cab, while the other, a lugubrious, be-spectacled, fat, freely perspiring man (fear or heat?) whom I would judge to be in his 30's, follows her into the passenger compartment where she reclaims her seat. The standing passengers have been too scared in her absence, to pinch it. From this throne, she continues to harangue him. It's a bit like a spectator sport at the Colosseum– a cruel combat. I don't know what possible defence he can have. After all, the bus should have left 20 minutes ago. He speaks in a calm measured voice, flaps fat flippers of arms from desultory shoulders but which are worse than useless flails against the barrage of words spitting from her lips like machine gun fire. Even I feel like ducking, and I'm on her side, but I feel I could easily be caught by a ricochet. It seems a bit obscene to be watching this unequal contest, which is confirmation to me that I would never have enjoyed being a spectator at the Colosseum. I am frankly relieved when he abandons valour in favour of discretion and, just before the door closes in that hiss which would have mimicked his deflated ego and utter public humiliation, he skips off the bus and into freedom as we eventually move off.

It's unbelievable! She who was so irate just a nanosecond ago, is now turning round and laughing and joking with her friend or acquaintance as if nothing had happened. How can she change her mood so utterly and so completely in such a short space of time? I feel she should deserve some applause. She got the bus moving after all, but perhaps everyone's too scared of her to make a wrong move. How long would we have sat there I wonder, if she had not taken the driver to his task? And what sort of public transportation system is this, where the drivers just park the bus and chat with their mates, ignoring such trivia as timetables? It must be Italian logic. If the Government has never heard of EU regulations, why should a bus driver have heard of timetables? It all makes sense, once you understand the Italian psyche.

On the journey, I have time to study this shaker and mover. She's probably forty-something, perhaps a well preserved early fifty and, I notice, just for confirmation of the absolute certainty, not wearing a wedding ring. She'd scare the pants off any man who came near her. A surreal vision springs to mind of them fleeing, hobbled, with their trousers round their ankles and she in pursuit: *Stop! I command you to make love to me!* She's wearing a dress in patrician purple and which no doubt explains why she is unafraid to attack those plebs of drivers in their den. She also carries with her the badge of her office – a matching purple handbag which, no doubt, she uses in the rare event of the purple prose of her invective being ineffective.

Travelling by public transport certainly gives you an insight into daily modern Roman life and so does getting off one stop too early, or otherwise we would not have seen the Smart car parked across the zebra crossing which shows it's not that smart after all. Or, more probably, being an Italian Smart car, it is probably smarter than it looks as it will not get a ticket on the grounds of never having heard of such a law as not parking on zebra crossings (what are they anyway?). All things considered, it is still smarter than us who got off at the wrong stop.

Back in our hotel we have no electricity which means we have no lights and it is a bit dull in here with the tinted windows and the brown gauze curtains. It makes the room look cold, even although it is warm. But more important than the lights, we're going to need the air-conditioning. No rest for the wicked. Iona's feet are blistered and she is not going to walk another step. Besides, it's a man's job. That's me, apparently.

I could use the phone, but judge I'll probably get a better result if I go to reception in person, especially since we are only on the first floor.

The urbane receptionist listens politely and solicitously. "Have you put the key in the slot, sir?" he asks unctuously.

What kind if a fool does he take me for? Really, I mean to say, I am not the most technically gifted person in the universe as I am the first to admit, but even I know that you have to put the key, which looks like a credit card, in the slot by the door to make the lights work. My innate politeness prevents me from uttering a scathing withering reply. I merely nod that I have.

"I'll send someone up right away, sir," he says, reaching for a telephone.

I have scarcely reached the room when there was a tap at the door. Incredible! It's the electricity repairman. I notice he casts a surreptitious glance at the key in the slot as he enters. He goes directly to a panel in the wall, flips it open and flips up a trip switch and lo! we have lights and the hum of the air-conditioning fills the room. Bloody hell! Why didn't I think of that and why didn't old oily receptionist down there not ask me if I'd tried that? Probably wanted to make a fool of me. The repairman smiles at my thanks and withdraws without saying anything but thinking: *Dragged me all the way up here just to do that. Bloody idiot! Ah well, if it weren't for morons like him, I'd be out of a job. And it's better than driving the buses. You're on the go the whole time.*

Iona has her feet plastered and has taken a Hedex to relieve the pain. I lie on the bed and let my feet throb and stoically refuse the medication. It's enough just to have the weight taken off them. Idly I pick up the literature at the side of the bed. It's about room service and such like and there is a laundry list. One item reads: *Mens' panties €2.* Fat chance! I didn't get to my present state of impecuniousness by paying other people to wash and iron my panties. For a start I'd be too embarrassed and secondly, I've never ironed my panties in my life as no-one ever sees them and if I'm run down by a bus, I probably wouldn't care anyway.

"I'm just going to have a shower," I say to Iona, "and I'm going to do some washing at the same time." I may as well as I'm not going to need my shorts for a couple of days and this will give them time to dry. I have been told that as we are going out for a meal tonight I have to wear my long trousers. Iona had spotted a street this morning, a lane off the Via Corso which had tables outside and advertised meals for €10. She knows I like to eat *al fresco*, but she also knows that I would like the sound of the price even better. And tomorrow, we are going to the Vatican and if we want to get into St Peter's we must wear trousers as they are extremely strict about the dress code.

"'bout bloody time!"

I strip off my lemon shirt and anything but mellow yellow shorts and throw in my green ensemble of Lincoln green for good measure, put the plug in the bath, pour shampoo over the clothes, turn on the shower and as I wash me, I trample the clothes underfoot. When I'm finished, the water is black. I don't know if it's primarily from me or from the clothes, but perhaps it would have been a good idea to have washed my feet before I began.

I wring the clothes out and pull the cord across the bath to hang them up to dry. It is then that I notice the hard lump in the breast pocket of my yellow shirt. What the hell is that? I pull out a squidgy mess of paper, just barely recognisable from the green writing on it. It is my bus, tram and metro pass.

I dry myself and wrap myself in protective folds of fluffy towel before I go to confess to Iona. I show her the sodden mass lying in the palm of my hand.

"What's that? It's horrible! Keep it away from me!"

For a moment I thought my towel had slipped. "It's my bus pass. I'm afraid I've laundered it!" It wouldn't have mattered quite so much, had we not being going into the centre with Bill and Pat for this *al fresco* meal.

"Perhaps I'll be able to borrow a ticket from someone else," I suggest in melioration, after the tide of insults to my intelligence has abated. "Someone who's not going out tonight. Maybe the Guttings. Don't expect they'll be wandering very far."

"Huh! And what makes you think that they'd trust you with their ticket? Don't you dare embarrass me by asking anyone for their ticket. Is that clear?"

"Jawohl, meine Fuhrerin!"

Not much chance of consummating Rome now in the interval before we have to meet Bill and Pat. About as much chance of resuscitating the squelchy mass that is my pass, but I squeeze the water out of it anyway and put the resulting pellet on the radiator. Since the radiator isn't on, I don't expect it to do much good. La-Belle-Dame-Sans-Merci watches me disdainfully.

When it is time to go, I think about taking the still sodden mass with me and explaining what has happened, but realising how pathetic an excuse that is, like pupils who say the dog ate their homework, I just chuck it in the bin.

Naturally, Iona complains to Bill and Pat about my accident. I am put out to see that Pat has not made Bill wear long trousers, but he doesn't wear swimming trunks as trousers either, it has to be admitted. As the bus lurches us towards our destination, I hope I'm not lurching towards another Nice crisis. I am on the alert for anyone who looks like an inspector and stand as close to the exit as other passengers permit. If one gets on, I'm getting off.

Pat is rummaging in her bag and produces a little phrase book. "I wonder what the Italian for *I washed my ticket* is?"

We all laugh merrily, but I am on tenterhooks the whole journey. We alight at the Piazza San Silvestro and, as we walk up the Via Poli, I like the colours of the building on our left, the same apricot and cream of the Keats house, but even warmer and seeming to glow in the evening sunlight. It is only when we reach the end and we emerge into the Piazza Trevi that I discover that it is the side of the palace the back of which forms the stage set to the Trevi Fountain. The Piazza is as busy as ever.

We take the Via della Muratte out of the square and there is the gold statue of Tutankhamen again, as still as ever. His hands are in the position adopted by footballers when they are defending a free kick. He must be doing all right though as the Lycra is stretched tight as a drum over a *puku* as good as mine. Iona, who nevertheless feels sorry for him, standing about for a living all day, puts some coins in his collection box and Tutankhamen bends over from the middle and straightens up again. Had it not been for this, I would not have noticed the white marble plaque on the wall of the house behind him, number 77. It says that Donizetti lived here.

We cross the Corso and enter the Via di Pietra. Tables run down its entire length. We choose a table about halfway down so we will not be bothered with any traffic noise. It's very ambient here, with the big red and white checked tablecloth and the candles encased in glass globes already lit, although it is still not yet dark.

Our waiter wants to know where we come from. Maybe he hopes we are American because he is anticipating the size of his tip, or maybe he just wants the excuse to tell us he is Romanian. I've not met a Romanian since I was in Romania in 1974. He wants to know what we would like to drink.

Bill and Pat order a half litre carafe of white wine. "I think that will be enough dearest, don't you?" says Pat.

I can scarcely believe my ears. It's not the endearment which horrifies me so much - they are always calling each other dearest. Although they are older than us, they have only been married half as long. Still, plenty of time to have stopped that kind of talk I would have thought. No, it's the baby carafe of wine between two people which horrifies me. I order a litre carafe and a beer, a *grande*. It's been hot work walking in these long trousers and I long to be like Bill in shorts. Bill thinks the beer sounds a good idea. Anything I can do, he can do smaller: trousers, wine and now beer, because he orders a *piccolo*.

The service is slow but it doesn't matter, we're here for the ambient atmosphere. I'm glad of the long beer to while away the time, whilst Iona makes a start on the white wine. It's not very cold and not very good though Bill and Pat pronounce it as delicious. I express my opinion and I can see they think I am being fussy. I used to like wine, any wine, the cheaper the better and I resisted developing a taste for good wine as long as I could, but alas the day came when I had to move upmarket. Still, I find the more you take of the cheap stuff, it does tend to taste better.

I have lasagne for my first course. It is only luke-warm and I beckon the waiter over and ask him to put it in the microwave again. He doesn't look too pleased. I don't know why he should feel insulted. It doesn't look as if it's been produced on the premises. When it comes back, it is so hot it is inedible: *That'll teach you, you miserable Scots haggis to complain about our frozen meal for one from the supermarket.*

My next course is *scallopine al limone* and I ask for it *senza fungi.* I shouldn't have done that really as I could have given the mushrooms to Iona, but I was just showing off my Italian.

When it comes, that is all it is, the escalope with a slice of lemon sitting on the top. If the plate had been blue, it would have looked like a lonely Caribbean atoll. Of course I should have known that if you want vegetables, even potatoes, you have to ask for them extra. I give Iona the lemon anyway to keep her sweet.

It's not the best meal I've had in my life and when the bill comes, it is €37, the same as last night, so that which had seemed so cheap turned out in the end to be no cheaper and not so good. There's a moral there somewhere but it was nice to sit out in the pavement in the gathering dusk of a velvet Roman evening sipping the white wine, which, although I had put it on the pavement away from the candle's heat, steadfastly refused to retain the little chill it had at the beginning.

It would be nice to see Rome by night. Well, the bits we can walk to at least, so we head back to the Trevi fountain. Like me, it is better by night. The upward floodlighting softens the grey stone of the palazzo and the pool shimmers in the reflected lights like an Impressionist painting. It's a place for romantics all right, so what am I doing here? A flower seller offers Iona a couple of long-stemmed red roses in a cellophane wrapping but she waves him aside like an irritating insect. She's well trained. I don't want her wasting any money on romantic trappings like this. She wouldn't say it with these flowers anyway. They probably don't have any thorns on them and wouldn't hurt very much if she slapped me with them.

Since the Trevi looks so good lit up, I would like to go to the Piazza Navona again as I reckon those fountains might look attractive illuminated and we never did go down to see the Fontana del Moro, but Iona vetoes it on the grounds that it is too far to walk and her feet are plastered. If she but knew it, she's not the only one. Underneath my trousers, my panties are plastered to my person and it feels as if the sweat is dripping off my – never mind. I bet I'm more uncomfortable than she is, so I am not too bothered really as unfortunately the Piazza Navona is in the opposite direction to the Spanish steps where we are now heading.

We approach them along the Via di Propaganda, a very pleasant street with impressive buildings sporting carved facades and intricate mouldings. From somewhere the sound of gentle music comes floating through the air to add to the general ambience. I would enjoy it more if I weren't waddling like a duck.

That store that I saw earlier in the Piazza Mignanelli looks even better and even more like a street in Amsterdam or Hamburg than it did earlier, the light in each window stronger now and the mouldings round the windows making them look like illuminated paintings.

"They're only dummies and you couldn't afford them anyway."

Iona interrupts my thoughts. I hadn't realised I'd been giving them such rapt attention.

"In any case, they've got too many clothes on for my taste," I reply with a sigh.

The Piazza di Spagna is as crowded as I had expected but there's a bit more room round the Fontana della Barcaccia now and it looks less like a gravy boat and more like a shark being pulled out of the water by an invisible line with water pouring obscenely from its eyes as if it were crying at its own imminent demise. In spite of this gruesome image, it's very ambient just to sit here and soak in the atmosphere and watch the people sitting on the steps and passing through the piazza. Rome in the gloaming as the song almost says, is a different experience from Rome in the daylight. I'm glad I'm here now, at this time, my time of day where the air is soft and warm, the lights mellow and yellow. It's what I like about the continent, this evening ambience when the speed of life slackens from the frenetic to this easy, strolling pace as if the people pick up, by some sort of osmosis, the mellowness cast by the lights. It is a privilege to be here, following the footsteps of the famous, seeing the sights they have seen, strolling as they have strolled in this piazza - and to think we so nearly didn't make it!

That reminds me! I need to make another pilgrimage. In the Keats house, I had learned that he had sent out to the nearby Caffé Greco for his meals and that this café was patronised by all the literati and artists of the 19th century: Byron, Wagner, Bizet and Liszt all got pissed here, not forgetting King Ludwig of Bavaria poor man, who was mad, and Casanova, who was mad for something else (maybe I could pick up some tips still lingering in the atmosphere) and Goethe. If I am to write another *Italian Journey*, I should follow in the maestro's footsteps and have a drink where he had drunk. Sounds logical to me. Even Iona can't object to that, in the interest of research, can she? There's only one problem - where is it?

For once, the gods seem to be on my side, or is it only an illusion, they are only leading me on? There are a couple of policemen passing by, just at that moment, except one is a woman.

"Scusi, dove e Caffé Greco per favore?"

It's about the limit of my Italian, learned from a TV programme thirty years ago, and I don't even know if it's right or not, so I am more relieved than insulted when the female of the species replies, in perfect English: *Via Condotti, just down there, but it is closed.* Of course the gods have to have the last laugh. It *would* be closed. We should have gone there after we came out of the Keats house.

Nevertheless, Iona is impressed by my Italian, a skill she never realised I possessed. Now that she thinks I have some brains, there is a slight chance that I may be able to use them on her tonight. As long as I don't do anything too foolish with them before we get back to the hotel, Rome might yet be consummated.

It's but a short stroll to this street, the one that you can see from the Steps pointing as straight as an arrow to somewhere in internal Rome. It's normally the sort of street I'd avoid like the plague. It's *the* designer shopping street: Versace and Armani have shops here as well as a host of other fashionable clothes and leather outlets. If there's one thing I can't stand it's fashion. Like jewellery, it's a mug's game. People with too much money spending it on things they don't need, to impress people who are not worth impressing in the first place.

The Caffé Greco is on the right hand side, number 86. There is a big rectangular sign in gold block lettering over the plain arched doorway which reads: ANTICO CAFFÉ GRECO. Too bad we can't get in, but it's good to stand on the threshold over which so many famous people have trod (and many millions more, less famous). The windows upstairs are lit up but the door looks like something they would use in Fort Knox. It looks like a lock-in and we've not been invited. Maybe they're only reading poetry but I know there's more than a whiff of sour grapes in that thought.

Looking up the Via Condotti, there is a splendid view of the Spanish steps and the Trinità dei Monti. The whole scene is bathed in a warm yellow glow, the shiny surface of the street picking up the glow from the lamps and shops and making it seem as if it were made of beaten gold. Maybe it is, paid for by all the fools who shop here.

Here is the Versace shop. The window display features a poster of a young man with a Chaucer's Pardoner's growth of russet hair on the point of his chin, and who is having a very bad hair day indeed. In front of this is a headless dummy, dressed entirely in black except for a silver belt at his waist. This is the new autumn/winter collection and the price list is below: *Chiodo Pelle € 807, Camicia €157, Cintura €121, Jeans €272 , Scarpe €258.* Bloody hell! If I wanted to look like that, and I wouldn't, how much would it cost me? I have to ask Iona to do the sums, or else we'd be here all night.

"€1615," she says, seconds later.

"And what's that in real money?" It sounds like a lot of euros to me.

"About £1000."

Good grief! It sounds even worse that way. I bet I've never spent that in total on clothes in practically half a century of enforced purchasing and here's this peacock wearing more money than I've got in the bank and that doesn't include his gold medallion either, as he's bound to have one of those nestling in the rug of his manly chest.

Funny I should think of the peacock, for as we walk along the Via Bocca di Leone, I am attracted by a window display in a shop called Moschino. It is a peacock, a midnight blue peacock and spread out behind it is a cocktail dress in the same sumptuous velvety blue material which the bird appears to be dragging behind it. That's all it is. The rest of the window is bare. The floor and walls of the display are yellow, which set off the colour of the dress perfectly. There is nothing so vulgar as a price tag to offset this remarkable scene. I have to admit I am impressed. Simple but staggering.

Here's another shop window. I never would have believed that window shopping could be such fun. It's on the Via Frattina and it appears to be an underwear shop. On a revolving pedestal, there is a male trunk. He's wearing underpants (or maybe they are trunks?) which are opaque at the front, but which allow you to see the buttocks as if through the mesh of a meat safe. You wouldn't want to have an accident wearing those. It would be like going through a mincer.

At the other side of the window is a female trunk. She has a top in the same material. She's wearing a bra beneath but I suppose you wouldn't necessarily have to if you wanted your nipples to poke through for a bit of fresh air. She is wearing a thong with silk ribbons. These are on sale, 30% off, a snip at €8.80. Hmm! About £6 and Iona's birthday coming up very soon. I suppose I could stretch to that. Still, it's a lot of money for not very much material but it's from a posh shop and it might be a good investment. It looks as if it may be fun tugging at those ribbons.

"What do you think you are doing? Come away from there before Bill and Pat think you are some kind of perv. What is it that you're staring at anyway?"

"Just a thong at twilight."

Whatever she thinks about that, Iona has no time to make a suitable rejoinder before we join up with Bill and Pat again.

"Look out, dearest!" says Pat, alerting Bill, who jumps back on to the pavement, and thus avoids being nearly mown down by a speeding Vespa as we cross the Via del Gambero.

"Phew, he was nearly a god there!" says Iona.

"Almost the dearest departed," I add *sotto voce* and I think, rather wittily, but Iona flashes me one of her looks.

We soon reach the Piazza San Silvestro and look at the timetable to see when our bus is due. Can you credit it? In the height of summer, the height of the tourist season, and I wouldn't mind betting, the number one most visited capital city in Europe, and the last bus was at 9 o'clock! Unbelievable! There's nothing else for it, we'll have to get a taxi. There's a whole rank of them in the square, ready, waiting. I wonder if they are bus drivers during the day.

"It shouldn't cost too much between the four of us," says Bill.

It should be amongst of course, but it amounts to the same thing and he's probably right about that, only it could never be as cheap as a "free" bus journey, but at least, I won't have to be on the lookout for inspectors. I can relax and watch the taxi meter instead.

The first one on the rank is one of those Fiat Uglymobiles. There is a bit of a scramble but I end up in the front seat, beside the driver, which means I get a good view of the meter.

It may be ugly, but the taxi is roomy, at least for me, and by the smell of it, new. Pat, however, who is tall, has less room in the back. She is sitting in the middle and has her legs stretched out, one foot resting on the central console. The driver is watching in his mirror and waggles his finger at her and gestures her to get her foot down, like a teacher admonishing a small child. I give Pat you-*are*-a-naughty-little-girl sort of look, in support, but as I turn round again, the driver fixes me with a steely glare. Did he see my expression, or is he annoyed at me squirming round in my seat, or both? After that, I am frightened to move in case I touch something and he stops the car and throws me out. I feel I should apologise for my buttocks wearing out the seat material. Can you credit it! A car-proud taxi driver, though how you could be proud of such an ugly vehicle beats me. Not even a toad could love this bulbous, squat shape. I'm a frog and I should know. An embarrassed silence descends in the cab.

It's a relief to arrive at the hotel. The figures on the meter read €8.37. That's handy as it solves the dilemma if we should give him a tip or not: *Look, mate, I think you should realise if you're going to use your Uglymobile as a taxi, people are going to come in it and sit on the seats.* We give him ten, which means it only cost €5 a couple. Can't complain at that, considering the wear and tear we did to his vehicle.

I can't wait to get to my room and tear off my trousers. Maybe those underpants I saw in the Via Frattina weren't so daft after all, with all those little perforations to let the heat and sweat out.

"You needn't think you're going to be getting up to anything," says La-Belle-Dame-Sans-Merci, sternly, misunderstanding my motives. "My feet are aching." Since she takes headache tablets for her feet, she is probably really telling me she has a headache.

"That's all right, dearest. We have another night left in Rome. Just you put your feet up, dearest." When in Rome, I may as well try the romantic talk.

She gives me one of those Frau Ning looks. I might have known it wouldn't cut any ice with her. I get her a Hedex instead.

Chapter 9
Con Molto Catholici

What's that noise? I lie awake, listening, straining my ears in the darkness. There it goes again. It sounds like a dog whining, as if in pain or dying of hunger.

"Iona?" I whisper. Although it is dark and our beds are far apart, I know she is awake although it is only 6:45.

"Mmm. What is it?" She sounds cross.

"Can you hear something?"

She takes the pillow off her head. It's one of her foibles. She's such a light sleeper that she puts her head under a pillow and if I am snoring, she uses ear-plugs as well.

"What is it *now*? I am trying to get some sleep!" She sounds even more irritable.

"Can you hear something?"

There is just enough light for me to make out that she has lifted the pillow from her shell-like. Obligingly, the dog performs again, a long protracted high-pitched howl.

"There!" I say triumphantly. "Did you hear that? Sounds like a dog whining."

She makes a non-committal sort of sound and makes a big production of turning over. But wait a minute! There's no sound of any traffic and the glass is three inches thick, so how come I can hear a dog whining? Where is it coming from?

I concentrate all my hearing powers to this mystery. I am now convinced it is coming not from outside, but from the wall behind my bed and I no longer think it is a dog whining.

"Iona! Iona! Listen! I think it is someone doing it!"

"Oh, for God's sake, what is it now?"

"That noise. I think it's someone doing it!"

Amazingly, she doesn't seem to have the same interest in this phenomenon as me.

"How disgusting! So what! You don't need to listen! And thank you for telling me! Thank you very much!" She beats the pillow up as if it were a substitute for my face.

I listen in the darkness to the sounds of ecstasy emanating from next door. Maybe it's not ecstasy, maybe it's pain. It brings to mind an experience I had once once when I was staying at my sister's at the end of the north, in Thurso. During the night I was afflicted with such a sharp pain in my chest, in the very heart of me, that I thought I was having a heart attack, dying even, like Keats, in a bedroom far from home. The stabbing pains came on which such suddenness and violence, that I could not help but cry out in anguish.

"Shut up! Shut up!" cried La-Belle-Dame-Sans-Merci in panic. "Iain and Margaret will think we're doing it!" Although the pain was so severe, I was in no position to notice precise details, I'll swear she was reaching for her superfluous pillow with which to smother me. Fortunately, after this last attack, the pain disappeared as suddenly as it had arrived. La-Belle-Dame-Sans-Merci had apparently put the fear of death into Death and Death fled, which only confirmed her opinion that I had just put these cries of anguish on in a sudden bout of eccentricity, but which left my hosts thinking - what?

Next morning, they were giving me what our parents would have called old-fashioned looks. I felt an explanation was necessary.

"Er, I hope that I didn't disturb you last night. I had a terrible pain in my chest. Thought I was dying of a heart attack, in fact!" I gave a weak little laugh, and I knew, even as I was saying it that they didn't believe me: in fact they thought it the most pitiful excuse they had heard in years.

"Yes, that's right, David," said Iain, with heavy irony. "That's what we thought, wasn't it, Meg? There goes David having another heart attack! Isn't that what we said, Meg?"

So they *had* heard me then! I suspected that they had. "No, really, it was really sore!" And I described the symptoms in graphic detail but Iain and Margaret just looked at each other and back at me with a when-you're-in-a-hole-stop-digging, sort of a look. And there was something else Iain had said. What did he mean by *again,* like I was some sort of serial heart attack victim?

To this day, they still think that I was enjoying connubial bliss. That was the day that I started calling Iona after the heartless lady in Keats's poem since apparently she was more concerned with her reputation than the fact that I thought that I was dying. It's not as if, had we *really* been doing it, that we didn't have a licence for it. I suppose it has something to do with the Calvinist doctrine that if you must do it, do it quietly, and for God's sake, whatever you do, don't enjoy it.

At last the sounds subside. Lucky bugger. Must keep my eyes open and see if I can spot who's in the next room. In the meantime, time for a little nap. We're not leaving until 9:30 this morning, so don't need to get up until after 8. Ah! The bliss! It's almost better than sex.

*

Poor Guttings! When he was in Florence, he didn't go to the expense of buying a pair of trousers and would like to visit St Peter's. Iona offers him a sarong. Typically, he doesn't show much reaction. Iona explains when we were in Konya in Turkey a few years back, visiting the home of the Whirling Dervishes and the tombs of (for Turks) some very famous mystics, there was a man at the door giving out skirts with elasticated waists to visitors like me who were unsuitably dressed in shorts. This was a great source of amusement to Iona who, when she got her laughter under control, said I reminded her of the King of Tonga with my *puku* bulging over the waist. It might just work for St Peter's, she explains and is worth a try. At least I wasn't sporting a beard, but by now Gutting's growth has attained reasonable proportions and could fairly be described as a beard without contravening the Trades' Descriptions Act. His hair is very dark and although his stomach is as flat as a ruler, he could never be mistaken for the ruler of the Tongans, but still, the sight of him in Iona's sarong should still be a sight worth beholding. I am quite looking forward to it.

Donald, my fellow Scot, is wearing shorts and so is Gordon. Perhaps they have an alternative plan to circumvent the dress code, or perhaps they are not going to bother with the basilica, as that is only part of our tour. We are going to be visiting the Vatican museum as well, and of course, St Peter's Square itself is worth a visit.

But first we have to get there. That means another of those nightmare bus journeys. As we wait for the bus to come, I sympathise with Angela who will have more than double the charges to take care of next week.

"Why don't they get the bus driver to take you? I mean, you've got a full bus load."

"Can't be done. Parking for one thing and the traffic is a nightmare."

It doesn't sound that convincing to me. I think it has probably got more to do with finance and the likes of Giancarlo's days off. It's not much less of a nightmare travelling by public transport but by this time in the morning, it shouldn't be too bad, should it? After all, the rush hour should be well and truly over, shouldn't it?

You wouldn't think so by the number of people squashed onto the bus when it comes. Where are all these people going to at this time in the morning, if they don't have to get up to go to work? Why don't they stay in bed and have a heart attack? Travelling by public transport like this is more than likely to induce a real one.

"Think of me next week," says Angela as we push our way on.

The bus journey is just the *hors d'oeuvres*; the real assault course is just about to begin. There is a collective groan from all of us as we see how crowded the carriage in the metro is.

"Line A, direction Battistini. Get off at Ottaviano San Pietro. Ottaviano San Petro," says Angela before we join battle and push our way on.

The short bus journey from the Campo dei Miracoli in Pisa, I realise now, plus the journeys we have undertaken in Rome, has been but mere training for this moment. We are packed like sardines. My hands are tight by my sides, my Panama and my camcorder clutched in one hand. The first stop is Repubblica. Surely to God some people will get off there and relieve the pressure! But it's worse. Even more people crowd on and we shuffle up even closer and more intimately together. There is a woman standing on one of my feet. Fortunately she doesn't weigh very much but she is completely unaware of what she is doing. I try to slide my foot from underneath but it doesn't make any difference.

There is no air-conditioning or if there is, it is hopelessly ineffective against the mass of bodies. As far as I can tell, we are all *living* bodies, at least for the moment. The thought occurs: *What if there's a fire down here or if there's a power failure? Imagine being stuck in here with all these people in the dark for God knows how long?* It doesn't bear thinking about and I try to suppress it. By now I am beginning to sweat. I can feel it oozing out of my armpits and trickling down my neck. And that's just what's happening under my short-sleeved shirt. I don't like to think what's happening under my long trousers, but I can feel the sweat trickling down my legs. I can see a dark blue stain under my pits already. God knows what my trousers look like.

Maybe it's because we are at least still moving, without accident, realising that things, however unpleasant this is, could be a great deal worse, that we turn adversity into light-hearted banter. Perhaps it's a way of suppressing the too awful thoughts that we might all be thinking or perhaps just a way of making this nightmare of a journey pass more quickly:

Where's Angela?

I don't know.

Are you sure you're not standing on her?

Don't worry. If we lose her, we'll just follow a nun!

But where are they? There's not a nun in sight. Travelling by Metro under these conditions would give any self-respecting nun a fit. To be so close to a man – too horrible to contemplate.

Spagna. We must be underneath the Spanish steps. Three down, three to go, and I hope I that's not the bodies which have succumbed to suffocation. Oh, hell! We're only half way there. And, if anything, the net gain of passengers is worse. Everyone in Rome seems to be hell-bent on getting to the Vatican. By now the front of my shirt is stained dark blue and I imagine the back is looking the same. People are beginning to notice, especially my companions who are passing the message down the line and, in spite of these hellish conditions, are smirking at the performance of my poor plumbing. Why aren't *they* sweating like me? I can see that the hair at the back of Tom's shirt is wet with perspiration and there are beads of sweat on his upper lip, but his shirt seems dry. Meanwhile, the natives don't even look warm.

"If this were cattle," says Usha, "it would be forbidden."

I can believe that, but not in Italy. Cattle probably do move like this.

At last we arrive and as expected, there is a mass exodus but yet as we make our way to the *Uscita* there is a hold up and our nightmare is not yet over. For some reason, the platform does not clear rapidly and now grinds to a complete halt. What's the problem now? I can't see over the heads of the hordes ahead of us.

At last, as we mount the stairs, the reason for the delay becomes obvious. There are three men resting from their labours of wrestling an enormous box down the stairs and we are forced to pass them in single fire. What can be in the box and how are they going to get that on the train? Thank God there wasn't a fire down here either! I think I'd rather walk back to the hotel than face that again.

I am an object of mirth and amazement when we emerge into the daylight and sunshine. Apart from my breast pockets, my entire shirt is dark blue where it was a paler blue before. Fortunately, my panties must have done their job and as far as I can tell, no unmentionable stains have permeated to the outside but it is very uncomfortable indeed. Isn't it ironic? I wear my swimming trunks and am dry, wear my underpants and I soak them. Like a cormorant holding its wings out to dry, I hold my arms out, to let the warm air percolate to my pits. If anyone gets lost they could follow the trail of steam as I dry off, if only I knew where I was going myself. Iona makes me stand still whilst she takes a photograph.

"Next time," she hisses, lest anyone can hear, "use an anti-perspirant!"

Under a big yellow sign which reads, in lower case lettering: *musei vaticani* and underneath that, *cappella sistina*, Yole is waiting for us with her trademark car aerial with scarf attached.

Of course the Vatican is another country, a state within a state since the Lateran treaty of 1929 but to enter it is more like boarding an aircraft than entering a foreign country. Once through massive glass revolving doors, we pass through a metal detector where a guard is waiting with one of those electronic paddles in case we fail, whilst our bags, on a conveyer belt, pass through x-ray machines.

We sit on some benches which look more like coffee tables and wait whilst Yole buys the tickets. Whilst I am waiting, I think I may as well pass the time by filming the entry procedures.

Ah, hah! What's this that I see? This guard, who is meant to be looking at a screen, is reading something, something about the size of a diary. Perhaps he's looking to see if he has any dates in his diary. But surely he shouldn't be doing that, should he?

I have just finished filming and put the camera away in my bag when another of the uniformed guards comes striding over.

"Filming not allowed!" he says brusquely.

Well, I'm pretty sure that's what he's saying although he is saying it in Italian but he looks angry enough to leave no doubt as to that's what he's saying. I suspect he realises that I may have picked up his colleague doing what he shouldn't have been doing. There are no signs that I can see which says that filming is forbidden. Is he going to demand my film?

I nod and show him that the camera is safely stowed away in its bag. He stares back at me. Is he sizing me up? If he demands my film, what would be my reaction? Am I going to meekly hand it over, or will I protest and when the cause of the fuss is investigated, will his colleague be exposed?

"Not my camera," I say. "Hers." I indicate Iona, sitting beside me, improving the shining hour by studying the guidebook. She has been blissfully unaware that I was even filming.

He gives her a lingering look. She looks back, unflinchingly. Today she is wearing her Chinese face. She is Scow Ling. He blinks and goes away.

"What did he want?" she wants to know.

"Search me. Maybe he fancies you."

Just then Yole comes along with our tickets and we follow her up some stairs and along a corridor. She stops us in a corner and points out the dome of St Peter's. The sun is streaming relentlessly through the glass but Yole says it's the only place in the Vatican where you can see the entire dome and we fry like eggs whilst she tells us that the dome was designed by Michelangelo but he died in 1564 before it was completed. He nicked Brunelleschi's idea though, as it consists of an inner and outer skin. There was an earlier church here built by Constantine in the 4th century and the dome of this replacement church is supposedly built over the site of St Peter's tomb who was crucified here about 64 AD. Peter asked to be crucified upside down because he said he wasn't worthy to be crucified like Jesus but I suspect he was using his head and reckoned the whole ghastly business might be over quicker that way.

Yole leads us outside now to a courtyard where there are huge posters of *The Last Judgement* and the Sistine Chapel ceiling. It's called the Cortile della Pigna because of an enormous bronze pine cone - it must be at least 10 feet high, which once was part of a fountain and which now, guarded by two peacocks, sits in front of a massive alcove in the Belvedere Palace which was commissioned by Innocent VIII at the end of the 15th century.

Speaking is not allowed in the Sistine Chapel, so Yole is going to tell us about the frescoes now. Some of the men commandeer a nearby bench so the ladies can sit down but there is still not enough room for them all. It looks as if we are going to be here some time, so I flop on the ground for the lecture. The secret about walking in cities is to grab a seat whenever you can, but some of my colleagues prefer to stand. Perhaps they think it is undignified to sit on the dusty flagstones or maybe their clothes are too good. I don't have to worry about that.

I am more interested in *The Last Judgement* than the frescoes on the ceiling, or at least the way that Yole tells it. It was completed in 1541, nearly 30 years after the ceiling. I like the subject matter of this. It's an unusual subject for an altar painting apparently, the dead being torn out of their graves on the left of the painting, to be judged by an uncompassionate Christ in the centre of the painting who, with upraised left arm is condemning the pour souls to hell in the bottom right. I can't help recalling the lines from *Holy Willie's Prayer: Sends ane to Heaven and ten tae Hell/ A' for Thy glory.* It seems a very Calvinist message for a Catholic painting. Ironically, Paul III who became Pope in 1534 and who commissioned the painting, was the leader of the Catholic Reformation against the Protestants, so no doubt it's Protestants like me who are being pitch-forked off the boat by Charon into Hades as a reminder to stick to the true faith.

In the bottom right hand corner is the character of Minos, judge of the dead in the Underworld. He's an evil looking bugger, with asses' ears and a serpent twined round his body. The joke is that this is a caricature of one of the Pope's entourage, Biagio da Cesena who fell out with Michelangelo about the number of nudes in the painting. Last laugh to Michelangelo, but then again, maybe not, because Paul's successor, Pius IV, nearly had the painting removed and was only prevented by doing so by the intervention of Michelangelo's pupil, Daniele da Volterra who covered the most flamboyant nudes and thus earned for himself the unenviable soubriquet of *breeches-maker*. But then maybe he preferred that to a girl's name.

The other item of interest for me in this painting is in the centre of the painting. It depicts St Bartholomew kneeling on a rock beside a human skin, the grotesque head and arms draped limply over the rock. The slack, empty face on this skin, in shape, like one of Salvador Dali's melted clock faces, looks tortured, and recalls a line from Wilfred Owen's *Dulce et Decorum Est*: *Like a devil's, sick of sin* and is said to be a portrait of Michelangelo himself, in which case, he had no high opinion of his looks. I suspect it's another message and that the anguished face, if it does represent Michelangelo, depicts his displeasure at being forced to work on this painting instead of finishing off the tomb of the deceased pope, Julius II. First and foremost, Michelangelo considered himself a sculptor and he resented the years spent painting this and the ceiling of the Sistine chapel, a total of 11 years. Still, no one could say they were wasted years, that's for sure, not even the artist himself.

Yole tells us about the Sistine chapel ceiling, that it depicts scenes from the Old Testament from God dividing Light from Darkness to the Drunkenness of Noah. Which just goes to show you, that you learn something new every day – I never knew that Noah *was* drunk, though I have to admit I have not read The Bible from cover to cover, though it is a Good Book. I know he lived for 900 years or something and he was spared for being so good, so drinking the Cabernet Sauvignon to excess can't be bad and it can't be so bad for the liver either. In fact, it seems to have some remarkable pickling properties. But more likely after enduring all that water, he just overindulged a bit: *Sorry Mrs Noah, light of my life, Joan of my ark, hic!...just got a bit fed up of drinking nothing but water. First time I've been drunk in 600 years. I swear by that rainbow I won't let it happen again, hic! Not if I live for another 300 years. Please, just don't hit me again! I'm an old man.* Or maybe he'd just been bitten by a mosquito and realises what a great opportunity he could have had with a little selective amnesia: *Sorry God, I totally forgot about the mosquitoes and the wasps but I did put in the midgies to annoy the Scots like you said, just so Scotland wouldn't be totally perfect.* But he was too much of a wimp and now he's drinking to drown his sorrows, and starting a new trend.

This was the first painting and as they progress towards the altar, you are meant to see how Michelangelo got into his stride and as he loosened up, the figures become less stiff and formal. Certainly I wouldn't have argued with God in the second last panel, where he is commanding the Sun to shine upon the earth. No Mr Nice Guy this with fluffy cotton-wool hair, but a greying, bad tempered looking hombre with forked beard who is not going to take any Nonsense or No for an answer either.

I am interested to note that in the Original Sin scene where Adam and Eve are eating the forbidden fruit, that Michelangelo has chosen to depict the Serpent with the torso of a woman. Interesting idea, Michelangelo, but I couldn't possibly comment.

The panels are surrounded by triangular lunettes depicting the Ancestors of Christ, then there are the Prophets and the Sybils and in the corners, Old Testament Scenes of Salvation and all these separated from each other by pillars with carvings and friezes which give the illusion of being three dimensional, so that there is not an inch of ceiling which has escaped the Michelangelo brush.

It may not have been a labour of love and there was no love lost between Michelangelo and Julius II. Michelangelo binned the Pope's plan for the ceiling in favour of his own design and even locked the Pope out at certain times when he wanted to see how the work was progressing. The artist finished not a moment too soon, for Julius lived only a few months after the ceiling was finished. And, when it was, it is hard not to imagine Michelangelo looking at the finished work and even if he didn't want to do it, saw that it was good.

Incredible to think that the walls barely get a mention, which, in a different setting, would be the focus of admiration themselves. It was Sixtus IV who commissioned the painting of the walls under the direction of none other than my hero, Pinturicchio. Here there are paintings by Botticelli, Perugino and Ghirlandaio. I nod sagely as if I'd heard of all these people all my life. I can't remember when I first heard of Botticelli, it was so long ago, but I know my familiarity with Pinturicchio goes back only four months and I've never heard of the other two before in my puff. But that's why I'm on an Italian Journey after all, to listen, to see and to learn and it's not as if I'm an art specialist like I suspect Mr Yorkie is and should know this stuff already.

Right! We're off! Hopefully we have learned enough to appreciate what we are going to see in the Sistine Chapel. But that is not all we are going to see, it's more like the icing on the cake, because we are going to be passing through some of the amazingly extensive Vatican museum on the way.

First stop is another grave for my collection – a really good one! I don't know how many saints I've got in my collection – I suspect this is my very first, but maybe not as I don't keep records as I feel that to do so would make me, in modern parlance, a sad person, like those people who write numbers of planes and trains in a notebook. Although, for a grave collector, the term would not seem altogether inappropriate.

It is the grave of St Helena, the mother of Constantine, a monstrous sarcophagus executed in the hated porphyry. It must be as deep as I am short, with figures in high relief mounted on rearing horses parading around the bottom, whilst the lid, with reclining figures at each corner, boast garlands of laurel wreaths. She took up religion after her husband, Constantius, divorced her on the grounds she wasn't posh enough after he was named Emperor elect. How come his parents got his name so wrong? A bit ironic to say the least.

Amongst her various claims to fame, she brought back a piece of the supposedly True Cross from Jerusalem. I suppose it was, or maybe it wasn't. It's now meant to be in an iron cross at the top of the obelisk which now marks the centre of the piazza in front of the basilica. Well, who's going to get up there and see? And how could you tell anyway? It might just as well be the finger of John the Baptist.

We're in a long corridor now. It's the Gallery of the Candelabra, so called because set in square niches, are massive Roman marble candlesticks, and it displays Greek and Roman sculptures. We're on a march through really; there isn't the time to stop and stare as W H Davies would have us do as this is just an artery en route to the Sistine Chapel, but we pause nevertheless in front of a statue of a well-endowed goddess, not because of the size, but the number of her endowments. In fact, they are not breasts at all, but bulls' testicles, according to Yole. They look more like plum tomatoes to me, except the Romans never knew tomatoes as I discovered a few years ago. Isn't that amazing?

But surely they are breasts, meant to feed all these children she has since she's so fertile? And why would anyone choose to string necklaces of bulls' testicles round your neck anyway like the onion Johnnies from France who were a common sight in my youth? Unless, of course, they are trophies of her suitors who were all hung like bulls and *that's* why she was so fertile! This sounds like a plausible explanation, as she was a bit of a hard woman in mythology, not averse to loosing off arrows at all and sundry and vindictive too, turning poor Actaeon into a stag to be devoured by his own hounds just because he happened to catch sight of her in the buff. Yes, this is none other than Artemis - but not the Greek Artemis whom we all know and love; this is Artemis of Ephesus, a fertility goddess who somehow acquired Artemis' name.

There are other busts in this gallery, but they are just heads and shoulders of blokes and of no interest to us, nor are any of the other exhibits, although I notice an amusing sculpture of Pan tickling some naked guy's foot. By the look on his face, he is making a great deal of noise about it. Perhaps the lady I mistook for a howling dog in the early hours of this morning was only having a foot massage.

We press on in a relentless tide and enter the next gallery, the Gallery of Tapestries. On our left are Belgian tapestries which depict the life of Christ and here is a really amusing one. Well, it may be amusing for us, but not for the diners. It's *The Last Supper*, and there, splayed out on a dish in front of Christ is a succulent roast suckling pig! Actually, there are two of them. One has been cut in half and separated on either side of the splayed out animal. No wonder Christ nor any of the disciples seem to be amused. At the centre of the table, one of them has swooned away completely in front of the offending fare whilst Christ comforts him by stroking his luxuriant blonde locks (a common colour in the eastern Mediterranean). His eyes are closed in horror: *In the name o' the wee man! Whit kinda grub is this tae gie a Jewish man for his last meal wi' his mates! I mean tae say!*

Colourful though the tapestries may be, it's the ceiling of the Gallery which gets my admiration. It's illusionist architecture at its best. Incredible to think that these panels containing figures which look as if they had stepped out of a piece of Wedgewood pottery, in their sugar-icing frames and Greek keys and laurel wreaths, are in fact, one dimensional and as flat as pancakes. I would love to reach up and touch them, just to make sure, the illusion is so perfect.

As we progress down the gallery, there is a huge tapestry of the Resurrection. Christ, in a red robe, and with his dazzlingly white skin, appears in 3D emerging from the blackness of the rock tomb but his eyes have an intensity which would be remarkable enough in a painting, but in a tapestry, all the more incredible. The gaze seems to hold you and as you get closer, Christ appears to be returning your gaze and as you get level, then pass, his eyes follow your progress. It's enough to make you want to repent.

From here we enter the Gallery of Maps, the idea of Gregory XIII, the same who gave us the new calendar, to show all of Italy and the islands in the Mediterranean as well as the siege of Malta and the battle of Lepanto, great Christian victories over the heathen Turks. Because of our recent visit to Tuscany, Iona and I stop and look for Stigliano where we were based, and there it is, even although it is a tiny little village! And here is Sicily where we were the October before, only the cartographer, for some reason, has painted it upside down so that the Straits of Messina appear on the bottom left instead of top right.

If the ceiling of the Gallery of Tapestries was wonderful in its tastefulness and use of restraint, this ceiling takes the breath away in its overstated show of opulence. There are so many panels, all of different sizes, it's impossible to make sense of it, to see what the focus is. In any case, there is so much gold paint, that the eye is dazzled. The impression I have, standing at one end and looking down the massive length of the corridor, is as if I have, like Alice, fallen into burrow, only in my case it is roofed with gold. It is a rest and a relief for the eyes, to look out from an open window and see the verdant greenery of the Vatican gardens, though marred somewhat by the ugly skeleton of the transmitting tower built by Marconi, rising like a pylon above the trees and still used by Radio Vatican.

Over to the left, is a good view of the dome, so Yole talked with forked tongue when she told us earlier that this was the only place where we could see the entire dome. But then, I am probably not meant to be leaning half out of the window. One little push from Iona and I would be strawberry jam. But too many witnesses for her to collect the bread from the insurance.

Next stop is the Sistine Chapel. Yole tells us before we go down the stairs that photography is expressly forbidden, whether or not you use a flash and that you are not allowed to video either. Even more than that, we are not supposed to talk. We are to be given 20 minutes in the chapel and we are to meet at the far end.

Off we go. As we descend the stairs, there are numerous signs saying that photography is not permitted. Yes, I get the message. This has to be one of the highlights of the trip which has been so full of highlights already. But before we enter the chapel, there is an added, unexpected attraction. We pass through a room which appears to be dedicated to the Doctrine of the Immaculate Conception, the Colonna dell' Immacolata which commemorates this event I had seen in the piazza Mignanelli and had set me thinking how this could happen some 2000 years after the event and in the 11th year of Pope Pius IX's reign. Presumably in this room of documents behind all these glass cases is the answer, but I am on the conveyer belt of mass tourism and to stop would be to create a logjam of tourists and block up the way to the Sistine Chapel. I don't suppose anyone else is interested or perhaps they are good Catholics and already know the answer.

Wow! The colours are amazing, so fresh, so clean, so new, like Pinturicchio's frescoes in Siena, that these also could have been painted yesterday. I am lucky, not for the first time on this trip, to benefit from restoration works. No eggshell cracked faces but creamy skin; no drab and dark garments but vibrant raiment; no lank hair in desperate need of a wash, but lustrous locks. I can see them perfectly and in close up because I have had the good sense to bring along the small pair of binoculars which is, and has been, an indispensable part of my travelling equipment for a good number of years. I focus on possibly the most famous image of them all, the creation of Adam, his outstretched arm, his fingers oh so nearly touching those of the outstretched arm of God, but minutely apart so that you can almost feel the energy passing between the two.

There are benches round the walls so you can sit and look at the ceiling in a bit more comfort, rather than breaking your back and putting your neck out of joint (pity poor Michelangelo who spent 4 years like that) and there is not a spare seat to be had but all the seated people do effectively block off the view of the walls. No one seems to be paying them the least bit of attention.

Neither do a lot of people seem to be paying attention to the no talking and no photography rules. Every so often there is a flash of brilliant light which seems to fill up the whole room and there are people unashamedly using their video cameras. There are guards patrolling the floor on the lookout for the flashers and filmers. I watch as one approaches a young Japanese who is aiming his camera at the ceiling and so is totally unaware that he is about to be caught. What will happen? He needn't bother to plead lack of English or Italian or any other language as there were plenty of signs of a camera with a dirty red cross through it. So, will his camera be confiscated? Will he be thrown out of the chapel? Not a bit of it. The guard taps him on the shoulder, nods at the camera, lifts a cautionary forefinger and shakes his head, before moving on again. In fact he has scarcely paused. The Japanese gentleman looks around him and after a moment, re-aims his camera whilst his companion keeps guard. No wonder that everyone is at it, except me. I had a much harder time for filming in the entrance where it didn't say filming was banned. I daren't now in case Iona catches me.

Every so often there is a Tannoy announcement reminding us that we are not to talk and not to take photographs either and for a moment, there is a hush, but it's a hopeless task. It's impossible to fill this room with silence. So many people, so awed by the spectacle; so natural to want to point out something special which has caught the eye. I bet the announcement is on a loop and time switch and comes on every two minutes or something for all the notice anybody takes of it. They ought to draft in one of those fierce nuns from Assisi if they want silence.

But talking of the absence of silence, I recall that this chapel is the setting for one of my most favourite pieces of music. From time to time, I indulge in the frivolous pursuit of making a list of the records I would take to a desert island after the style of the radio programme and this one is always there, although others may come and go from time to time. I am referring to Allegri's *Miserere*, his arrangement of Psalm 51, composed in 1638. If there *are* angels, then this surely must be the way they sing, but they performed it here as the culmination of the service known as Tenebrae in which the candles are extinguished one by one until, in complete darkness, the *Miserere* is sung. That must be one of the most spine-tingling experiences ever.

The popes retained copyright of the manuscript and we only hear it today because the 14 year old Mozart heard it once and wrote the whole thing down from memory! No doubt whoever was pope at the time, in 1770, was fizzing and quite possibly steam came out of his ears which reminds me that this is the place too, where the cardinals meet to decide who is to be the next pope. So where is the chimney then?

Outside, the chapel looks plain, non-descript and uninspiring. Who would believe that it contains such treasures within? Talk about an inner beauty! Anyway, high up, close to the pitch of the roof is the window from which the smoke comes. Yole says that they bring in a portable chimney for the purpose.

We're out in the glaring heat again and standing on the steps of the basilica. This is our first view of the piazza which looks surprisingly empty and nun free. Probably there are hundreds of people there, it's just the piazza is so vast that it swallows them up.

Now for the moment of truth for the underdressed! Guttings looks fetching in Iona's black and yellow sarong but it doesn't melt the hearts of the two men in suits at the entrance. One looks like a negative of the other, his light suit contrasting with the dark suit of his companion but both have greasy slicked back hair and both mean business. Probably that's why they are wearing business suits. If Guttings had shaved off his beard he may have passed as an underdeveloped girl, if a rather ugly one, but it's too late now. He tries again, this time pulling his shorts down from his hips and his socks up so that they cover his knees and they practically meet, apart from a small slit. He leans forward to cover the gaps but it's still not suitable say the suits. He's not going to be visiting St Peter's on this trip, neither unfortunately is his missis who nobly stays to keep him company.

Likewise Gordon. He has his partner's wrap round his middle, and he *would* look like the King of Tonga if he worked on his belly a bit, but his royal status cuts no ice with these cool dudes. Rejected. Bombed out.

Not so Donald, the crafty Scotsman. Here, at the top of the steps, at the entrance to the basilica, he pulls from his rucksack what looks like a couple of sleeves, steps into them, zips them to the bottom of his shorts and presents himself for inspection. Transformation. Pass. Smart move. Well that's all that's smart about them. My son wears this sort of baggy attire with pockets and pouches and zips in the unlikeliest of places. They would never make it in Saville Row, but Donald is young enough not to worry about being seen dead in such things and, I have to admit, they are practical. What would I have given to have been wearing shorts on that Metro trip, which, with apologies to Apsley Cherry-Garrard, was for me, the worst journey in the world.

Yole is unsympathetic and unrepentant. "You were warned," she says, "that they are very strict here. All right, we'll meet you over there -" she indicates with a flourish of her wand some indeterminate point over to her right and with a glance at her watch, "- in half an hour." I have a feeling that she is not best pleased with them.

Guttings looks glum, but then he always does. If his suitcase had not been lost, would he have had a pair of trousers to procure access? Still, he knew in Florence that trousers were a necessity, but maybe he thought his insurance wouldn't stump up. It reminds me I still don't know if I'm going to be reimbursed for the extra £310 I paid, just to get here. I had forgotten all about it. Thank you, Guttings, for reminding me. It's not your fault, but now I feel like you look.

Inside the basilica, to our right, is Michelangelo's *Pietà*. Iona is confused. She is sure that when she was here before, that it wasn't there, in that location. Yole confirms that her memory is like an elephant's, which I already know. It was moved to this site after some madman attacked it with a hammer, in the year of our marriage, 1972. Thanks a lot, buddy. Now it's even harder to see. Apart from the tourists who form a human shield round it anyway, there is now 6 inches of bullet-proof glass. Actually, I just made that last statistic up, but that's what it looks like and it sounds reasonable.

Poor Mary! She looks so young, not a wrinkle on her face. She scarcely looks old enough to have produced a son as long, as limp, as dead as he. For the worst of all things must surely be to witness the death of your child. It goes against the tenets of nature. It is not right, it should not be; all of Nature cries out against such an abomination, yet Mary does not rage at his going into that good night like Dylan Thomas, but accepts the weight of her dead son in her lap with a sadness and resignation as if she is beyond grief.

Apparently it was the only *pietà* he ever finished; he was just 25 and signed it on a sash across Mary's chest but a combination of the glass, distance and the heads in front of me make it impossible to see such detail. He made Mary so youthful, Yole says, to show her innocence and purity. Now I know why people can't believe that Iona is so young-looking for her age. All that confining herself to birthdays and anniversaries with the occasional consummation of new places has really done wonders for her skin tones. So why then, do I have a face like a crumpled brown paper bag? I'd really like to know, Michelangelo.

It's impossible also for the eye not to be attracted to the bronze monstrosity under the dome, in the centre of the nave. The basilica is light and airy but this is dark and brooding and funereal. It marks the spot supposedly under which St Peter lies buried and forms a canopy over the Papal altar where only the Pope is allowed to perform Mass. It is Bernini's *baldacchino,* made from bronze stripped from the roof of the portico in the Pantheon, as Yole had told us earlier. I wish they hadn't. The four enormous pillars, twisted like barley sugar sticks spiral upwards to support the crown of the fringed canopy. The design is bad enough, but it's the colour that offends me more than anything, so black and sombre, the gold filigree not withstanding, that you can't help feeling depressed. Imagine that lunatic with his hammer attacking the *Pietà* when he could have turned it into a weapon of Mass destruction instead.

At the bottom of the columns is the coat of arms of Pope Urban VIII, a reminder that, apart from Bernini, we have him to blame for this. It features two crossed keys, the keys to the Kingdom of Heaven, but heaven knows why they would want to destroy the effect of the dome's cupola by plonking this thing, this monstrosity, at the bottom of it.

Yes, the dome is a magnificent sight, supported on its massive four piers. Shafts of light are streaming in from the gallery of windows, illuminating the gold lettering which encircles them beneath and below them, at the top of the piers, are medallions which from here look like paintings, but which are, in fact, mosaics. The bottom of the piers depict the relics which St Peter's supposedly has in its possession and being St Peter's, they are good ones: St Veronica's hankerchief, which bears Christ's image after she used it to wipe his face; the lance of St Longinus, which pierced the side of Christ on the cross; a piece of the True Cross (another); and the head of our patron saint, St Andrew - whom a 5th generation Scottish American of my acquaintance once referred to as "the greatest Scotsman who ever lived". Imagine that, not just a tooth, but the whole headful, only apparently Paul VI gave it back to the Eastern Church in 1966. Not that it makes any difference to me. You never get to see any of these relics anyway.

Through the dismal frame of the *baldacchino*, and glowing all the more intensely perhaps because of it, is a golden light in the apse. It is the image of the Holy Spirit, shown as a white dove in the centre of an elliptical window, from which radiate golden rays which turn to red at the outer edges, so that the impression is of a diamond flashing fingers of fire. To the right of this is the tomb of Urban VIII who gets a position of honour here, in the apse of the basilica, instead of down below in the crypt.

Also in the main body of the church, intriguingly, is the body of Pope John XXIII. I can recall the television broadcast of his funeral in 1963 maybe because television was still something of a novelty for our impoverished family in those days, but who could forget that great aquiline nose as he lay in his open coffin? Yole waves her hand to indicate that he lies somewhere over on the right, as if it's only a matter of slight significance. He's on his way to sainthood. Apparently, when they examined his body in the crypt, there were no signs of deterioration, which is one of the signs that you may be a saint. There are other tests besides, but in the meantime, until they make their minds up, they have brought him up here, and put him in a glass coffin. I can scarcely believe what Yole is telling me. This is as good, if not better, than any relic, and I can scarcely believe either that she is not including him in the tour. Just as well we have the afternoon free and I can come back and see him for myself. A grave is one thing, but the real body of a famous pope is something else! For once, I consider myself dead lucky.

We pass the entry to the crypt. Must go down there too this afternoon; there must be popes galore down there, though to be honest, I don't know much about popes or one from another, but I'd like to find John Paul I if I could, the one who died suddenly in mysterious circumstances. And down there too, there must be the graves of the Stuart would-be Kings of Scotland, Bonnie Price Charlie, the Young Pretender and his father, whom, strangely enough, they called the Old Pretender. I know because they died in Rome and one of the few things I knew about St Peter's before I came here, is that there is a memorial to them in here, somewhere. No doubt I could find it on my own later, but it might save a bit of time if I ask Yole where it is.

She says we're on our way there now. It's not a bad memorial at all. I think the Stuarts would be pretty chuffed with it really. There are two pretty glum looking angels with

319

bent heads and drooping wings standing on either side of a door, presumably the gates of death, but just like the sort of door you would expect to see on a stately home with panels and a couple of brass knockers. Above the door is the legend: BEATI MORTVI QUI IN DOMINO MORIVNTVR. In the panel above that is a whole lot more Latin. Not for the first time, I regret my wasted time in the Latin class, but I recognise IABACO III and underneath IABACO II MAGNAE BRIT REGIS FILIO which I take to read: James III, son of James II, king of Great Britain. Then beneath: KAROLO EDVARDO. That's him all right, Prince Charles Edward Stuart, popularly known as Bonnie Prince Charlie. There's a reference to HENRICO also, the younger son, Prince Charlie's brother who became a cardinal, and who, after the death of Charles Edward, styled himself Henry IX. That would have been a hard act to follow and how ironic, if he had been king, for a cardinal to follow in name, at least, that arch anti-Catholic and womaniser, Henry VIII!

Well, Henrico may have called himself king and so may his father who was never king either, but that doesn't alter the facts. Nevertheless, here it is, written in stone as if it were a fact. But one thing is for sure - Shakespeare wasn't right when he made Juliet say: *What's in a name? That which we call a rose,/ By any other name would smell as sweet.* I bet the Old Pretender, James Stuart, thinks Iabaco III sounds a whole lot better than either of the other two.

"Can you tell us about them?" This is my reward for declaring an interest. Yole wants me to address the group on the Stuarts. Had she seen me earlier acting the guide in the Piazza del Popolo? Surely not. She probably doesn't know much about them and wants to learn so she can pass the information on to later tours.

So I tell them about the Old Pretender and the First Jacobite Rebellion in 1714 and the Young Pretender and the Second Jacobite Rebellion in 1745, and the retreat from

Derby and how, if Bonnie Prince Charlie's troops had only gone on, if they'd had the promised support from France which failed to materialise, London could well have fallen and we might all be Catholics now. I expand about the inconclusive second battle of Falkirk and the butchery of Culloden, the last battle fought on British soil in 1746 and how after that, the wearing of the tartan was forbidden and the playing of the bagpipes also. I pause for breath.

"That was very interesting," says Yole. "Thank you."

I am warming to my task. "Ah, but the story didn't end there. You see –"

Someone is putting a steady pressure on my foot. It's La-Belle-Dame-Sans-Merci and her look says: *Shut up!* I have my mouth open, ready to tell the group all about Charlie's flight to Skye and his escape to France, dressed as a washerwoman, Flora MacDonald and all that, but clearly they are going to have to remain in ignorance as we are already making our way to the exit.

"What's the matter?" I hiss as the foot-stomper and I follow in the wake.

"Couldn't you see that everyone was bored to tears?"

"No!"

"Well they were! They didn't want a bloody history lesson!"

Ooooh! She swore and in a church too and in St Peter's as well! She must be really mad at me this time for embarrassing her again.

Out in the piazza, we are reunited with the shorts people. God knows what they did with themselves all this time in the frying pan heat of this cauldron of a piazza. They do look a bit fed up. Well, nothing new for the Guttings I suppose, but Gordon and partner don't look too happy either. Maybe they've got an attack of the miseries from the Guttings having spent all this time with them in this intense heat, exchanging few words.

In front of us, in the centre of the piazza is an obelisk brought to Rome by Caligula in 36 AD. Interesting to note that, unusually, it does not have hieroglyphics on it. Maybe Caligula's men nicked it before it was finished or else he said: *I want one of those pointy Egyptian things but not with any of that funny writing on it or I'll stick it up your toga* and they had to sandpaper all the writing off as, if any Emperor would do as he said, Caligula would. It's not in its original position though. Nero's Circus used to run through half of the present day piazza and basilica and beyond and the obelisk supposedly marked its centre.

The piazza is the design of Bernini and this is splendid, a complete contrast to his dire *baldacchino*. How could anyone who designed that, design this? The twin arms of the four columns-deep colonnade sweep round in an encompassing arc which remains open at the bottom and gives on to the Via della Conziliazone. Bernini had planned to build a triumphal arch there but it was never built, so the arms of the colonnade remain symbolically open as if welcoming the world into the piazza and the protective arms of the Catholic Church. In the piazza, Yole adds, there are a couple of points where if you stand on them, the seemingly impenetrable forest of columns all melt into one single row. Must go and try that!

Of course, the Via della Conziliazone wasn't there either in Bernini's day. This was part of Mussolini's settlement with the Church, the so called Lateran Treaty of 1929 when the Vatican was accorded independent city status, so Mussolini tore down the houses to make way for this broad avenue and thus infuriated a great number of residents at the same time. Actually, the houses are not all in line, so a row of columns was introduced on either side to convey the impression that the road runs perfectly true and straight. The best view of the piazza and the Via della Conziliazone is from the top of the dome and I shouldn't think there's a person here who hasn't seen that view on a million postcards and posters.

Over to the left, Yole indicates the papal apartments and says that the second from the end is the Pope's bedroom. How does she know that then? Maybe when she was here before with a tour she saw him at the window in his pyjamas, getting a breath of fresh air. But there's no chance of us catching a glimpse of him today. The air in Rome is too hot and he's retreated to the mountains. Quite right - he didn't know I was coming or I am sure he would have stayed. Too bad, I'll not find out now if that itchiness on my shoulder blades is due to budding wings or not. But if he can't be sure yet about John XXIII, I don't suppose I would have got a definitive answer today anyway.

To our left, there's a couple of Swiss guards. They were first introduced by Julius II in 1506 to protect the Holy See. You have to be aged between 19 and 30, unmarried and Swiss of course. But you don't seem to have to be able to see that well to protect the See apparently, as one of them is wearing spectacles. You just don't have to mind making a spectacle of yourself dressed in that yellow, blue and red stripy outfit designed by Michelangelo on one of his off days.

"Are there any more questions?"

It's time for Yole to go. Her last office for us is to explain how we can go back by tram if we want to avoid the Metro. Don't we just! Only, if we take the tram, we are to watch out for pickpockets. True enough, there isn't room for pickpockets to operate in the Metro, their arms are pinned to their sides.

"Erm...could you tell us, where are the toilets?" says Tom.

I hated that as a teacher. You've just finished explaining something and you ask if there are any questions, hoping that the pupils want elucidation on some arcane point and

323

they say something like: *Do French sheep speak French?* or: *Do we **have** to know all this?*

They are right behind him, which is why he can't see them of course, but just as soon as Yole goes, that's where I am going. In Iona's bag I have my shorts and I can't wait to get out of these trousers and expose my legs to the fresh air.

I dive into the nearest cubicle. I take off my pouch, colour co-ordinated with my shirt of Lincoln green of course, (naturally, as best dressed tourist of the year I would ensure that it did) and which contains my visa card and, unusually, some euro notes which Iona has allowed me to carry which is only fair really as she is carrying my clothes. I place it on top of the cistern. Then I take down my trousers, followed by my panties. Ah, the relief! To let the air in is bliss. I encourage the circulation amongst the recently liberated by having a jolly good scratch. I wish I had my kilt with me. How comfortable it would be to stride across the piazza and the Via della Conciliazione with the air circulating freely! Suddenly, a thought occurs. What if I had turned up at St Peter's wearing my national dress? Would I have been allowed in? And if not, what fun I would have at the Race Discriminations Board. Only it's Italy and they would never have heard of it. Wait a moment, though - it's not Italy, it's the Vatican. I am so transfixed by the thought that I stop my scratching. Maybe *they* have heard of it. The scenario intrigues. I imagine presenting myself before the business suited:

No!

What do you mean, no?

No skirts on men allowed.

This is not a skirt! This is a kilt. Gordon tartan for your information, not that an ignoramus like you would know any better - or care.

334

Don't you dare swear at me! This is a church. We can still see your knees. Don't care what you call it, it's still a skirt. And you look like a man, sort of.

You insult my national dress. I am going in!

Oh no you don't! Guards!

*Look at them, with their funny stripy trousers! They think they're the cat's pyjamas but no self-respecting cat would be seen dead in them. But I bet you'd let them in, yet you won't let **me** in with my tasteful tartan.*

It's still a skirt! Now gedda outta here!

You'll not hear the last of this! I'm going to report you to the Race Relations Board.

So whadda I care! What's that anyhow, you Scots git! Now piss off!

I slip out of my reverie and into my swimming trunks. When I get back to the piazza, everyone is gone except for Iona and Bill and Pat and Tom, Dick and Harriet.

"What took you so long?" says Iona with more than a hint of irritation in her voice. I have apparently been keeping them waiting but I didn't know they were all waiting for me – no one bothered to tell me.

I hand her my trousers with my panties discreetly hidden rolled up inside them, but for some reason, she doesn't want to touch them and presents her back so I can stuff them into her rucksack.

I hadn't realised I had taken any time at all, just time enough to change out of my trousers. As I unzip her bag, suddenly I feel ice-cold as if someone had squeezed all the blood out of my heart. I can't say whether it was the act of unzipping the bag or the recollection of what I did in the cubicle, perhaps both, which triggered the memory. My pouch! I don't know why I took it off in the first place but I can see it now, lying on top of the cistern. I drop my trousers and bolt down the stairs without explanation and make straight for the cubicle. Thank you, God! The cubicle is unoccupied and there is my pouch, just as I had left it. I seize it, relieved beyond belief to see that it is not a mirage. If we had had to cancel our visa with the holiday not yet half over and very little cash…

The wrath of La-Belle-Dame-Sans-Merci doesn't bear thinking about. Last time I lost it, that time in Nice, she wasn't with me and I took a gamble and didn't report it, only for it to turn up intact at a police station after a couple of days. But, had I lost it this time she would have made me cancel it, I'm sure, and we wouldn't have been able to do the exploring we had planned for the second week in Sorrento. Imagine us lying round the pool unable to go anywhere because of my stupidity. It doesn't sound all that bad to me, but it would have been intolerable for Iona who hates the heat and for whom sitting around a swimming pool for longer than an hour drives her to distraction. Life for her would have been unbearable and she would have made it unbearable for me also.

It's with an enormous sense of triumph therefore that I return, waving my pouch in the air.

"Oh, for goodness sake!" says Iona in exasperation. Apparently it had not dawned upon her till then the reason for my precipitant departure. You might have thought that she would have been pleased and full of praise for my remembering so quickly and being so lucky to find it still there. But no! Not a single word of appreciation.

I test the spot on the piazza where the columns are supposed to meld into one and it works! I wish I could do a disappearing act like that! It could be very useful at times of embarrassment. There is another one at the other side but I can't get on to that as there is an American standing on it whilst his Italian friend tells him his life story. I give up waiting.

The plan is that we will have some lunch and then we will make an ascent of the dome and pay another visit to the basilica. We exit the piazza through the colonnades to the left, or the right if you are facing the basilica, and make our way down the Via di Porta Angelica and there on the left, is another of the Swiss guards. This one has the same style of uniform, only his is one shade of blue with a black beret and leggings and white gloves. He seems to be there as a traffic obstacle as he has to step in front of the oncoming traffic to allow the traffic coming behind him to pass, such is the narrowness of the street that it will not allow two cars in addition to him all abreast at the same time. An unconventional but effective way of controlling the traffic. We have sleeping policemen to do that but here they have real live upright Swiss guards. They should give him the striped pyjamas to wear though. Everyone would avoid them.

At the Bar Moretto, we split up, Iona and I outside, the others in search of air-conditioning in the inside. I don't want anything to eat really, liquid refreshment would do me nicely but Iona insists that I eat something. She says I need my protein and me with a hump like a camel, except I carry mine at the front, not the back. Ridiculous!

It looks like you can order a slice of pizza, not the whole thing. We ask the waiter who looks Jewish and a bit puzzled at my question. He says in a heavy accent, yes we can do that and do I support Manchester United?

"Not on your life! Me not English. Me Scottish. Me support Aberdeen."

He looks blank.

"Aberdeen. You not heard of? Aberdeen. Football team, same colours Man U."

He shakes his head. "Two pizza. Cheers, mate."

I am surprised and impressed at his use of the idiom. "Where you learn speak like that? *Cheers, mate*?"

"Lots of English visitors. I pick it up. Like to talk English."

"You English very good," I compliment him, although it is not.

"Cheers, mate," he says and goes, hopefully for my beer. I am dying of thirst.

La-Belle-Dame-Sans-Merci is glaring at me balefully.

"What is it? What have I done now?"

"What are you speaking to him like that for?"

"Like what?" I am puzzled. I thought I had been perfectly polite, even especially friendly, saying his English was good, when it wasn't.

"Talking to him like he was an idiot and you are mentally defective. *Me Scottish, me support Aberdeen*, indeed!"

I am stunned. She is right of course. I was hardly aware of having done it. His English had been so halting, it had seemed right at the time to reduce it to baby language for easier comprehension, but I see now that I was wrong and that his English will never improve if native speakers insist on sounding like Red Indian chiefs, though I should say Native Americans of course.

I am not surprised when it comes, to find that instead of one slice of pizza each, we have a whole one each and they are not that small either. I hate eating a lot in the middle of the day. It takes me to about this time to shake off the ties of sleep, and a heavy meal just makes me want to revert. But this is my humble piece of pizza pie so I do not complain about the misunderstanding. Instead, I just eat it and swallow hard when the bill comes and I discover it's about what I would have spent on an evening meal. Not that I'll have to do that tonight however, as it is our last night as a group and we are going out to a restaurant. But now I'll probably not have room for the feast which, like the meal at the Palazzo Borghese, I've already paid for, included in the price of the tour.

I leave the waiter a tip, although I never felt like less like it in my life.

"Cheers, mate!"

I am unhappy also at the prospect of having to wear my trousers again, exacerbated by the thought of having to climb all those stairs in them, but there is nothing else for it but to descend to the toilets and put them on again. It feels like descending to Hades.

Eventually we find the ticket office by the side of the Sistine Chapel and discover that a lift will transport us part of the way. Tom, Dick and Harriet have gone back to the hotel so it is only Bill and Pat and Iona and I, we intrepid upwardly mobile travellers who are undertaking the steps.

We are first in the queue for the lift but by the time it comes, we have been joined by many more. There is a lift driver and he crams us all in but does not whisk us upward until even more people have been pressed into service. The air in the lift is clammy, the atmosphere unbearably humid. Packed together in this forced intimacy with complete strangers for this brief period where our lives cross, I avoid eye contact. It's quite intimate enough without gazing into the eyes of the person whose body is pressed against you. I gaze over the heads of my fellow passengers to the driver by the door standing by his panel of buttons. It has *Schindler's* written above it. Ah! Schindler's Lift. That explains it.

We are decanted onto a courtyard. Over to our left I can see the backs of the statues which adorn the top of the façade of the basilica, so I know just exactly how high we are and how high we have yet to climb for the dome towers over us to our right. I'd like to go and have a closer look at the statues, but that can wait till later, once I've been to the top.

Like the Duomo in Florence, we emerge initially inside the dome. Now we are so close, we can indeed see that the paintings in the medallions above each of the great plinths and below the six foot high gold lettering, are in fact, mosaics. Gazing up at our destination, where the light comes bursting through the cupola, the panels spread out like a starburst.   Below is Bernini's *baldacchino*. From below it looked immense, which it is, at 66 feet high, but from here it looks tiny and such a long way down to the top of the cross which draws the four corners of the canopy together.

The four arms of the church spread out from this central point, though because of the wire mesh which prevents would be suicides from casting themselves onto the variegated marble floor beneath, it is not possible to lean over and I can only see two of them. Nevertheless, from here it still impresses more than from at ground level, just how enormous is the scale of this building and reminds me that I am inside the largest church in the world, ironically, in the smallest country in the world.

From the splendours of the interior, it's but a small step to the exterior or rather the gap between the inner and outer dome but a giant leap as Neil Armstrong might have said, in terms of architecture. It's a bit like entering a toilet, with glazed gold tiles but without the graffiti which usually adorns such establishments, or which defaced the Duomo in Florence for that matter.

It's well worth the climb. If only one could escape the bird-brains chattering on their mobile phones, it would be perfect for a bird's eye view of Rome.

"Rome with a view," I quip wittily to Iona.

"Very amusing!" she replies without humour.

There's the famous view of Bernini's twin colonnades sweeping like a pair of cupped arms with Caligula's obelisk marking the centre of the piazza, which even from this height, still looks enormous and at the far end, like a gaping wound, the Via della Conciliazione leading straight to the Tiber.

It's fun trying to spot the other landmarks. The Pantheon, circular and grey, looks like a flying saucer. I can see the Forum and the arch of Septimus Severus. The Wedding Cake rears huge and white over everything, like a great white pimple, easily the most recognisable structure in the landscape, and, you would have to say, completely out of place. The Colosseum is much harder to spot, only confirmed by the use of the binoculars, indistinct and grey amidst the tumble of terracotta roofs and much smaller than you would expect. There is a surprising amount of greenery all over the city.

And at our feet is much more greenery, the elegant and spacious Vatican Gardens, mature trees and manicured lawns and a couple of formal gardens, one shaped into a coat of arms on the lawn in the centre of a huge house but what it is and whose coat of arms it is, the guide book does not say. The railway station is to the left, only used for freight nowadays and the papal heliport is at the furthest extremity of the gardens and not visible from here. There's the courtyard where we had our talk on *The Last Judgement* and the ceiling paintings of the Sistine Chapel, so all those buildings must be the Vatican museums. Blimey! (Because I am remembering where I am).

I take a last look around. Even if I do come back to Rome, I'll probably never come here again and make my way down to the courtyard where the lift stops. I make my way over to have a closer look at the saints standing patiently on the roof of the monument. I can look along the line of them, but I can't get very close because of the ten foot high railings which no doubt are another suicide deterrent. Just as well really as it would confuse the nuns if I appeared amongst them: *Who's that new saint up there?...Don't know. The one standing next to David Addison you mean?*

You wouldn't guess it, but behind these figures standing on the balustrade, it's like a little village, and all completely invisible from below. In addition to the two mini cupolas above the ends of the transepts, there are little buildings like

331

garden gazebos as well as other buildings, with terracotta tiled roofs, and even a post office. If I had a postcard, I could post it here in the blue post box outside the post office and it would probably arrive quicker than if posted in Italy, so they say.

I make for the lift, post haste. My companions will be fed up waiting for me I imagine. I am right of course. Time now to go to the opposite extremity, to the crypt, and visit some dead popes but the ladies are wearied and after the descent from the lift, just want to sit and rest their legs. There aren't any seats but they prop their bums as much as they can on some poor blighter's monument. I think it could well be the Stuarts'. Bill is off to the loo, so I look for the crypt.

The good news is that it's free and I would have actually *paid* to have been amidst such illustrious company. Down here, it is wall to wall popes. Some hopes amidst all these popes, of finding one that means anything to me. Some of the sarcophagi look very old indeed, but wait a moment, here's one that looks very new. I can scarcely believe my luck! If there's one I would have hunted for, it would have been this one. IOANNES PAVLVS PP I. Until I came here and learned about some other popes who seem to have been megalomaniacs or patrons of the arts, or both, this is about the only pope I've heard of, apart from John XXIII and I'm going to visit him shortly, I hope. As my memory serves, John Paul was the first to have a double-barrelled name and only lasted a month. Some say he was murdered. And here I am, standing, not at a memorial, but where he actually is. I wonder how he's getting on in there. Do they check him to see if he's a saintly candidate?

I could go rummaging around looking for some of the popes I've come across on this trip, like Julius II and Innocent X but they may not even be here and before I came here, I'd never heard of them, so what's the point unless you know their place in history? I dare say I'm missing something by not leaving the main thoroughfare and examining some of the serried ranks of sarcophagi in this vault, but it's altogether too easy and doesn't mean a thing to me. Here's Innocent IX for example. Sorry, Pope, but I don't know anything about you. My fault I'm sure. It probably means you were a good, average guy or I would probably have stumbled over you by now on this trip. You were only one out from notoriety, but not close enough to get into my collection. Sorry about that. To be remembered, you have to be very good or very bad, which is why I only remember a handful of my hundreds of ex-pupils.

So I zip through the hundreds of dead popes down here, my appetite whetted to see a real live dead pope. Pat and Iona are still where I left them, Iona fanning herself with her Chinese fan and Pat flapping some sort of pamphlet, probably less ineffectually. St Peter's greatest fans, I don't think. All this Cathedral to explore and there they are, still sitting on their bahookeys.

Bill is down in the crypt they say, yet I didn't see him. How cryptic! I remember how he side-stepped me on the Spanish Steps. I'm beginning to think he doesn't want to be left alone with me. He would have been behind me and perhaps he was following me, ready to duck down behind a sarcophagus in case I turned round. Or down there, amongst all the dead, where the living are in the minority, I really am just a dead loss.·

"Right, I'm off to find John XXIII. Anyone coming?"

The fans flutter agitatedly as if they were wafting away a foul smell, instead of issuing an innocuous invitation. As if I would do such a thing in such a holy place! All right. I'll go on my own, but go I must.

I head off to the right and it doesn't take me long to find him. After all, he is lit up like a fish in an aquarium. He is in a glass coffin beneath a huge Renaissance painting of wot I know naught. There are candlesticks burning above him and spotlights burning inside the coffin. He looks like a wax-work, like something out of Madame Tussaud's, yet he died forty years ago and if he were wax, surely those lamps would have melted him by now, especially that famous nose which comes within a centimetre of the top of the glass? And how long has he been on public display like this, under the spotlight?

If this is death, it looks OK. Maybe it's worth being dressed up like Santa Claus to have this sort of peace. His head rests upon a red cushion and he wears a red night-cap, trimmed with white fur, a red cape with gold trimmings, a white nightie and red slippers which rest upon a red cushion. Very comfy. He looks composed. Very composed. That's all right, he's doing the right thing. As long as he does not decompose, he'll be all right and he might make it as a saint yet.

There are rows of seats here, so we can view the corpse in comfort, yet there are only two others, apart from myself. How bizarre! You can't get near the Pietà, made of stone, yet here there is the real body of a pope, and no-one seems remotely interested, except for a Protestant like me. How ironic life is, or should that be death! I wonder if he minds being made an exhibition of like this. Would he mind, would anyone, if I pulled out my camcorder and filmed him? There are no notices to say that I shouldn't, yet it seems not right somehow, so I do it half-expecting a hand to descend on my shoulder, or a lightning bolt to come from the skies. But nothing happens: no-one seems to notice, or if they do, they don't mind and John XXIII sleeps on regardless.

He looks a lot more comfortable than me, that's for sure. I am desperate to get out of my trousers, although there is a lot more to do here. We haven't even scratched the surface of the Vatican museums for example but I am desperate to scratch somewhere else and the ladies pronounce themselves too tired to do any more sightseeing. We have to go out tonight so we all agree that we'll call it a day. It's been quite a successful day: one confirmed saint, one saint in waiting, three Scottish kings in waiting and one pope which I'll count.

Oh, and there was the Sistine Chapel

Chapter 10
Con Molto Alcol

At the Bar Moretto we stop for the compulsory daily *gelati* and continue down the Via di Porta Angelica until we come to the Piazza del Risorgimento where we can catch the pickpocket tram back to the hotel.

It's a leafy sort of a place and very crowded which is a good sign for the thieves and us as it means we probably don't have too long to wait for the tram. It's 4:50 and according to the timetable, if we are not mistaken, there should be one along in five minutes.

"Be a good frog and hop across to that corner shop and get some water," says Iona, "this stuff is revolting."

She's right enough about that. The water, even in its insulated bottle, as usual, feels as warm as a baby's bathwater. Just because I'm a frog, she thinks it's easy for me to hop across the road and get some more water, except she's wrong about that - hopping across the road is not the sort of thing you can do in Italy without the risk of being one very squashed amphibian.

The stream of traffic seems endless and looks as if it will never cease. Time is passing and the tram may appear at any moment. There's no sign of it but I can't tell from which direction it will come and I'm still stuck on the pavement. There's only one thing for it, I am going to have to step into the stream and let the drivers steer around me. With what may be a final look at Iona who has sent me on this perilous expedition and who is sitting on the kerb in the shade, chatting unconcernedly to Bill and Pat, I take the first step off the pavement on this Herculean labour. The things we do for love or out of fear, even if we have to face fear itself. It's just a question of prioritising your fears.

If I could, I would have done it with my eyes closed. For a start it means I wouldn't see the vehicles bearing down on me and secondly, I wouldn't see the irate faces of the drivers as they swerve around me without seeming to slacken speed. In a hopeless gesture, I raise my right hand as if to fend them off, like Canute ordering the tide to retreat, but it means they can't see the face of the *pazzo* who is attempting this death-defying feat.

Safely across! I grab a bottle and pay for it. I have a feeling that the tram may already be there. Like a swimmer entering a cold pool, it is better not to hesitate but to plunge right in as soon as I judge the time to be right. After this Mercedes, I can make a start, but I don't know about this red car hurtling down in the next lane. I take the plunge, and then an incredible thing happens! The mass of metal which had been hurtling towards me stops. I risk a quick glance at the driver. He doesn't seem in the least put out and in the meantime, the car in the next lane has slowed down and stopped too! I feel like Moses cleaving the waters as I make a gesture of thanks to these two untypical motorists and dodge the next three cars and arrive safely at the other side. Has the world gone mad? Two Italian drivers actually stopped and there wasn't even a zebra crossing in sight!

I needn't have feared that I was going to miss the tram though, there's still no sign of it. I hand the precious water to Iona.

"This is not *frizzante*," she complains. She still does not realise that she is lucky to get me back all in one piece. "It'll do though," she adds. She must have seen the sign of rebellion clouding my brow.

As usual, she is right. In my haste, I had just grabbed the first bottle my hand closed upon, but I'm damned if I am going to cross that stream of death again, however charmed a life I seem to have at the moment. I think I've probably used up a lifetime's luck in the last few minutes.

I move off to sit further down on the kerb out of the shade of the trees and incredibly, my luck is still in! The world has certainly gone mad. As I lower myself to sit in the first available space of unadulterated sunshine, I accidentally get a pretty good eyeful down the front of a voluptuous young lady in a mini skirt, bulging out of her bra. The view is best seen from above and I wonder how long I can wait before if I can pretend I have sat on some ants and stand up again. She's with a much older man, as old as me at least. I don't know how some blokes do it. It isn't fair. Now he's nuzzling at her neck and I don't like to stare, but I can see that he's peeking at her Dolomites as well he might. The way they are jutting out like that it would be difficult not to, and his right arm is around her and I presume from the movement of his shoulder, massaging the thigh I can't see, though I can see plenty of the one round my side. Dirty old man! Bloody hell! They are practically doing it! It's going to be a race to see who comes first, the tram or them. In fact, it's getting too embarrassing to look really. They don't seem to be concerned that they are making an exhibition of themselves. This is Italy and this is Rome after all. It's all part of the culture, and the climate must bear a lot of the responsibility for this hot Latin blood behaviour. It's time I got up and had a drink of water, to restore my Calvinist blood to its traditional coolness.

Having slaked my thirst, I return to my lowly perch and in that brief moment before I sit down, I believe I can see all the way from the swelling foothills of the Dolomites to Naples, practically. Italian topography in one fell swoop.

And still there is no tram. The piazza is now full of would-be passengers. I know what's going to happen now. When the tram does come, it's going to be a mad scramble for a seat and we'll probably not get one and it's a long journey back to the hotel.

But at last a tram does shamble into view and stops. It is the oldest, most rickety tram in all of Italy. It has wooden slatted seats and I wouldn't mind betting it was built in the thirties, if not the twenties, so redolent it is of that sort of smell which comes from the accumulated dirt of decades. Amazingly, we have a seat and so it seems, does everyone else.

Although it is 20 minutes late, the tram does not move off and the slats of the seat start to bite into my bum. I can imagine the excess material of the green swimming trunks dripping through the slats like the ruched curtains in an undertaker's window. We sit and we wait and we wait. No purple clad matriarch this time to get this show on the road. By co-incidence the other show is sitting in front of me, but the participants seem to have spent their passion or are holding themselves in check. What a relief! I wouldn't want Iona getting any inspiration. I have to think of my heart at my age. Though, if Rome has to be consummated, tonight has to be the night as we leave for Sorrento tomorrow morning. Must remember to keep the noise down though. Don't want the people next door phoning reception: *Sounds like the short, fat geezer next door is having a heart attack. Think you should send for an ambulance!*

Suddenly, there is a mass stampede; everyone seems to be leaving the tram. The doors were never closed and people are streaming out until, in a matter of seconds, we are left alone. We look at each other in speechless bewilderment. What on earth is going on? The world *has* gone suddenly mad. Has there been some word of a terrorist attack? We decide we'd better leave too and follow the exodus.

We step out of the tram and follow the crowd. It then becomes apparent why everyone was leaving. On another track, a brand new tram has just pulled up. This is more like it! Much more comfortable seats, which although plastic, are moulded to the posterior. I wonder how many tests, how many moulds of bums they took before they got it right: *Now young miss, if you would just plonk your lovely bum into this gooey substance so we could get a perfect mould of your bum...yes, I'm afraid it does have to be done in the nude but I assure you I am a scientist and derive absolutely no pleasure from this whatsoever, heh! heh! heh!* It has air conditioning and a LED display so you can tell where you are which would be useful if you know where you are going in the first place.

Hope this one is going to where we want. What if it's not? I just presumed that because the tram was late, two arrived together. Now what's happening? The driver from the old rickety tram is standing in the doorway and haranguing the passengers: *Well, that's charming I must say! I was here first, so you can just get your butts back into my old tram right this minute!* That's what he must be saying because he's looking pretty upset about it and the passengers are evacuating and rejoining the old tram. There are one or two others who have stayed put, including us. What should we do? We remain where we are, in an agony of indecision. Oh, to be able to speak a bit of Italian!

At last we glide away from the stop, leaving the old tram still standing. You would have expected that to go first, but not according to the rules of Italian logic of course. The only thing is, are we headed in the right direction? Well, here is the Tiber which we are crossing. That's a good sign. Now we are at an iced cake of a building, the Galleria Nazionale d'Arte Moderna on the Viale delle Belle Arti which is an even better sign as it means we are definitely on the right tram track.

Bill and Iona have a map and reckon that the next stop or the one after that will be ours. It's nice to relax and put your faith in others, so when Bill says when we arrive at the stop that the next one will do, I slip out of my shoes again, only for Bill to change his mind again as soon as I have completed the manoeuvre.

"No, this one. This is the one we want!" and off he hops, with us scrambling after him at his heels, me with my toes in my shoes but not the heels.

It's a good decision, because right at the stop, there is a supermarket. I've been here a week practically and it has been a bit of a holiday for my liver. Apart from the lunchtime beer and the wine at the Villa Borghese in Florence, I've had nothing to drink. This is the first supermarket or shop that sells alcohol I've come across and I began my search in Naples! I don't give my liver a holiday when on holiday. In fact, the poor organ never gets much of a rest at all, but on holiday it's expected to work overtime.

I decide I'd better buy a couple of bottles of gin. Gin is the preferred summer drink, especially on the continent. There's no telling when I'll come across another supermarket again and with a week in Sorrento to come, there will be plenty of time for aperitifs. As I clink them into my basket, I catch Bill looking at them. He doesn't have time to disguise the look of surprise on his face.

"One for today and one for tomorrow!" I explain. "Hopefully I'll get some more in Sorrento."

He laughs but I can tell he doesn't know if I'm joking or not. He thinks it might well be true.

Alas, Slim-line tonic doesn't seem to have arrived in Italy yet. Ah well, fat tonic will have to do then. It suits me better anyway. I think of getting some beer but my purchases are heavy enough already and there's no chance of persuading Iona to backpack it although half of the gin is nominally hers but I know I'd be lying if I didn't admit that the lion's share will be mine. But it would be interesting to see Bill and Pat's reaction all the same. They've just bought some herbal teas. I'm sure they're very refreshing.

It turns out that we have come off at a stop too early. It gives us a chance to look at this part of Rome though. It's a leafy suburb this, obviously one of the more select suburbs of Rome. The streets are lined with oleander and the buildings are elegant edifices with stone balconies but here's one that's different, shaped like a wedge with wrought iron balconies at the thin end with luxuriant foliage and windows with green shutters. *The House with the Green Shutters*, one of my favourite Scottish novels. It would never have looked like this though.

Back at the hotel, it's into the mini-bar with the gin and tonic which means that just about everything in the mini-bar has to come out, but I won't be drinking any of that, not at those prices, so it doesn't matter if they get warm. The interior of the mini-bar itself feels warm, so I have little hope that my gin will be sufficiently cooled down by the time it's aperitif time. Why don't they have ice-trays in these contraptions?

In the meantime, I'll have a shower. I may be a beast, and in spite of whatever La-Belle-Dame-Sans-Merci thinks, at least I'm not a dirty beast. I may be mad, but at least I am clean round the bend.

The maids have nicked my soap! Can you Adam and Eve it! It was scarcely used! I had taken it from Florence and it was good for quite a few washes yet, notwithstanding the skin area it has to cover. I am building up quite a collection in what I call my pabby bag. *Pabby* was my childhood word for toilet and no one knows why, least of all me. Iona can't bear the sound of the word. It's another of her little foibles. At the very least it means a Frau Ning or a Scow Ling when I say: *I'm just off to the pabby. I may be gone some time.* I have tried to pass the word down to my children so it will not die with me, but I suspect it is on the endangered list. It doesn't seem to have caught on, regrettably. My late, lamented aunt used to use it but now she is gone, and as far as I know, it leaves me the sole user. Imagine that! The last pabby speaker in the world!

It's not that I'm mean, but I mean to say, if you're paying for it anyway, why not pinch the soap? Except *pinch* isn't the right word for something that is put in the toilet for my personal use each morning, is it? And it does happen each morning for each morning it miraculously renews itself because I put the soap and the shampoo into my toilet bag as well as the little sachet for cleaning your shoes, though I do not clean them often, I must admit, but now I've got these handy little sachets maybe I will more often. And not forgetting the body lotion and the skin moisturiser of course. The one thing I do not bag is the shower cap. I can't think of a use for it, but maybe I should start stacking them up in case an idea turns up later. Maybe I could put them on my feet if I got verrucas but that would be going to extremes, like taking a headache pill for sore feet and nobody in their right mind would do that, would they?

You should see our toilet back home. It is full of toiletries from all over the globe. They are not souvenirs, it's just that I am already in the shower before I remember them as they are stowed tidily away out of sight and therefore, out of mind. She'll never be as rich as me if she keeps on parting with good money for these things that we get "free." And what's more, she can't believe that I'm still using the bottle of shampoo from Naples. She finished hers ages ago - in Naples. She can't believe her ears, or *gears* as we call them in our family, as that is the way that George, our son, who is deaf, says it. She thinks that there can't be enough left to work up a lather at all; that these little bottles only do two washings.

"What! You must be joking! What a waste!" If there's one thing I can't stand, it's waste, even when it's other people's money.

"All right then, let's see how much you use and how much lather you get!"

"I'd lather have a shower with you, dearest!" I know it's a feeble joke and the endearment Iona will treat as sarcasm and the lowest form of wit which makes it doubly contemptible.

I can't help it. I keep picking up other people's idiosyncrasies. Bill and Pat are to blame for this latest, dearest, lapse. I say things like: *Well, that's the way it is* because I have cousins who can not bear a pause in conversation and must fill the silence. I used to say: *Definately* because footballers, and one in particular, used to pronounce it this way in interviews, probably when asked if Aberdeen were the team most likely to be relegated this season. It may be all right for footballers to put the emphasis on the way that they would spell the word but it is definitely not all right for English teachers. Thank you, Iona for all the foot-stomping that cured me of this pernicious habit. If not for you, I would have been considered a complete moron, a disgrace to my profession. I expect it's because I was either a parrot in a previous existence or I'm not imaginative enough to invent my own turn of phrase. It did take some stomping out though, so deep-ingrained was the habit. I am definately cured now though; that's the way it is after your feet get stomped upon or you're nagged so much you discover your gears don't have synchromesh with the rest of your head.

As predicted, the witticism is given short shrift. "Huh! Call me when you are ready."

I really don't know why I bother! Here I am, trying to do my bit for the family economy, my pabby bag bulging with so many goodies after so many hotels, so many days, that

344

I am in danger of being over my weight allowance for the return flight, but I know she'll just go and buy more soap and shampoo, regardless of my foreign imports. She still needs training. Maybe if I can prove to her this time, the economy of my method, she will mend her ways.

This means she has to see me naked. Now, if we are to consummate Rome, this is not a good idea. I may be almost an anagram of the Greek god, Adonis, but I am the first to admit that I do not have a heavenly body, though there is that photo of me in Olympia, sitting in my shorts (I was more sartorial then) with a mahogany tan (the best I ever had) and flat stomach (though I never carried a six-pack - I was not on the beer then) and almost shoulder length raven hair (I am a member of the Crow family on my mother's side) and if I weren't me, I think I would quite fancy me, especially as it's a grainy picture from a distance. But that was thirty years ago and this is now and I have no illusions about the repugnance of my physique. I know I am not a pretty sight with my clothes on and worse with them off.

There is a further problem. The bottle from Naples is at the end of its life. There is barely a smidgeon left in the bottle, but I have a cunning plan, something which will convince Iona of the economy of my methods.

"Ready!"

Try not to picture the scene. I have already completed my ablutions, apart from the thinning hair. Like a magician, I demonstrate to the rapt audience, (only Iona, thankfully, with averted gaze) just how little shampoo there is in the palm of my hand after I have turned it upside down and smacked its bottom to get the last of the blue liquid out of the bottle. This I plaster to my hair and rub in. Now for my cunning plan. I hold the bottle up to the spray and let it fill up, then I empty the contents over my head. Would you just look at all that foam! QED!

"You are the meanest creature in Christendom! I don't know why I ever married you!" And with that, she flounces out.

I know what I've done wrong this time: I've proved *her* wrong. You should never do that to a woman, not if you want to consummate a foreign part, or even a part with which you are quite familiar. Except that's her idea in the first place, so she may well get a disappointment tonight. Anyway, if I had not been so economical, she would not have got such a magnificent diamond and sapphire engagement ring which I paid for out of the savings from my student grant. Even in those pre-tuition fees days and student loans, it was considered a bit of a feat to save money off a grant and I derived a great deal of kudos (I think that is the correct word) for my achievement. Anyway, it was a waste of money as she threw that ring away, by mistake, admittedly, several years later and I had to buy her another one, this time a magnificent emerald which I bought in Charlotte Amalie on St Thomas in the US Virgin Islands. Well, it is a tax-free zone and was a bargain and I can't resist a bargain. Besides, we had never been there before and it worked a charm, as far as I can remember.

But that was a good number of years ago, the charm of the ring has worn off and now I have completely blown it. I need a good stiff drink. Thank God I bought that gin. I don't care how warm it is. Perhaps it will melt the heart of La-Belle-Dame-Sans-Merci, - but I doubt it.

*

We are all dressed in our finery as we gather in the foyer prior to our visit to the restaurant for tonight we are dining with the tenors. Tenors it may be but it sounds more like terrors to me. I ask Angela what we can expect.

"Don't worry," she says, "it's very light stuff."

That doesn't help much. Will it just be some background singing that I'll maybe be able to put to the back of my mind, like musak in a supermarket, or will it be something else? As long as it's tenors though and none of those terrible sopranos.

We have to catch the bus again, for the first time a relatively empty one and then walk to the restaurant, in a street somewhere near the terminus. To be honest I am not paying a great deal of attention to where we are going, just following our leader. Perhaps those warm gins I had before we came out have blunted my interest. I made the most of Iona's absence in the shower to keep my gin topped up.

We pile downstairs into a basement and it becomes obvious as soon as we arrive that unlike the meal at the Palazzo Borghese, we are not going to be the only ones as it's rather a large room set with many more tables than we require. In fact, we are in the minority. Our party can be accommodated at just three tables. Iona and I find ourselves at the same table as Bill and Pat, the young Scottish couple and the Guttings. Gordon and partner and the Yorkies are at the adjacent table to us. Behind the Guttings, who are across the round table from me, there is a small stage with a grand piano on it. It looks like it is going to be live music after all.

There are only two bottles of wine on the table. I should have sat at a table which has fewer people at it, since, regardless of size, each table has only two bottles each, one red and one white. That's not enough to drown a gnat. But maybe it's going to be the same as the Palazzo Borghese, and we can get more on demand.

Here come our fellow diners, trooping in. There's hundreds of them. The guides, including our Angela, have their own table.

"Welcome to our friends from Japan!" says our host and MC when everyone is seated. Clap! Clap! "Welcome to our friends from Israel!" Clap! Clap! "Welcome to our friends from England!" Clap! Clap!

"And Scotland!" someone shouts out. It could be my voice. I hate it when people say England when they mean the UK.

"Anyone here from Scotland?" asks the MC.

Cheers and raised hands from our table.

"Welcome to our friends from Scotland!" Clap! Clap! "Anyone here from Wales?" Silence. "Anyone here from Ireland?" Silence.

"They haven't got the clap!" This *sotto voce*, under the influence of the gin, to Iona who returns my witticism with a look which says: *How pathetic! Why don't you just shut up!*

"Now may I present to you the artistes for tonight!"

First to appear is an older man in a white tuxedo with a red rose in his buttonhole, one of those bootlace ties and his grey hair tied back in a pony-tail. Second is a younger man in a penguin suit, and to my dismay, a woman in a black evening dress. Her mouth is a gash of red lipstick and she has her hair scraped back in a bun. Her shoulders and bust are erupting out the top of the dress. Not too much bust, so perhaps her singing will be commensurately restrained. But it's still against the Trades' Description Act to have her in the act, although she is much more comely than the others by a mile. The trouble is she's not just there for the looks, she's going to be opening that gash of a mouth of hers.

Having made their appearance, they now disappear to let the waiters perform their duties. To my relief, after a moment's pause, when I am within an inch of saying: *Well, that's how it is,* Bill starts to pour the wine. I had wanted to, but didn't like to be the first. It looks better coming from him. I don't want them to know my tongue is hanging out. Uh! Uh! Here's mine host coming over here. Wonder what he wants?

"Excuse me," he says. "Sorry for my little mistake just now."

"What?"

"Saying you were from England just now."

"Oh, that's all right," I say. "A lot of foreigners make that mistake."

"I'm from Lancashire. Been here five years now!"

I am a bit stunned and amazed by this revelation. "I thought your English was very good!" That's what I say but I am thinking: *In that case you should have known better, you English ignoramus.*

"Anyway. Is everything all right? Can I get you another bottle of wine?"

What a wise man! What a nice man! Yes, he certainly can. He comes back a moment later, not with one bottle, but one in each hand! He is a really, really nice man now. I catch Gordon's eye at the next table and tip him a wink, raising my glass in salutation. My look says: *It's easy when you know how.* He looks back: *I wish I had your charisma.* Or, it might just be: *You're a jammy bastard! How did you do that?*

The first course is some sort of risotto. I notice that Guttings hasn't touched his. The waiter wants to know if he can get him something else, but he just shakes his head and the waiter clears away.

Pause for a song. A young man, casually dressed in a black T shirt and jeans makes his way to the piano. It looks like this is going to be the pattern, a song for every course. We're going to be here all night at this rate. The younger tenor takes to the stage and lets his tonsils vibrate, then the soprano. She may not have the build of the stereotypical soprano, but she can screech with the best, I mean the worst, of them. Then the older man joins them and they perform a trio. Bloody hell, but these people can project! I expect they are used to being in a theatre, and here, in this room with the low ceiling, it's an assault on the ears like the skirl of bagpipes herded from the glens and confined and restricted to someone's front room. One is powerful enough on his own, but all three at once is deafening and the voice of the soprano soars above them all. It's a good job that I keep my glass topped up as there's every chance that she could crack it at this range. She's wreaking enough havoc on my ear drums as it is.

The songs don't mean anything to me. They might be Neapolitan songs or songs from an opera. The Japanese kids at the table behind me, to my right, are ending themselves. I don't suppose they have ever heard anything like it in their lives. Neither have I really, not so many, not all the way through and certainly not so loud. I don't think it's anything to laugh about but I'm glad they are enjoying themselves. I am getting more fun from watching them helpless with mirth than I am the singing, but then I am a bit of a Philistine.

Phew! Relief! They've gone now – for the moment. Now for the main course. It's pork in some sort of sauce. Ooops! *The Last Supper* tapestry in the Vatican Museum revisited. I watch with interest. The meat is smothered in sauce, so it may not be immediately obvious. It reminds me of the time I took a party of pupils on a Rhine cruise and one of the boys was apparently allergic to pork. There was no menu but, as becoming our status, we teachers were served first, so it was my daily duty to examine the fare of the day and if it was pork to leap up and race to his table and say: *Don't eat that!* For the amazing thing was that although he was allergic to pork, he couldn't recognise it at a hundred paces. But then again, why should he? If he's allergic to it, presumably he's never had it put before him again, maybe since he was a baby. It was easy for Jesus and his disciples on the tapestry as the whole body was there (enough to turn you vegetarian) unless they thought it was some sort of skinned dog.

I recall another time when an uncle and aunt arrived unexpectedly, and my uncle who said that he couldn't eat pork, not on religious grounds, on grounds of taste – he just didn't like it, pronounced the cold chicken he had just eaten, the best he'd had. No doubt he was just being polite, but maybe not, as what he'd just eaten was pork and why it tasted so good was possibly because he'd never eaten a chicken before which tasted like this. His aversion to pork was more to do with a prejudice than a genuine dislike. So will our Israeli friends be able to spot the difference?

I needn't have worried. Whatever the Israelis are having, it is not the same as us. Maybe Guttings is Jewish, because he's not eating this either. He picks at some of the potatoes and some of his vegetables, but leaves the rest alone. Mrs Guttings explains that he's very picky. I feel like asking if I could eat it, to prevent the waste, but it would just have gone to waist anyway.

One thing about all this entertainment is that although we can't eat, we can drink. In fact, there is nothing else to do, so even with our extra bottles, we need more wine now that the main course has arrived.

"Would you like some more wine?" I ask Bill.

He would. Good. I go over to Angela's table.

"Excuse me, er... What's the deal about the wine?"

Angela looks up with what can only be described as an astonished stare. She cannot have failed to notice how we had already received two extra bottles. She doesn't know, I hope, that the Guttings are generously donating most of theirs towards the common weald.

"I mean, if we want any more, do we have to pay for it or is it included?" Sensing an atmosphere, I plough on to cover the awkward silence. "I'm just a delegate, Bill was wanting to know." I indicate my companion with a wrist as limp as my excuse.

"Just see your waiter," she says in a tone as if I'd asked her how to breathe. What she's actually saying is: *Look, you're not fooling anyone. You've got a boozer's face if ever I saw one and you'll drink as much wine as you can as long as it's free, but if you have to pay for it, you won't have any more at all, because you are a mean miserable git from Aberdeen and I don't know why your lovely wife married you. I pity her.*

"Er...right thanks!" I beat a hasty retreat. "Waiter!" Best not to lose any time. It would hell to be stranded at the next piece of entertainment without anything to make it more bearable, to dull the senses, to flatten out the soprano's piercing high notes.

Already! Here they come again. This time it must be a Spanish song because the soprano is striking a flamenco pose and she is playing air castanets as the younger tenor serenades her. Enough to make her run a mile I would have thought, someone waggling his tonsils at you like that with the power of a ten force gale. Now the older one is wandering amongst us singing to individual tables which sends the Japanese kids into paroxysms of hysterics again.

The younger one comes back on to the stage. I think there may something familiar about this song. Well, I recognise one line. Suddenly the older one makes another appearance and has a verbal dual with the younger one. We are caught right in the middle. I can see now how the walls of Jericho fell down. To think that people actually pay good money to hear this! I feel more inclined to pay them to go away.

At last they stop and everyone claps, including me. The difference is, as far as I can tell, that I am clapping because they are finished. This part is concluded by the soprano and the older tenor hurling notes at each other. It sounds as if he's made a very improper remark, the way she's screeching notes back at him: *No I will not...not...not - definitely not rip them off, rip them off, rip them off! Screeeeeech!* But it's all right really, they seem to make some sort of compromise because they end up having a little waltz together and above all, praise be, they stop singing. If this is meant to be light stuff, what is the heavy stuff like? My head is throbbing. Thank God for the wine to make the pain go away.

"Waiter! More wine here!

The artistes are mingling, accompanied by a photographer. I am used to this sort of trick. On the Caribbean I have been photographed with a pirate with a parrot on his shoulder which is appropriate since it's a form of daylight robbery. However I have my own secret weapon. I am so unphotogenic that even they would not expect me to buy a photo. At least I hope I am unphotogenic, that the camera *does* lie and I am not so ugly in real life as I am in photos.

When we get the results, true to form, I have not come out well. It's better than many photos I've seen though. At least both eyes are open and I do not look like a drooling idiot, just an idiot. My face looks like a side of raw roast beef or as if I had been dragged over a glacier, so we do not purchase a photograph, even although we could have it signed by the pony-tailed terror (sic) to remind us of how much we have enjoyed his singing and so attractively priced at an eye-watering €20.

It annoys Iona that she can't be photographed with me without it looking like an advert for *Beauty and the Beast*. On our silver anniversary, on the Caribbean cruise and determined to mark this millstone, (sic) she was reduced to covering my face with foundation makeup before the professional photographers were let loose on me at the captain's reception. Each evening our dining companions would seek out my photograph from the hundreds of others for their daily post-prandial entertainment.

The sweet is a gâteau. Not the most Italian meal I've ever had in my life but we're not so much here for the food but the music and if music be the food of love, play on! Play on and on and on because tomorrow we move to Sorrento. But I wish I had earplugs because they are sure to be back for a finale and I have a feeling I am going to have a headache and we can forget the Roman consummation.

I donate my sweet to Iona as I am not a sweet person, as you know by now. I'd rather have more wine. This will be my sweet course and hopefully the sweet people will not want any more wine after this, so there should be plenty for *little moi* and perhaps it will induce me to have a sweeter attitude towards the music even if it can not totally anaesthetise the ears.

Guttings is not a sweet person either. He's eaten practically nothing. At least I've eaten the other courses, and am drinking more than my fair share of wine, but he's had practically nothing of either. Perhaps he likes the music, but he doesn't look as if he is. He doesn't look as if he likes anything, ever.

I like this music now. Actually I don't, it's doing my head in, but the entertainment makes a good cover as my partner's rapt, singing along in bits and clearly enjoying herself. And this wine, a bit thin and watery is starting to seem quite palatable after all, even for a 11.5%. No more red left. Oh, well, I'll just have to move on to the white then. Hmm! A bit warm and a touch acidic. But the second glass is better and by the third I scarcely notice these faults at all.

Now the pony-tailed tenor is wandering amongst the audience of diners singing something I have heard before and which I actually recognise. It's from *The Marriage of Figaro* with lots of la la la's and repeated phrases in it. He has now got a hold of Usha and is leading her reluctantly up to the stage, all the while doing his la la la's. Poor Usha looks a bit embarrassed, especially when he points to a place on the stage and seems to be singing to her: *Stand there and don't move!* whilst he goes in search of a second victim. He is back a moment later with Mrs Yorkie whom he places on his left with Usha on his right, all the while blasting them with: *Figaro! Figaro! Figaro!*

Behind his back, Mrs Yorkie is imitating him. As he raises his arm to declaim, she raises both arms, one of which is thrust right in the tenor's face, whilst she shakes her hips and waggles her bosoms. The tenor pulls her arm down, never missing a beat, but she breaks free singing: *Figaro!* and comes to the front of the stage and waggles her assets in time to his tonsils.

"Figaro!" we sing back, even me.

The tenor continues his aria or whatever it's called whilst Mrs Yorkie spreads her arms out wide like some member of the chorus in the finale of some popular musical. She is completely upstaging him. Poor Usha doesn't know where to look or what to do. She raises an arm in imitation of Mrs Yorkie but no doubt she's not had as much wine as she and in any case has a much quieter personality.

I think it's the funniest thing I have seen in a long time, or perhaps ever, as the tears are rolling down my cheeks. The room is in an uproar. The Japanese kids are in serious danger of splitting their sides or laughing themselves to death. Meanwhile, Guttings watches the whole performance, impassive, unmoved. It really is incredible that he can sit through all this poker-faced. It's a kind of a talent in a way. He should dress up like the Sphinx and stand on a box in the Piazza Navona and make his fortune.

Mrs Yorkie goes back to her seat amidst rapturous applause. Of all the people in all this room, that the tenor could have picked, he picked probably the only person who would have reacted in this way. It is almost too good to be true, as if, somehow they had secretly rehearsed this little act. But of course that was impossible and I would never have suspected she had such hidden talents. Perhaps she didn't know herself until she found herself on the stage, Italian wine coursing through her arteries and arias blasting through her ears.

They should have stopped there, the tenors, but they have to spoil it all by *deaving* us some more, this time with a tambourine and the soprano rising above all the cacophony like the sparrow who soared higher than the eagle. At last it is over. Once again rapturous applause breaks out; they take their bows and leave. I applaud also, it would be churlish not to, but not too much - don't want them thinking they have to come back and do an encore. Oh, God, please, God no! It's all right, they've finished. The waiters materialise again to serve coffee.

I go over to congratulate Mrs Yorkie on her performance and tell her I think it's the funniest thing I've ever seen. They are all looking very mellow at this table, compared to the sober people at the one I have just vacated, so I stay and talk. It's only fair that after Mrs Yorkie has entertained me so royally, that I try to reply in kind.

"Do you mind if I tell you a wee joke?"

They don't mind.

"All right then, here's a *wee* joke." I slap Gordon on the back, just to emphasise the word. "Three pigs went into a restaurant to have a meal. The waitress asked for their order for the first course. The first pig asked for pâté, the second for soup and the third said he would just have a large glass of water. The waitress then took the order for the main course. The first said he would have duck, the second asked for beef Wellington and the third said all he would like really is another large glass of water. The waitress was puzzled and said to the third diner, "Excuse me for asking but why are you only wanting to drink water?" The pig answered, "So that I can go *wee wee wee* all the way home!"

They laugh the sort of easy laughter that only comes from a well lubricated larynx. I even laugh myself to see such fun but suddenly I am serious. I have just thought of something exciting I can tell them, probably triggered by the animal sound I have just made which makes me think of the whining dog I had heard this morning.

"Here, listen to this," I say excitedly, "this is a true story!" They are leaning over the table the better to hear my every word. "This morning, in my bed, I heard what I thought was a dog whining and guess what it was?" It is a rhetorical question, so I plunge on. "It was people doing it in the room next door! Ha! Ha! Ha!"

No one is laughing. The smile leaves my face and a tsunami of shame and embarrassment sweeps over me. In spite of the heat in this room and the gallons of wine I've consumed, flushing my face, I can feel the blood draining from it and I'm sure if I looked in a mirror now, I would be as pale as a ghost. The horror of the situation dawns on me. Although I have no idea who is in the room next door, it seems logical that it would be one of our party, and just because I don't know who it is, it doesn't mean to say that the Yorkies or Gordon and Blondie haven't seen me or Iona go into our room, so they know we are next to them.

"Ha! Ha! Ha! It was you, wasn't it!" I slap Gordon on the back, trying to make light of it. Blondie is occupying herself by lighting up a cigarette and not looking at me. "Ha! Ha! Ha! Caught you!" It reminds me of what I said to the Yorkies in Pisa when I caught them buying their brass tower. They must think I have a brass neck. What if it's *them* next door, not Gordon and Blondie? Oh, God! How do I get out of this? The silence is becoming oppressive. I can think if nothing else for it but to flee.

"Well, I'd better be getting back to my table. See you!"

I slink back to my table, fill up my glass again. I wish that the floor would open up and swallow me. Why, why, why, did I not stop and think? What made me think that they'd be interested in my story in the first place? Now they must think I'm some sort of perv who probably stays up half the night with a jam jar at the wall hoping to hear some heavy breathing. Thank God Iona hasn't found out about this one.

I sit in solitary contemplation, peering moodily into my wine. The others are engaged in conversation, apart from the Guttings of course, but I am too gutted to think of anything to say to them. Iona is talking across me to Bill and Pat. I haven't a clue what she's warbling on about. Donald is looking adoringly at his wife and I hear him say: *But not yet dearest!* Has he caught it from Bill and Pat or is this what people are meant to say to their spouses? Maybe if I said it to Iona once in a while she wouldn't hit me so much. But she'd only think I was being sarcastic and probably hit me. I am the most miserable creature on earth and I wish I was lying in it.

I think the safest thing for me to do in future is to keep my trap shut. I should be a Guttings. No one loves me, not even my trouble and strife, the love of my life. I have no social graces, keep putting my foot in it and all I'm trying to do is be friendly. And I'm a boor. Now I'm sure. I've actually hated the musical provision tonight, probably the only person in the room who hasn't enjoyed it. My idea of hell, but other people's idea of culture. It shows I've got no breeding, no culture. I'm just an idiot. I think I'll be a hermit. Hermit the Kermit because I am a frog. Yeah, that's me. I'll not open my mouth again. I've got foot in mouth disease. This whole holiday has been a succession of disasters. What impression have these people got of me who knew nothing of me at the start of this holiday? And tomorrow we'll part, except for Tom, Dick and Harriet, Bill and Pat and Donald and his wife – what was her name? If I ever knew, I have forgotten. You see, I just don't listen. That's the trouble with me. I just don't listen and I don't think. No wonder everybody hates me. I can't think of a single person on this trip whom I've not offended. I wish I were dead.

It's time to go but there's still the best part of a bottle of wine in the bottle. Pity to waste that. The waiter will probably just pour it down the sink. I'll smuggle it out. Drown my sorrows. Couple of problems though. It doesn't have a cork and how to get it past Iona, never mind the waiters and carry it home on the bus? It's not so much that she'll think it's stealing, it's that she's always trying to limit my alcohol intake.

I let everyone else at the table leave first and hold the bottle down by my side. It's pretty obvious really and as I pass Gordon's table, he notices it. He's talking to the soprano like they were long lost friends. He gives me a look of approval and nods. I remember how he had taken a bottle from the Palazzo Borghese. He's got a couple of unfinished bottles at his own table. I bet he liberates them. His nod in my direction has been encouraging, as if he harbours no hard feelings towards me. I decide I'll continue with the pretence that I'm unaware of having committed a *faux pas,* that I don't really think it was them next door.

"The trouble is, there's no cork," I tell Gordon. "Hope I don't spill it all on the bus before I get back to the hotel!" I don't tell him about the other, bigger, Iona problem. She's bound to notice as soon as she turns round.

We set off up the street. It's another of those close Italian evenings. I breathe in the warm Roman air. There is the scent of fear in the air. It's coming from me. I walk alone behind the group which has Iona in it. At the bus stop, I talk to Tom, Dick and Harriet and in due course along come Gordon and Blondie and the Yorkies. As I predicted, they have purloined their wine bottles, only they have corks in theirs. This is a chance to make some conversation, to test the atmosphere. I am hopeful that our wine marks us out as kindred spirits and my embarrassing remark can be attributed to too much wine being in and the wit being out, which indeed is no less than the truth.

"How did you manage to get corks?"

"I asked the soprano," says Gordon.

I am amazed. "And she just went and got them like that? What did you say to her?"

"I said: *Excuse me, but didn't I meet you before in New York?*"

"And have you ever been in New York?"

"Never!"

I look at him in admiration, then chuckle at his boldness. I would never have thought of something like that to say! After that it was easy, he just charmed her like a bird off a tree and she went and got him a couple of corks. If I'd tried it she probably would have said: *I'm calling the management. You're not allowed to take wine off the premises. Besides, by the look of your face, you're taking plenty back inside you, you pint sized Scottish git.*

In the bus, I stick my finger into the neck of the bottle. No one else has to have any if they don't want any. By now Iona must have noticed but perhaps she doesn't want to create a scene and perhaps Gordon's trophies have put my contribution a bit into perspective. I am feeling a bit more relaxed. It looks as if I may have got off with everything after all.

In the lounge of the hotel, we commandeer a couple of flowery Chesterfields and some chairs. We are nine: The Yorkies, Gordon and Blondie, Tom and Harriet (Dick has gone to e-mail his friends) Angela, and Iona and me. We need glasses. Gordon is dispatched to procure them, who else? Presently he comes back armed with an armful of them. Unfortunately it is also a meeting of the smokers' union: Mrs Yorkie, Angela and Blondie, all women and confirming the statistics that more women than men smoke nowadays.

So we drink, and chat, we who have only known each other for not quite a week and who know really nothing about each other. We don't even know each other's names. It's inevitable I suppose, that we should ask each other what we do for a living. Mr Yorkie admits to being an art teacher. Hah! Hah! I knew it! I knew I was right! Harriet, I have marked down as a primary school teacher, a nursery teacher actually.

"I don't work," says Harriet.

"Yes," I pursue, but what did you do before got married?"

"I was a primary school teacher."

I can scarcely contain my delight. "Which class?"

"The babies, the new ones."

I can scarcely resist the urge to get up and punch the air. My observations of human nature are not so wide of the mark after all. I can still get some things right. It's impossible, however, to guess what Gordon and Blondie do, nor Mrs Yorkie and they're not telling. Tom's a doctor. I had him down for that, or a lawyer.

My earlier maudlin mood has now disappeared. I no longer seem like a pariah. I have not been ostracised. There doesn't seem much to talk about, now that we've done that. The silence is awkward. I feel like saying: *So that's the way it is* but that annoys Iona. I think I'll tell them a joke. Since we were at the Vatican today, let it be a pope joke. Anything's better than this silence which is creeping ever more uncomfortably over us like a wet blanket.

"Listen to this! Do you want to hear a joke?" There's no objection. Perhaps there's some relief that someone has broken the silence. "Right," I begin. "The pope's chauffeur arrives to take the pope for a drive in the country. "Look," says the pope, "it's a long time since I drove anywhere and I'd really like to drive today." The driver protests: "I'm sorry but I can't let you do that. I'd lose my job. And what if something should happen?" "Look here," says the pope. "Am I or am I not the pope?" Reluctantly, the driver gets in the back as the pope climbs in behind the wheel. But when they reach the motorway, the Supreme Pontiff floors it, accelerating the limo to 105 mph. "Please slow down, Your Holiness!" pleads the worried driver. But the pope keeps the pedal to the metal until they hear the sirens. "Oh, my God, I'm gonna lose my license," moans the driver. The pope pulls over and rolls down the window as the cop approaches, but the cop takes one look at him, goes back to his motorcycle, and gets on the radio. "I need to talk to the Chief," he says. The Chief comes on the radio and the cop tells him that he's stopped a limo doing a hundred and five. "So whaddya talking to me for? Book him!" says the Chief. "I don't think we want to do that, he's really important," says the cop. "So what!" exclaims the Chief. "All the more reason!" "No, I mean *really* important," says the cop. "Well, who is it?" asks the Chief. "The Mayor?" "Bigger," says the cop. "President?" suggests the Chief. "Bigger." "Well," says the Chief, "I give up. Who is it?" "I think it's God!" "God! What makes you think it's God, for God's sake?" "He's got the pope for a limo driver!" replies the cop.

Well, that seems to go down quite well. It could have been risky but for once I don't seem to have put my foot in it. If anyone is a Catholic they don't seem to mind. They want to know if I have any more jokes. Unfortunately I have a very bad memory for jokes, but there's one I always remember.

"Well, there's this one about beans -"

"No!" It is La-Belle-Dame-Sans-Merci with the Viagra eyes.

"Aw! Go on, let him tell it!" It is Mr Yorkie who is speaking. He is on the same Chesterfield as Iona and is leering at her as if she were an oil painting. I can tell by the way that she is retreating into her corner that she does not reciprocate the attention and if she is representing an oil painting then from where I am sitting, it is Munch's *Scream*.

What am I to do? The company clamours for my joke, but yet I am forbidden from on high to tell it and if I do, Rome will not be consummated, not on this trip at least. Oh, what the hell! Rome was not built in a day, so why should it be consummated in two? I bow to my fans and tell them the joke, with all the actions.

I am a hit! And I probably will be when La-Belle-Dame-Sans-Merci gets me upstairs. I think these people like me! They will all be gone tomorrow, apart from Tom and Harriet and they look the least amused apart from Scow Ling, my Chinese wife. But of course, she has heard the joke before, many, many times. Isn't it amazing how fickle life can be! Less than an hour ago, I considered myself a leper, but now here I am the life and soul of the party! Maybe, at the last gasp, I have redeemed myself! I am ecstatic. Gordon and Blondie and the Yorkies will go away with a good impression of me after all.

I could go on all night like this, if only the jokes would come but they probably wouldn't, though now I think about it, there's the one about Maltesers... but the wine is finished and Iona is standing over me as if about to make a citizen's arrest.

"It's time we were going to bed," she says, unashamedly announcing her intentions towards me, to the whole company. "We've got an early start tomorrow."

Eh? We're free tomorrow, doing our own thing. So there's no rush to bed. I'm just coming alive. Tomorrow, Rome is ours for the taking. To begin with, we could have a really long lie in; that would be my desire. Iona must have plans for us. Or maybe she just wants to break this up before we head for the bar. Hmm. Maybe she's right. That would cost money, but what I really want to do is to go up last. I want to follow Gordon and the Yorkies and see who goes into the room next door. I do not suspect Tom and Harriet, yet how ironic it would be if it were they! No! Quite impossible and I've been right about them already. No! It has to be Gordon and Blondie or the Yorkies, given my reception at the table, but which one? How to find out? I must play it cool. Probably they are as anxious to cover up as I am to find out. But now Iona has blown it. It looks like we are to be the first to leave. Besides, the fires are still burning. Mrs Yorkie and Blondie are still inhaling their cancer sticks. They could be some time yet.

We bid each other good night. Now we are leaving, Tom and Harriet decide to leave too, as often happens at parties. It just takes one to go for the party to break up. That leaves the hard core, as in Firenze. I could have been a member of that club if things had been different. Now they'll probably talk about us, but maybe they'll say what a hoot I am and I'm not such an idiot as I look.

In our room, we prepare for bed. Time has passed. Iona is in the pabby, scrubbing her teeth by the sound of it. I have time on my hands. Perhaps, if I open the door of our room and peer out into the thickly carpeted corridor, I might be able to solve the mystery of the occupants next door, though there is no logical reason why I should be able to do so.

The gods are at it again. Who should be coming up the corridor towards me, but Gordon and Blondie! And there am I with my *It's not a bald spot – it's a solar panel for a sex machine* T shirt which I use as nightwear only - with no earthly reason to be peering out of my room except to catch a glimpse of who might be in the room next door.

"Good night!" I say with a frog in my throat, although it feels as large as a person, and since I am a form of low life, it probably is.

"Good night!" they reply and I'm sure they must be thinking, although their faces do not show it: *What's that mad Scotsman doing sticking his head out of the room like that? And did you read his T shirt? Do you think he's advertising? He'll have some bloody wait!*

Mortified, I shut the door softly.

Damn! Damn! Damn! And double damn! I could punch myself, kick myself to death. They've caught me! They must think I'm a right perv. I tiptoe hastily back to the room before Iona completes her ablutions. God! If she finds out what I've just done! I just can't believe it. Five seconds later and they would have passed me, and I would have seen if they had gone next door or not and they probably would not have been aware of my snooping. After all, it's not for prurient reasons I wanted to find out, but to ease my mind. My gaffe at the restaurant would be far less embarrassing if it were *not* them. Now I'll never know but they will forever think that I am some sort of weirdo. All my good work of tonight, of winning them over, has evaporated like morning mist. This, instead of that, will be their abiding memory of me. Tomorrow we part forever. How can I possibly give them an explanation? How can I possibly face them tomorrow? I know I can't. I feel lower than a frog's belly. I crawl between the sheets, put the pillow over my head and wish to die.

Chapter 11
Arrivederci Roma

Ever loath to get up in the mornings, I am especially reluctant to do so this morning. I have not slept well; my little piggy eyes stare back at me gloomily in the bathroom mirror. Perhaps I should skip breakfast in case I run into Gordon and Blondie. He's probably told the Yorkies about last night by now.

"What's the matter with you?" says Iona. The tone is more inquisitorial than solicitous.

"Just didn't sleep well, that's all."

There's nothing new in that, so she makes no more of it. For once we are going down to breakfast together. I need Iona for moral support. If Gordon and Blondie are there, I can pretend to be so deep in conversation with her that I haven't noticed them. That, in itself will be a test of my stamina and ingenuity. As I've already said, if there's one thing I can't stand first thing in the morning, it's conversation, especially if it's deep and meaningful, or even worse, cheerful.

I'm in luck. There doesn't seem to be any sign of them. Now I want to gulp my breakfast and get out of here before they arrive, in case they are even later than us. It's only putting off the evil hour as we will have to travel together back to Naples but I may be run down by a bus this afternoon and it may never happen. Must check my swimming trunks are clean.

We're having our second cup of coffee and I'm just beginning to relax when in come the Yorkies. Eyes down.

What an interesting pattern there is on this plate! I've never really looked at it before. Fascinating! Please let them choose a table where I can pretend to not see them.

No chance, there they are just a few tables away, right in my line of vision. The gods are turning the screw again. They led me on to think I was safe and then this happens. Typical! I can't keep studying the crockery forever. Our eyes meet as they come back and sit down with their fruit juices. I give them a wan smile and they smile back with barely more enthusiasm. Never mind, I'll soon be out of here, but oh, no, Mrs Yorkie is coming over! Bloody hell! She's not going to say anything here, is she, in front of all these people, especially in front of Iona? I lower my eyes and hold my breath. Flight is impossible.

"Good morning!" She doesn't sound too belligerent. "I was wondering…" she pauses and looks at Iona. Come on, spit it out! Maybe she's going to be sarcastic. Are you going to say: *Do you realise you are married to the biggest perv in Scotland?* Or something else, even worse like: *Did you hear us all right last night then? Were we loud enough for you? I hope you derived some satisfaction from it!"* Then she'll turn on her heel and I will look at Iona and shrug my shoulders with wide-eyed innocence as if to say: *Search me! Some people! Completely mad! Expect she's drunk!*

I can't bear the suspense. My mind is racing ahead, thinking of other gambits Mrs Yorkie might be about to deploy and thinking of possible plausible explanations. If Iona finds out about my activities last night, I'll get such a foot stomping and hair pulling I'll baldy be able to walk.

"I was wondering…" Mrs Yorkie says again. She looks a bit nervous. In fact, she looks as nervous as I feel. Maybe she's lost the courage. Maybe she is thinking: *What if she likes being married to a perv? Maybe she's in on it too!* "…if you wouldn't mind - posting these cards for us?"

Relief, then amazement washes over me. What an odd request!

"Certainly," says Iona. I notice it's not me who is being asked. She takes the bundle of cards Mrs Yorkie must have been holding behind her back. Iona doesn't seem to think there is anything the slightest bit peculiar about the request.

"Thanks," says Mrs Yorkie.

What's going on here? They've still got half a day in Rome, like us, not to mention the airport where they could post the cards. Even the hotel reception would post them for them - when they remembered. No wonder she looked nervous. I presume they have stamps on them?

She must feel like some sort of explanation is necessary, the unspoken question in my eyes hanging in the air between us like something tangible.

"I don't trust the hotel to do it and we're not going out today (animal impressions in the room perhaps?) and in case there isn't a post box at the airport..." her voice tails off. So? There is still something not right about this. I'm not convinced. How ironic! A moment ago, I had thought I was going to be the one who was embarrassed to hell. Aware of the awkwardness in the atmosphere, she plunges on: "Actually, we'd like them posted in Sorrento - if you don't mind."

Ah, hah! This sounds a bit more like the truth. I don't mind at all, but I do mind not knowing why.

"It's just a joke, really," she says. "Thanks!" And she turns on her heel and goes back to her table before we can say any more.

Bizarre! What kind of joke would that be? Maybe when I read the postcards, I'll get a clue. But, up in our room, preparing to go out, Iona will not let me see them.

"They're private!"

"No, they're not! Everyone reads postcards! Especially the posties! And that's what we are."

"You do, maybe."

"Aren't you in the least curious to know why they have to be posted in Sorrento?" I can't believe her lack of curiosity, her total indifference towards this intriguing mystery.

"No!" The tone has a certain ring of finality about it.

I sulk. There's no point in arguing. She'll not change her mind either. And she'll hide the postcards from me now that I've expressed an interest. I just think it's a natural curiosity. It's in my nature to be curious. My mother used to say I always wanted to know the far end of a fart. Anyway I am relieved that Mrs Yorkie wasn't coming over to give me a character assassination. Maybe they haven't yet seen Gordon though. But now that they've asked a favour and such a strange one at that, I feel the moral high ground has shifted considerably back in my favour. They have some sort of secret and perhaps all I need to say if they say anything is: *Postcards* as if I knew what it meant.

*

We are going back to Roman Rome. There are so many other things we could do, but we're more interested in archaeology than art, so we've decided to try and make some sense of the Forum and we'll go to the Palatine. Besides, it's free.

We buy travel passes at the nearest tobacconist and in due course, arrive at the Colosseum. What I'd not been able to work out before was what the ruined building facing the Colosseum was. It turns out, according to our guidebooks, that it is the apse of an enormous basilica, with half a dozen white columns standing lonely sentinel on either side. It is the Temple of Venus and Rome, another of Hadrian's building projects. This was the largest temple in ancient Rome, actually two temples with their apses back to back, as if they couldn't tell their apses from their corbels. The pillars, so far away from the basilica as to seem part of another construction altogether, are in fact all that remain of the 150 which formed a portico. The temple facing us is the Temple of Venus, the other, the Dea Roma, faces the Forum. They contained two huge seated statues of the goddesses. When the architect Apollodorus remarked that the statues were too big, that if they stood up (as if they would) their heads would hit the ceiling, Hadrian had him executed. It doesn't pay to criticise the architect, especially if he's Emperor. If I'd been around, I could have told him that. Never criticise your boss. That's why I have been married for so long - and am still alive.

It doesn't look much now, but in the first century it was really something as our book with the transparent overlay shows. It stands on the site of Nero's mansion, the Domus Aurea or house of gold. After the fire of 64 AD which some say Nero started, he built this outrageous new palace. No expense spared. The walls were covered in gold leaf and mother of pearl. The bedrooms showered guests with flowers and perfume, the dining room rotated, probably the first rotating restaurant in the world. And in the baths you could have a choice of either sulphurous or sea water. Not much of a choice really. No wonder you needed to be showered with perfume if you've just come from the sulphurous bath: *Have you been bathing in that pool again, Domestus? You may think you are clean but your pong is driving me round the bend.*

But the lake would have been the best – banquets on barges and brothels on the shore and high-class hookers to boot - none of your riffraff. Maybe Nero was on the fiddle after all: *So they won't let me have a new palace, huh? Well, they'll have to if it burns down. Heh! Heh! Heh! Now where did I put my bloody violin?* As things turned out, he committed suicide in AD 68 so he didn't have much time in the new place. The Colosseum now stands where the lake used to be. Perhaps I'm standing at this very minute on a pile of passion, 2000 years ago. Perhaps their ghosts are still there, beneath my feet. Is that why they feel so hot, already, at this time in the morning?

The Colosseum was Vespasian's contribution to the expurgation of the hated Emperor's memory. The Temple of Venus and Rome was Hadrian's. And in its turn, it too became a marble quarry. The Popes looted it for their own constructions. How handy to have a ready supply of marble on your doorstep! The gilded bronze roofing tiles were used by Honorius I for the roof of St Peter in the Vatican and it, in its turn was demolished by Julius II to make way for the present church. Never mind *caveat emptor!* Caveat Emperor more like. Nero, Vespasian, Hadrian, no building was safe. And who's to say what will happen to St Peter's in the centuries to come? If history is anything to go by, it will not last forever. On the bright side, anything they do to Bernini's *baldacchino* would be an improvement, like melting it down for a start.

We circumnavigate the Colosseum, peering in, through barred gates, into the interior to see what we can see. You can see what there is to see on post cards anyway and it mostly looks like a pile of bricks. Time is short and we have other priorities, so we'll not bother going in. Now we have come half way round and what's this? They have put a lift in the Colosseum! No kidding, are you looking at this, Vespasian? See what they have done to your monument – are they taking a rise out of you or just providing one for the tourists? It's good to see that the tradition of desecration of ancient monuments is alive and well in the 21st century, (though this was probably done in the twentieth) and that the ancient customs are still holding good. If I were you, St Peter's, I'd be shaking in my foundations. How about a nice speedy glass elevator to the top of the dome? After all, it's not pc to discriminate against those who can't manage the steps, such as the arthritic and obese, is it?

We retrace our steps of this morning, past the Arch of Constantine and on to the Via Sacra and then take a left turn instead of going down to the Forum and go up the hill towards the Palatine. We can see people wandering around in the cool and green leafy slopes, but there are high railings between us and them. It's rather like looking at wild animals in a zoo, though they look rather tame, I must say. Well, I trust we are on the outside, looking in but I suppose it depends upon your point of view.

Eventually we come to a turnstile, but there's a problem. It won't turn. Iona pushes it but it won't budge. I find a similar problem, but manage to move it a bit and squeeze through, by sucking in that lump of emergency rations I carry around before me, just in case I am stranded in a desert without any food or water. I have done it. I am in.

Bang! Bang! Bang! Bloody hell, what was that? At the same time, Iona is saying, "David! David! You've to get out!"

I look up to see that she is pointing to a man in a green wooden booth a few yards away and there is no mistaking his body language. He is waving at me but I can't tell how many of his fingers he is using. I suspect not more than two. He is telling me to get out of there, and not tomorrow either. All at once it becomes clear. I have gone in the exit, that's why the turnstile would not turn. It turns all right when I push it to come out. The man in the booth gives me a contemptuous look as we pass: *Thought you could get in for free? You didn't reckon on me!* Should I explain that I didn't realise that was the exit? No, it's not worth it. I'll let him think I'm dishonest. Better than admitting I'm an idiot. Hopefully he'll think I'm English anyway.

The entrance is further along, up a steep flight of stairs and there is a sign which says *Tickets*. You have to pay to get into the Palatine apparently. We have a choice. We can either go there and visit the House of Augustus and the House of Livia, the Huts of Romulus and other such attractions or we can continue with the original plan and try to make sense of the Forum. We don't have time for both. We opt for the latter. The fact that we have to pay for the Palatine is not a factor. No, I really do want to see if I can make more sense of the Forum first and foremost.

So we make our way down to the Forum and exit as before, along the Via dei Fori Imperiali so we can explore it from the other end, from the arch of Septimius Severus. This means that we come first to The Forum of Caesar which is closed but we can look down on it from the Via dei Fori Imperiali and the Via di San Pietro in Carcere and see all there is to see, namely the three Corinthian pillars which is all that remains of the Temple of Venus Genetrix or the Temple to Caesar's geriatric granny. There are some more columns which are all that remain, probably of some shops which flanked the temple, and burnt grass littered with piles of stones and broken columns.

Close up, the arch of Septimius Severus towers over us and the Forum. Only from close up do you get the true scale of how immense it is. It's looking a bit the worse for wear these days. It was half buried up until the 18th century but it's had 200 hundred years of exposure to the Roman atmosphere and pollution since then and is pockmarked like a youth with a bad case of acne.

Near the arch, on a stump of a pillar of red brick is a stone on which is carved: VMBILICVS VRBIS ROMAE. There used to be a circular temple here which marked the centre of Rome, so this is the spot that marked the centre of the Empire. There used to be a marble column near here – the Milarium Aureum, on which were carved in gold letters, the distances to all the major cities of the Empire. This is where all the roads began or stopped. They have the same idea at John O' Groats except that there it is a wooden signpost with black lettering, one arm of which has movable letters so you can have your photograph taken with the distance to your own town: *Thurso 20 miles.*

Like John O' Groats, or Land's End, the Milarium Aureum was probably a tourist trap in those days too: *Clever Dick's Instant Portraits* and an army of similar sketchy folk all queuing up to trap all these barbarian tourists standing at the Milarium Aureum to prove that they had been at the hub of the Empire: *Just seventy sesterces, sir, to show the folks back home, that you were really here! ...Well, OK, but only sixty sesterces and make sure you get how many miles it is to Corinium Dubunnorum. And I don't want the column growing out of my head, Dick.*

Nearby is the Temple of Saturn, the oldest ruin in the Forum, dating from 497 BC but it was rebuilt several times apparently and the present eight columns date from 42 BC only. The columns themselves are massive, but it stands upon an enormous platform which doubles its height and dwarfs people below. The symbolism of the construction conveys the power of the god over puny man.

Saturn probably would have been my favourite god. He was favoured especially by the poor and slaves, a mythical god-king in whose reign there were no such things as slavery, private property, war and crime. His reign is still celebrated today, except we call it Christmas – they called it Saturnalia, a week of feasting and sacrifices in which the normal social order was reversed, the world turned upside down, so that slaves would be served by their masters. It was also celebrated by people at home. They would exchange gifts, like wax dolls which doesn't sound like a good idea to me. I wouldn't give my wife a wax doll of me for a lorry load of pins, never mind two. I have a good idea where she would stick them - in the sorest place she could think of. One in each.

Running at right angles to this, along the Via Sacra, is the Basilica Julia – named after Julius Caesar though I should think he was hardly amused at them getting his name wrong and giving him a woman's name to boot. It may be close, but it's still a bit of an insult. It used to be the civil law courts. There's not much to see now, only the steps and stumps of pillars but it seems to stretch along the Via Sacra forever. And it was three storeys high, so there must have been plenty of cases to try. There were 180 magistrates, all sitting separately and lawyers would hire spectators to applaud palpable hits at opponents and boo and hiss at rivals. A bit of a pantomime in fact. Another thing the Romans gave us. Anyway, it probably was more entertaining than going to the real theatre and far better than going to the shows running daily with gore at the Colosseum.

On the steps there are supposed to be board games scratched onto the surface by bored punters waiting to be hired by the lawyers. I wonder if this is one. It's a big circle with the letters ORMO at the bottom and some other letters too faint to read now and there's a piece broken off anyway. Perhaps it's just a bit of graffiti but it's Roman graffiti all the same; someone must have sat here for hours and laboriously carved this into the stone. It's not as if he could just give a quick spray with his can and skulk off. Apparently no one came up to him in all that time and said: *I say, old chap, but would you mind not defacing this public building?* No doubt he was a big bruiser with bulging biceps and a hairy chest and tattoos and that's why no one thought to mention it to him.

This looks as if it might be a game though. It's a whole series of shallow holes of regular size and depth though there doesn't seem to be any recognisable pattern to them as far as I can see. I press my thumb into one and it takes it quite comfortably. I've no idea what they did with it, but I'm sure it must be a game of some sort. I expect you had to throw

375

marbles at the holes but I suppose a lot of them missed and a lot of people lost their marbles which they must have found rather maddening.

At the end of the Basilica Julia is the Temple of Castor and Pollux, its three elegant pillars projecting into a cloudless sky. There is a path here, to the right of the Basilica Julia and on a whim, we decide to take it. It's another one of those serendipitous finds. There's some steps going downwards, some ancient brickwork, a recess in which is set a barred gate and a white marble plaque on which is written CLOACA MAXIMA. I don't know why I remember it, but the Cloaca Maxima is one of the few things I do remember from my days of studying Latin. Now here I am all these years later face to face with it, but to be honest, there's not that much to see from here. There's a whole lot of Italian written on the plaque but I don't need to be able to understand it to know what this is. It's the sort of thing that a guide would never take you to. It's the main sewer of Ancient Rome and goes all the way to the Tiber. I mean what sort of person would get a thrill out of seeing a sewer? Iona has often accused my mind of being like a sewer. She thinks that I have a one track, dirt track mind. I'm not sure how she can tell my mind's a sewer as I keep my dirty thoughts to myself but I remember how she read my mind about Pink Top in Naples.

We come back down towards the Curia again, this time on the road which runs parallel to the Via Sacra and we come to the Rostra. Now this is another very interesting place! It's a bit like Hyde Park Corner where you can go to get things off your chest. Julia, Augustus' nymphomaniac daughter, literally did. It is said that from here she acted the prostitute which did not go down too well with the old Emperor and ended up with her being chucked out of the house, not to say the country.

Also here, even more interesting, but gruesome, Cicero's head and hands were displayed after he was put to death by the Second Triumvirate consisting of Augustus, Mark Antony and the lesser known Marcus Lepidus. Mark Antony's wife, Fulvia, it is said, stabbed the silver-tongued orator's tongue with a hairpin. What had he said, I wonder to offend her so much?

I know how he used to feel, apart from with his hands, that is. I have often been accused of rabbiting on, of never using one word when twenty would do. I am heading off to the other side of the Rostra. I've had an idea. There is something I want to do. Who knows, I'll probably never get another chance.

"And just where do you think you're going?" I am stopped dead in my tracks by the imperious command.

"Er..erm...I just thought I'd go and stand on the Rostra."

"Why?" Her voice is dripping with suspicion.

"Why not? A good view of the Forum."

"Just as long as there's no speeches! Don't make a bigger fool of yourself than you already are."

It's unbelievable! She knows me better than I know myself! How did she know that I was going to do my *Friends, Romans, Countrymen,* speech? For it must have been from here that Mark Antony incited the mob against Brutus by delivering his immortal lines, or at least, the additional dialogue written for him by Shakespeare. From here, the Rostra looks like a solid platform on top of a high wall, but the other side is a disappointment. The platform from where the speeches were made is long gone – too easy a marble quarry for the subsequent generations of builders to ignore.

In front of the Rostra is a tall, slender, single column. No one knew what it was until the pedestal was excavated. It turns out that it was erected in AD 608 to commemorate

377

the visit of the Byzantine Emperor Phocas which makes it the youngest erection in the Forum and it has been standing like that since the day it was put up by the architect Viagra. Actually, I don't know who did put it up, but that is an impressive amount of time to maintain an erection. I think I might just go over there and stroke it. Maybe some of the power will rub off on me.

"Where are you going to now?"

"Er...erm. Nowhere really." Bloody hell! Is she dirt-track mind reading again? She *does* know me too well. Like the boar's nose in Florence, it doesn't look as if I'll be able to stroke Phocas' column either. Probably wouldn't have been done me much good anyway.

Just beneath the Rostra wall, there is a hole in the ground fenced off with black iron railings. I go over to see what it could possibly be. It must be my lucky day! There are some steps leading down into the bowels of the Forum and once again, the way is barred, but on the wall there is a plaque similar to the one at the Cloaca Maxima only this one says NIGER LAPIS and in smaller letters beneath, TOMBA DI ROMOLO. Does this count for my collection? Can you actually include the tomb of a mythical figure? Well, in Cyprus, I visited the beach where Aphrodite wearing nothing but a languorous smile, was washed ashore on a sea-shell, as in Botticelli's celebrated painting. Yes, why not? A myth's as good as a smile.

The Curia is next door, so we wander over to have a look inside. It's a repository for bits and pieces of marble statuary, including two relief panels which used to decorate the front of the Rostra, one of Trajan sitting on a throne and the other of him destroying records of unpaid taxes to free the citizens from debt. I bet that made him popular all right and there's no harm in reminding everybody of the fact each time they come to the Forum and listen to some geezer like Cato who says: *Carthago Delenda Est - Carthage must be destroyed* and they must raise taxes. At the far end there is the headless figure of a person in a toga executed in porphyry. I wish they'd executed the sculptor instead. It glistens like a wet seal. If you could hold it, it would probably slip through your hands like a piece of raw lamb's liver. No doubt it is somebody extremely worthy to have the honour of being sculpted in this special stone. Perhaps it's Trajan himself, in gratitude for the tax break.

We can't go in and look around, but we can see all there is to see. It is very plain and very high and there is a patterned marble floor in a strip down the centre. It doesn't look like any representations of the Senate I've ever seen in films or TV. That straight marble strip surely suggests that the senators were seated in tiers at either side of the marble floor in adversarial style, like the House of Commons. Anything I've ever seen of the Senate had them in a horseshoe shape or semicircle. There are three very shallow, wide steps at each side. Apparently the senators took along their own collapsible chairs and sat on these platforms. They must scarcely have been able to see over the heads of the senators in front and hardly any room to move. And if you wanted to go to the toilet, it would have been like at the cinema today – everyone would have had to stand up and collapse their chairs to let you past. Maybe it was a tactic they used if they felt the debate was going against their point of view: *No, by Jupiter, you're not getting past Incontinentus. You should have gone before you came. That's what you get a lunch hour for. Have you got a medical problem or something? You're always going this when Cicero is speaking...* So why didn't they build proper tiered rows with benches with plenty of legroom? The Curia is certainly wide enough. And why is the Curia so incredibly tall? And why does it look nothing like it is depicted in films? The guidebooks are no help. We'll just have to be curious about the Curia.

Adjacent to the Temple of Castor and Pollux is the temple of Julius Caesar, erected by Augustus on the spot supposedly where Caesar was cremated. There's not much of a temple left to see now, but there are the remains of a straight wall and then a curved one behind that, like the apse of a church with an ugly temporary-looking roof over the whole. There is a guide rabbiting on in Italian to a small group of tourists. It looks like a private party. There are two kids who are looking extremely bored and not having a party at all. He must be giving Caesar's life story because he is taking forever. There is a railing round the straight piece of wall and I want to squeeze in between the railing and the circular wall but I can't because his group is blocking the passage.

At last however, he leads them away and I squeeze into the narrow passage. There is a stump of a broad pillar here and on the top, a bunch of wilted flowers. So this is where Caesar's body lay and was burned to ashes! According to one of the guidebooks, this is where Mark Antony made his funeral oration. But he wouldn't do it here would he? Surely he would be on the Rostra where everybody could see him? Caesar's body would have been plainly visible from there, it's not that far away, if you could see over the heads of the crowds that is, but the funeral pyre presumably would have been built high enough for everyone to see the flames. But then again, maybe he *would* do it right next to the body? Who knows? You can't trust all you read in guidebooks, nor can you trust Shakespeare either. I point this out to Iona and add, "Surely Mark Antony should have said: *Friends, Romans, Countrymen, lend me your ears. I come to burn Caesar, not to praise him. The evil that men do lives after them –*."

"Shut up!" She realises that by this cunning ploy I have sneaked my speech in after all, even although it may or may not be, at the right spot.

"Of course, if he had said that," I plough on, "the next bit wouldn't make much sense. *The good is oft interred with the bones –."*

"I told you not to do that."

"I apologise from the heart of my bottom, dear trouble and strife. I shall remain speechless from now on," I say contritely. It's no less than the truth. I'm not very sure how it goes on after that, so I would have stopped there anyway. It must be 40 years since I was made to learn it at school and I never taught it, so it's not surprising that I'm not sure how it continues. What is surprising is that I can remember even that much.

We make our way up the Via Sacra and now we are on the territory we trod earlier in the day. Here is the Temple of Antoninus and Faustina, Picasso's cow still peering forlornly over its pen at me: *Yoohoo! Moo! You back again? Say pal, you can't get me outta here can you? I haven't even room to turn around in this bloody pen!*

It's amazing how the level of the ancient Forum is so much lower than it was in the 17th century, for the green door to the church of San Lorenzo in Miranda is stranded thirty feet or more above the level of the present excavations and floor of the Forum. No wonder they didn't know what the heck the Column of Phocas was. There was probably only about 15 of its 44 feet sticking above ground. The funny thing was they had been getting it right all along when they accidentally stubbed a toe on it or bumped into it like people nowadays who walk into lamp posts, and cursed: *What the Phocas column doing here?*

Across the way, now that I have seen the whole Forum, is my favourite building on the site – the Temple of Vesta. I like the curved shape and how the slim pillars seem to soar into the air, especially as we see them from below like this. It's got nothing whatsoever to do with an interest in virgins.

What we didn't see earlier however, was the House of the Vestal Virgins which is right nearby. All that's left are the ruins of the house around the central courtyard. It's an oasis of green amidst all the burnt grass and broken stones which make the Forum look like a building site. There is a central strip of emerald grass, with fishponds in the middle and round the perimeter there are marble statues looking coolly white on their pedestals. These are statues of Vestals. Most of them seemingly have lost their heads. Maybe that's symbolic of their decision to turn their back on the world of men and adopt this nun-like existence. Apparently there is one there who has had her name removed. It is thought that it might be a lady called Claudia who committed a terrible crime and brought the cult into disrepute. No, she did not lose her virginity – her crime was she became a Christian. Isn't that terrible? It doesn't get much more sordid than that.

It would be lovely to shake the dust off my feet and walk in that peaceful garden and meet the virgins. You don't often get the chance to meet so many these days all gathered in one spot like this. But it is not allowed. All the best bits of the Forum seem to be out of bounds. Just like the Vestals in the olden days.

Well, we're finished with the Forum now. I have a much clearer idea of it now. All the same, it is still hard to visualise it at any given period of time as I can't hold the dates in my head. The successive building programmes make it difficult to imagine what was there, let's say in 200 AD. I suppose I could work it out, but I can't summon the effort to do the sums and besides, we had better be heading back. We musn't be late to catch the bus, whatever we do. Some people have flights to catch.

Back at the Colosseum there is a *gelati* van, unfortunately. €10 for two ice creams! That's like £7 in real money! You can buy a whole businessman's lunch for less than that.

They think by sticking a stick of chocolate in it that they are creating something exotic that gives them the right to charge you an exorbitant price. They didn't even ask us what size we wanted or if we wanted the chocolate, just stuck it in and stuck out their hand and demanded a ten euro note in it. How convenient! No change needed. I'd like to tell them where to stick their ice cream but it's too late now.

We go off to a low wall to sit and eat them. Of course I sit in the sun whilst Iona chooses a place in the shade. You would think we weren't speaking to each other, to look at us. I plonk my posterior on the stone and leap up immediately with an involuntary cry of pain and surprise. The stone is red hot and my bum is burnt. I have a good mind to rub the ice cream on the spot. That seems a more appropriate place for it. It's the worst ice cream we've had since we came to Italy or is it the price of it which is leaving a nasty taste in my mouth? I go over to the van and show the rich (he must be a millionaire) vendor my burnt bum: *I'd like to compliment you on your bum cream. You know, for a minute I thought you were meant to eat it! Very cool and soothing. I don't suppose you would divulge the recipe, would you?* Well, I don't really, but I'd like to.

Over to my left, in a swathe of grass in front of the Colosseum, there is some entertainment to take my mind off the burning issue. A bride and groom are having their photographs taken. She is in the traditional white dress and he is in a white suit, complete with waistcoat. He must be sweltering under all that. There's a long haired photographer with cameras strapped across his body like a guerrilla's bandolier of bullets, appropriately enough as he's going to do plenty of shooting by the looks of it. To his left there is a young man with a microphone with one of those square little boxes at the top that you see on newsreels and the wire disappears into a bag which he has on his shoulder. To his right, there is an older man with a ponytail and a massive camera with a microphone which projects over the lens like the snout of a swordfish. There seems to be a power pack on his back. He hefts the camera onto his shoulder as his knees buckle under the weight.

The young couple are posing for a still. He has his hand resting on the pocket of his trousers so that the tail of his jacket is pushed to the side, like someone showing off the cut of his suit. She is snuggling up to him, so that her voluminous dress totally obscures his left leg, her bouquet of white lilies held across their waists. He is staring adoringly at the Colosseum whilst she gazes off into the middle distance at an object to the right of the camera. But a lot of the time they are apart. At the moment, he is striding up and down in front of the photographer whilst she stands demurely, holding her bouquet. Now she is picking up her skirts allowing a breeze to balloon them out and I get a flash of white shoes and ankles. Yes, it's probably pretty sweaty under all that brocade. It is his turn now to stand and wait.

Wait. Yes, that's what the wedding guests are doing in an hotel somewhere in Rome. These two look as if they have got all the time in the world and God knows how long it took them just to get here just for the Colosseum backdrop, not to mention the time it will take to get back. But the photographer, with euro signs in his eyes suggests: *Why not have one in front of the Temple of Vesta to commemorate your last day as a virgin? Heh! Heh! Heh! (Well pretend then!).* These bloody photographers! They are up to all the dodges and rule weddings nowadays. I know I have been kept waiting for an hour or more whilst the bride and groom go off somewhere "romantic" for photographs. Normally I wouldn't care but the guests are left to wait in swanky surroundings with the price of alcohol to match, so there is no chance of getting legless, not at those prices.

But I have a feeling about this. I don't think this is a real wedding. I suspect it's an advert of some sort, but what it's for precisely, I'm not sure. There seems to be too much equipment and the pose doesn't look as if they're having a memento of their happiest day together. They look more like models than newly weds. And it looks as if the man with the movie camera is more interested in the Colosseum than the couple. They're not in the shot he's filming just now anyway. Maybe he's got nothing to do with them after all. But what is the young man doing holding the microphone? Is he going to interview them for the radio: *Tell, me you happy newly weds, what do you think you'll be doing tonight? Have you got any special plans at all?*

What can it all mean? Suddenly the penny drops. I am as thick as a brick sometimes. Iona puts it down to excess of alcohol. She says not only has it destroyed my face but destroyed the brain cells as well. But I get it now. No wonder they are apart so much of the time. No wonder they are not gazing fondly into each other's eyes. No wonder the movie man is so interested in the Colosseum. No wonder the microphone man is ready. Voice over: *Tired of him already? Marriage in ruins? Don't want to see him? For free advice, see us at our office near the Colosseum!* (*We'll fleece you later*).

Well, I'm glad I got that worked out before we had to go. One mystery is plenty. I've still got the riddle of the postcards on my mind. The *gelati* are finished and we must be going. We cross the road and burrow down into the Metro. There is no sign of a train so, faithful to my maxim that in cities, you should grab a seat whenever you can, I sit down to wait.

Gradually, I become aware of the woman to my right. She's a flamboyant character dressed in a yellow and red dress. To say it is loud would be an understatement. It is positively screaming at me. Although I judge her to be in her forties, her hair is jet black and tied back in a pony tail and unless I am much mistaken, it's not out of a bottle. She is wearing great hooped earrings, the sort that I could put my fist through, two on each side. The bangles on her swarthy brown arms jangle and set up an accompaniment with the earrings so at each slight movement she's like a human Aeolian harp. The line from the nursery rhyme floats into my head: *And she shall have music wherever she goes.* And indeed, she certainly seems to be listening to music, though there is no sign that she is plugged into a Walkman or CD player, for although she is sitting down, her feet are moving, not just tapping in rhythm to some inaudible and invisible source of music, but moving in some sort of dance rhythm. I don't know much about dancing, but I would say these are dance steps. I wonder if I went up to her and asked: *Are you dancing?* she would say: *No, it's just the way I'm sitting.*

I nudge Iona in the ribs and give her the eyes right sign. She looks suitably impressed at this eccentricity.

"I think she has a touch of the gypsy in her, don't you think?" I say *sotto voce.*

Iona does think so and we continue to watch fascinated as the performance continues. Then abruptly it stops as the woman stops, stands up and takes up a position on the edge of the platform as if she expected the arrival of a train imminently. And indeed, a few seconds later, I hear or rather sense, the rush of air that always presages the emergence of a train from the tunnel. But she knew about it *before* that happened. Did she have some sort of sixth sense that the train was coming?

We scramble on board. As usual, it is packed but not so solidly as on that nightmare trip to the Vatican. In fact, there is sufficient room for a quartet of musicians. They are dressed in gold shirts and black trousers with black cummerbunds. No sooner have we departed when they strike up a tune. The sound of the fiddles and Pan pipes give it an unmistakeable Romanian gypsy-like air. What! Two gypsy events in such a short space of time? A co-incidence, or what? Could it possibly be that our gypsy-looking lady on the platform who seemed to anticipate the arrival of the train was actually tuned in to the music of this gypsy band? Surely not, but yet...

The music is certainly very catchy and I don't mind in the slightest throwing a euro or two into the hat they are passing around. Unfortunately, they get off at the next stop – Cavour. We have one more stop to go.

But there seems to be a problem. The train is not moving. The doors have closed, we are all ready to go, but we're not going anywhere. The doors open again. Some people get off but the majority stay put in the train which looks as if it is staying put. Nothing happens. Presently there is a banging at the window. It looks like a guard gesturing that we should get off. Get off? But why? The guard has already disappeared down the platform, banging on the windows as he proceeds. Not that I would have been able to ask him anyway, but no one else is getting the chance to either.

The platform is now crowded with people, the train is empty, the guard hops on to the last carriage and without further ado, the empty train draws out of the station. What on earth is going on? It just doesn't make sense. But that's Italy for you. Obviously, the train is working perfectly well, at least as far as we can see. The natives are restless. It's plain to see they are as mystified as me and more than a little peeved into the bargain.

After five minutes and another train has not appeared, Iona is getting worried. What if the next train has been cancelled? What if they have all been cancelled? How are we going to get back to the hotel in time? Although I don't say anything, I am a tad worried myself. I am worried I am going to have to pay for a taxi. We should be all right for time – we still have half an hour before we are due back.

Still plenty of time - if a train comes soon and we don't have to wait too long for a bus once we get to the Terminus. Iona hates this sort of situation but I tend to thrive on it. I hate arriving early for anything and hanging about. I like the excitement of arriving just in time; she loves the quiet life, to leave plenty of time for possible unforeseen events like this. It looks as if it's going to be my sort of day.

I just hope it's not going to be one of the times when I judged it too finely for comfort, like the narrow miss catching the train in Paris, all because there was a bill board in the Metro of a little girl who was the spitting image of Hélène which I wanted to photograph. I can remember calculating the number of stations, the number of minutes left and coming to the conclusion that it was mathematically impossible to catch that train to Dover. Yet we made it, by the skin of our teeth, and not due to a miscalculation in my Maths either. I sank back in the seat, sweating like a pig, and in celebration, buying a can of coke even at SNCF prices to ease my parched throat. As the train drew out of the station, I checked my watch to see by how many minutes it was late – and poured the contents of the can down my front as I flicked my wrist over, to the amusement of the people sitting opposite me.

Then there was the time we arrived in Dunkirk just in time to see the ferry sail away leaving us with four hours to waste and not enough money to buy a sandwich. We spent some of the time getting the kids to walk round the car park in the vain hope that they would find a franc someone had dropped so we could buy the sandwich. I think that's the only time I've ever actually missed something, apart from the infamous trip to New Zealand, but that wasn't my fault.

Iona looks at her watch in agitation. "We're never going to make it!"

"Oh yes, we will!" I don't want her to think that we'll need to get a taxi. In any case, surely if we are a little late, they will wait for us, for a little bit anyway, but she is clearly getting her knickers in a twist about this. "If you hadn't insisted on getting that bloody *gelati* -" I just have to add, "- we wouldn't be here now. We'd probably be back at the hotel."

I don't really know why I said it. Perhaps I am still rankling at the cost of it, but more likely I am preparing my defence against the attack which will come if we do arrive late at the hotel, letting her see that it wasn't *my* fault, that it was hers for having to have a bloody *gelati* every day. Just because we're in Italy and they make the best ice cream in the world, there's no need to go bloody mad. But of course I am not a sweet person. Actually, I'm getting quite stressed myself about the non-appearance of the next train. Perhaps that's why I said it. It was a stupid thing to say anyway.

But fortunately, like a glowing blue angel on wheels, the train arrives just at that moment before Iona has time to make a suitable riposte, like hurling me onto the line, which is the most likely sort of line she'll take.

There's a whole train-load to get on to a train which is already a train-load, so once more it's sharpened elbows to the fore as we fight our way on. We *have* to catch this one. We can't afford to wait for another one. I follow close behind Iona. No one is going to stand in her way, my very own WMD – woman of mass destruction as she cleaves a path through the mass of bodies.

It's crowded, but it's only one stop. Besides, I'm used now to a close encounter of the Italian kind. I just hope it's a nubile young lady that I get to rub my body up against. In the event, one out of three isn't bad for me. At least she is female, even if she is someone's great granny. She's dressed completely in black. She probably went to her husband's funeral round about the time I was born. If we don't get a bus right away when we get off the Metro, I'll probably be going to my own.

Out of the Metro and a mad dash to find the stance for the bus to the hotel. We need an 86 or a 92. But where to begin? It seems this is the Terminus for all of Rome. With impeccable logic for once, that's why the Italians call it *Terminus.* There are buses everywhere, but of course there appears to be no logic in the way that they are distributed. We race from stance to stance, from bus to bus, looking for the magic numbers, splitting up in order to optimise the chances of hunting one down, and at last I find the one we want. Now I have to find Iona before the bus goes. Phew! There she is at the end of the row. No mistaking her. She must be the pinkest person in Rome.

Sitting, waiting for the bus to depart, in an agony of impatience, Iona kneads her knapsack. She kneads it even more than I need a beer and I need it a lot, or rather, I need a lot of beer. All this rushing about in the heat has given me the mother of all thirsts which the warm water in the insulated bottle does nothing to assuage, but to tell you the truth, at least half of my mouth's dryness is due to the fear, not that the bus will have gone, but they are waiting for us and cursing us for putting their flight in jeopardy. For anyone whom I have yet failed to insult or offend, (is there anybody?) this could be their moment. This holiday began with a missed flight and it might end with missed flights for half the company thanks to me. It's not the disapprobation that worries me, so much; it's the thought of the compensation I might have to pay which terrifies me.

As we draw near the hotel, we are scanning the street for landmarks. We can't afford to over or undershoot our stop. The trouble is there are no landmarks that automatically leap out and hit us between the eyes. Is this it? Iona and I look at each other. Yes, we think it is. It seems we have been on the bus for about the right length of time. We press the bell and are decanted, mercifully at the end of the street that we want and hasten our steps towards the hotel which is half a mile distant, if not more. My watch says we have ten minutes to the deadline. The way Iona is charging up the street, we are going to make it with five minutes to spare at least. That's what I call good timing. An otherwise dull journey has been turned into an exciting adventure with this race against the clock.

The bus is there and some of our fellow passengers are already on board, while others are hanging around in groups. But there is something about the way they are standing which tells me they have been waiting for some time. What I expected to see was luggage being loaded onto the bus, travellers idly chatting and joking, taking a leisurely departure. But there is no luggage on the pavement and the luggage compartment gapes ominously open. Angela is looking down the street, in the direction from which she would expect us to come. She spots us and looks at her watch. There is something in the atmosphere of the waiting group as they watch our approach, which strikes fear into my heart. Have we possibly got the time we were to meet wrong? I can believe I would, but not Iona, not both of us.

As we skid to a stop, Iona pants out a breathless apology. "I'm so sorry! Did we get the time wrong?" she asks of Angela. She's probably blushing. She blushes when she's innocent, at the mere thought that someone may suspect her of a solecism. In a court of law, the jury would always judge her guilty, but here it's impossible to tell, flushed as she is with the rush and the heat.

"No, no, it's just I like to get away as promptly as possible. You never know with the traffic. And we've *got* to get to the airport on time," she adds, I think, rather darkly.

I wonder how long they have been waiting as we go to fetch our luggage from the luggage room. If we had been there, would we have gone perhaps half an hour ago, even more? Well, that's not our fault if we make the most of our time in Rome, yeah even unto the last minute.

Everyone is aboard when we return with our luggage and see it safely stowed away by Giancarlo in the bowels of the bus. I am practically hugging myself with the masterly management of my timing. I think I have a bit of a genius for this sort of thing. If we hadn't stopped and waited for that *gelati*, if that train hadn't dumped us, we would have arrived far too soon and I would have had a potentially embarrassing encounter with Gordon who by now is bound to have informed the Yorkies about my eccentric behaviour of last night, to put the kindest interpretation upon it. As it is, there is no need to avoid them, no need to pull out my ace postcard. They are at the back of the bus somewhere; we are at the front. The evil moment when I may have to face them is postponed at least and may never happen. As Robert Louis Stevenson said: *To travel hopefully is a better thing than to arrive.*

We negotiate the suburbs of Rome without any hold up and in due course hit the A1 or E45 if you prefer, and travel, on course and on time, hopefully, south to Naples, to journey's end which was journey's beginning. Perhaps the Guttings will be reunited with their luggage. To all intents and purposes, the Italian Journey is over bar the travelling.

Like the travellers of old, I have had my education rounded off. But am I a more rounded being, more cultured as a result of my experiences, of my exposure to some of the world's greatest artistic achievements spanning a millennium? Well certainly the former, with all those breakfasts. But have I been made more of a gentleman, the rough edges smoothed off? There is only one person to ask. We are, for once, sitting together like a real married couple; she has not yet moved off to her own domain across the passage.

"Well, I'm not sure. You're probably still a boor. I don't know how much you've learned or for how long you'll remember anything you may have learned. I wouldn't say you're a culture vulture exactly, but you could be one of those things."

Before I have time to consider which is the better, a culture grown in some Petri dish or a hideously ugly scavenger, she goes on, "I'll have to wait and see what you are like in bed."

What? I give her a sideways glance. Is that meant to be an encouragement or what? Does she mean that after all these places she thinks that I have learned new skills and wonders if they will last till her birthday, not long after our return? Her face holds no clues. It is as straight as the Via Caslina which was the old Roman road for the A1. (A first-class name, much better than a letter and a number).

"What do you mean?"

"Well, you would be less of a boor if you controlled your flatulence in bed and stopped fluffing up the blankets afterwards."

I might have known. So that's boorish behaviour is it? I thought it was normal, manly behaviour. I thought everyone did that.

Something is wrong. We are slowing down. Ahead, traffic is piling up, red brake lights are coming on and further ahead, traffic is at a standstill, stretching to the horizon. That's the trouble with Roman roads, efficient but boring. Pity the poor soldiers, marching, marching, carrying all that equipment in the fierce sun and not even a slight bend or even a curve in sight to relieve the monotony. Tramp, tramp tramp in their sockless sandals in a straight line, mile after mile, towards the horizon. How utterly sole destroying.

Our situation is scarcely much better. We are scarcely moving, sometimes not moving at all and whatever is causing the hold up is not even in sight yet. I don't know how far we can see ahead, but it looks like miles. We are going to be here for some time evidently, at this rate. Presumably it is an accident. What a rare thing! In spite of the way they drive, like bats out of hell, practically bumper to bumper, lights flashing to say: *Get out of my way you bastard, I'm coming through anyway!* So unlike our own dear country, where flashing lights for us mean: *Please go ahead, old chap, after you!* or *Thank you!* And yet, in spite of all this aggressiveness, in all the weeks, in all the hundreds upon hundreds of miles I've travelled in Italy, this is the first accident I've come across.

Boring! Boring! Iona goes across the passage to have a nap. May as well. Nothing to look at that is going to change in the foreseeable future and yet I can't help opening my eyes after what seems five minutes, but is probably no longer than a minute, if that. I keep thinking that I might possibly just be missing something and would you believe it, my curiosity is rewarded. I might have known it! We are in Italy and trust an Italian driver to deal with a traffic jam in a typically Italian way.

I am at the right side of the bus which is in the slow lane. Well, of course we are all in the slow lane now, but this is the lane with the emergency lane on the right and here is a car steaming down it quite the thing. The cheek of the driver beggars belief. Even if he does have a flight to catch, he shouldn't be doing it. *I hope the cops catch you, you cheeky bastard*, I say to myself.

But Nemesis takes a different form. A driver, seeing this performance in his mirror, straddles both lanes. There is not enough room for the Smart Alec to get past on either lane. As the Smart Alec tries to pass on the right, the other driver pulls right and as he tries to pass on the left, the other pulls left. Thus they weave their way at a snail's pace down the motorway.

"Ya beauty!" I cry out involuntarily, like Tam O'Shanter who couldn't control his enthusiasm for the delectable Cutty Sark and thus revealed his presence to the witches.

Iona, across the passage is Frau Ning. I'm not suggesting she's a witch, just that I've interrupted her nap and made her aware of my presence. I explain the situation to her and she watches the proceedings with interest over the heads of the Guttings and Giancarlo. Guttings of course is staring ahead, his face mask-like and unblinking as usual. I wonder what will happen. We are moving so slowly there is nothing to prevent Smart Alec from leaping out of his car and in a rage, hauling our hero out of his car and giving him a good doing.

But the gods have got a laugh up their sleeve. Would you believe the cruel injustice of it? The gods have created a lay-by off the emergency lane. Smart Alec swerves into it, overtakes our hero on the wrong side, nips out of the lay-by again and tools off down the emergency lane again. Curses! Well, let's hope the cops do catch him after all. Iona and I look at each other in dismay. The good guys don't always win, not in real life. I wouldn't mind betting that Smart Alec gets off with it completely.

If Angela is feeling worried about this delay, she's not showing it too much. Once again I reflect on the perils of being a travel rep. She's got to decant all these people at the airport on time and is at the mercy of idiots who prevent an early start and unforeseen circumstances like this. God knows how long we'll be stuck in this. Presumably, she has built in a good measure of time for this sort of eventuality, but all the same, I wouldn't care to be in her shoes.

I slide over the passage to sit beside Iona. "You know, do you think anyone has organised a tip for Angela and Giancarlo? I don't think they have," I whisper. I've been on a holiday like this before, in Turkey and I know it's customary to tip the guide and the driver. Maybe the others are unaware of this, or maybe they are waiting for someone else to initiate it.

"Good idea! Go on then!"

"What?"

"Well, go and collect some money from them."

"Me?"

"Yes, why not?"

"I...I...I've no idea how much it should be." I am filled with horror at the idea of having to go up the bus and speak to Gordon and the Yorkies, but of course, I can't tell her that. I fumble in my brain for an excuse. "You'd be better at it. Why don't you go and discuss it with Bill and Pat?"

"Oh, all right then. Out of the way!" She's not best pleased, but when it comes to handling money, she knows I'm best left out of it.

I move back to my own seat. The traffic crawls on into the distance and is still crawling when Iona comes back and reports that each couple is contributing €20 for Angela and 10 for Giancarlo.

"And who's going to present it?"

"I've asked Gordon to do it. They're giving him the money." That makes sense. We can't collect the money down here and we can't tell the Guttings either. Somehow or other, we'll have to let them know.

At last the traffic clears. It seems that a lorry has shed its load of onions. There are onions all over the side of the road. It's going to take forever to pick them up and there's nothing to indicate what caused it to happen in the first place. Alas, there's no sign of Smart Alec having been detained by the police either.

We are stopping at Cassino again for a toilet stop and a drink. No wonder Angela wasn't looking agitated. If needs be, we could just have missed this out and if anyone was desperate, well that would just have been too bad.

As we are first off the bus, the Guttings and us, I take it upon myself to tell them about the contribution. He takes this blow to his finances stoically, as I knew he would.

"Give the money to Gordon," I say and press on, so as to be first in the queue and to maximise the amount of rays I can get.

Only when I get to the counter, there is not enough change in my pouch and Iona has none either, the tips have broken the bank. We are practically euroless.

"What's the matter?" It's Mr Yorkie who has come up and seen me raking without success and increasing embarrassment through the various compartments of my pouch.

"Er...I seem to be financially embarrassed."

"Is that all you want?" he asks, nodding at the single can of Coke.

"Yes, I'm afraid I'm that poor."

"Here," he delves into his pocket and brings out a fistful of change which he wants to pour into my palm.

"Oh, no! I couldn't possibly," I fluster.

"Go on! We're going home, I don't need them."

Don't I know it! I am posting his postcards in Sorrento for him. "Oh, all right then, I'll just take a couple of euros, thanks very much."

As I walk away with the can, I think: Well that was nice of him! Maybe Gordon hasn't told him. Maybe he has and just doesn't care. It probably wasn't him next door after all. Hmm! That means my noisy neighbour probably *is* Gordon after all.

Angela is sitting alone at a table, like me, except she is inside and I am outside. I can see that the others are huddled in a group and there's a lot of whispering going on. It must be blindingly obvious to Angela that a plot is being hatched. It's probably Gordon trying to conjure up a couple of envelopes from somewhere. If anybody can do it, he can. Angela is pretending not to notice. She's probably thinking: *You had me worried there. I thought it was never going to happen.*

We're all on board. As the doors hiss shut, Gordon comes down to the front.

"Just before we move off," he says, "we've got a little present for you." He makes a little speech and says it's compensation for him being such a pain. Well, it's true, he did hide from her when she was trying to count us but if Angela were asked who should get the prize of most painful person on this trip, with all due modesty, I think she'd pick me. Ironic really then, that if not for me, she probably wouldn't be getting this tip at all. It would have been more fitting therefore, that I made the speech. I would have mentioned some highlights from the tour, some funny incidents and put in some jokes if any sprang to mind. But perhaps we'd still be in the car park now, instead of bowling along the motorway to Naples.

"If you look to your left now," says Angela, "the castle you can see now amongst the trees is the Palace of Caserta. Palace of Caserta. It was begun in 1752 for the Bourbon King Charles III. The façade is plain and only the back is decorated to avoid annoying the peasants in case they revolted. It was the Italian HQ during the war and where the armistice was signed in 1945."

How daft is that! These Bourbons must have been off their heads, completely *pazzo,* if they thought that by keeping the decorations to the back of this amazing pile that the peasants would be appeased by an apparently plain mansion: *No, we don't mind at all if you have a house a million times bigger than our shit holes of pigsties. Just as long as there is no fancy stonework OK?* Sounds plain daft to me.

It comes upon us suddenly, Naples airport. We are back in the very spot a week ago where I watched Pink Top go off on another tour and where the Guttings waited in vain for

398

their luggage. It's all bustle as we retrieve our luggage from the hold of the bus and find a place out of the way to stand beside it and await developments. Angela has told us that a couple of taxis will whisk us away to Sorrento. Meanwhile, she has gone into the terminal to find out at which desk the homeward-bound people have to check in.

A man in a short-sleeved white shirt appears holding a card with ADDISON written on it. I identify myself.

"Follow me, please," and he seizes Iona's bag and starts marching off.

What! So soon, just like that! We haven't had time to say goodbye. I seize the handle of my case, wave to my ex-companions. "Goodbye, everyone!" I call. Half of them haven't even noticed, they are still lugging their luggage from where Giancarlo has placed it; some are away, presumably looking for a trolley.

I start to move off.

"Just a minute, David!"

It's Gordon. He's pulling a little notebook out of his pocket. "Can I have your e-mail address?"

I write it down hastily in my neatest printing and read it back to him. He nods as if he understands it. There's no time to ask for his. We shake hands and I set off in pursuit of Iona and the driver.

"Don't forget the postcards!" shouts Mrs Yorkie.

"Don't worry!" I shout back.

And that's the last I see of them. Never even got a chance to say goodbye to Angela or kiss Usha goodbye. We'll never meet again, unless by some twist of fate, some joke of the gods, they throw us together again for their sport.

At least Gordon must think I'm not such a bad chap after all. He didn't *have* to ask for my e-mail address. Sometimes people who meet on holiday do that, just as a less embarrassing way of saying goodbye. They've been friends for the holiday but they both realise that like the wine which tastes so good abroad, it's not quite the same thing when you get home, but exchanging addresses keeps up the pretence that you will continue the friendship and once back home, you can lose it.

But he didn't have to do that and he actively sought me out. The two clowns of the tour. He, at least, seemed to appreciate my jokes and we had a common interest in wine, not to say debauchery. I hope my writing is legible and he does get in touch. I would like to get to know him better. I still don't even know his real name.

In the meantime, I hurry after Iona. I have a mini-bus to catch. The Italian Journey may be over, but the Sorrento extension is about to begin. A whole new adventure is just beginning, a new start, albeit with some of the other people from The Italian Journey.

Whatever happens, it won't be peaceful. We're not going to sit by the pool all day. There's Herculaneum just up the road, and probably Pompeii again, Vesuvius to climb and the Amalfi Coast to explore and that's just for starters. Plenty of things to do and plenty of scope for things to happen. That at least is certain, for nothing ever seems to run smoothly. Trouble seems to be attracted to me like a magnet.

As I stow my luggage in the mini-bus, I just hope I can keep embarrassments to a minimum and avoid disasters completely. Like Queen Victoria, I will try to be good. The problem is, I never have been much good at anything.

Printed in the United Kingdom
by Lightning Source UK Ltd.
105626UKS00001B/1-21